A

Philip E. Lilienthal

BOOK

The Philip E. Lilienthal imprint honors special books in commemoration of a man whose work at University of California Press from 1954 to 1979 was marked by dedication to young authors and to high standards in the field of Asian Studies. Friends, family, authors, and foundations have together endowed the Lilienthal Fund, which enables UC Press to publish under this imprint selected books in a way that reflects the taste and judgment of a great and beloved editor.

Wandering Spirits

Jiang Yan dreams that his brush has become multicolored flowers. From *Mr. Cheng's Garden of Inks* (*Chengshi moyuan*, ca. 1601), an illustrated catalogue of designs for ink-cakes manufactured by Cheng Dayue (fl. 1550–1606).

Wandering Spirits
遊神

Chen Shiyuan's
Encyclopedia of Dreams

Translated with an Introduction by
Richard E. Strassberg

UNIVERSITY OF CALIFORNIA PRESS

University of California Press, one of the most
distinguished university presses in the United States,
enriches lives around the world by advancing
scholarship in the humanities, social sciences, and
natural sciences. Its activities are supported by the
UC Press Foundation and by philanthropic contributions from individuals and institutions. For more
information, visit www.ucpress.edu.

University of California Press
Oakland, California

First Paperback Printing 2022

© 2008 by The Regents of the University of California

Library of Congress Cataloging-in-Publication Data

Chen, Shiyuan, b. ca. 1500.
 [Chen Shiyuan de bai ke quan shu de meng xiang.
English]
 Wandering spirits : Chen Shiyuan's encyclopedia of
dreams / translated with an introduction by Richard E.
Strassberg.
    p.   cm.
 Includes bibliographical references and index.
 ISBN 978-0-520-25294-3 (cloth);
 978-0-520-38969-4 (pbk.)
 1. Dreams—China. 2. Dream interpretation—
China. 3. China—Civilization. I. Strassberg,
Richard E. II. Title. III. Title: Chen Shiyuan's
encyclopedia of dreams.
 BF1098.C5C46   2008
 135'.3—dc22   2007050925

For all dreamers

Dreaming is spirit-wandering and a mirror for knowing the future.
Chen Shiyuan

For, from where does one know that thoughts that occur in dreams are any more false than others, seeing that they are often no less vivid and definite?
René Descartes

No small art is it to sleep: it is necessary for that purpose to keep awake all day.
Friedrich Nietzsche

Dreams are true while they last. Can we at the best say more of life?
Havelock Ellis

Contents

Preface ix

Editorial Notes xi

Chinese Dynasties xiii

Introduction 1

LOFTY PRINCIPLES OF DREAM INTERPRETATION BY CHEN SHIYUAN

Preface 51

PART I · *The Inner Chapters*

1. The True Controller 55
2. The Long-Willow Method 58
3. Day and Night 60
4. The Various Forms of Divination 63
5. The Disciple of Emptiness 66
6. The Sage 78
7. The Six Types of Dreams 80

8. The Ancient Methods of Interpretation	84
9. Auspicious Events	88
10. Influences and Abnormal Conditions	91

PART II · *The Outer Chapters*

1. Heaven	103
2. Sun and Moon	108
3. Thunder and Rain	115
4. Mountains and Rivers	120
5. Forms and Appearances	130
6. Food and Clothing	138
7. Utensils and Things	147
8. Valuables and Goods	154
9. Brush and Ink	158
10. Written Graphs	169
11. The Official Examinations	177
12. Gods and Strange Things	191
13. Longevity and Destiny	208
14. The *Feng* and Other Birds	215
15. Animals	220
16. Dragons and Snakes	228
17. Turtles and Fish	234
18. Plants and Trees	239
19. Reward and Retribution	244
20. On General Analogies	251

| List of Sources | 257 |
| Index | 273 |

Preface

Over the past century, psychology, and in more recent decades, cognitive science and neurobiology, have been working to bring the understanding of dreams down to earth from the lofty realms of the religious and artistic imaginations. Yet we still dwell in a world in which premodern beliefs remain pervasive. In mainland China, where the revival of pre-Communist culture has been widespread, there has been a rise of new publications investigating traditional understandings of dream content. Meanwhile, many of these ideas have continued to be transmitted in Taiwan, Hong Kong, and among overseas Chinese. As this book demonstrates, dreams have been taken seriously in China for at least three millennia and are preserved in a rich, diverse literature.

One of the most extensive compendiums of traditional Chinese dream culture is Chen Shiyuan's *Lofty Principles of Dream Interpretation,* which was completed around 1562. Chen's unique treatise is an encyclopedic compilation of various theories together with close to seven hundred examples assembled from a wide range of literary sources. These are presented along with his own comments on some of the perennial issues concerning the nature of dreams and their role in waking life. His work appeared at a timely moment in Chinese cultural history, contributing to the new degree of interest in dreams that arose among an expanding reading public during the Ming and Qing dynasties. Chen himself became recognized as an authority on the subject, and his encyclopedia has continued to be reprinted into the modern era.

In the West, articles and individual studies by Sinologists have shed more light on various aspects of Chinese dream culture in recent decades, but it would still require extensive reading in the original sources to gain a broad overview of its diverse manifestations. There is no better introduction to this rich corpus than Chen Shiyuan's encyclopedia. It not only contains an abundance of material, but also reflects the premodern mentality of a judicious scholar whose opinions are representative of the educated mainstream of his time. Unlike Chen, I cannot claim that this book was prompted by a divine revelation in a dream. But I hope that an English version of his *Lofty Principles* will make an important aspect of traditional Chinese culture more available in our global age and stimulate further humanistic inquiries into the universal phenomenon of dreams.

I would like to thank my colleagues in Chinese studies who kindly answered various questions in the course of producing this translation, especially Professor Hung-hsiang Chou, as well as Professors William Bodiford, Paul Kroll, David Schaberg, Hongyin Tao, and Ye Yang. At UC Press, I am grateful to Reed Malcolm for his support and guidance, to Mary Severance and Christopher Pitts for their expert editorial assistance, as well as to Kalicia Pivirotto and Claudia Smelser. I am also indebted to Professor Robert Hegel of Washington University, whose own interest in Chinese dreams preceded mine, for his helpful suggestions as a reader of the original manuscript. Following Chen Shiyuan's lead along the many byways of Chinese dream literature has not only resulted in a deepened appreciation of a civilization that has preserved such a wealth of material, but has also encouraged me to pay greater attention to my own dreams. His encyclopedia, though compiled four and a half centuries ago, can remind us of the continuing mystery of human consciousness.

Editorial Notes

This translation presents the complete text based on the 1833 *Guiyun bieji* 歸雲別集, the 1850 *Yihai zhuchen* 藝海珠塵, and the 1939 *Congshu jicheng chubian* 叢書集成初編 editions. The original division into "inner" and "outer" chapters has been preserved as parts I and II, but Chen's interlinear commentaries, which include the texts of the dream narratives and their sources, have been configured as endnotes to each chapter. Thus, the reader who is more interested in the general flow of Chen's discussion can read through the main text unimpeded. This was the case with the earliest extant version in the *Menglin xuanjie* 夢林玄解 of 1636, an abridgement which did not include the valuable commentaries at all. Chen, like most Chinese encyclopedists, usually condensed his sources, but he occasionally transcribed them, sometimes with minor differences and occasional mistakes. I have translated what he wrote, rather than what appears in extant editions of his sources, but have consulted the latter to correct obvious misprints, missing words, and factual errors. Problematical sources are followed by a bracketed question mark [?]. Multiple names and titles referring to the same individual have also been consolidated. When necessary, individuals whose names are identical in romanized form are distinguished by their dates, such as: Emperor Xuanzong of the Tang 唐玄宗 (r. 712–756) and Emperor Xuanzong of the Tang 唐宣宗 (r. 846–859); Fu Jian 苻健 (r. 351–355) and Fu Jian 苻堅 (r. 357–385); Gao Yang 高颺 (n.d.) and Gao Yang 高洋 (529–559). I have also added Chinese character graphs, additional information in brackets, and remarks in italics where translation alone is not sufficient to convey the original Chinese. References to the text of the *Lofty Principles* follow the form: I:5n35 = part I, chapter 5, note 35. A list of sources cited in Chen's encyclopedia has been provided that includes additional bibliographical information, and the index of motifs will enable the reader to search for related dream narratives that are recorded in part II.

ABBREVIATIONS

BBCSJC	*Baibu congshu jicheng* 百部叢書集成
CSJC	*Congshu jicheng* 叢書集成
ICS	*Chinese University of Hong Kong ICS Ancient Texts Concordance Series*
SSJZS	*Shisanjing zhushu* 十三經注疏
ZZJC	*Zhuzi jicheng* 諸子集成

MEASUREMENTS

The following equivalents are all approximate and differ to varying degrees depending on historical period and locality:

> A *li* is 1/3 of a mile (0.56 kilometers), a *mu* is about 1/6 of an acre, and a *qing* is equal to 100 *mu* or 16.2 acres.
>
> A catty *(jin)* is 1.3 pounds (603 grams) and a *dan* is 133.3 pounds (60.5 kilograms).
>
> A *sheng* is 1.87 pints (about 1 liter) and a *dou* of liquid is equal to 10 *sheng* (2.3 gallons or 10 liters). As a dry measure, a *dou* was standardized in the modern period as 316 cubic inches. A *hu* was an earlier equivalent to ten *dou* and later five *dou*, and a *zhong* was about 100 *dou*. These and other Chinese measurements are rendered into approximate English equivalents when possible.

Chinese Dynasties

Xia		ca. 21st cent.–ca. 17th cent. BCE
Shang		ca. 17th cent.–ca. 11th cent. BCE
Zhou		ca. 1056–221 BCE
Western Zhou Period		ca. 1056–771 BCE
Spring and Autumn Period		770–476 BCE
Warring States Period		475–221 BCE
Qin		221–206 BCE
Han		206 BCE–220 CE
	Western Han	206 BCE–8 CE
	Xin	9–23 CE
	Eastern Han	25–220 CE
Three Kingdoms		220–280
	Wei	220–265
	Shu-Han	221–263
	Wu	222–280
Jin		265–420
	Western Jin	265–316
	Eastern Jin	317–420

Southern Dynasties		420–589
	Liu Song	420–479
	Southern Qi	479–502
	Liang	502–557
	Chen	557–589
Northern Dynasties		386–581
	Northern Wei (Tuoba)	386–534
	Eastern Wei	534–550
	Western Wei	535–556
	Northern Qi	550–577
	Northern Zhou	557–581
Sui		581–618
Tang		618–907
	Zhou	690–705
Five Dynasties		907–960
	Later Liang	907–923
	Later Tang	923–936
	Later Jin	936–946
	Later Han	947–950
	Later Zhou	951–960
Ten Kingdoms		902–979
	Wu	902–937
	Former Shu	907–925
	Wu-Yue	907–978
	Chu	927–951
	Min	909–945
	Southern Han	917–971
	Jiangnan	924–963
	Later Shu	934–965

Chinese Dynasties

	Southern Tang	937–975
	Northern Han	951–979
Song		960–1279
	Northern Song	960–1126
	Southern Song	1127–1279
Liao (Khitan, Qidan)		907–1125
Jin (Jurchen, Nüzhen)		1115–1234
Western Xia (Tangut, Xixia)		1038–1227
Yuan (Mongol, Menggu)		1279–1368
Ming		1368–1644
Qing (Manchu, Manzhou)		1644–1911

Sun Xian dreams that an imperial emissary has arrived to announce his success in the official examinations as the principal graduate. The graphs *zhuangyuan* on the banner indicate "principal graduate," which Sun became in 1454. From *Illustrated Survey of Principal Graduates of the Ming Dynasty* (*Ming zhuangyuan tukao*, 1607, 2:11b).

Introduction

Dreams are such a universal human experience and have been so widely believed to carry significance that virtually every culture from antiquity to the present has encouraged people to recount and transcribe them. In the course of some three thousand years of written civilization in China, an abundance of dream narratives has been preserved in various genres of literature; this probably constitutes the greatest corpus in any single language before the modern age.[1] Chinese dream culture contains a fairly diverse range of opinions about what oneiric experiences were, including skepticism about their interpretability and value as a guide to waking life. Broadly speaking, however, three main generalizations can be made about Chinese views of dream interpretation. Firstly, most traditional Chinese maintained an attitude of pragmatic spiritualism: they were primarily concerned with the implications of dreams for personal welfare both in this world and in the afterlife. Secondly, they commonly regarded the origins of their dreams as contingent on a web of external stimuli rather than arising independently from purely psychological factors. Lastly, the act of dreaming was widely characterized as an out-of-body state that was often termed "spirit-wandering" 神遊 *(shenyou)*.[2] These included both local and distant interactions with other people, as well as with gods, demons, ghosts, and strange creatures.

Techniques of dream interpretation often eclectically combined magical elements from shamanistic and occult practices along with Confucian, Buddhist, and Daoist beliefs, precedents from the literary tradition, as well as empirical insights. Such methods were frequently framed within intellectual systems that comprised what has been called "correlative cosmology."[3] Archetypal patterns such as yin and yang and the five agents

五行 *(wuxing)* were employed to classify phenomena and define intricate relationships of cosmic response that linked the microcosm of the individual with the macrocosmic forces of the universe. In contrast to this widely accepted approach, however, were philosophical and religious views that regarded dreams as mental illusions. There was also an advanced strain of speculation that regarded dreams as thought processes, and literary representations of dreams as autonomous zones of desire beyond the constraints of conventional social morality. Such was the diversity among these conceptions that they never coalesced into a single, universally accepted theory. Dreams were seen as both a confirmation of and a threat to the sense of order in waking life, as factual and as fabricated, as meaningful and as delusional.

This range is apparent in Chen Shiyuan's 陳士元 (1516–1597) *Lofty Principles of Dream Interpretation* 夢占逸旨 (*Mengzhan yizhi*, 1562). Writing at the beginning of the late Ming dynasty, when the publishing industry entered a new phase of expansion, Chen was heir to a large, heterogeneous corpus of textual material on dreams that had been transmitted from the past.[4] This included: documented ancient practices; theoretical discussions in Confucian, Daoist, and Buddhist texts; philosophical essays; official and unofficial historical accounts and biographies; anomaly accounts; miscellanies; poems; dramas; short stories; as well as popular dream manuals. An eminent and prolific scholar who wrote for a broad readership, Chen compiled his encyclopedia during a period when interest in dreams had spread among all levels of society. His intention was to elevate knowledge beyond popular beliefs, arguing that dreams were a legitimate subject of inquiry for the educated class. The brief survey that follows traces the evolution of the key elements of traditional Chinese dream culture that formed Chen's intellectual horizon and that of his readers during the sixteenth century.

THE EVOLUTION OF CHINESE DREAM CULTURE

The pragmatic approach to dreams is evident in one of the earliest definitions, which appears in the philosophical work *Master Mo* 墨子 (*Mozi*, ca. late 4th cent. BCE): "A dream is that which is taken to be real when asleep."[5] While evidence remains scarce for how prehistoric people in China regarded dreams, the late Shang dynasty tortoise-shell and oracle-bone inscriptions, dating from the thirteenth to eleventh centuries BCE, indicate that the kings at this time, if not before, regarded their oneiric experiences as highly consequential. They thus regularly consulted their

Introduction 3

highest, ancestral gods for explanations of their dreams, as well as those of their wives and officials. These rulers demonstrated their concern as they posed questions about warfare, hunting, sacrifice, rain, travel, and health. With the help of diviners, pyroscapulamancy was practiced by heating specially prepared tortoise plastrons and animal bones, and then reading the resulting cracks to learn whether a dream was ominous or not. Some examples of the dreams of King Wuding 商武丁王 (r. ca. 1250–1189 BCE) were inscribed afterward in simple, formulaic language on the shells and bones:

> On the day *bingzi*, Gu divined whether the king's dream about his wife meant calamity or not.
> On the day *xinwei*, Gu divined whether the king's dream about his elder brother Wu following him with a dagger meant calamity or not.
> On the day *guiwei*, the king divined if his dream of a demon meant that he should proceed with offering the *yu* sacrifice or not.[6]

The Shang rulers maintained frequent communication with their ancestral gods on many other matters and interpreted certain signs as indications of divine approval. However, the shell and bone inscriptions suggest that they generally regarded dreams fearfully. Such events were mostly assumed to convey the dissatisfaction of their ancestors in heaven who might send down punishments or catastrophes. Few among those that were divined were initially thought to be auspicious.

Some etymological interpretations of the Shang form of the graph for dream 夢 focus on its pictographic elements. These might indicate a person pointing to his eye to signify a palpable visual perception (right-hand component) while dreaming in bed (left-hand component).[7] It is clear from the records of these divinations that methods of interpretation had already evolved that both framed dream experience in language and sought to integrate the experience into broader cosmological patterns that could be rationally understood. This not only involved organizing its content into a brief, coherent narrative and classifying its character as auspicious or inauspicious, but also verifying it afterward based on various divination systems and the observation of portents or subsequent events in waking life. Corroborating subjective events with what were regarded as objective forms of evidence remained a prominent technique of Chinese dream interpretation, and can be seen as having an early origin, particularly with regard to dreams that were of national political importance.[8]

While the Shang kings were prognosticating their dreams, other forms of interpretation probably already existed among the population transmitted through popular religion and folklore. These were performed by spirit-mediums or other occult specialists. Pyroscapulamancy continued to be practiced in later periods, and recent archaeological evidence suggests that it was also popular among non-aristocrats during the Western Zhou period (ca. 1056–771 BCE).[9] Two poems in *The Book of Songs* 詩經 (*Shijing,* ca. 11th–7th cents. BCE) indicate that dream interpretations were provided by "great men" 大人 *(tairen),* who may have been people of rank, while another mentions "elders" 故老 *(gulao)* as being consulted.[10] There are also conventional associations of dream imagery with fixed interpretations similar to the content of dream manuals 夢書 *(mengshu).* In the song "The Beck" 斯干 ("Sigan"), traditionally read as the dream of King Xuan of the Zhou 周宣王 (r. ca. 827–784 BCE), images of black and brown bears are interpreted as indicating the birth of sons while snakes and serpents indicate daughters.[11] The song notes that the king later produced both a son and a daughter as predicted. That dream manuals existed at an early point is confirmed by an anecdote in *The Compendium of Master Yan* 晏子春秋 (*Yanzi chunqiu,* Warring States period) where a professional interpreter summoned to the court of Duke Jing of Qi 齊景公 (r. 547–490 BCE) states that he must consult his manual before attempting to decipher the duke's dream about battling two suns.[12]

The use of dream manuals is among the most pervasive and enduring practices with counterparts in many other cultures. They have remained a regular feature of Chinese almanacs down to the present, and their popularity may be attributed to empowering a reader to decipher dream imagery without requiring any training, spiritual abilities, or professional status. Many of these were attributed to the famous Wei dynasty official and dream interpreter Zhou Xuan 周宣 (d. ca. 239). A few lines from the chapter on clothing in the oldest surviving text, *A New Version of Mr. Zhou's Manual for Interpreting Dreams* 新集周公解夢書 (*Xinji Zhougong jiemengshu,* 966), indicates the kind of fixed interpretations they provided:

> Dreaming of wearing new clothes means illness.
> Dreaming of taking off clothes means a dispute.
> Dreaming of wearing blue clothes means becoming an official.
> Dreaming of wearing yellow clothes means great happiness.
> Dreaming of green clothes means a wife will become pregnant.
> Dreaming of white clothes is very auspicious.[13]

Dream manuals also underscore the important role that symbolic images 象 *(xiang)* have always played in Chinese dream interpretation, for such images often served to mark linkages or correspondences between the individual and the cosmos. Primary reliance on dream manuals was a characteristic practice of marketplace professionals. Hence, these texts were often looked down upon by scholars and the more sophisticated interpreters who catered to the elite. A similar skepticism is reflected in the story of the previously mentioned dream of Duke Jing of Qi. The astute official Yan Ying 宴嬰 (d. 500 BCE) orders a professional dream interpreter to ignore his dream manual and cleverly provides him with an optimistic explanation to tell the duke instead. This placebo succeeds in curing the duke's illness because Yan recognized that the duke shared the popular faith in the skill of these interpreters and in the reliability of their manuals.

With the growing use of written texts during the Warring States period (ca. 475–221 BCE), dream narratives began to be recorded at length. Against the backdrop of increased competition among the feudal states for hegemony, the intellectual life of this period was transformed as schools of educated advisors proffered text-based knowledge to rulers in the hope of gaining patronage. The courts were thronged with a variety of experts, including military strategists, historian-astrologers, philosophers, diplomats, bureaucrats, physicians, spirit-mediums, and *fangshi*-wizards 方士. Included in the books that have come down to us from these groups are dream narratives designed to demonstrate their particular worldviews and skills, as well as those that functioned politically in policy discussions. This early literature reveals a characteristic of many traditional Chinese accounts of dreams: their questionable status as actual or accurately reported oneiric experiences. Whether presented within historical chronicles at one end of the literary spectrum or as philosophical allegories at the other, they tend to follow similar narrative conventions. Such ambiguity continued throughout the development of Chinese literature as it expanded to include new kinds of private, unofficial historical writings as well as overtly fictional works. With the exception of verifiably autobiographical accounts, dream narratives in prose typically employ a third-person, objective narrator who omnisciently records the private experience of a dreamer. Along with other rhetorical features, they utilize the conventions of an official biography to create an effect of verisimilitude, factuality, and authority. The origin of the account is rarely disclosed, and the relationship between the narrator and the dreamer is generally not apparent, especially if the two were not contemporaries. Most of the narratives compiled by Chen Shiyuan in his encyclopedia conform to this generic code, which was accepted by readers as the normative framework for transmitting dream experiences.

One of the largest collections of stories from the early period can be found in *Zuo's Narratives to the Spring and Autumn Annals* 春秋左傳 (*Chunqiu zuozhuan*, Warring States period), an assemblage of explanatory anecdotes embedded within a historical chronicle from the feudal state of Lu, covering the years 722 to 481 BCE.[14] Most of the thirty-plus dreams included are spiritual communications that transmit literal or symbolic messages which, once interpreted, usually offer clear guidance for action to members of the ruling class. The response of the dreamer to the dream is generally consistent with the book's central theme of the unfolding of history based on individual virtue or lack thereof. When the arrogant prime minister of Chu, Ziyu 子玉 (d. 632 BCE), is about to attack Duke Wen of Jin 晉文公 (r. 636–628 BCE) at the battle of Chengpu in 632 BCE, he dreams that the God of the Yellow River requests the sacrifice of some elegant caps and martingales designed for the prime minister's horses. In return, the god would grant Ziyu a strategic piece of territory. In keeping with his character, Ziyu begrudges these petty items and also refuses to listen to his loyal ministers who remonstrate with him. He later loses the battle and, finally, his life. The moral thematics of *Zuo's Narratives* not only suggest that Ziyu has obstinately rebuffed spiritual support through his selfishness, but also that his own actions are the real origin of his doom. One of his ministers remarks in despair, "It will not be the gods who defeat the prime minister. He takes no care for the people of the country. In truth, the prime minister will defeat himself."[15]

Not all of these dreams, however, are so obvious. There are some that the reader of the text, as well as the dreamer, initially finds ambiguous, calling into question the ability of dreams to clarify events in the human world. In what have been called "equivocal dreams," a certain opacity may lead to the wrong assumptions until a clever interpretation manipulates the symbolic images to provide the kind of meaning consistent with the moral trajectory of the story.[16] Just prior to the battle of Chengpu, Duke Wen has a terrifying dream in which Ziyu wrestles him to the ground and sucks out his brains. Despite its apparent inauspiciousness, the duke's uncle and minister, Zifan 子犯, adroitly proclaims, "Good Fortune! You were facing up to heaven but Chu was bent over, as though being punished for some crime. And your brains would soften him up!"[17] In these kinds of dreams, the text evokes skepticism about the uses of interpretation that occasionally surfaces in Chinese writings. Still, most historians, official or not, continued to document dreams as verifiable portents. It is clear from these and other early narratives that interpretations were performed by a variety of figures beyond spirit-mediums, court officials, and professional diviners. Talented guests at the feudal courts were also consulted, and, in some cases, individuals could also decipher their own dreams unaided.

Zuo's Narratives is also the locus classicus of a concept of human nature used to explain the physical entity that experiences dreams. This asserted the existence of an ethereal soul 魂 *(hun)* and an earthly soul 魄 *(po)* that normally were conjoined within the body during waking life. In sleep, as in death, the bonds between these souls dissolved, freeing the ethereal *hun*-soul to wander while the earthly *po*-soul remained within the body. In an entry about the appearance of a ghost in 534 BCE, the aristocrat Zichan of Zheng 鄭子產 (ca. 580–522 BCE) explained, "Man at his birth undergoes a transformation, and this is called the '*po*.' As soon as the *po* has taken form, it also contains a yang part which is called the '*hun*.' If he can consume a great amount of the vigorous essence 精 *(jing)* of things, then his *hun* and *po* will be strong. Thus, his essence will become supple and his spirit 神 *(shen)* will be luminous."[18] Later theories further elaborated the notion of these dual souls and also spread the idea that the *hun*-soul did not leave the body of its own volition, but was attracted to wander elsewhere by spiritual forces outside the body. This supported a simple etiology of dreams based on a kind of seduction of the individual by external powers. A more complete correlation of the two souls with yin and yang cosmology probably did not reach its final formulation until the second century BCE. However, the idea that the substance of the *hun*-soul is vital *qi*-energy 氣 and characterized by rapid movement beyond the grosser physical limitations of the body can already be found in pre-Han texts. In the *Songs of Chu* 楚辭 (*Chuci*, ca. 3rd cent. BCE), a number of poems present the *hun*-soul as capable of traveling beyond the normal limits of time and space. These poems are thought to contain literary transformations of religious material that reflect the heavily shamanistic culture of the south. A few, such as the "Summons of the Soul" 招魂 ("Zhaohun") and the "Great Summons" 大招 ("Dazhao"), describe a common funeral ritual in which a spirit-medium or ritual specialist attempts to recall the *hun*-soul back to the body immediately after death. Other pieces, such as "On Encountering Sorrow" 離騷 ("Lisao") and "The Far-off Journey" 遠遊 ("Yuanyou"), are more like daydream fantasies in which the aggrieved official Qu Yuan 屈原 (4th cent. BCE) leaves the Chu court in search of sympathy and encounters divine figures in the course of his celestial peregrinations.[19] While none of these poems are specifically cast as a dream, their thematic structure offered prototypes for several kinds of later dream narratives. Among these are: ascents to heaven where transcendents 仙 *(xian)* who have mastered the techniques of longevity are encountered, journeys to hell and back by those who report religious views of the afterlife, and erotic encounters with goddesses who may seduce, instruct, harm, or disillusion humans.

Another early form of descriptive poetry, the *fu*-rhapsody, arose around this time and flourished during the Han. A courtly genre with highly rhetorical language, it often celebrated a centralized world of plenitude dominated by imperial power and the kind of ordered cosmos that was characteristic of correlative cosmology. At the same time, many of these works also continued the shamanistic religious traditions present in the *Songs of Chu*, such as the use of incantation and enumeration, to create a magical counterpart in language to the objects and experiences described. This created a dynamic tension between the circumscribed political world of courtly values and transgressive elements that threatened to escape human control. In the *fu*-rhapsody, the dream began to emerge in poetry as a liminal zone defined by pleasurable journeying, ambiguous encounters with divinities, and sensual landscapes of momentary enchantment. The "Rhapsody on the Gaotang Shrine" 高唐賦 ("Gaotangfu"), by the poet Song Yu 宋玉 (ca. 290–ca. 223 BCE), is among the earliest examples of poems about dreams of erotic encounters between humans and goddesses. In this piece, King Xiang of Chu 楚襄王 (r. 298–263 BCE) visits the Yunmeng Terrace with Song Yu and gazes at the mist-enshrouded Gaotang Shrine from a distance. Informed by the poet that this mist is called "Dawn Cloud," he learns upon further inquiry that his predecessor, King Huai 楚懷王 (r. 328–299 BCE), had a dream here in which he encountered a goddess from Shaman Mountain who transformed from the rain and mist.[20]

The following night, Song Yu himself has a dream vision of encountering the same divinity, which he described in a sequel, "Rhapsody on the Goddess" 神女賦 ("Shennü fu").[21] Her encounter with the poet, however, is presented as ambiguous, emotional, and spiritual rather than physical, even though symbolic landscape imagery was abandoned in order to directly describe her appearance, movements, and sensual qualities.[22] Typically, in later Chinese literature, the different quality of *qi*-energy possessed by humans and divinities and the living and the dead is cited as a major reason why such unions are fated to be brief, occasionally disastrous, and usually impossible to recapture. Nevertheless, literary descriptions of such encounters in dreams formed a genre of fantasy that aroused similar passions among many readers.

Neither of these two poems overtly draws the conclusion of later religious Daoist and Buddhist beliefs, which is that the ephemeral character of oneiric experiences proves that waking life is illusory, and that the only solution to the problem of human desire is ultimate detachment through spiritual enlightenment or transcendence. Still, around the same period as these poems, early Daoist philosophers were employing the dream to advocate complex and often paradoxical considerations about consciousness, self, and the nature of language and of the world. Some of the most skeptical arguments are contained in the *Master Zhuang* 莊子 (*Zhuangzi,* ca. 3rd cent. BCE), which have had widespread influence. The eleven anecdotes that relate to dreams fall roughly into three categories.

Firstly, there are fairly straightforward narratives based on the concept of wandering souls, where the body is thought to be closed down during sleep so that the *hun*-soul is free to depart and interact with others. These dream states enable the philosopher to advocate radical, antithetical views whose subversive character is given a protective coloration by locating their exponents outside of waking reality. For example, the character Master Zhuang comes across an old skull on the road. He questions it with an air of commiseration about its unhappy fate, resulting, he assumes, from suffering one of the many dangers inherent in human existence. Then he uses it as a pillow. The skull comes to Master Zhuang in a dream to berate his entanglement in conventional thinking and to assert the superior happiness of the dead in comparison with the pain experienced by the living.[23] In another dream, an oak tree at a shrine appears to a carpenter who had dismissed it as useless for woodworking. The tree exalts the worth of its perceived uselessness from the point of view of a higher value—survival. He caustically contrasts his existence to that of other, more desirable trees that have been cut down, and derides the carpenter for his anthropocentric ignorance.[24] Both anecdotes employ humor and reversals of the reader's assumptions to undermine common values, privileging the world of dreams as a place of superior understanding.

A more original use of dream in the *Master Zhuang* questions even this function. Instead, a dream reveals the instability of one's waking identity, resulting in existential doubt. Unquestionably, the most well-known example is the "Dream of a Butterfly" 蝴蝶夢 ("Hudiemeng"):

Once Zhuang Zhou dreamt he was a butterfly, a butterfly flitting and fluttering around, happy with himself and doing as he pleased. He didn't know he was Zhuang Zhou. Suddenly, he woke up, and there he was, solid and unmistakable Zhuang Zhou. But, he didn't know if he was Zhuang Zhou who had dreamt he was a butterfly, or a butterfly dreaming he was Zhuang Zhou. Between Zhuang Zhou and a butterfly there must be *some* distinction! This is called the "Transformation of Things."[25]

Here, the dream is equated to waking consciousness as a ground for apprehending the self. But, because of the ceaseless alternation between these two states, neither is able to serve as an ultimate basis for certainty. This can only be found in the constant change that is the nature of the Way 道 *(Dao)*.

Finally, in a more theoretical mode of speculation, the *Master Zhuang* also contains the statement that ultimate enlightenment is like "a great awakening when we know that this is all a great dream,"[26] a conceit that later was also widely disseminated by Buddhism. As an end point to the entire problem of dreaming, the text affirms that the perfected gentleman 真人 *(zhenren)*, having arrived at the highest state of spiritual cultivation, no longer dreams at all because he is without persistent thoughts or worldly attachments.[27] This suggests that some of the early Daoist philosophers regarded dreaming as a pathological symptom of waking self-consciousness. It indicated a mind entangled in dualistic thinking and a body that was vulnerable to harmful external agents.[28]

Despite the philosophical appeal of the *Master Zhuang* among the educated, oneiric experiences, especially nightmares, continued to be widely understood as emanating from powerful forces in the environment that could threaten personal welfare. Incantations found in occult texts dating from the late third century BCE suggest a well-developed tradition that employed magical curses to expel demons in nightmares.[29] Shamanistic medicine generally posited dreams as the result of demons that had penetrated the body and lodged themselves there. Such invasions could result from the inexplicable malevolence of these forces, from the individual's unwitting transgression of divine prerogatives, or as retribution for past offenses. The solution usually involved techniques of exorcism. Wang Yanshou's 王延壽 (fl. mid-2nd cent. CE) "Rhapsody on a Dream" 夢賦 ("Mengfu") narrated such a frightening experience and recorded incantations designed to neutralize these horrors.[30] This may be one of the earliest attempts by a writer to document his dream. However, its purpose was not merely clinical or an act of self-exorcism. Rather, Wang sought to create a literary piece with magical elements that readers might recite in order to deal with their own nightmares.

Theories about the origins and nature of dreams in early China also appeared in medical treatises. A danger connected with the wandering of the *hun*-soul at night was its possession by forces while outside the body so that it could not return. This prevents the dreamer from awakening despite the wandering *hun*-soul's natural desire to reunite with the *po*-soul. Various techniques recorded in later texts were apparently used. These included enticing the wandering spirit back by gently calling out the dreamer's name in a darkened room so as to physically shock the sleeper into awakening, as well as the use of ritual incantations. Preventative methods were also advocated, such as clasping the thumbs within the fists prior to falling asleep.[31]

The more sophisticated medicine practiced by physicians during the Warring States period also acknowledged the possibility of the invasion of "evil energy" 邪氣 *(xieqi)*. It defined the body as a holistic, microcosmic system in correlation with the universal activity of yin and yang and the five agents. Normally, yin and yang types of vital energy 精氣 *(jingqi)* harmoniously circulated along networks of vessels 脈 *(mo)* and meridians 經 *(jing)* administered by the five *zang*-organs 五臟 *(wuzang)* and the six *fu*-organs 六腑 *(liufu)*, the latter two groups generally corresponding to the vital organs. The consequences of the disruption of the regular rhythms of the patient's vital energy were diagnosed through examination of the pulse along with other symptoms, including dreams. *The Yellow Emperor's Inner Canon of Medicine* 黃帝內經 (*Huangdi neijing*, ca. 2nd–1st cent. BCE) advised that "dreams can also help us diagnose a person's illness. If one dreams of fearfully crossing a large body of water, this indicates an excess of yin. If one dreams of flames or fire, this indicates an excess of yang."[32] In this classic medical treatise, certain fixed associations with symbolic images characteristic of dream manuals have been grafted onto a system of pathology. The variety of these images was seen as due to the physiological differences among the elements of the body reflecting twelve kinds of excess or fifteen kinds of deficiency of yin and yang vital energy. The content of dreams may indicate such internal imbalances of physiological forces and also the exact location in the body of the highly mobile, invading elements.[33]

One typical practice in early Chinese theorizing about dreams was to categorize them, and many of these categories continued to be referred to by later writers.[34] *The Government Organization of the Zhou* 周禮

(*Zhouli*, ca. 3rd cent. BCE), later canonized as a Confucian classic, records an idealized version of the early Zhou dynasty government. It promoted the rationalistic view that dreams primarily originate from external stimuli combined with psychological factors. These were then interpreted and confirmed by various divination systems. In discussing the duties of the official interpreter of dreams 占夢 *(zhanmeng)*, it indicated that he used a system based on the calendar, yin and yang qualities of atmospheric vapors 氣 *(qi)*, and the astronomical positions of the sun, moon, stars, and asterisms to decide whether the ruler's dreams were auspicious or not. These were classified into six types: 1) normal 正夢 *(zhengmeng)*; 2) nightmares 噩夢 *(emeng)*; (3) dreams about waking thoughts 思夢 *(simeng)*; (4) dreams about waking statements 寤夢 *(wumeng)*; (5) happy dreams 喜夢 *(ximeng)*; and (6) fearful dreams 懼夢 *(jumeng)*.[35] Another official, the grand diviner 大卜 *(taibu)*, was supposed to be in charge of personnel who interpret three kinds of dreams of the king by comparing them to the halos of atmospheric vapors around the sun the next day.[36]

During the Eastern Han dynasty, another typology was put forward by a private scholar, Wang Fu 王符 (ca. 90–165 CE), in his *Discussions from a Gentleman in Hiding* 潛夫論 *(Qianfulun*, ca. 111–152 CE). In a chapter especially devoted to dreams, he created a classification of ten types: 1) dreams of direct correspondence 直 *(zhi)*, which are predictive of events that later occur; 2) symbolic dreams 象 *(xiang)*, which are encoded in imagery that could be interpreted, for example, by the use of dream manuals; 3) fixation dreams 精 *(jing)*, resulting from recurrent thoughts during waking hours; 4) imaginative dreams 想 *(xiang)*; 5) dreams based on status 人 *(ren)*, whose content is influenced by the dreamer's social role; 6) dreams in response to stimuli 感 *(gan)*, resulting from rain, hot or cold weather, or from wind; 7) seasonal dreams 時 *(shi)*, whose content reflects the agricultural cycle, such as growth of crops in summer or storing the harvest in fall and winter; 8) contrary dreams 反 *(fan)*, whose interpretation is the opposite of the normal logic of the dream; 9) dreams caused by illness 病 *(bing)*, resulting from an imbalance of yin and yang in the body; and 10) dreams based on the dreamer's nature 性 *(xing)*, whose content reflects individual preferences and tastes.[37]

This grouping combined several different kinds of criteria. Wang essentially offered a summary approach for his time period that took into account occult, moralistic, cosmological, physiological, and psychological factors. Furthermore, while he regarded certain conventional types of imagery as auspicious or inauspicious, he felt that methods of divination were effective only when some spiritual entity had definitely affected the individual. In such cases, interpretations of dreams ought not be limited to conventional approaches. Interpretation for Wang was a skilled art, and he noted that dream manuals were easily misunderstood by ordinary people and amateurs. Lastly, he considered the reaction of the dreamer to an interpretation to be a valid aspect of the total significance of the dream. If a person responds to an auspicious dream with bad conduct, it would be, functionally speaking, the same as if the dream had been initially inauspicious.

Previously, another independent thinker of this time, Wang Chong 王充 (27-ca. 100 CE), voiced skepticism about a number of dreams recorded in early literature in his iconoclastic essays, which touched on such topics as birth, death, premonitions and portents, demons, and poison. In his *Judicious Discussions* 論衡 (*Lunheng*, ca. 70–80 CE), he did not question the veracity of these accounts, but rejected reliance on overly literal interpretations. Dreams, he argued, arose from encounters that engaged the individual's vigorous essence and spirit. Though they were composed of symbolic images, these were different from phenomena in waking reality. Such images should not be interpreted as if they existed in real life, he argued, for it was preferable to confirm dreams with other forms of divination, such as those that observed corresponding portents. Wang also challenged the prevailing notion of the *hun*-soul leaving the body and wandering off during sleep, as well as concepts of an afterlife where people preserved their identity and consciousness. Both Wang Fu and Wang Chong have been termed "materialists" by some modern scholars. In the case of their theories of dreams, this meant affirming primarily mental and physiological bases, although these did not preclude correspondences with macrocosmic patterns and the use of divinatory methods.[38] In both cases, their theories were aggregates of disparate etiological factors rather than single, synthesized explanations. This syncretistic approach remained typical of Chinese theorizing and is also reflected in Chen Shiyuan's views.

The medieval period (3rd–10th cents.) marked an important new phase in both the understanding of dreams and in their literary representation while earlier textual traditions continued to be selectively transmitted. With the collapse of the centralized empire of the Han dynasty, the high culture was now largely sustained by local aristocratic, scholarly, and religious communities that focused on individualistic concerns and on comprehending the dislocations produced by a chaotic age. The court-centered focus on the grand ethical and political programs of Confucianism gave way among many of the educated class to the desire to inquire more deeply into the naturalistic relationships between the three realms of heaven, earth, and man. Within intellectual discourses characterized as "mystical learning" 玄學 *(xuanxue)*, "pure conversation" 清談 *(qingtan)*, "universal learning" 博學 *(boxue)*, and "knowledge of things" 博物 *(bowu)*, the dreams of a broader range of people beyond rulers and the political elite were scrutinized. These were documented in an expanded range of narrative genres that included official and unofficial historical accounts and biographies, anomaly accounts, short stories, miscellanies, and encyclopedias. Propelling the cultural energy of this period was the spread of Buddhism and religious Daoism, which evolved in tandem by appropriating elements of each other's theologies, rituals, texts, and institutions.

Buddhism had begun to be introduced from India and Central Asia in the mid-first century CE. According to various later and probably spurious accounts, this followed a visionary dream of Emperor Ming of the Eastern Han 漢明帝 (r. 57–75 CE) in 60 CE.[39] The imported beliefs of various schools introduced among other elements a more complex universe of heavens and hells, a deeper sense of causality behind events, and a greater awareness of the role of consciousness in the construction of reality. Buddhist culture most commonly employed the dream as a metaphor of the illusory nature of all dharmas, as stated in *The Diamond Sutra* 金剛經 (*Jin'gangjing*, ca. 400): "All the dharmas that are produced are like dreams, phantasms, bubbles, shadows."[40]

There were also more specific theories such as the typology in *The Commentary on the Discipline that Sees Well* 善見律毘婆沙 (*Shanjianlü piposha*, 489), which distinguished four categories. Two of these were based on the dreamer's physiology and quotidian experiences and considered illusory. The other two types were dreams caused by divine beings and prophetic dreams caused by past merit or demerit. These were regarded as more real.[41] The last category introduced the roles of karma and reincarnation into the etiology of dreams. These ideas were also to have profound influence on later, secular theorizing by Chinese scholars. The Buddhist view asserted that the auspicious or inauspicious quality of prophetic dreams was directly related to the virtuous acts or sins of the dreamer in a former existence. Some theorists regarded sinful acts in dreams as only valid on a metaphysical level, while others regarded dreams as an intermediate state between human existence and nirvana. Dreams also played a role in Tantric rituals and appeared in stories of the Buddha's life and other miracle tales. They revealed apocalyptic predictions and were popularly sought by people for guidance about personal destiny through incubation in temples.⁴² In addition, individual monks sometimes kept notes of their dreams and those of their disciples, even compiling dream diaries to chart spiritual progress. In these latter activities, the consciousness of the dreamer was regarded as playing a creative, rather than passive, role. For, compared to waking life, the dream state was felt to be closer to the bliss of enlightenment.

Buddhist theories influenced more secular views as early as that of Yue Guang 樂廣 (252–304), an expert in mystical learning. In replying to a question about the nature of dreams from his future son-in-law, Wei Jie 衛玠 (286–312), Yue identified their origins as either thoughts or "contingent causes" 因 (yin).⁴³ The former were understood to be internal desires, hopes, or intentions, while the latter were defined as mental processes generated by perceptions of external stimuli. Yue phrased his discussion of such associations negatively: no one dreamt of entering a rat hole in a carriage, pounding leeks, or eating an iron pestle, because these actions did not exist in waking life and, so, had never been perceived.

Religious Daoism, which also arose in the first century CE, incorporated many of the philosophical and cosmological concepts of earlier Daoist schools. The *Master Zhuang* was canonized as a sacred scripture and grew in influence, especially among devotees of mystical learning. The *Master Lie* 列子 (*Liezi*, ca. 4th cent.), written in the same vein, also appeared. Its anecdotes and short discussions transmitted both pre-Qin (before 221 BCE) and later material including yet another typology that defined eight kinds of waking consciousness and six categories of dreams for interpretation. It included the medical concept that "influences" 感 (gan) produced "altered conditions" 變 (bian) indicated by dreams, as well as the influential formulation, "What the spirit encounters becomes a dream; what the body comes in contact with becomes an event. What we think about by day and dream of by night results from whatever our spirit and body encounters."⁴⁴

Among the anecdotes in the *Master Lie* is a dream narrative that reiterates the earlier skepticism found in the *Master Zhuang*. A court case arises between a woodcutter who has caught a deer and a thief who steals it. Both confuse their waking actions with their dreams, and the judicial authorities, considering the matter to be undecidable, propose to arbitrarily divide the deer. Two other dream anecdotes contrast the enlightenment of the mythical Yellow Emperor 黃帝 (Huangdi), who journeyed out-of-body to heaven in the company of a wizard, with the experience of King Mu of the Zhou 周穆王 (r. ca. 956–918 BCE), who made a similar but ultimately unsuccessful tour. The Yellow Emperor, who had spiritually prepared himself for the experience, returns to earth, awakes, and finally becomes a transcendent. King Mu, however, did not cultivate himself sufficiently and is described as sensually overwhelmed by the intense, rarefied energies of the celestial realm. Suffering from overexposure to these perceptions, he can only beg to be taken back to earth, where he lives out the rest of his mortal life traveling through the terrestrial world.[45]

The latter two dreams reflect the ideals of meditation and alchemy in religious Daoism. These introduced a more complex understanding of the *hun*- and *po*-souls, their relation to dreaming, as well as new techniques for directing their wanderings. Both souls were still regarded as spiritual in nature. However, the goal of transcendence was now to preserve their unity in the process of transformation as the individual abandoned the grosser form of the physical body and ascended to heaven as pure *qi*-energy. Dreams like those experienced by the Yellow Emperor or historical Daoist masters who received revelations were encouraged if they involved the wandering of the *hun*-soul together with gods, transcendents, and perfected gentlemen. Typical dreams, in contrast, where the *hun*-soul ventures away from the body and becomes vulnerable to possession or disturbing influences, were regarded as obstacles to spiritual progress. Even worse, the hitherto sedentary *po*-soul could also roam by itself along more earthly routes. During these peregrinations, it might encounter demons and engage in sexual activities resulting in mental obsession and a loss of vigorous essence. To prevent such dangers during sleep, it was considered necessary to restrain both wayward souls with the help of guardian spirits through visualizations, incantations, and talismans.[46]

Religious Daoism developed a vast sacred literature of esoteric, visionary revelations that was disseminated among educated believers through scholarly and missionary efforts. Dreams formed an important channel of communication between leading Daoist adepts and various divinities, as well as among adepts themselves both in life and after death. These involved the bestowing of secret techniques of spiritual cultivation as well summonses to become officials in heaven. Yang Xi 楊羲 (330–386), who received divine instructions at midnight on Mount Mao from 364 to 370, sent records of his dreams to his patrons in the Xu family; the Xus exchanged notes of their own experiences with him. Similar instances were documented by Tao Hongjing 陶弘景 (456–536), who organized the sect of Maoshan 茅山 (or Shangqing 上清) Daoism. The pattern of receiving empowering religious revelations through dreams and using these as a justification for legitimization or rebellion became a recurrent feature of Chinese political life.⁴⁷ Reigning emperors could claim new forms of divinity after dream encounters with Daoist gods, some of whom revealed themselves as ancestors of the imperial family. Emperor Xuanzong of the Tang 唐玄宗 (r. 712–756) met the seminal Daoist philosopher Laozi 老子 (trad. fl. late 6th-early 5th century BCE) and Emperor Zhenzong of the Northern Song 宋真宗 (r. 998–1022) received sacred texts from the Supreme Jade Emperor 玉皇上帝 (Yuhuang shangdi).⁴⁸ Similarly, Zhu Yuanzhang 朱元璋 (1328–1398), the future Emperor Taizu of the Ming 明太祖, dreamt of encountering Daoist gods in the course of establishing the dynasty and recorded the experience himself.⁴⁹ On the microcosmic level, Daoist dreams could also indicate the state of the body's progress in realizing transcendence by refining itself into pure *qi*-energy through diet, exercise, meditation, and alchemy. Some dreams enabled the practitioner to identify internal demons such as the three "corpse-worms" 尸蟲 *(shichong)*, who dwelled behind the forehead, heart, and navel. A dream of intercourse with a woman indicated that the three were holding a meeting to plot against the dreamer, while a dream of one's home going up in flames was said to indicate that the ingestion of longevity drugs was having a positive effect combatting them.⁵⁰

Both Buddhism and religious Daoism promoted new, extensive arrangements of heavens and hells that closely mirrored the Chinese government of the human world with its complex hierarchy of officials and bureaucratic procedures. These were popularly disseminated through a variety of media such as pictorial albums, temple murals and sculptures, sacred texts, oral storytelling, and ritual plays that vividly detailed an array of rewards and punishments. In contrast to earlier fears of the unpredictability of strange creatures, this view of the afterlife offered the possibility that these ruling divinities not only possessed superior powers, but also followed common ethical and legal practices that humans could understand, rely upon, and, in some cases, influence. A narrative genre developed during the medieval period that was particularly suited to exploring problems between the yang world of the living and the yin world of the supranormal: the "anomaly account" 誌怪 *(zhiguai)*. Anomaly accounts continued earlier tendencies to collect and categorize strange phenomena as part of the cultural process of defining the normal and domesticating the threats of the unknown, foreign, and uncontrollable.⁵¹ Written mostly by officials and private scholars, some of whom also compiled more orthodox histories, they made use of previously documented events and also incorporated legends, folklore, oral history, and religious elements to explore the kind of themes that preoccupied people during this period. These included return-from-death experiences, journeys to heaven and hell, encounters with gods, goddesses, demons, and ghosts, as well as the appearance of strange portents and anomalies. Some of the motivations for compiling such stories included explaining why humans and spirits wandered across the boundaries that separated yin and yang worlds, as well as publicizing the consequences of these transgressions. Dream was highlighted as a dimension where these acts often occurred. Just as the Chinese state during this time could not always prevent the incursions of foreign tribes, neither could local societies resist mass internal migrations; each anomaly account can thus be seen as a case history illustrating a problem resulting from porous boundaries. This literature not only sought to prove that such events did indeed occur, but also to serve as guides to similar situations.[52]

One of the best-known early collections of anomaly accounts, *In Search of the Supernatural* 搜神記 (*Soushenji*, ca. 335–ca. 349), compiled by the Eastern Jin dynasty historian and official Gan Bao 干寶 (fl. ca. 317–ca. 349), contains twelve dream narratives that focus on the consequences of strange phenomena intruding into waking life. One example demonstrates how Xu Tai 徐泰 overcomes the underworld bureaucracy when he dreams that deputies arrive with orders to fetch his sick uncle. In response to Xu's pleas and moved by his devotion to his relative, they agree to substitute someone else with a similar name.[53] This story highlights the popular Chinese belief in reciprocity or repayment 報 (*bao*) as a means of sustaining the moral balance of the universe. Dreams were sometimes a medium for carrying out this mechanism or for communicating subsequent events in waking life that were responses to previous actions.

As narratives, the conventions of anomaly accounts are virtually indistinguishable from the historiographical style of official biographies in the standard dynastic histories, even though the tendency to separate out more fantastic content from the latter genre had already begun. Both genres include anecdotes about charismatic individuals with spiritual abilities such as *fangshi*-wizards and other practitioners of occult magic. A few of these achieved enduring fame as dream interpreters. Zhou Xuan became one of the most celebrated practitioners throughout later dream culture in China. Originally a local official at the end of the Eastern Han dynasty, he rose to prominence at the court of Emperor Wen of the Wei 魏文帝 (r. 220–225) and was known for his accurate predictions. Over the centuries, he has been credited as the author of various dream manuals, but such claims are unlikely. He was recorded as not only employing more subtle methods, but also rejecting any reliance on interpretive texts. Zhou went further than his predecessors in seeing dream thoughts as essentially no different from waking thoughts and in asserting that the consequences would be the same regardless of origin. As he wrote, "The fact is dreams are nothing more than ideas 意 *(yi)*. If they take form enough to be articulated, their auspicious and inauspicious meanings can be divined."[54]

A type of dream interpretation not noted by earlier theorists, yet recorded as being employed from this period on, is the so-called glyphomantic dream 拆字夢 *(chaizimeng)*. In this type of interpretation, Chinese graphs are analyzed in order to reveal hidden meanings. One method is to uncouple the elements in a graph and reassemble them into a meaningful sequence to create paranormal readings. Such wordplay can be traced back at least to *Zuo's Narratives,* though in the medieval period this skill was credited to the Yellow Emperor in remote antiquity.[55] At some point in time, perhaps as late as the Sui dynasty, it was developed as a professional fortune-telling technique that was often practiced along with other forms of divination.[56] However, to judge from several anecdotes, its use in interpreting dreams may have occurred somewhat earlier. One instance involved Zou Zhan 鄒湛 (d. ca. 291), a high official during the Eastern Jin dynasty who rose to the positions of chancellor of the National University and chamberlain for the palace revenues. His recurrent dreams occurred at the permeable boundary between living and dead because of overlapping claims to the same space. Zou solved the problem by performing a glyphomantic analysis of the name of a plaintive ghost and thereby demonstrated his command of one of the magical dimensions of the Chinese language:

> Zou Zhan dreamt of a man who gave his name as Zhen Shuzhong 甄舒仲 but then said nothing more. This occurred on more than one occasion. After a while, Zou understood and said, "West of my house is a mound of earth and broken tiles—there must be a dead man buried there. 'Zhen Shuzhong' means a man 亻 in 中 the earth 土 and broken tiles 瓦 west 西 of my 予 house 舍." He investigated and found it to be so. Zou collected the remains and generously reburied them. Afterward he dreamt that the man came and thanked him.[57]

A related technique of magical interpretation involves the use of homophonic puns. In these cases, the limited number of sound categories in Chinese facilitates lexical slippages, permitting the interpreter to substitute one meaning for another. Rather than appearing arbitrary, such associations reflect a general belief in a mystical structure of phonic signification embedded within the pronunciation of a graph or compound.[58]

With the rise of a genre of classical short-stories known as "transmissions of unique events" 傳奇 *(chuanqi)* during the Tang dynasty, the boundary began to erode between earlier anomaly accounts, which were presented as records of actual events, and more creative fictionalizing. As practiced by scholars and officials largely in and around the capital city of Chang'an, these tales were designed to entertain, display literary talent, satirize public figures, disguise political views, and explore aspects of private life. Dreams, like other strange phenomena, were suitable subjects. These narratives spanned the range from philosophical allegories to autobiographical anecdotes. Among the most famous allegories is Shen Jiji's 沈既濟 (ca. 740–ca. 800) *The World Inside a Pillow* 枕中記 ("Zhenzhongji"), which, like the *Master Zhuang,* expresses the illusory nature of worldly ambition.[59] A frustrated scholar named Lu 盧生 encounters a Mr. Lü 呂翁 at an inn, borrows a pillow from him, and dreams of fame and fortune. Lü may well be Lü Dongbin 呂洞賓, a Daoist god whom people invoked at incubation temples in hopes of obtaining dreams that would reveal their destinies. The dream episode in this piece parodies the form of an official biography and subverts its canonical role in literature as the most legitimate representation of a human life. By the end of the story, the hero's vicissitudes as a high official recounted in this inverted dream-biography convince him of the illusory nature of an official career, resulting in Daoist enlightenment.

Among more factual *chuanqi* is Bo Xingjian's 白行簡 (775–826) "A Record of Three Dreams" 三夢記 ("Sanmengji," ca. 809–826), which purports to document three unique types not commonly experienced or transmitted by classical sources. The first is a dream in which someone in waking life simultaneously experiences events occurring in someone else's dream. A high official, Liu Youqiu 劉幽求 (655–715), discovers his wife attending a banquet on her own, although the escapade turns out to be what she was dreaming about while at home. The second is autobiographical and involves a circle of poets and officials including the author's eminent brother, Bo Juyi 白居易 (772–846), and Yuan Zhen 元稹 (779–831). It is a dream about actual events occurring at a distance: Yuan Zhen, who is far away, dreams that the two Bo brothers and another friend visit a temple at the same time that they made the excursion. The last involves two simultaneous, identical dreams: the scholar Dou Zhi 竇質 (fl. 785–804) dreams of encountering a spirit-medium at a temple and meets her the next day; the spirit-medium had also dreamt of meeting the scholar.[60] In addition to individual accounts, the Tang also witnessed the rise of special collections of dream literature such as the *chuanqi* anthology *Ex-*

ceptional Dreams 夢雋 (Mengjuan), now mostly lost, which was attributed to the Tang grand councilor, Liu Can 劉燦 (fl. 888–904).⁶¹

One of the most important developments of the medieval period was the identification of dreams as a separate category of knowledge in encyclopedias 類書 *(leishu)* and miscellanies 筆記 *(biji)*. Only about one-third of the six hundred or so known encyclopedias from the third through the eighteenth centuries survive today, but these have preserved excerpts from numerous individual works that later disappeared. Some encyclopedias were designed to aid writers with literary allusions, as well as to provide students with a simplified digest of canonical texts and the high points of the literary tradition. This coincided with the growing popularity of writing poems about one's dreams.⁶² Miscellanies reflected the growth of a private narrative literature that randomly accumulated curious facts including personal experiences and observations about things. Some of the taxonomies employed in both genres provide indications of changing attitudes toward the intellectual status of strange phenomena and a desire to comprehend them more systematically. Generally speaking, though, the early examples of both encyclopedias and miscellanies continued to express ancient and medieval Chinese attitudes toward strange phenomena by regarding them as anomalous occurrences. They collected information with a high degree of historical and factual content, in addition to stories that appeared more fabricated and bizarre. The *Encyclopedia for Literary Composition* 藝文類聚 (*Yiwen leiju*, 604) by Ouyang Xun 歐陽詢 (557–641) combined a selection of thirteen dreams taken from classical, philosophical, and official and unofficial historical writings together with such pieces as Wang Yanshou's "Rhapsody on a Dream." Although certain aspects of this work precede the arrangements of later encyclopedias, the dreams are all classified under the category of "divine and strange" 靈異 *(lingyi)* and located in between sections on gods and the *hun-* and *po*-souls.⁶³ The Buddhist encyclopedia *A Grove of Pearls in the Dharma Garden* 法苑珠林 (*Fayuan zhulin*, 668) compiled by the monk Daoshi 道世 (ca. 600–683) contains several typologies. In a chapter devoted to dreams, examples are additionally divided into three types: auspicious 善行 *(shanxing)*; inauspicious 不善 *(bushan)*; and neutral 無記 *(wuji)*, which were intended to reveal the karma of the dreamer. Dreams recorded within narratives in other chapters included miracles, events in the life of Buddha, and eschatological prophecies.⁶⁴ Miscellanies of this time, such as Dai Fu's 戴孚 (ca. 724–ca. 794) *An Extensive Record of Anomalies* 廣異記 (*Guangyiji*, preface 806) and *Miscellaneous Morsels from Youyang* 酉陽雜俎 (*Youyang zazu,* ca. 850) by Duan Chengshi 段成式 (803–863), also contained dream narratives which were transmitted in later encyclopedias, including Chen Shiyuan's.[65]

By the late tenth century, the scholar-gentry of the Song dynasty had largely succeeded the aristocratic families of the medieval period as the arbiters of cultural tastes and political power. They promoted a revival and redefinition of Confucian values to support an imperial state with a more merit-based bureaucracy. Among the results was a clearer definition of orthodox and unorthodox subject matter in official literature. A pair of court-sponsored encyclopedias formalized this shift, which can be seen in their respective classifications of dream narratives. *The Imperial Digest of the Taiping Era* 太平御覽 (*Taiping yulan,* 984) and *The Taiping Miscellany* 太平廣記 (*Taiping guangji,* 978), both compiled by Li Fang 李昉 (925–996), were originally intended for the edification of Emperor Taizong of the Northern Song 宋太宗 (r. 976–997). The former collected more orthodox material suitable as precedents for governing and generally chose excerpts from classical and historical works. Its four chapters on dreams were placed under "human affairs" 人事 *(renshi)* inasmuch as the dreamers are mostly notable historical and political figures. The nearly two hundred examples were further divided into auspicious dreams, those that resulted in some kind of divine response, and inauspicious dreams, with further sub-categories. The remaining kinds of material from Buddhist and Daoist sources, unofficial histories, anomaly accounts, miscellanies, *chuanqi* stories, and other kinds of fictional narratives were placed in seven chapters in *The Taiping Miscellany.* This was a loosely structured compendium that continued Tang dynasty views regarding strange phenomena. Its 170 examples were subdivided into auspicious, inauspicious, gods and demons, and dream journeys. Each is titled according to the names of the dreamers, who are also presented as historical figures, though most are far less prominent personalities than those in *The Imperial Digest.* One may see emerging from these two encyclopedias a clearer bifurcation of attitudes toward dreams in the Song with regard to their role in public life. At one extreme, some scholars espoused a rationalistic, ethically oriented philosophy that was skeptical of occult knowledge following the model of Confucius 孔子 (551–479 BCE), who declined to discuss strange phenomena in *The Analects* 論語 (*Lunyu,* Warring States period).[66] Others published their orthodox and unorthodox writings separately and often adopted a conventionally apologetic tone in their prefaces to the latter.

Nevertheless, dreams continued to be generally regarded as an important part of human experience and surfaced in court politics, especially the dreams of the imperial family. Another court-sponsored encyclopedia of the period, *A Giant Divination Tortoise for the Imperial Library* 冊府元龜 (*Cefu yuangui*, 1013) compiled by Wang Qinruo 王欽若 (962–1025), devoted two chapters to the dreams of various rulers throughout Chinese history.[67] Some Song dynasty Neo-Confucian intellectuals sought to incorporate a new understanding of the causes and nature of dreams within the broader metaphysical framework they were evolving, seeking to normalize them along with other strange phenomena as natural events.[68] One of the earliest Song thinkers to reconsider dreams in this vein was Zhang Zai 張載 (1020–1077), who argued in *Correcting Obscurity* 正蒙 *(Zhengmeng)* that dreams, like all phenomena, were forms of *qi*-energy that followed universal patterns 理 *(li)*. Traditional explanations such as the wandering of the *hun*-soul and the activity of the five *zang*-organs were likewise seen in this light. Zhang, however, contributed two new emphases related to the Daoist idea that the body was quiescent when dreaming and not in direct contact with the real world. He argued that dreams as a form of mental activity were directed by the will 志 *(zhi)*, which gave them their motivation and coherence. But, because the will during sleep was detached from perception, the content of dreams was derived exclusively from memory.[69] "Nothing more purely follows the activities of the mind than dreams," he wrote, reducing the traditional role of the vigorous essence and spirit.[70] A related idea had been voiced by Li Taibo 李泰伯 (1009–1059) that the concerns of the dreamer were determined by what the mind had been immersed in during the waking hours. These views, which have their roots in earlier Daoist and medical beliefs, can be seen as a bridge to later Ming writers who located a cause of dreams in emotional obsession.[71]

Another influential thinker, Cheng Yi 程頤 (1033–1107), also located dreams within the bipolarity of universal patterns and *qi*-energy while specifically inquiring into the moral status of dreaming. Both he and his elder brother, Cheng Hao 程顥 (1032–1085), regarded the origin of dreams as a natural response of the mind and the five *zang*-organs to universal patterns. The character of a dream, though, depended on the mind's state of sincerity. Thus, the dreams of sages praised in the classics reflected their perfection, but ordinary people, whose minds are composed of muddled *qi*-energy, have more confused experiences.[72] Zhu Xi 朱熹 (1130–1200), later canonized as the paragon of Confucian orthodoxy, summarized these views when he wrote, "Being awake is yang; being asleep is yin; being awake is clear; being asleep is muddled. Being awake is to have a master 主 *(zhu)* in control; being asleep is to have no master in control."[73] His political metaphor of the mind as containing a ruler governing a numinous consciousness implies that dreams occur under more chaotic conditions. But, unlike Cheng Yi, Zhu also felt that the mind was continuously active even when in a state of comparative tranquility, so that everyone, even a sage, has dreams.

The Neo-Confucian program of moral and intellectual self-cultivation emphasized the exhaustive investigation of universal patterns of phenomena through the observation and classification of things 格物 *(gewu)*. This spirit of classification pervades miscellanies from the Song period onward, especially Shen Gua's 沈括 (1031–1095) *Jottings from Dream Stream* 夢溪筆談 *(Mengxi bitan)*.[74] Shen's taxonomy of phenomena sought to reexamine the medieval sense of the anomalous and magical qualities of the supranormal by employing analogy, standards of plausibility and verification, and by recognizing processes of transformation. The miscellany itself is named after the estate where he spent his later years in retirement, which he claimed to have envisioned in his dreams before having acquired it. When he finally visited the property, he named it "Dream Stream" 夢溪 (Mengxi), stating that it must have been his destiny to dwell there.

One entry treats the dream of Emperor Xuanzong of the Tang (r. 712–756) concerning the legendary demon-queller Zhong Kui 鍾馗 and a famous painting that resulted from this dream. What is distinctive is Shen's framing of a medieval anomaly account within the history of its representation as a painting, treating it more as an actual object in the world than as a strange event. Moreover, Shen normalizes the miraculous transformation of the historical Zhong Kui (fl. early 8th cent.), who later became a popular household god, by investigating his name and finding that it had been used by both men and women in the past.[75]

Meanwhile, a parallel line of inquiry into dreams was pursued by the eminent literary figure and official Su Shi 蘇軾 (1037–1101) both in theory and by recording his own experiences in miscellanies such as the *Forest of Jottings* 志林 *(Zhilin)*. This was also an extension of the Neo-Confucian interest in the mind, but was less focused on identifying ethical functions than on describing cognitive processes and subjective experience. Su was more receptive to Buddhist views of consciousness and his theoretical speculations, expressed in a short piece, "Preface and Poem on the Studio of Dreams" 夢齋銘並序 ("Mengzhaiming bingxu"), can be traced back to Yue Guang's earlier identification of thoughts and causal contingencies as the dual origins of dreams:

The human mind depends on stimuli 塵 (*chen*) for it has never been an independent entity. As stimuli arise and disappear, the thoughts they engender never remain fixed. Dream consciousness is formed by a succession of stimuli, which lose their original character after many have been perceived. Therefore, though neither the spirit nor the body has directly encountered such thoughts, how could they not be understood as arising from these contingent causes? Take someone who sleeps after herding sheep. The sheep become a contingent cause that gives rise to thoughts about horses, the horses lead to thoughts of carriages, the carriages lead to canopies, and then, one may dream of canopies and processional music, imagining oneself as a king or noble. Now, though the distance between a king or noble and sheep is considerable, why should one regard this as strange when one realizes how thoughts are dependent on causal contingencies?[76]

The mental processes Su describes might be understood today in terms of memory and imagination. The significance of his discussion compared to other Song Neo-Confucian views lies in his emphasis on the mind's dependency on perception and its unavoidable focus on the diverse minutiae of the world. This idea is largely derived from Buddhism, as indicated by his appropriation of the term *chen* (from the Sanskrit *guṇa;* literally, "dust"), a pejorative word that denotes the deceptive, sensual aspects of the world. The inner mental processes described by Su Shi are more freely associative in their operation than the disciplined rigor of classifying things. But his example of the sheep eventually yielding images of a king or noble still traces a plausible sequence.[77]

In the early Ming dynasty, Ye Guang and Su Shi's theories were combined in a more precise formulation by Ye Ziqi 葉子奇 (fl. late 14th cent.). Ye specifically identified the origin of thoughts as visual perceptions while considering causal contingency as a form of associative thinking based on linking similar categories of phenomena. However, he still did not discuss how such associative thinking could yield dream imagery that was not based on actual, perceived phenomena. "Southerners do not dream of camels while Northerners do not dream of elephants because they have never seen these animals," Ye stated.[78] All these thinkers shared Zhu Xi's aversion to discussing what he called "wild dreams" 胡夢 (*humeng*). It was left to later generations of thinkers to account for strange, hitherto unknown dream imagery and to articulate a more unified theory that linked perception with mental processes. This was expressed most coherently by Wang Tingxiang 王廷相 (1474–1544) just a few decades before Chen Shiyuan compiled his encyclopedia.

Wang began his discussion by identifying the roles of sensory perception and thoughts in the creation of dream imagery. He called the former "activation by *po*-soul consciousness" 魄識之感 *(poshi zhi gan)* and the latter, "activation by thoughts" 思念之感 *(sinian zhi gan)*. He held that dreams were nothing other than thoughts occurring while asleep. Wang then recognized two origins and characters of these thoughts: familiar images were produced by "activation from experience" 緣習之感 *(yuanxi zhi gan)* in daily life, while another kind of imagery resulted from a different process termed "activation through fluid contingencies" 因衍之感 *(yinyan zhi gan)*. Fluid contingencies produce images that have never before been encountered or even imagined. By using the word *yan* 衍 (fluid, amorphous, expansive), he was suggesting an uninhibited process of cognitive activity beyond associations based on analogies, and thereby provided an explanation for the existence of Zhu Xi's wild dreams:

> After we have talked about anomalies, images of ghosts, spirits, and demons appear in our dreams; after we have seen terraces and pavilions, imperial watchtowers and palaces appear in our dreams. Annihilating toads is caused by having stepped on eggplants by mistake; encountering a woman in a dream is brought about by having done the good deed of burying some skeletons. Images like these change again and again: now fish, now people, until we forget the distinction between sleeping and waking, and attempt to interpret dreams while we are still dreaming. Given these examples, we can see that the excitation in the thoughts in our minds is very obvious. Moreover, things in dreams are the very same things as in the world. As we form categories from mental images, how can there be no coincidences between dream images and real life events? Yet, the things in dreams are so diffuse and scattered that we cannot find any verification for them. The dreams that offer us no portents are many indeed.[79]

Wang Tingxiang was a particularly advanced theorist whose ideas foreshadowed a later flowering of similar speculations in the seventeenth century. Indeed, Ming literati culture can be said to represent the peak of interest in dreams among the educated elite, which was fueled by a new autobiographical impulse to record and examine personal experiences. Following Emperor Taizu's publicizing of his dreams about founding the Ming dynasty,[80] his son Emperor Chengzu 明成祖 (r. 1402–1424) sponsored a massive scholarly project to compile a new encyclopedia, *The Yongle Encyclopedia* 永樂大典 (*Yongle dadian,* 1408), that would contain a larger number of dream narratives than had appeared in any previous work. Though the original manuscript copy that resulted was intended only for the use of the emperor and his officials, the wide range of source material indicates the abundance of dream literature available to the compilers and other readers at the time.[81] The commercial publishing boom that later began during the Jiajing era (1522–1567) provided a broader range of more affordable books for both elite and middle-brow readers. It disseminated an even greater corpus of dream narratives in a variety of literary genres at a time when individualism and intellectual syncretism flourished, state-sponsored Neo-Confucian orthodoxy was being challenged, previous social distinctions were eroding, and an early modern, urban culture was superseding the influence of court taste. It was at this opportune moment that Chen Shiyuan compiled his encyclopedia for an expanding reading public thirsty for self-empowering knowledge. Through his *Lofty Principles,* he sought to counter popular views of dreams by presenting a convenient summary of traditional theories preserved in canonical texts together with an abundance of examples selected from credible literary sources.

CHEN SHIYUAN AND HIS ENCYCLOPEDIA

Chen Shiyuan was born in 1516 into a prominent landowning family in Chenjialing (Chen Family Ridge), a suburb of Yingcheng in Huguang (modern Hubei province). Originally a military family, the Chens had risen in status to become literati, and under the Ming system were allowed to participate in the civil service examinations. Chen Shiyuan's father, Chen Zheng 陳正 (1495–1563), was a child prodigy who went on to attend the National University in Nanjing as a tribute student. Noted for his poetry, he was said to have rejoiced when his son later succeeded in the higher examinations, announcing that his son had freed him from having to pursue a career in government. Chen Zheng was thus content to live on the income from his property and earned mention in a local gazetteer for his philanthropy during famine relief. His wife, Mistress Hua 華氏 (n.d.), also from Yingcheng, was the daughter of a metropolitan graduate of 1472 who had served in the Shaanxi circuit of the censorate.[82] The eldest of seven sons, Chen Shiyuan was later described as possessing an extraordinary degree of energy and rarely yielding to distractions as he concentrated on nurturing his talent.[83] At twenty-two, he, too, began to climb the traditional ladder of success by following in his father's footsteps as a National University student in Nanjing, where he specialized in *The Book of Changes* 易經 (*Yijing,* ca. late 9th cent. BCE–Han). In 1544 he surpassed his father by earning the metropolitan graduate degree at the age of twenty-eight. This catapulted him into the highest echelon of the educated class and provided him with lifelong elite status. The following year Chen then began a promising official career as magistrate in Luanzhou, a district not far from Beijing in Beizhili (modern Hebei province). As a student at the National University, he had already begun to assemble collections of his writings and soon began to author scholarly works. While in office, he compiled the district's first local gazetteer. A rising fellow provincial, the future grand secretary Zhang Juzheng 張居正 (1525–1582), added a preface praising Chen Shiyuan for his able administration.[84]

Despite this auspicious beginning, Chen abruptly resigned as magistrate in 1549, supposedly because of a dream.[85] According to the story, his father had dreamt that the Confucian sage Mencius 孟子 (ca. 372–ca. 289 BCE) appeared to him shortly before Chen Shiyuan's birth. Consequently, he gave his son the courtesy name of "Minister of Mencius" 孟卿 (Mengqing). However, while Chen Shiyuan was serving as magistrate, the tablet of Mencius mysteriously fell down one day and knocked a sacrificial vessel to the ground during a ceremony in the local Confucian temple. Chen interpreted this as an evil omen: he quickly resigned from his position and never again served in office.[86] A later writer remarked sympathetically that he had been unhappy with the career of an official,[87] but an earlier source stated more directly that he resigned because his talent had provoked jealousy.[88] Thus, the thirty-one-year-old Chen Shiyuan again found himself following in his father's footsteps, as his own son would do after him, when he adopted the identity of a retired scholar dwelling in political reclusion. He chose the artistic names "Cultivating Myself" 養吾 (Yangwu) and "The Old Fool in the Empty Circle" 環中迂叟 (Huanzhong yusou), both of which allude to Daoist ideals in the *Master Zhuang,* as well as the "Scholar Hiding in the Jiang-Han Region" 江漢潛夫 (Jiang-Han qianfu), an allusion to the Eastern Han dynasty scholar Wang Fu. Upon his return home, the local magistrate bestowed the name "Hall of Boundless Energy" 浩然堂 (Haorantang) on Chen's residence, alluding to Mencius's practice of self-cultivation.[89] The persona of a retired scholar became increasingly acceptable to many of the educated elite during the late Ming, as population growth reduced the chances for success in the official examinations and political life grew more dangerous due to factional struggles. For anyone entering the cultural world with the ambition of becoming known as a famous scholar, a high degree and previous official rank were distinct advantages. Chen was among those who were able to successfully capitalize on such credentials. He combined them with his gentry status to live comfortably as he produced authoritative scholarly works for the commercial book market. His subsequent indifference to an official career may also reflect his early Confucian studies with a prominent local scholar, Yu Yinxu 余胤緒 (d. 1569). Yu promoted his teacher Zhan Roshui's 湛若水 (1466–1560) version of the School of Mind 心學 *(Xinxue)*, which challenged state-sponsored Neo-Confucian orthodoxy, and he urged Chen to pursue sagehood through a combination of firm determination and the relinquishing of selfish desires.[90]

After leaving office, Chen first fulfilled a desire to see the wider world by traveling to the five sacred mountains, authoring accounts of these journeys. The ensuing four decades were mostly spent at home producing more than thirty known titles on such topics as the Confucian classics, history, phonetics, geography, local culture, surnames, and epigraphy, in addition to compiling two more local gazetteers. He established a marketable reputation through his abundant writings, while in Yingcheng he was regarded as the personification of the ideal Confucian scholar. Thus, when the scholar Cheng Renqing 成仁卿 (fl. ca. 1572) visited the area seeking information in order to compile a regional gazetteer, he sought out Chen. The result was a short but engaging work, *Collected Conversations about the Jiang-Han Region* 江漢叢談 (*Jiang-Han congtan*, 1572) in which he discusses local myths, legends, and history in the form of recorded answers to Cheng Renqing's inquiries. Then fifty-six years old, Chen noted in his preface that he was beginning to feel the onset of old age and no longer engaged in the more demanding research of his earlier years. Instead, he described himself as leading a leisurely, pleasurable life in his Garden Surrounded by Greenery 環碧園 (Huanbiyuan).[91] Unfortunately, little has survived of Chen's poetry and other informal writings that might have provided more details of his personal life.[92] However, he continued to write sporadically and issued collections of his earlier works. By 1584, when he had reached the age of seventy by Chinese reckoning, he had apparently overcome his earlier aversion to Buddhism and authored the first of two studies on Buddhist topics. Later, he stated that the second of these, focusing on Sanskrit expressions in Buddhist texts, was motivated by a dream in 1587 where he discussed Sanskrit with a foreign monk who then wished him long life in a glorious ceremony.[93] Indeed, Chen lived on to the ripe age of eighty-one.

It was later estimated that his unpublished works amounted to some four hundred chapters.[94] Many of these circulated in manuscript and were subsequently lost. Toward the end of his life, the bibliophile Zhou Lianggong 周亮工 (1612–1672) lamented that he had only been able to collect some six or seven copies of Chen's works and that only two of these still remained in his possession.⁹⁵ Later, Cheng Dazhong 程大中 (fl. 1757), a fellow local of Chen's who compiled a list of his writings, compared Chen to two other polymath scholars of the Ming with a similar range of interests, Yang Shen 楊慎 (1488–1559) and Zhu Mouwei 朱謀㙔 (d. 1624).⁹⁶ Some of Chen's titles were listed in the bibliographical section of the *History of the Ming Dynasty* 明史 (*Mingshi*, 1739), and eleven were reviewed in *Summaries of All Titles Collected for The Imperially Sponsored Complete Works of the Four Libraries* 欽定四庫全書總目提要 (*Qinding siku quanshu zongmu tiyao*, 1781). Of the latter group, five were judged worthy of being reprinted in *The Complete Works of the Four Libraries* 四庫全書 (*Siku quanshu*, 1772–1782).⁹⁷ The success of Chen's publications was based on his ability to digest previous scholarship, include material from a wide range of sources, and judiciously offer his own opinions on specific issues. From the Qing dynasty on, he was praised for carefully documenting his sources. His methods were seen as similar to the practices of the later schools of Han Learning 漢學 (*Hanxue*) and Evidential Research 考證 (*Kaozheng*) and contrasted with the contemporaneous essay-based approaches regarded by many as a characteristic weakness of Ming scholarship.⁹⁸ The general conservatism of Chen Shiyuan's writings, while not placing him in the ranks of the most advanced thinkers or prose stylists of his time, nevertheless served him well as an encyclopedist, and it earned him a lasting place in the intellectual life of the Ming and Qing dynasties.

According to the author's preface, *Lofty Principles of Dream Interpretation* was completed around 1562, when Chen was forty-six. Years later, he included this work as one of ten in *A Further Anthology of Returned Clouds* 歸雲別集 (*Guiyun bieji*) printed in 1583. At some point in the late Ming, an abridged version of *Lofty Principles*, which included only the main text without the annotated sources, was reprinted in *Explanations of Subtleties in the Forest of Dreams* 夢林玄解 (*Menglin xuanjie*). This was a compendium of several works on dreams aimed at a more popular audience that appears to have appropriated Chen's name as one of the editors.⁹⁹ In 1833, *A Further Anthology* was reprinted by an admiring local, Wu Yuping 吳玉坪. The complete *Lofty Principles* was again included in the collectanea *Tiny Pearls from the Ocean of the Arts* 藝海珠塵 (*Yihai zhuchen*, 1850) and the *First Grand Anthology of Collectanea* 叢書集成初編 (*Congshu jicheng chubian*, 1939). Thus, including more recent reprints, Chen's work on dreams has remained in circulation for almost four and a half centuries. Of all his writings, it is the one for which he is remembered today.¹⁰⁰

Introduction

In his preface to *Lofty Principles,* Chen presents himself as a retired scholar and pays tribute to the spirit of Su Shi and to the role of Daoism in Chinese dream culture. He records a dream of his that occurred in 1562 on the day just after the moon's height in the eighth lunar month of the year *renxu.* This is the same day and year in the horary cycle of the first of Su Shi's visits to Red Cliff in 1082. Su's outings yielded valuable philosophical insights, which he expressed in two *fu*-rhapsodies that achieved a canonical status in Chinese literature.[101] It is in the second rhapsody that Su describes a dream in which he encounters a transcendent whose enigmatic question enables him to suddenly grasp Master Zhuang's concept of the transformation of things. Chen alludes to both rhapsodies when he invokes similar moments in his preface. Like Su, he discovers a cosmic principle from contemplating the waxing and waning of the moon while enjoying wine one night. In the dream that follows, a question posed by a mysterious old man suggests that dreams are not illusions, but constitute a part of reality. This becomes one of the central themes reiterated throughout the *Lofty Principles.* In addition, the old man's revelation of a sacred scripture invokes the ethos of religious Daoism: it is a motif that appears in a number of other dreams recorded in Chen's encyclopedia. Chen concludes by offering his work as but a crude attempt in the human world to make sense of his experience, whose undecidability for him alludes to the conundrum of Master Zhuang's "Dream of a Butterfly."

In what may be a more overt reference to the *Master Zhuang* and other Daoist texts, Chen followed a similar organization and divided the *Lofty Principles* into two parts, the "inner" and "outer" chapters. The ten inner chapters are a series of concise introductory discourses that present traditional cosmological and historical frameworks as well as Chen's views on several perennial themes in Chinese dream culture. This section displays a generic affinity with the views in Wang Chong's *Judicious Discussions* and Wang Fu's *Discussions from a Gentleman in Hiding.* In contrast to the advanced psychological speculations of Wang Tingxiang and others, Chen's presentation of the nature of dreams primarily follows mainstream assumptions widely held by the educated class. Some of these ideas, originated in the anecdotes of the *Master Zhuang* and *Master Lie,* were systematized in the essays of the *Master of Huainan* 淮南子 (*Huainanzi,* ca. 139 BCE) and in the classic medical treatises, and later incorporated into Zhu Xi's orthodox Neo-Confucianism. Chapter 1, "The True Controller," employs a Daoist term and summarizes the basic principles of correlative cosmology, whose key elements for Chen are the bipolar activities of yin and yang, heaven and earth, and the *hun-* and *po-*souls, all acting in accord with the movement of the Way. Chen tends to highlight the role of the dreamer's spirit rather than the *hun-*soul. The former concept, which appears in early philosophical and medical texts, can suggest a more purposeful, coherent aspect of the personality, and his preference for it may reflect late Ming culture's interest in individualism. Still, Chen largely subscribes to the traditional view that most dreams result from the spirit's wandering away from the body during sleep rather than from purely internal mental processes.

Chen's historical perspective likewise reflects traditional philosophical attitudes toward the present as an era of decline far from the golden age of the sages. He asserts that this has created a problem for the correct understanding of dreams, inasmuch as the ancient techniques, discussed in chapters 2, 4, and 8, have not been transmitted. Moreover, he voices doubt that even the ancient forms of divination alone could reveal the deeper meaning of a dream for his contemporaries. Adopting a pluralistic view of the matter, Chen advocates employing a variety of techniques that are basically eclectic assemblages. These include referencing conventional meanings of dream imagery, the use of divination, numerology, homophonic and glyphomantic analysis, recognizing typologies and the influence of medical conditions, correlation with astronomical phenomena, drawing comparisons with documented dream narratives of the past, as well recognizing contextual and personal factors. This last component is particularly critical for arriving at a successful interpretation and lies at the core of what Chen means by "lofty principles" 逸旨 *(yizhi),* in contrast to popular and occult techniques that primarily rely on mechanical rules and the fixed associations found in dream manuals.[102] The title *Lofty Principles,* however, is a bit misleading—his encyclopedia does not propound a particular interpretative technique for readers to learn and practice. Rather, it offers an abundance of evidential cases from the past that utilized a variety of more sophisticated methods. Despite several personal dream experiences that were life-altering, Chen himself remained a scholar in the Confucian mode, a transmitter of traditional knowledge who is not known to have performed interpretations for others. Ultimately, he felt that such a skill depended not only on broad technical expertise but, more importantly, on profound spiritual insight as demonstrated by unusually perceptive individuals such as Zhou Xuan. While he undoubtedly agreed with the famous interpreter Suo Dan 索紞 (fl. early 4th cent.) that this art could not be learned from books alone, Chen maintained that neither was practical experience in itself sufficient without an understanding of the nature of consciousness.[103]

To clarify his position that dreams are real, Chen takes issue with the Buddhist view by fashioning a debate (part I, chapter 5) between his spokesman, the Master Who Understands the Subtle 通微主人 (Tongwei zhuren) and the Disciple of Emptiness 宗空 (Zongkong). The latter espouses the belief that dreams are merely insubstantial mental events that, like all phenomena, have no abiding existence. In reply, the Master cites the authority of antiquity and the existence of numerous dream narratives recorded in classical, historical, and Daoist texts, in writings of eminent scholars of the past, and even in apocrypha and anomaly accounts. This signals the broad range of source material that Chen goes on to present in part II. The Master, like a solidly orthodox scholar, argues that the transmission of these narratives, especially in canonical texts, is itself convincing proof of the reality of dreams: they are valid, firstly, because they have been clearly iterated and historically documented. Secondly, they are fully shaped in these stories by including a valid interpretation, as the Chinese term *yuanmeng* 圓夢 (literally "rounding off a dream") connotes. Lastly, they are shown to have been confirmed by subsequent events in waking life, which completes the proof of their substantiality. Each dream narrative he selects thus possesses a tripartite form: a verbalized oneiric experience 夢 *(meng)*; an interpretation 占 *(zhan)*; and a resulting confirmation 徵 *(zheng)*. Conversely, it is suggested that a dream may sometimes be neutralized and its inauspicious effect suspended by the dreamer's refusal to express it in language.[104] Most of the dreamers in Chen's encyclopedia are historical figures and members of the elite: rulers, officials, and scholars, or their wives and relatives. These would have been regarded by readers as credible individuals and the recorded accounts of their experiences as plausible evidence. By patterning the fluid events of memory into conventionalized stories, the dreamers affirm their reality, and many of them are shown by the narrators to have thereby gained some control over the effects of their dreams in waking life.

Not only do dreams matter, but Chen also regards dreaming as a universal human activity. In "Sages" (part I, chapter 6), he rejects the Daoist philosophical notion that sages and perfected gentlemen do not dream because they supposedly have developed such concentrated spirits that they do not have thoughts when asleep. His counterargument that everyone possesses the same kind of mind is an affirmation of the philosophy of Mencius, who defined the sage as someone who has preserved an innate moral nature common to all humanity. If dreaming is inevitable, though, it does not follow for Chen that all dreams are valid or interpretable. There is a distinct set of criteria at work in his material that emphasizes public and ethical content, a focus that sets the *Lofty Principles* apart from later developments in Chinese dream culture, which explored the role of private emotions and desires. Ruling the state, giving birth to an heir, managing human relations, obtaining official position, prolonging longevity, recovering from illness, as well as achieving success in the official examinations are among the most common motifs in part II. In the strata of society that Chen presents, everyone is coherent and articulate, regardless of their moral status or whether the dream is auspicious or not. Even seriously ill dreamers are capable of recounting their dreams in stories that make sense.[105]

In "Ancient Methods" (part I, chapter 8), Chen discusses five kinds of dreams that should not be interpreted as well as five kinds of errors in the practice of interpretation. Like Zhu Xi, he rules out a wide spectrum of private imagination as perverse or immoderate and blames the occurrence of such dreams on the moral deficiencies of the dreamer in waking life. Displaying an orthodox Confucian suspicion of emotions and desire, Chen erects a barrier of decorum to the investigation of bizarre imagery and sexual fantasy. These elements, however, were to become fruitful themes for succeeding generations of scholars and writers. Some of these figures were more willing to record intimate modes of self-scrutiny and embraced Buddhist ideas of illusion as a positive creative force. The results were later expressed in autobiographical writing and influential works of fiction and drama, and even led to organized clubs where people met to discuss their dreams.[106] This phase, which was most energetically pursued during the seventeenth and eighteenth centuries, brought Chinese dream culture closer to the psychological and artistic inquiries of the modern West. But such visions clearly lay beyond the horizon of the *Lofty Principles*. If Chen's intention stopped short of validating highly subjective content, the copious information he gathered probably contributed to legitimizing these later explorations.

Chen's most distinctive contribution to dream theory appears at the end of "Influences and Abnormal Conditions" (part I, chapter 10), where he presents a typology of nine types. Most are based on the pathology of traditional Chinese medicine where internal or external influences can produce abnormal physical conditions that generate dreams. Despite its indebtedness to Wang Fu and the *Master Lie,* Chen's nine types of dreams share a more coherent origin than those in earlier classifications.[107] These ten chapters in part I together represent the most extensive treatment of dream theories up to its time, for previous, surviving texts on the subject are mostly brief remarks, pithy anecdotes, evocative poems, or short essays. It is perhaps for this reason that recent commentators of the *Lofty Principles* regarded Chen Shiyuan as having demonstrated the deepest grasp of theories of dream interpretation among traditional Chinese writers.[108]

Part II constitutes the encyclopedia proper. This section collects almost seven hundred examples of dream narratives, which are strung together in Chen's text to substantiate his central argument about the reality of dreams. They are organized into the standard categories of Chinese encyclopedias based on their content. Beginning with dreams of heaven, chapters 1 to 3 present the macrocosm of celestial phenomena and are complemented by chapter 4, which deals with the topographical features of earth below. In chapters 5 to 13, the focus then shifts to the middle dimension of human affairs, including interactions with gods and strange creatures, followed by a survey of the microcosm composed of various flora and fauna in chapters 14 to 18. Chapter 19 illustrates how dreams reveal the moral mechanism of repayment at work in the universe. In the final chapter, Chen concludes by again advocating the use of "lofty principles" in dream interpretation. Still, he does not entirely reject the kind of ready-made interpretations found in popular dream manuals. In his theory of nine types, he also transmits some of these inasmuch as they were incorporated into the classical medical treatises he references. But his skepticism remains apparent in his closing remarks when he states, "Some dreams may contain identical elements but their meanings are actually different, while others appear to be different but their meanings are the same—one cannot depend on fixed rules."[109]

It is chapters 9 to 11, however, that best reveal the core of his intended readers. These focus on the essential concern of the educated class with writing. In "Brush and Ink" (chapter 9), dreams about acts of writing result in notable artistic achievement or reveal destinies. "Written Graphs" (chapter 10), focuses on glyphomantic and homophonic analyses of graphs that demonstrate an esoteric understanding of language by various interpreters. Lastly, "The Official Examinations" (chapter 11), deals with one of the most pervasive anxieties of the educated class during the Ming. As the possibility of obtaining degrees and entering official life receded for the increasing number of educated students, competing in the examinations became a recurrent activity that consumed many of them throughout their adult lives. Dreams were looked to for signs of success or failure, and certain incubation temples became known for their power to disclose impending results. Chen himself asserts that "the highest rankings in the official examinations have always been presaged by auspicious signs."[110] From this we may surmise that a primary audience for Chen's encyclopedia was the substantial group of some five to six hundred thousand first-degree holders during the late Ming. Required to undergo retesting every three years in order to advance or maintain their status, they were never able to free themselves from the subculture of the examinations. For the overwhelming majority facing certain disappointment, obtaining the higher provincial and metropolitan graduate degrees was indeed regarded as a dream come true.[111] Not surprisingly, these three chapters together contain the largest number of narratives with a common theme—that of achieving status through literary culture—followed next by those involving encounters with gods and strange creatures. In contrast, one of the shortest chapters is "Wealth and Goods" (chapter 8), a subject that Confucians theoretically regarded as a degrading obsession characteristic of the merchant class.

Chen Shiyuan's encyclopedia remains the earliest surviving work that attempts to present a broad and coherent summary of the diverse strains of Chinese dream culture. Its author invited readers to peruse it at leisure, and its organization encouraged many, no doubt, to consult it at random, a few dreams at a time, while mulling over his theories and judgments. The modern reader should likewise feel free to do the same, savoring it bit by bit while considering both the differences and similarities between these oneiric events from the past and those experienced today. Does the *Lofty Principles* make a persuasive case for the reality of dreams? Perhaps. We can at least acknowledge the example of a pair of dreamers compared in an anecdote from the *Master Lie* that Chen included.[112] The servant of a Mr. Yin was practically worked to death by his wealthy master, but at night he dreamt that he was the ruler of a state and enjoyed all the pleasures of noble rank. In response to the commiseration of a friend, he replied that he was, nevertheless, content with his lot because of his dreams. Mr. Yin, in contrast, spent his days worrying about the burdens of wealth while at night had nightmares that he had become a menial slave. This story suggests that dreams may function to address the imbalances of our waking lives. Mr. Yin is urged to lessen his demands on his servants and scale down his responsibilities whereupon his dreams improve. Might this not teach us to accept that our dreams are an inalienable part of our existence? To employ the discourse of the *Lofty Principles,* Chinese dream culture maintains that the quality of our total life experience is an inescapable combination of the yin world of our wandering spirits together with the yang world of our waking consciousness.

NOTES

1. For modern Chinese summaries of traditional dream culture, see the two recent books by Fu Zhenggu 傅正谷, *Zhongguo mengwenhua* 中国梦文化 [Chinese dream culture] (Beijing: Zhongguo shehui kexue chubanshe, 1993) and *Zhongguo mengwenhua cidian* 中国梦文化词典 [Dictionary of Chinese dream culture] (Taiyuan: Shaanxi gaoxiao lianhe chubanshe, 1993). Another important study in recent years is Liu Wenying 刘文英, *Meng de mixin yu meng de tansuo* 梦的迷信与梦的探索 [Superstitions about dreams and investigations into dreams] (Beijing: Zhongguo kexue chubanshe, 1989), which contains additional material. A useful study produced in the West is Roberto K. Ong, *The Interpretation of Dreams in Ancient China* (Bochum: Studienverlag, 1985).

2. A statistical survey grouped pre-Communist China with other cultures that have the highest proportion of the population believing in out-of-body experiences (OOBE) and that also interpret most dreams as OOBEs. See Dean Sheilds, "A Cross-Cultural Study of Beliefs in Out-of-Body Experiences, Waking, and Sleeping," *Journal of the Society for Psychical Research* 49, no. 775 (March 1978): 697–741, esp. pp. 717, 728, 734.

3. For studies of correlative cosmology, see John B. Henderson, *The Development and Decline of Chinese Cosmology* (New York: Columbia University Press, 1984) and the articles collected in the special issue "Reconsidering the Correlative Cosmology of Early China," *Bulletin of the Museum of Far Eastern Antiquities* 72 (2000).

4. For a collection of studies on the boom in the publishing industry that began in the mid-16th century, see Cynthia J. Brokaw and Kai-wing Chou, eds., *Printing and Book Culture in Late Imperial China* (Berkeley: University of California Press, 2005).

5. *Mozi jiangu* 墨子閒詁 (ZZJC 4:193). A subsequent definition found in the earliest dictionary, *Shuowen jiezi* 說文解字 (Explanations and analyses of single and composite graphs, 100 CE), states that "dreams are what one is aware of during sleep." See *Shuowen jiezi* (Beijing: Zhonghua shuju, 1977 ed.), 153.

6. Translated from Hu Houxuan 胡厚宣, "Yinren zhanmeng kao" 殷人占夢考 [A study of dream interpretation among the Yin (Shang) people], in Hu, *Jiaguxue shangshi luncong chuji* 甲骨學商史論叢初集 [A first collection of essays on tortoise shell and oracle bone studies and on Shang dynasty history] (Hong Kong: Wenyoutang shudian, 1970), 1:4a-8a, nos. 1, 4, 7. See also Song Zhenhao 宋镇豪, "Jiaguwenzhong de meng yu zhanmeng" 甲骨文中的梦与占梦 [Dreams and dream interpretation in the shell and oracle bone inscriptions], *Wenwu* 文物 600 (June 2006): 61–71.

7. For a discussion of the etymological meanings of the Shang dynasty graph, see Liu, *Meng de mixin*, 157–59.

8. See Ong, *Interpretation of Dreams*, 145–50 for examples of what he terms the "corroborative" approach.

9. Poo Mu-chou, *In Search of Personal Welfare: A View of Ancient Chinese Religion* (Albany, NY: State University of New York Press, 1998), 34n100.

10. Kong Yingda's 孔穎達 (574–648) commentary suggests that the "great men" designated the official dream interpreters who held the rank of middle-ranked servicemen according to *The Government Organization of the Zhou Dynasty* 周禮周禮 (*Zhouli*, ca. 3rd cent. BCE). They served under the grand diviner 大卜 (*taibu*) who, in turn was under the diviner of dreams 占夢 (*zhanmeng*). According to Kong, the graph 人 *ren* in "great man" (*tairen*) in *The Book of Songs* was a mis-transcription for 卜 *bu* in *taibu* 大卜 (grand diviner), and the elders did not designate an official rank but were respected members of the society. See *Maoshi zhengyi* 毛詩正義 11:2 (SSJZS 1:437) and *Lofty Principles*, I:5.

11. See the poems "The Beck" 斯干 ("Sigan"), "No Sheep?" 無羊 ("Wu yang"), and "The First Month" 正月 ("Zhengyue") in *Maoshi zhengyi* (SSJZS 1:436, 438, 441). Translated in Arthur Waley, trans., *The Book of Songs: The Ancient Chinese Classic of Poetry* (New York: Grove Press, 1996 ed.), 161–63, 163–64, and 167–70, respectively. These are discussed in *Lofty Principles*, I:5 and 5nn32-4. For more examples, see Ong, *Interpretation of Dreams*, 151–55, which classifies these as dreams of "direct association."

12. *Yanzi chunqiu* 宴子春秋 (ICS 6.6/51/25–52/8). In the "Treatise on Arts and Literature" in the *History of the Western Han Dynasty* 漢書: 藝文志 (*Hanshu:* "Yiwenzhi," 92 CE) eighteen divination manuals are listed of which the first two are specifically concerned with dreams: *The Yellow Emperor's Long-Willow Method of Dream Interpretation* 黃帝長柳占夢 (*Huangdi changliu zhanmeng*) and *Gan De's Long-Willow Method of Dream Interpretation* 甘德長柳占夢 (*Gan De changliu zhanmeng*). Both works have been lost. The bibliographer commented that, "Of all the methods of divination, dream-interpretation ranks foremost." See *Hanshu* 漢書 [History of the Western Han dynasty, 92 CE] (Beijing: Zhonghua shuju, 1975 ed.), 6:1772–3; also *Lofty Principles*, I:2.

13. Zheng Binglin 郑炳林 and Yang Ping 羊萍, eds., *Dunhuang ben mengshu* 敦煌本梦书 [Dunhuang manuscripts of dream manuals] (Lanzhou: Gansu wenhua chubanshe, 1995), 13; also Liu Wenying 刘文英, *Zhongguo gudai de mengshu* 中国古代的梦书 [Ancient Chinese dream manuals] (Beijing: Zhonghua shuju, 1990), 347–48. These texts have been studied in Jean-Pierre Drège, "Notes d'Onirologie Chinoise," *Bulletin de l'École Française d'Extrême-Orient* LXX (1981), 271–89 and "Clefs des Songes de Touen-houang" in Michel Soymié, ed., *Nouvelles Contributions aux Études de Touen-houang* (Geneva: Librarie Droz, 1981), 205–249.

14. See Zhang Yaquan 张亚权, "*Zuozhuan* mengshi kaobian" 左传梦事考辨 [Investigation into dream incidents in *Zuo's narratives*] in *Dongfang wenhua* 东方文化 (Nanjing: Dongnan daxue chubanshe, 1991), I:183–91.

15. *Chunqiu zuozhuan zhengyi* 春秋左傳正義: "Xigong 28" (SSJZS 2:1826); Burton Watson, trans., *The Tso chuan: Selections from China's Oldest Narrative History* (New York: Columbia University Press, 1989), 63.

16. Wai-yee Li, "Dreams of Interpretation in Early Chinese Historical and Philosophical Writings," in David Shulman and Guy Stroumsa, eds., *Dream Cultures: Toward a Comparative History of Dreaming* (Oxford: Oxford University Press, 1999), 24–29.

17. *Chunqiu zuozhuan zhengyi:* "Xigong 28" (SSJZS 2:1825); Watson, *Tso chuan,* 59–60.
18. *Chunqiu zuozhuan zhengyi:* "Zhaogong 7" (SSJZS 2:2050). Zichan's statement asserts that these souls are stronger among the elite, who possess the power to consume more sustenance. Therefore, in some cases after death, an aggrieved *hun*-soul of an aristocrat can linger in the human world as an angry ghost. In addition to Zichan's correlation of *hun* and *po* with yin and yang, the Confucian philosopher Zheng Xuan 鄭玄 (127–200) later equated the *hun*-soul with *qi*-energy 氣 and regarded it as the basis for human spirit and intelligence while the *po*-soul was the source of the senses. Also see Yü Ying-shih, "'O Soul, Come Back!' A Study in the Changing Conceptions of the Soul and Afterlife in Pre-Buddhist China," *Harvard Journal of Asiatic Studies* 42, no. 2 (Dec. 1987): 363–95. Some popular dream manuals indicated the existence of three *hun*-souls and six *po*-souls. See Liu, *Zhongguo gudai,* 38. For Chen Shiyuan's views on the two souls, see *Lofty Principles,* I:1.
19. See Fu, *Zhongguo mengwenhua,* 102–20 for analyses of several poems that appear to follow the structure of daydreams in the *Songs of Chu.*
20. Translated in David Knechtges, trans., *Wen xuan, or, Selections of Refined Literature* (Princeton: Princeton University Press, 1996), 3:325–27.
21. Translated in Knechtges, *Wen xuan,* 3:339–49.
22. For a discussion of these two poems, see Wai-yee Li, *Enchantment and Disenchantment: Love and Illusion in Chinese Literature* (Princeton: Princeton University Press, 1993), 23–30.
23. *Zhuangzi zhuzi suoyin* 莊子逐字索引 (ICS 18/48/19–26); Burton Watson, trans., *The Complete Works of Chuang Tzu* (New York: Columbia University Press, 1968), 193–94; also Victor H. Mair, trans., *Wandering on the Way: Early Taoist Tales and Parables of Chuang Tzu* (New York: Bantam Books, 1994), 170.
24. *Zhuangzi* (ICS 4/11/21–4/12/2); Watson, *Chuang Tzu,* 63–64; Mair, *Wandering,* 37–38.
25. *Zhuangzi* (ICS 2/7/21–23); Watson, *Chuang Tzu,* 49; Mair, *Wandering,* 24. It is interesting to note that among the Burmese, the soul that leaves the body and wanders during sleep is called the "butterfly." Sheilds, "A Cross-Cultural Study," 716.
26. *Zhuangzi* (ICS 2/7/1–4); Watson, *Chuang Tzu,* 47–48; Mair, *Wandering,* 22–23.
27. For Chen Shiyuan's critique of the *Master Zhuang*'s view that the perfected gentleman does not dream, see *Lofty Principles,* I: 6.
28. See the classification of the graph 夢 *(meng)* in *Explanations and Analyses of Single and Composite Graphs (Shuowen,* 153) under the radical for illness. Although Liu, *Meng de mixin,* 158 believes this to be an error, it might also reflect early beliefs that dreams could have pathological origins.
29. See Donald Harper, "A Chinese Demonography of the Third Century B.C.," *Harvard Journal of Asiatic Studies* 45, no. 2 (1985): 459–98 for a discussion of two such manuscripts uncovered from a tomb at Shuihudi in modern Hubei dated ca. 217 BCE.
30. Translated in Donald Harper, "Wang Yen-shou's Nightmare Poem," *Harvard Journal of Asiatic Studies* 47, no. 1 (1987): 243–46.

31. See Michel Strickmann, "Dreamwork of Psycho-Sinologists: Doctors, Taoists, Monks," in Carolyn T. Brown, ed., *Psycho-Sinology: The Universe of Dreams in Chinese Culture* (Washington, D.C.: Wilson International Center for Scholars, 1988), 29–31.

32. Ren Yingqiu 任應秋, ed., *Huangdi neijing zhangju suoyin* 黃帝內經章句索引 [Index to the Yellow Emperor's inner canon of medicine] (Beijing: Renmin weisheng chubanshe, 1986), 17:51–52. Translated in Maoshing Ni, trans., *The Yellow Emperor's Classic of Medicine: A New Translation of the* Neijing Suwen *with Commentary* (Boston: Shambhala, 1995), 66. See also chap. 80 of the *Huangdi neijing,* which likewise diagnoses certain dreams as reflecting excess or deficiency of *qi*-energy in various organs; translated in Ni, *Classic of Medicine,* 299–300. Some of these ideas are summarized in *Lofty Principles,* I:10.

33. See the anecdote in *Zuo's Narratives* where Duke Jing of Jin 晉景公 (r. 599–581 BCE) dreams of two demonic boys who state that they will hide between his heart and his diaphragm to avoid the effects of medical treatment. *Chunqiu zuozhuan zhengyi:* "Chenggong 10" (SSJZS 2:1906); also *Lofty Principles,* I:5n27.

34. For a summary of some of these categorizations, see *Lofty Principles,* I:10.

35. In addition, the interpreter of dreams is supposed to present the king with interpretations of his auspicious dreams during the third month of winter. He also makes offerings to the four directions to expel the bad dreams and orders the commencement of the *nuo* 儺 exorcism ceremony at the end of the year to purify the palace and cleanse it of any disease. See *Zhouli zhushu* 周禮注疏 25 (SSJZS 1:807–808).

36. Commentators differ regarding the content of the three kinds of dreams interpreted by the grand diviner. See Fu, *Zhongguo mengwenhua cidian,* 847–48. These translations follow Zheng Xuan's commentary, which is cited by Chen in *Lofty Principles,* I:2n2. The grand diviner used several other methods to prognosticate state affairs besides shell and bone divination and the hexagrams of *The Book of Changes* 易經 (*Yijing,* ca. latter half of 9th cent. BCE–Han). His methods of dream interpretation died out, according to Zheng Xuan. The logic behind comparing the king's dream with the halos around the sun is that the king was regarded as the earthly correlative of the sun. See *Zhouli zhushu* 25 (SSJZS 1:803).

37. See *Qianfulun zhuzi suoyin* 潛夫論逐字索引 (ICS 28/52/14); also Anne Behnke Kinney, trans., *The Art of the Han Essay: Wang Fu's* Ch'ien-Fu Lun (Tempe, AZ: Center for Asian Studies, Arizona State Univ., 1990), 119.

38. See *Lunheng zhuzi suoyin* 論衡逐字索引 (ICS 47/215/15 ff).

39. In 60 CE the emperor dreamt of a golden man who arrived by flying through the air. The figure was identified by an interpreter as the Buddha, which led to the dispatching of a mission to India that was regarded as the beginning of the importation of Buddhism to China. See Daoshi 道世, ed., *Fayuan zhulin* 法苑珠林:12 (Beijing: Zhongguo shudian, 1991 rpt. of ca. 1912 ed.), I:206; also Rudolf G. Wagner, "Imperial Dreams," in Brown, *Psycho-Sinology,* 13, who dates such accounts to various sources from the 4th century on and *Lofty Principles,* II:12n8.

40. Translated in Shuen-fu Lin, "Chia Pao-yü's First Visit to the Land of Il-

lusion: An Analysis of a Literary Dream in Interdisciplinary Perspective," *Chinese Literature: Essays, Articles, Reviews* 14 (1992): 82.

41. Strickmann, "Dreamwork," 38–39. On Buddhist dreams in general, see G. Sundara Ramaiah and S. D. A. Joga Rao, "Buddhist Interpretation of Dreams," *The Tibet Journal* 13, no. 1 (Spring 1988): 30–37; also Alexander L. Mayer, "Dreams," in *Encyclopedia of Buddhism,* ed. Robert E. Buswell, Jr. (New York: Macmillan, 2004), 1:238–239.

42. Dream incubation in temples was by no means limited to Buddhist deities but was widespread in Daoism and in local cults. For brief discussions of this practice, see Ong, *Interpretation of Dreams,* 39–46 and Lienche Tu Fang, "Ming Dreams," *Tsing Hua Journal of Chinese Studies* n.s. 10, no. 1 (June 1973): 64–66.

43. Yue Guang's ideas were briefly recorded in Liu Yiqing 劉義慶, *Shishuo xinyu* 世說新語 [A new account of tales of the world, ca. 430] (Beijing: Zhongguo shehui kexue chubanshe, 2003 ed.), 103; translated in Richard B. Mather, trans., *A New Account of Tales of the World* (Minneapolis: University of Minnesota, 1976), 98 and in Lin, "Chia Pao-yü," 88. For a discussion of Yue Guang on dreams, see Liu, *Meng de mixin,* 224–26. Yue and Wei are also referred to in *Lofty Principles,* II:20, 20n1.

44. *Liezi zhuzi suoyin* 列子逐字索引 (ICS 3/18/1–10). These six types of dreams are virtually identical to the typology in *The Government Organization of the Zhou Dynasty* described above. See also *Lofty Principles,* I:7, 7nn1, 2, I:8, 10.

45. For these three dreams, see *Liezi zhuzi suoyin* (ICS 2/6/15–2/7/2, 3/16/10–3/17/10, 3/19/6–15); translated in A. C. Graham, trans., *The Book of Lieh-tzŭ* (London: John Murray, 1960), 33–35, 61–64, 69–70.

46. See Stephen R. Bokenkamp, trans., *Early Daoist Scriptures* (Berkeley: University of California Press, 1997), 287–89, 387.

47. An example in more recent times was dream of the leader of the Taiping Rebellion, Hong Xiuquan 洪秀全 (1814–1864), in 1837 that he was a son of God and, like Jesus, destined to inaugurate the Kingdom of Heavenly Peace on earth. See Wagner, "Imperial Dreams," 16 ff.

48. For a study of the visitations of the god Laozi to Emperor Xuanzong, see J. J. L. Duyvandak, "The Dreams of Hsüan-tsung" in *India Antiqua: J.-Ph. Vogel Festschrift* (Leiden: Brill, 1947), 102–8. Also Wagner, "Imperial Dreams," 19–20, who notes that such imperial dreams were not usually recorded in orthodox historical sources.

49. See Romeyn Taylor, "Ming T'ai-tsu's Story of a Dream," *Monumenta Serica* 32 (1976), 1–20; also Fang, "Ming Dreams," 55–57.

50. Corpse-worms are discussed in Zhang Junfang 張君房, ed., *Yunji qiqian* 雲笈七籤 [The bookcase of the clouds with the seven labels, 1019.] (Beijing: Huaxia chubanshe, 1996 ed.), 83:516–19. See also Strickmann, "Dreamwork," 35; Fang Jing Pei and Zhang Juwen, *The Interpretation of Dreams in Chinese Culture* (New York: Weatherhill, 2000), 43; Fu, *Zhongguo mengwenhua cidian,* 847.

51. For a study of anomaly accounts, see Robert Ford Campany, *Strange Writing: Anomaly Accounts in Early Medieval China* (Albany: State University of New York Press, 1996). Individual translations appear in Karl S. Y. Kao, ed., *Classical Chinese Tales of the Supernatural and the Fantastic: Selections from the Third*

to the Tenth Centuries (Bloomington, IN: Indiana University Press, 1985). The later tradition of the strange in Chinese literature is discussed in Judith Zeitlin, *Historian of the Strange* (Stanford, CA: Stanford University Press, 1993), 15–58.

52. For a discussion of the role of return-from-death narratives and ghost tales in anomaly accounts, see Robert F. Campany, "Return-From-Death Narratives in Early Medieval China," *Journal of Chinese Religions* 18 (1990): 91–125 and "Ghosts Matter: The Culture of Ghosts in Six Dynasties Zhiguai," *Chinese Literature* 13 (1991): 15–34. For a study of ghosts in Chinese fiction, see Anthony Yu, "'Rest, Rest, Perturbed Spirit!' Ghosts in Traditional Chinese Prose Fiction," *Harvard Journal of Asiatic Studies* 47, no. 2 (1987): 397–434.

53. Translated in Kenneth J. Dewoskin and J. I. Crump, Jr., trans., *In Search of the Supernatural: The Written Record* (Stanford, CA: Stanford University Press, 1996), 122.

54. *Sanguo zhi* 三國志 [History of the three kingdoms, 297] (Beijing: Zhonghua shuju, 1963 ed.), 1:810–811. Translated in Kenneth J. DeWoskin, trans., *Doctors, Diviners, and Magicians of Ancient China: Biographies of Fang-shih* (New York: Columbia University Press, 1983), 138–40.

55. See *Zuozhuan zhengyi*: "Xuangong 12" (SSJZS 2:1882) in which the graph 武 (*wu*, military) is analyzed as 止 (*zhi*, to stop) and 戈 (*ge*, spears). The attribution of glyphomancy to the Yellow Emperor appears in *Annals of the Thearchs and Kings* 帝王世紀 (*Diwang shiji* [BBCSJC 7b-8a]) by Huangfu Mi 皇甫謐 (215–282). By performing a glyphomantic interpretation of his own dream, the Yellow Emperor obtained the names of two talented men whom he later found to serve as officials in his government. This anecdote is also recorded in *Lofty Principles*, I:5. For two other examples, see Ong, *Interpretation of Dreams*, 169–72.

56. "Glyphomancy" 拆字 (*chaizi*, literally, "disassembling characters") is a term coined by Joseph Needham in *Science and Civilisation in China* (Cambridge: Cambridge University Press, 1956), 2:364. Its practice as a popular fortune-telling method involved a variety of other techniques. See also Wolfgang Bauer, "Chinese Glyphomancy *(ch'ai-tzu)* and Its Uses in Present-day Taiwan" in Sarah Allan and Alvin P. Cohen, eds., *Legend, Lore, and Religion in China: Essays in Honor of Wolfram Eberhard on His Seventieth Birthday* (San Francisco: Chinese Materials Center, 1979), 71–96. Bauer dates the origin of this as a commercial profession back to the Sui dynasty and the earliest detailed manuals to the 10th century.

57. *Jinshu* 晉書 [History of the Jin dynasty, 646] (Beijing: Zhonghua shuju, 1974 ed.), 2380. The anecdote may well be apocryphal and is abridged in *Lofty Principles*, II:10n31.

58. See, for example, *Lofty Principles*, II:11n35. The anecdote originally appeared in the miscellany *Trifling Words from Beimeng* 北夢瑣言 (*Beimeng suoyan*) by Sun Guangxian 孫光憲 (d. 968).

59. Translated in William H. Nienhauser, Jr., trans., "The World Inside a Pillow," in Y. W. Ma and Joseph S. M. Lau, eds., *Traditional Chinese Stories: Themes and Variations* (New York: Columbia University Press, 1978), 435–38.

60. "A Record of Three Dreams" is typical of the obscure origins of many dream narratives, even those that purport to be historical. It was apparently not

printed until centuries later during the Ming, and there are several printed versions of the first dream with different casts of characters. Conversely, the incident involving the author Bo Xingjian has been accepted by many as genuine. For remarks on its textual history, see Wang Pijiang 汪辟疆, ed., *Tangren xiaoshuo* 唐人小說 [Fiction by men of the Tang dynasty] (Shanghai: Shanghai guji chubanshe, 1978), 110-11.

61. A surviving remnant of this work containing four short dream narratives was reprinted in Ma Guohan 馬國翰, ed., *Yuhan shanfang jiyishu* 玉函山房輯佚書 [Collected remnant texts from the Mountain lodge of jade book boxes] (Yangzhou: Jiangsu Guangling guji keyinshe, 1990 rpt. of 1884 ed.), 7:175.

62. Sixty-eight dreams from lost works preserved only in Tang and Song encyclopedias are recorded in Liu, *Meng de mixin*, 338-43. In general practice, the autobiographical impulse to record dream experience was expressed in poetry rather than in prose. See Fu, *Zhongguo mengwenhua cidian*, 499-845 for a selection of dream poetry.

63. See Ouyang Xun 歐陽詢, ed., *Yiwen leiju* 藝文類聚 [Encyclopedia for literary composition] (Beijing: Zhonghua shuju, 1965 ed.), 2:1355-57.

64. Daoshi, *Fayuan zhulin*: 32 (1991 Beijing rpt.), I:491-99. For other dream typologies in this encyclopedia and in other Buddhist texts, see Liu, *Meng de mixin*, 250-52.

65. For recent studies on these two works, see Glen Dudbridge, *Religious Experience and Lay Society in T'ang China: A Reading of Tai Fu's* Kuang-I chi" (Cambridge: Cambridge University Press, 1995), 50-64 ff and Carrie E. Reed, *A Tang Miscellany: An Introduction to* Youyang zazu (New York: Peter Lang, 2003), 56ff.

66. See *Lunyu zhuzi suoyin* 論語逐字索引 (ICS 7.21/16/17): "Confucius would not discuss strange things, power, disorder, or gods."

67. See Wang Qinruo 王欽若, ed., *Cefu yuangui* 冊府元龜, chaps. 892-893 (Beijing: Zhonghua shuju 1960 rpt. of early Ming ed.), 11:10552-10575.

68. For discussions of the views of Song intellectuals toward dreams, see Fu, *Zhongguo mengwenhua*, 85-115; Lin, "Chia Pao-yü," 83-90; and Liu, *Meng de mixin*, 223-45.

69. For recent research on the role of memory that draws similar conclusions, see Cavallero and Cicogna, "Memory and Dreaming," in Cavellero and Foulkes, eds., *Dreaming as Cognition* (New York: Harvester Wheatsheaf, 1993), 38-57.

70. Zhang regarded the spirit as a natural force whose activity manifested the power of heaven. This was usually so subtle, though, that it was largely below the threshold of human perception. A later biographer of Zhang regarded the writing of *Correcting Obscurity* as a response to an unusual dream of his. See Fu, *Zhongguo mengwenhua*, 104-107.

71. See Liu, *Meng de mixin*, 220-21. Chen Shiyuan held a similar view and expressed this etiology as the "overflowing of emotions" 情溢 *(qingyi)* in *Lofty Principles*, I:10.

72. Cheng Yi reiterated the view in the *Master Zhuang* that the sage did not necessarily dream at all because his *qi*-energy was so pure that he had transcended all thoughts. Though this belief continued to enjoy a certain currency, it was by

no means embraced by other Confucian thinkers and was later rejected by Su Shi 蘇軾 (1037–1101) and Chen Shiyuan. See Fu, *Zhongguo mengwenhua,* 107–115; *Lofty Principles,* I:6.

73. Zhu Xi 朱熹, *Zhuzi daquan* 朱子大全 (Taipei: Zhonghua shuju, 1966 ed.), 7:57:17a; translated in Lin, "Chia Pao-yü," 84.

74. See Daiwie Fu, "A Contextual and Taxonomic Study of the 'Divine Marvels' and 'Strange Occurrences' in the *Mengxi bitan,*" *Chinese Science* 11 (1993–94): 24–35 for a discussion of Shen's taxonomy, which, he argues, occupies a middle position between the traditional "aristocratic-folkloric" culture of the Tang and the rationalistic views of Song Neo-Confucian thinkers.

75. See Shen Gua 沈括, *Xin jiaozheng mengxi bitan* 新校正夢溪筆談 [A newly edited version of *Jottings from Dream stream*], ed. Hu Daojing 胡道靜 (Beijing: Zhonghua shuju, 1957), 320–21. For a discussion of this dream as indicating a tendency among Song intellectuals to deprive ghosts of their power of enchantment, see Fu, "Contextual and Taxonomic Study," 18–19.

76. Su Shi, "Mengzhaiming bingxu" [Preface and poem on the Studio of dreams] in Kong Fanli 孔凡禮, ed., *Su Shi wenji* 蘇軾文集 [Collected prose of Su Shi] (Beijing: Zhonghua shuju, 1986), 575; also translated in Lin, "Chia Pao-yü," 89.

77. Fu, "Contextual and Taxonomic Study," 11.

78. See Liu, *Meng de mixin,* 232 and Lin, "Chia Pao-yü," 90.

79. Translated in Lin, "Chia Pao-yü," 91.

80. Zhu Yuanzhang's accounts of two dreams were printed during his reign and widely reprinted thereafter. The most important of these was "Jimeng" 紀夢 [Record of a dream] written after 1368. See *Ming Taizu yuzhi wenji* 明太祖御制文集 [Imperially composed writings by Emperor Taizu of the Ming] (Taipei: Zhongguo shixue congshu, 1965 ed.), 447–54; translated in Taylor, "Ming T'ai-tsu," 20. In addition, at least a dozen more of the emperor's dreams were recorded by others. See Fang, "Ming Dreams," 55–72.

81. *The Yongle Encyclopedia* contained 22,937 chapters of which only about 800 have survived. A second manuscript copy was later produced during the Ming, but access to it was also restricted. Chapters 13,135–13,140 were devoted to dreams. Chapters 13,137–13,138 are still missing today, but the remaining ones have been reprinted in *Yongle dadian* 永樂大典 [The Yongle encyclopedia] (Beijing: Zhonghua shuju, 1986 rpt. of 1408 ms.), 6:5663–5710.

82. *Yongzheng Yingcheng xianzhi* 雍正應城縣志 [Gazetteer of Yingcheng from the Yongzheng era, 1726], in *Zhongguo difangzhi jicheng* 中國地方志集成, vol. 11: *Hubei fuxian zhiji* 湖北府縣志輯 (Nanjing: Jiangsu guji chubanshe, 2001 rpt. of 1726 ed.), 82; Hu Mingsheng 胡鳴盛, "Chen Shiyuan xiansheng nianpu" 陳士元先生年譜 [Chronological biography of Chen Shiyuan] *Guoli Beiping tushuguan yuekan* 國立北平圖書館月刊 3, no. 5 (Nov. 1929): 605–606.

83. *Guangxu Yingcheng xianzhi* 光緒應城縣志 [Gazetteer of Yingcheng from the Guangxu era, 1882], in *Zhongguo difangzhi jicheng*, vol. 11, 338; Hu, "nianpu," 643.

84. "Ke Luanzhouzhi xu" 刻灤州志序 [Preface to the printed edition of The gazetteer of Luanzhou] in Zhang Juzheng 張居正, *Zhang Taiyue ji* 張太岳集 [Col-

Introduction 45

lected works of Zhang Taiyue (Juzheng)] (Shanghai: Shanghai guji chubanshe, 1984 rpt. of Wanli era ed.), 93–94. The preface was written about 1547–48. Zhang had just earned the metropolitan graduate degree in 1547 and began his official career as a Hanlin bachelor.

85. Hu, "nianpu," 614. Lienche Tu Fang, "Ch'en Shih-yuan" in *Dictionary of Ming Biography,* ed. L. Carrington Goodrich (New York: Columbia University Press, 1976), I:178 gives 1547 as the date of his retirement from office.

86. Fang, "Ch'en Shih-yuan," 179. The anecdote is also found in Zhou Lianggong 周亮工, *Shuying* 書影 [Book shadows, 1667] (Shanghai: Shanghai guji chubanshe, 1981 ed.), 224 and *Guangxu Yingcheng xianzhi,* 338.

87. Li Yan 李淡, *Donglindangji kao* 東林黨籍考 [Biographical research on members of the Donglin party] (Taipei: Mingwen shuju, 1991 rpt.), 006:805:75; also Bian Shiyun 卞士雲, "Guiyun bieji xu" 歸雲別集序 [Preface to *A further anthology of returned clouds*] (1833 Baoshantang ed.), 1a.

88. *Yongzheng Yingcheng xianzhi,* 82; also *Hubei tongzhi* 湖北通志 [Comprehensive gazetteer of Hubei, 1921], 51:40b, in *Zhongguo shengzhi huibian* 中國省志彙編 (Taipei: Huawen shuju, 1967 rpt. of 1921 ed.), 7:3572–73.

89. Hu, "nianpu," 615. Chen also took the courtesy name Xinshu 心叔 (Mind-gathering).

90. Hu, "nianpu," 607. From the age of about nineteen, Chen maintained a close relationship with Yu Yinxu and later composed his obituary. A metropolitan graduate of 1526 who rose to become vice minister on the right in the Ministry of Revenue, Yu had earlier studied with Zhan Ruoshui and became an influential teacher in Yingcheng after retiring from office.

91. Chen noted that his casual replies in the book to Cheng's questions were recorded by an assistant with little further editing. For praise of this short work in two chapters, see Ji Yun et al. eds., *Qinding siku quanshu zongmu tiyao* 欽定四庫全書總目提要 [Summaries of all titles collected for *The imperially sponsored complete works of the four libraries*] (Beijing: Zhonghua shuju, 1997 ed.), I:970. The chief editor Ji Yun 紀昀 (1724–1805) only had access to an incomplete edition, but it was among those chosen to be reprinted in the *Siku quanshu* 四庫全書 [The complete works of the four libraries, 1772–1782]. A more complete version that includes Chen's preface appeared in the 1850 collectanea *Yihai zhuchen* 藝海珠塵 [Tiny pearls from the ocean of the arts] (Taipei: Yiwen, 1968 rpt.).

92. Some of Chen's poems and prose were collected by him in *Guiyun ji* 歸雲集 [Collected works of returned clouds, ca. 1549–ca. 1582]. For a surviving set of poems by Chen on the pleasures of dwelling at home during the four seasons, see Hubeisheng difangzhi bianzuan weiyuanhui 湖北省地方志編纂委員會, ed., *Yingcheng xianzhi* 應城縣志 [Gazetteer of Yingcheng] (Beijing: Zhongguo chengshi chubanshe, 1992), 829.

93. Hu, "nianpu," 626.

94. Wu Yumei 吳毓梅, "Guiyun bieji xu" 歸雲別集敘 [Preface to *A further anthology of returned clouds*], (1833 Baoshantang ed.), 1a.

95. Zhou, *Shuying,* 223–24.

96. Fang, "Ch'en Shih-yuan," 178.

97. For the opinions of Ji Yun et al. on Chen's works, see Ji, *zongmu tiyao*, I:46 passim.

98. For one such opinion of Chen, see Ye Dehui 葉德輝, *Xiyuan dushuzhi* 郋園讀書志 [Notes on books from the Xi garden] (Shanghai: Zhanyuan, 1928), 9:56B–57B.

99. Chen's relationship to the *Explanations of Subtleties in the Forest of Dreams* is discussed in Michael Lackner, *Der chinesische Traumwald: Traditionelle Theorien des Traumes und seiner Deutung im Spiegel der ming-zeitlichen anthologie Meng-lin hsüan-chieh* (Frankfurt am Main: Peter Lang, 1985), 166–70, though without any conclusions as to the authenticity of the text's claim that Chen was the original compiler. See, however, the suspicions surrounding this work and its purported origins in Hu, "nianpu," 618–19 and in Ji, *zongmu tiyao*, 2:1458. Despite a preface supposedly written in Chen's own calligraphy in 1564, there is no mention elsewhere by either Chen or his bibliographers of his having authored a work titled *Menglin xuanjie* 夢林玄解. The only connection may be the inclusion of the abridged version of the *Lofty Principles* by the compiler He Dongru 何棟如 (fl. 1598), or, perhaps, by unscrupulous publishers seeking to capitalize on Chen's reputation.

100. For a recent edition with commentary, see Lu Yuanxun 卢元勋 et al., *Gudai zhanmengshu zhuping* 古代占梦术注评 [Ancient texts on dream interpretation techniques with commentaries and critiques] (Beijing: Beijing shifan daxue chubanshe, 1991), 1–143.

101. Su Shi's first visit actually took place in the seventh lunar month. For translations of both pieces about Red Cliff, see Richard E. Strassberg, *Inscribed Landscapes* (Berkeley: University of California Press, 1994), 185–88.

102. The term *yizhi* 逸旨 has been misunderstood as "free" or "untrammeled principles." See, for example, Lackner, *Chinesische Traumwald*, 169, which translates Chen's work as *Freien Hinweise zur Traumdeutung*. However, Chen's use of *yizhi* to mean "lofty principles" that are superior to popular practices appears in his discussion of the ancient official method of confirming initial interpretations of dreams with astronomical observations. See *Lofty Principles*, I:7n12.

103. *Lofty Principles*, I:8, 8n16. Suo Dan's remarks appear in *Jinshu* (1974 ed.), 1665.

104. See, for example, the dream of Earl Sheng 聲伯 (fl. 583–575 BCE) in *Lofty Principles*, I:5n19, 8n5 where he avoids its negative consequences as long as he does not have it interpreted.

105. For a critical study of the role of narrative forms in Western dream stories, see Bert O. States, *Dreaming and Storytelling* (Ithaca: Cornell University Press, 1993).

106. Dreams in later Ming and Qing culture are discussed in Zeitlin, *Historian of the Strange*, 132–81; see esp. 138–42 on Chen Shiyuan's encyclopedia. Also, Robert E. Hegel, "Heavens and Hells in Chinese Fictional Dreams," in Brown, ed., *Psycho-Sinology*, 129–41.

107. *Lofty Principles*, II:10, 10n18

108. See Lu et al., *Gudai zhanmengshu*, 1.

109. *Lofty Principles*, I:10.

110. *Lofty Principles*, II:11. For a study of the popular dimensions of the

official examinations, see Benjamin A. Elman, *A Cultural History of Civil Examinations in Late Imperial China* (Berkeley: University of California Press, 2000), 295–370, esp. 326–45 for the widespread belief in dreams that could predict success.

111. Elman, *Civil Examinations*, 140–42.

112. *Liezi zhuzi suoyin* (ICS 3/18/21–19/4); translated in Graham, *Lieh-tzŭ*, 68–69. The anecdote is abridged in *Lofty Principles*, I:8n14.

夢占逸旨卷之一　歸雲別集二十六

應城陳士元著

同邑後學吳毓梅玉坪氏刊
弟毓松秀巖氏
男道灼雲卿氏　仝校

真宰篇第一

真宰窈冥無象無形頑濛渾穆氣數斯涵莊子若有真宰而特不得其朕○廣成子窈窈冥冥至道之極○淮南子古未有天地窈窈冥冥芒芠漠閔頑濛鴻洞莫知其門
動靜陰陽數包終始　○列子太易者未見氣也 周子太極動而生陽靜而生

夢占逸旨　卷之一　歸雲別集二十六　三

Lofty Principles of Dream Interpretation
夢占逸旨

Chen Shiyuan
陳士元

Preface

On the day after the moon's height in the eighth lunar month of the year *renxu* of the Jiajing era [September 14, 1562], I was sitting in my studio in Puyang [Yingcheng, Hubei]. The sight of the moon slowly rising stirred me, and I was delighted when it attained its fullness. Moved by its cycle of waxing and waning, I pondered the succession of vigor and exhaustion. Then I ordered some wine and drank until I felt exhilarated, finally becoming drunk. I lay down with the wine ladle as a pillow, covering myself with the breeze as I sank into a deep sleep. I dreamt that an old man with white bushy eyebrows, wrapped in a robe as ethereal as the mist, descended into my room. He bestowed a set of volumes whose golden writing dazzled my eyes. They seemed to be in the ancient "tadpole-style" graphs, and I wanted to recite them but was unable to. So I hid them in my sleeve both from fear of losing them and to guard such a rare treasure. But doubts arose in my mind, and I politely asked the old man, "Isn't our encounter, sir, just a dream?" The old man laughed and replied, "What encounter isn't a dream, and what dream isn't real?" Suddenly, he emitted a sharp cry, and I was startled awake. When I arose, it was morning, and I let out a sigh. What kind of auspicious omen was this? I spent all day thinking it over, but I couldn't understand the reason behind it. Alas! Was my encounter with the old man at night real and my sighs during the next morning a dream? I consulted a dream interpreter about its meaning, for I was deeply affected that such a scripture was revealed on earth. Based on bits of things seen and heard, I compiled this work in two parts, as "inner" and "outer" chapters, recording trifles and delights for which I have fashioned the title *Lofty Principles*. Though I have eliminated both commonplace and abstruse language, how can I avoid the criticism that it resulted from a wine-soaked dream? Worthless gentlemen who have withdrawn from the world may find this no more than an aid to their jokes and conversations.

PART I
The Inner Chapters
內篇

CHAPTER I

The True Controller
真宰

The True Controller is fathomless and obscure, neither image nor material form. Though undifferentiated, turbid, and profound, it contains all the permutations of *qi*-energy.[1] *Qi*-energy divided into yin and yang forces, and numbers issued forth marking beginnings and ends.[2] Heaven swirled about and earth congealed as these two spaces became fixed in their proper positions. Then, mankind and all other things were born.[3] Man possesses within himself a fundamental, placid harmony resembling the relationship between heaven and earth. He is pervaded by a blend of vigorous essence and spirit, which do not conflict with each other.[4] The *qi*-energy of heaven became the ethereal *hun*-soul; the *qi*-energy of earth became the earthly *po*-soul.[5] When a person's *qi*-energy is pure, the *po*-soul follows the *hun*-soul. When *qi*-energy is impure, the *hun*-soul follows the *po*-soul. Following the *hun*-soul leads to nobility; following the *po*-soul results in lowliness. A pure *hun*-soul is worthy; an impure *po*-soul is stupid. These are the thresholds to longevity or a short life, good fortune or disaster.[6] There is nobility and worthiness, lowliness and stupidity, longevity and good fortune, short life and disaster. There is also nobility yet stupidity, lowliness yet worthiness, longevity yet disaster, short life yet good fortune. The transformations of this world are inconsistent, but their tendencies can be discerned from early signs. The *hun*-soul can know the future, the *po*-soul can conceal the past.[7] When men awake in the morning, their *hun*-soul becomes active in their eyes. When they fall asleep at night, their *po*-soul reposes in their livers. When the *hun*-soul hovers in the eyes, one can see things. While the *po*-soul reposes in the liver, one can dream. Dreaming is spirit-wandering and a mirror for knowing the future.[8] Therefore, it is said that when the spirit makes contact, dreams result, and when the body encounters things, events occur.⁹

NOTES

1. There seems to be a True Controller, but it is impossible to apprehend its appearance. According to Master Guangcheng, the absolute Way is fathomless and obscure. (From the *Master Zhuang*.) In antiquity, before there was heaven and earth, everything was fathomless and obscure, confused and murky, undifferentiated and empty, so that there was no gateway into it. (From the *Master of Huainan*.)

2. When the Great Ultimate moved, it gave birth to yang; when it became quiet, it gave birth to yin. (Master Zhou Dunyi.) The Great Generation occurred before *qi*-energy appeared. It lacked any form or definite borders, but then it transformed and became oneness. One transformed and became seven; seven transformed and became nine. "Nine" *[jiu]* is a homophone for "finality" *[jiu]*, so when nine transforms, it becomes one again. (From the *Master Lie*.) Oneness gave birth to two, two to three, and three gave birth to the myriad things. The myriad things carry yin and embrace yang. (From the *Laozi*.)

3. Heaven revolved while earth stood still as everything kept spinning about without diminishing. (From the *Master of Huainan*.) Heaven and earth were born of primal *qi*-energy and are the ancestors of all things. (From *A Summary of Ritual*.)

4. When *qi*-energy formed a harmonious blend, it became mankind. (From the *Master Lie*.) Man's vigorous essence and spirit flow together with the movements of heaven and earth. This is the basis on which dream interpretation was established. (From a commentary to *The Poems of Wang Jiefu*.)

5. Heaven in us takes the form of virtuous power while earth in us takes the form of *qi*-energy. Life occurs when virtuous power flows and *qi* blends with it. Thus, the arrival of life is called "vigorous essence." The interaction of the two kinds of vigorous essence is called "spirit." What accompanies the spirit as it comes and goes is called the "*hun*-soul" and what enters and exits along with the vigorous essence is called the "*po*-soul." (From *The Book of the Spiritual Pivot*.) What is called the "*po*-soul" is the initial transformation when something first obtains life. After birth, the yang part of the *po*-soul is called the "*hun*-soul." (Zichan of Zheng.) Vigorous essence and spirit are apportioned by heaven and the components of the body are apportioned by earth. What belongs to heaven is pure and disperses; what belongs to earth is impure and coagulates. (From the *Master Lie*.) The *hun*-soul rules the emotions and the *po*-soul rules the inherent nature. (From *Discussions in the White Tiger Hall*.) The *hun*-soul is the yang spirit of a person and the *po*-soul is the yin spirit of a person. (Gao You.) What man breathes in and out is *qi*-energy. The sensory perceptions of the eyes and ears comprise the *po*-soul. When these become *qi*-energy, it is called the "*hun*-soul." (Zheng Xuan.) The *hun*-soul is governed by the agent "wood," and the *po*-soul is governed by the agent "metal." That is why one speaks of the three *hun*-souls

and the seven *po*-souls, for these are the numbers of the agents "metal" and "wood" respectively. (Zhu Xi.)

6. A numinous *hun*-soul is worthy; a wicked *po*-soul is stupid. A light *hun*-soul is bright; a heavy *po*-soul is dark. Feathers elevate the *hun*-soul; hair weighs down the *po*-soul. (From *A Record of Textual Studies*.)

7. When the *hun*-soul is strong, one is adept at achieving a profound understanding and when the *po*-soul is strong, one is adept at remembering things. The sage uses his *po*-soul to take charge of his *hun*-soul while ordinary people use their *hun*-soul to direct their *po*-soul.

8. Whatever enters into the vigorous essence and spirit can flow and connect with heaven, earth, yin, and yang. Therefore, during daytime activities and nighttime dreams, good, evil, auspicious, and inauspicious events all occur according to their categorical natures. (Zhu Xi.) It is the reflector of heaven and earth and a mirror of the myriad things. (From the *Master Zhuang*.)

9. When the spirit makes contact, dreams result and when the body encounters things, events occur. Thus, we think during the day and dream at night as body and spirit encounter things. When the spirit congeals, thoughts and dreams dissipate on their own. (From the *Master Lie*.) The *hun*-soul interacts with others during sleep; the body is animated when awake. (From the *Master Zhuang*.)

CHAPTER 2

The Long-Willow Method
長柳

Guides to the practice of the Long-Willow Method are recorded in bibliographical treatises, but the details are no longer known.[1] Among the officials of the Zhou dynasty was the grand diviner in charge of interpreting the three patterns of tortoise shell divination, the three methods of hexagram divination, and the three types of dreams.[2] The three types of dreams are: dreams of arrival; dreams of obtaining things; and dreams of obtaining everything.[3] Moreover, the eight charges were applied to the interpretations of the three patterns of cracks in tortoise shell divination, the three methods of hexagram divination, and the three kinds of dream divination in order to observe whether these were auspicious or inauspicious.[4] The patterns of cracks utilize tortoise shells to disclose their meaning, while hexagram divination is revealed through the use of milfoil stalks. Milfoil and tortoise shells are external things that were established and taught by sages for practical use. They can aid in understanding the manifestations of divine spirit and resolve great doubts.[5] However, a dream is basically the experience of the *hun*-soul and is not created by such external things. How can one identify flourishing or decline and success or failure except by ascertaining a dream's general characteristics and investigating its deeper meaning?[6]

NOTES

1. The "Treatise on Arts and Literature" in *History of the Western Han Dynasty* lists *The Yellow Emperor's Long-Willow Method of Dream Interpretation* in eleven chapters and *Gan De's Long-Willow Method of Dream Interpretation* in twenty chapters.

2. The grand diviner interprets the three patterns of tortoise shell divination, namely, those cracks on the shells resembling striations on jade, those resembling the shape of clay roof tiles, and those forming a right angle. He also interprets the three methods of hexagram divination, which are called the "Connected Mountains," "Returning to Concealment," and the "Zhou Dynasty Hexagrams." (From "The Grand Diviner" in *The Government Organization of the Zhou*.)

3. Dreams of arrival are dreams where the dreamer arrives someplace. They were identified by the Xia dynasty people. "*Qi*" in "*qimeng*" [dreams of obtaining something] means "to obtain" and indicates that which is obtained in a dream—they were identified by the Shang dynasty people. "*Xian*" in "*xianzhi*" [dreams of obtaining all kinds of things] means "everything," and "*zhi*" also means "to obtain." It means dreams in which everything is obtained—they were identified by the Zhou dynasty people. (From Zheng Xuan's commentary to *The Government Organization of the Zhou*.)

4. *The Government Organization of the Zhou* states that the eight charges regarding state affairs concerned: war; astronomical omens; bestowals; strategies; results; arrivals; rain; and disease. These eight charges were applied to the interpretations of the three kinds of patterns of tortoise shell divination, the three methods of hexagram divination, and the three kinds of dreams in order to determine whether the response was auspicious or inauspicious for the state and to proclaim policies that would aid in government. A commentary states that there are eight fixed charges that are formulated in language and posed to the milfoil stalks of hexagram divination and to the tortoise shells of pyroscapulamancy, and these are also utilized in the interpretation of dreams.

5. "The Great Commentary" in *The Book of Changes* states that the sages established their teachings according to the Way of divine spirit. It also states that one should make advantageous use of the hexagrams when leaving home and returning. The common people all used them, and it is called "divine spirit." Furthermore, it states that they can be used to connect with the bright, virtuous power of the divine.

If you have great doubts, resolve them through divination with milfoil stalks. (From "The Great Plan" in *The Documents of Antiquity*.)

6. Although tortoise shells and milfoil stalks are external things, they can still be used to divine flourishing, decline, success, or failure. Yet, dreams arise from the vigorous essence and the spirit, which these external things cannot compare with. These methods can still be used in interpretation. However, if they do not produce an accurate result, then it is not possible to use them to determine a dream's general characteristics and hidden meaning.

CHAPTER 3

Day and Night
晝夜

Day and night are like a single breath; past and present are like day and night.[1] Heaven and earth regard spring and summer as day and consider autumn and winter as night; an era of good government as day and an era of chaos as night.[2] Heaven and earth produce auspicious signs that are expressions of their vigorous essence and spirit.[3] The appearance of things such as lucky stars, propitious clouds, bronze vessels, chariots, and sweet springs are considered auspicious omens. These are the auspicious dreams of heaven and earth.[4] Such things as baneful stars, dust-filled windstorms, malevolent vapors, earthquakes, droughts, and the god Yi-yang are called demonic misfortunes. These are the nightmares of heaven and earth.[5]

Since the auspicious dreams and nightmares of heaven and earth can be interpreted, why not the dreams of people? People live in servitude to their bodies as they follow regular patterns of sleep and wakefulness. When conscious and awake, their bodies are active. When they lie down and sleep, their bodies are quiescent. Yet, man's spirit-energy can roam about as he flows along with the transformations of nature.[6] It reverts to absolute vacuity and is gathered up within absolute numinousness. His luminous *hun*-soul never decays while the outer covering of his vigorous essence never becomes murky.[7] How could the spirit become activated or quiescent because of falling asleep or awakening? Therefore, even though the body may be asleep, the spirit is not asleep. It may be withdrawn when alone or communicate when in contact with things. Because it is sometimes withdrawn and sometimes communicative, one may or may not dream when asleep.[8] When the spirit makes contact with things, it may happen at a distance or it may occur nearby. It may last

Day and Night

an eternity or only briefly. There are different images that are light or dark, different postures of jumping up or falling down, different situations of success or disgrace, different outcomes of victory or defeat. Things classified as fortunate or malevolent are diverse and cannot be systematized. Although there may be things that have never before been seen or heard, they can all become condensed into a dream. And they can be experienced in just a single period of sleep. Whether these events are auspicious or evil can be identified and interpreted, but why was dream experience ever regarded like day and night?[9]

NOTES

1. One may know things by understanding the Way of day and night. (From "The Great Commentary" in *The Book of Changes*.) Life and death are like day and night. (From the *Master Zhuang*.) A sage appears once in a thousand years, yet this occurs as rapidly as dawn and dusk. (Yan Zhitui.)

2. In spring and summer, doors are kept open, and this enables sincerity to flow through. In autumn and winter, doors are kept closed so that sincerity returns to remain inside. During an orderly era, the yang force predominates and is luminous. During a chaotic era, the yin force predominates and is impure. These resemble the symbolic images of day and night.

Heaven creates the periods of spring, summer, autumn, winter, daytime, and evening. (From the Master Zhuang.)

3. The vigorous essence of yin and yang is rooted in the earth, but it rises to manifest itself in heaven. (From "Treatise on Astronomy" in *History of the Western Han Dynasty*.)

4. Lucky stars are shaped like a half-moon. A king dares not regard them as if he were an ordinary individual. (From *Mr. Sun's Illustrations of Auspicious Things*.) Resplendent and turbulent or lonely and spiraling—such are providential clouds. (From *Historical Records*.) When the Son of Heaven is filial, then auspicious clouds appear and float across the sky. (From *A Concordance to the Divine Significance of The Book of Filial Piety*.) When the virtuous power of a king reaches the mountains, then auspicious clouds float upward from them, and valuable objects and chariots appear. When his virtuous power reaches down to the watery chasms and springs, then sweet springs bubble forth. (From *Discussions in the White Tiger Hall*.)

5. Baneful stars belong to the category of comets. (Jin Zhuo.) Dust-filled windstorms are when the earth is mixed together with rain. (From *Commentary on The Book of Songs*.) Malevolent vapors are inauspicious *qi*-energy. (From *Ocean of Chapters According to the Five Sounds*.) Mountains collapsing and rivers drying up are signs of the destruction of the state. (From *Apocrypha to The Book of Ritual*.) The *Master of Huainan* states that Yiyang was sighted on the Plains of Mu, and a commentary added that Yiyang was an earth god who appeared at the suburban altar when the Shang dynasty was about to fall.

6. Man interacts with the vigorous essence and spirit of heaven and earth.

(From the *Master Zhuang*.) The lungs govern the eyes, the kidneys govern the nose, the gall-bladder governs the mouth, and the liver governs the ears. The external is that which is displayed outside, and the internal is that which lies within. Opening and closing, tensing and relaxing each follow a fixed order. Thus, the head is round in the image of heaven and the feet are squared-off in the image of earth. Heaven contains the four seasons, the five agents, the nine celestial regions, and the three hundred and sixty-six days. Man also contains four limbs, five *zang*-organs, nine orifices, and three hundred and sixty-six joints. Heaven controls wind, rain, winter, and summer. Man also engages in taking and giving, and experiences happiness and anger. He forms a trinity together with heaven and earth. Therefore, he can return to the fundamental principle of his nature and destiny by investigating the duality of life and death and by distinguishing the traces of identity and difference. In this way he can nourish and care for his vigorous essence and spirit as well as soothe and calm his *hun*- and *po*-souls. (From the *Master of Huainan*.) The heart responds to the jujube, the liver responds to the elm: thus do we connect with heaven and earth. As night approaches, one dreams of water, as daylight approaches, one dreams of fire: thus do heaven and earth connect with us. (From *A Garden of Stories*.)

7. Master Yang Xiong says that the luminous *hun*-soul never decays and the outer covering of vigorous essence is never murky. Liu Zongyuan's commentary says that the luminous *hun*-soul is in charge of the functioning of the eyes, and the outer covering is the surface of the pupil. Wu Mi's commentary states that the luminous *hun*-soul is the brilliant luster of vigorous essence, and the outer covering is the whiteness of the vigorous essence.

8. A dream occurs when the spirit makes contact with a form. No dream occurs without such contact even though one is asleep.

He was soundly sleeping and pleasantly awoke. (From the *Master Zhuang*.) Being awake and sleeping is the activity and quiescence of the mind. Whether or not there are thoughts reflects the activation or quiescence of the mind when it is active. Whether or not there are dreams reflects the activation or quiescence of the mind when it is quiescent. Yet, being awake is yang and being quiescent is yin. Wakefulness is a state of clarity and quiescence is a state of murkiness. When one is awake, there is a controller at work, but when one is asleep, there is no apparent controller. Therefore, the mystery of responding to and communicating with something when alone can only be spoken about when one is awake. (Zhu Xi.)

9. Life and death, survival and extinction, dire circumstances and success, poverty and wealth, worthiness and degradation, censure and praise, hunger and thirst, cold and heat—all are transformations of events and the workings of destiny. It is just like the succession of day and night, and this is even truer for dreams. (Confucius.)

CHAPTER 4

The Various Forms of Divination
眾占

There are various forms of divination, but those involving dreams are the most important.¹ Dreams can be correlated with tortoise shell and hexagram divination. Therefore, the three dynasties of Xia, Shang, and Zhou all emphasized them. When the Luo River produced the "Cinnabar Text," the nine divisions were defined, and the method of tortoise shell divination became clear. When the Yellow River produced the "Green Diagram," the eight trigrams were displayed, and the method of divination by hexagrams became possible.² The secrets of dream interpretation can firmly determine the patterns of human nature and destiny as well as the calculations of tortoise shells and hexagrams.³ As for the three patterns of cracks in tortoise shell divination, there are 120 basic forms and 1,200 possible laudations.⁴ The three methods of hexagram divination contain eight basic forms that are further differentiated to form sixty-four permutations.⁵ There are the ten halos with ninety variations related to the three kinds of dreams.⁶ If dreams are compared to tortoise shell or hexagram divination, how could any one of these be considered superior to the others? When King Wu attacked King Zhou of the Shang, his dream was in accordance with the divination.⁷ Shi Chao of Wei said that since the divination with milfoil stalks confirmed his dream, King Wu utilized the result.⁸ Unless one has attained a thorough understanding of yin and yang and has profoundly investigated the horizon where heaven and man meet, how can one engage in such things?⁹

NOTES

1. The various kinds of divination bring order to symbolic images connected with all kinds of events, and they prognosticate according to the signs of good

and evil. There are many kinds of divination, but those involving dreams are the most important. Therefore, there were special officials for this purpose during the Zhou dynasty. (From "Treatise on Arts and Literature" in *History of the Western Han Dynasty*.)

2. The rounded form of heaven is revealed by the calculations of the Yellow River Diagram and the squared form of earth is indicated by the patterns of the Luo River Text (Shao Yong). The Yellow River Diagram understands the creative principle and reveals the plan of heaven, and the Luo River Text flows together with the receptive principle to reveal the symbolic images of earth. (From *Apocrypha to the Spring and Autumn Annals*.)

3. The vigorous essence and spirit of man flow in conjunction with heaven, earth, yin, and yang. Therefore, every dream can be categorized. If one recognizes this, then it is possible to use dreams to articulate the patterns of human nature and destiny. (From *Mr. Lü's Readings of The Book of Songs*.) Dream interpretation and tortoise shell divination are the same. (From Wang Chong, *Judicious Discussions*.)

4. The word "laudation" [*song*] means the pronouncement of the divination. The number of pronouncements for each of the three kinds of patterns is the same, only the names and techniques differ. Each of the 120 basic forms in each pattern has ten kinds of pronouncements. Each pattern can have five different colors. These patterns are doubled and their boundaries indicated with ink. (From Zheng Xuan's commentary on *The Government Organization of the Zhou*.)

5. In the three methods of hexagram divination, the hexagrams and their permutations are the same but their names and divination techniques differ. There are eight trigrams, and their permutations result from doubling them to form hexagrams. (From Zheng Xuan's commentary on *The Government Organization of the Zhou*.)

6. *The Government Organization of the Zhou* says that the reporter of ill omens is in charge of the method of the ten halos, which is used to observe evil and auspicious signs and to distinguish between good and bad fortune. The first kind of halo is called "malign," the second, "symbolic image," the third, "engraved," the fourth, "examined," the fifth, "dark," the sixth, "obscure," the seventh, "complete," the eighth, "ranked," the ninth, "increasing," and the tenth, "imagined." Zheng Zhong's commentary says that "halo" [*hui*] means brilliant vapors. Zheng Xuan's commentary says that the king is represented in heaven by the sun. After he dreams at night, one can observe vapors around the sun the next day and interpret whether they are auspicious or not. There are ten kinds of vapors that can be interpreted, and each vapor has nine variations. This method has disappeared nowadays.

7. "The Oaths of Tai" in *Documents of Zhou* states, "My dream is in accordance with the divination, and both indications are auspicious." Kong Rong's commentary says that this means that both the dream and the divination were positive.

8. Kong Chengzi dreamt that Kangshu told him to establish Yuan as the heir. Moreover, Kong had also used the milfoil sticks according to the Zhou dynasty method of hexagram divination to obtain the hexagram *Jun*: "Difficulty at the Beginning." The historian-astrologer Shi Chao of Wei said that it meant "sub-

lime success," so how could Kong have had any doubts? Furthermore, when divination with milfoil stalks confirmed his dream, King Wu employed the result. How could he not have followed it? (From *Zuo's Narratives to the Spring and Autumn Annals*.)

9. What gives us auspicious dreams and sends us nightmares lies along the horizon where heaven and man meet each other. This requires judicious investigation and absolute respect. (Zhu Xi.) Heaven and man flow along together. They respond to each other and are never distant from each other. The former kings considered it necessary to establish officials to observe malevolent or auspicious signs and to distinguish between lucky and unlucky omens. Thus, they achieved a harmonious identity with the horizon where heaven and man meet and eliminated any gap between the two. (Wang Huishu.)

CHAPTER 5

The Disciple of Emptiness
宗空

The Disciple of Emptiness initiated a discussion with the Master Who Understands the Subtle by stating, "All dreams are but illusions, no different from such things as dew, lightning, bubbles, and reflections.[1] Everything arises and is destroyed; all returns to emptiness and futility." The Master replied, "Why have you not investigated antiquity regarding this? The Yellow Emperor Xuanyuan dreamt of Huaxu, the Register-Diagram, Feng Hou, and Li Mu.[2] Yao dreamt of clambering up to heaven and of riding on a dragon.[3] Shun had dreams of long eyebrows and beating a drum.[4] Yu the Great dreamt of a book about mountains, washing himself in a river, and sailing past the moon in a boat.[5] Tang dreamt of licking heaven.[6] Jie and Zhou had dreams of a malevolent whirlwind and a great bolt of lightning.[7] King Wen dreamt of the sun and moon, an elder, and a fisherwoman.[8] Jiang Taigong dreamt of the Supporting Star.[9] Confucius dreamt of his late lord, a boy, three sophora trees, and red vapor.[10] Nüjie dreamt of receiving a star.[11] Taisi dreamt of pines, junipers, and oaks.[12] Yi Yin's mother dreamt about water issuing forth from the mortar.[13] The mother of Confucius dreamt about Kongsang and green dragons.[14] These events are all credible. How can they be regarded as empty delusions?" The Disciple said, "These are all apocryphal writings and stories collected from the streets. *The Six Classics* never recorded such things."[15] The Master replied, "The addition of nine more years of life[16] and the dream of sitting peacefully between two pillars[17] are recorded in *The Book of Ritual* while dreams are especially abundant in *Zuo's Narratives to the Spring and Autumn Annals*, such as Duke Ping of Jin dreaming about a bear and the Duke of Song dreaming of birds.[18] Lü Qi dreamt that he shot at the moon, and

The Disciple of Emptiness 67

Earl Sheng dreamt that he crossed the Huan River.[19] Duke Zhao of Lu dreamt of Duke Xiang, and Duke Yuan of Song dreamt of Duke Ping.[20] Duke Wen of Jin dreamt of the ruler of Chu, and Duke Zhuang of Wei dreamt of Hun Liangfu.[21] Kong Zhengchu dreamt of Kangshu, and Yanji dreamt of Boshu.[22] A man of Cao dreamt of Caoshu Zhenduo, and a man of Zheng dreamt of Boyou.[23] Zhao Dun dreamt of Shudai, and Xun Yan dreamt of Wu Gao.[24] Wei Ke dreamt about an old man, and Han Jue dreamt of his father.[25] Shusun Muzi encountered a woman of Gengzong, and Meng Xizi obtained the daughter of a man of Quanqiu.[26] As for the well-known examples of the naked youth, the two boys, the celestial emissary, and Hebo, God of the Yellow River—none of these has been misrepresented or falsely recounted.[27] Moreover, Yijiang's dream about Yu was fully described by Zichan of Zheng, who possessed a universal knowledge of things.[28] The men of past generations read about these dreams and utilized this knowledge, and so it has been manifest for a thousand years. How could all of them have engaged in preposterous talk or upheld spurious notions?" The Disciple replied, "All the chapters of *The Book of Ritual* contain some expressions dating from the Han dynasty while *Zuo's Narratives,* in an attempt to be comprehensive, was unable to avoid the unreliable and the exaggerated. How can anyone believe them word for word?" The Master said, "You are still following the narrow knowledge of your own mind, which is impeding complete spiritual understanding![29] Are not the chapters on the Shang and Zhou dynasties in *The Documents of Antiquity* and the 'Lesser Odes' in *The Book of Songs* writings that were carefully edited by sages? When King Gaozong of the Shang dreamt of Fu Yue, an exact portrait of him was made, and Fu Yue was searched for everywhere.[30] King Wu of the Zhou swore to his army, 'My dream is in accord with the divination.'[31] And, when King Xuan built his palace and inspected his herds, there were dreams of bears, vipers and other snakes, locusts turning into fish, and flags of tortoises and snakes turning into those of birds.[32] Moreover, the king had an official explicator interpret it, which showed how seriously he took these dreams, for he was unwilling to disregard them.[33] Since the court of King You was beset by slanderous statements that could not be verified, he summoned elders and asked them to interpret his dreams.[34] Thus, when did the ancients ever neglect to interpret their dreams? The apocrypha and popular stories collected by officials contain some reliable things worth carefully selecting. How can one entirely dismiss these sources without discrimination as if they just contained mumblings while asleep?"[35]

NOTES

1. According to a Buddhist sutra, all active dharmas are like dreams, illusions, bubbles, and reflections, or like dew and lightning. One should look upon these from the perspective of thusness.

2. The Yellow Emperor took a nap and dreamt that he traveled to the Land of Huaxu. No one knows how many thousands of miles it is from the central states of China. No boat, carriage, or traveler on foot can reach it. It can only be reached by spirit-wandering. After the Yellow Emperor awoke, he was overjoyed and completely satisfied. Twenty-eight years later, the world was well governed, almost as well as the Land of Huaxu. (From the *Master Lie*.)

The Yellow Emperor summoned his official Tianlao and questioned him. "I dreamt that two dragons held out a white diagram and presented it to me in a city beside the Yellow River." Tianlao said, "The Yellow River produced the Dragon Diagram and the Luo River produced the Tortoise Text. These record emperors and list the names of sages. Isn't heaven about to bestow a diagram on Your Majesty?" The Yellow Emperor then purified himself and fasted for seven days. Then he went to Cuigui River, where a large perch bore a white diagram with vermillion graphs written on *lan*-flower leaves that was bestowed on the emperor. It was titled the "Register-Diagram." (From *The Yellow River Diagram Offered as an Aid to the Emperor*.)

The Yellow Emperor dreamt that a great wind blew away all the dust in the world. He also dreamt that someone picked up a crossbow weighing about four thousand pounds and drove a herd of ten thousand sheep. After he awoke, the emperor sighed and said, "The wind *[feng]* stands for a command and is a sign for government. When one removes the element for 'earth' 土 from the written graph for 'dust' 垢, what remains is the graph 后 *[hou]*. Could there be someone in the world named Feng Hou? A four-thousand-pound crossbow requires unusual power *[li]*. Anyone who can drive a herd of ten thousand sheep is capable of shepherding *[mu]* people toward goodness. Could there be someone in the world named Li Mu?" The Yellow Emperor searched for them based on these two interpretations of his dream, and he found Feng Hou and Li Mu. He made them, respectively, general and prime minister. Based on this experience, he wrote *The Book of Dreams* in eleven chapters. (From *Annals of the Thearchs and Kings*.)

3. Empress Hexi dreamt of rubbing against heaven. The body of heaven resembled the roof of a cavern with stalactites. The empress looked up and inhaled. She reported this to an interpreter of dreams who told her that Yao had dreamt of clambering up to heaven, and Tang licked heaven when he reached it. These are all the dreams of sage-kings. (From *History of the Eastern Han Dynasty from the Dongguan Pavilion*.) *Bo and Kong's Encyclopedia* states that Yao and Shun were superior sages, causing auspicious signs to appear throughout the world. A commentary quotes a dream manual that states that Yao dreamt of ascending Mount Tai by riding on a green dragon. Shun dreamt that he was beating a drum. The *Grand History* states that Yao dreamt of riding on a dragon up to heaven and then gained possession of the entire world.

4. Shun dreamt that his eyebrows grew as long as his hair, and Yao therefore bestowed upon him the Brilliant Ornamented Jade. When Yao became old, he

appointed Shun to take over the government. (From *Annals of the Thearchs and Kings*.) Wen Zisheng of the Northern Wei dynasty wrote in a composition for the Temple to Shun that "he was moved to dream of long eyebrows; he enlightened and elevated the narrow and lowly." For the dream about Shun beating a drum, see the preceding note.

5. When Yu the Great climbed Mount Heng, he dreamt of a boy in embroidered red clothes who called himself the "Emissary of the Black Yi Tribe by the Green River." He told Yu, "If you want to obtain my book about the mountains, purify yourself at the sacred mountain of the Yellow Emperor." So Yu withdrew and purified himself for three days, then climbed a long, winding path and discovered a rock where he obtained a book written with jade graphs on gold slips that disclosed the principles of curbing floods. Subsequently, he traveled throughout the world and had his official Yi record it. The title of the book was *The Guideways Through Mountains and Seas*. (From *The Spring and Autumn Annals of Wu and Yue*.) Yu dreamt that he washed himself in the Western River. (From *Annals of the Thearchs and Kings*.) Before Yu of the Xia dynasty was discovered, he dreamt that he sailed on a boat across the moon. (From *Bo and Kong's Encyclopedia*.)

6. See above [note 3].

7. *Bo and Kong's Encyclopedia* states that when the kings Jie and Zhou ruled, their actions provoked rebellions throughout the world. A commentary cites a dream manual that states that Jie dreamt that a malevolent whirlwind destroyed his palace, and Zhou dreamt that a great bolt of lightning struck his head.

8. King Wen of the Zhou dreamt that the sun and moon illuminated his body. (From *Annals of the Thearchs and Kings*.) When King Wen was touring Zang, he observed an old man fishing and wanted to entrust the government to him. The next day he told his officials, "Yesterday, I dreamt of an excellent man with a dark complexion and whiskers who was riding on a dappled horse with vermillion hooves. He urged me, 'Turn the government over to the old man of Zang. Will he not minister to the common people?'" Therefore, King Wen welcomed the old man of Zang and entrusted him with the government. (From the *Master Zhuang*.)

When Jiang Taigong was the magistrate of Guantan, King Wen dreamt of a woman who blocked the road and wept, "I am the daughter of the Eastern Sea who is to be married to the Western Ocean. Now the magistrate of Guantan is blocking the road and preventing me from proceeding to the wedding. There is bound to be a great storm when I proceed, but since Jiang Taigong possesses virtuous power, I dare not create such a violent disturbance when I pass by." The next day, King Wen summoned Jiang Taigong. For the next three days and nights, there was indeed a tempest that passed by the outskirts of Jiang's town. (From *A Record of Manifold Things*.)

9. Before Jiang Taigong met King Wen, he was fishing at Pan Stream and dreamt at night that the god of the Supporting Star in the Northern Dipper gave him the idea of overthrowing King Zhou in the future. (From *The Central Omens in The Documents of Antiquity*.)

10. When Confucius was stranded without food between the states of Chen and Cai, he took a nap. Then he arose and said, "Today I dreamt of our late lord." (From *The Compendium of Mr. Lü*.)

Confucius dreamt of a boy who beat a *lin*-beast and injured its left front leg. (From *The Central Concordance to The Book of Filial Piety*.) Confucius had a dream at night of a red vapor among three sophora trees in Fengpei. He drove his carriage forward and saw that a boy had injured the left leg of a *lin*-beast. Confucius looked for some brush and spread a cover over it. (From *History of the Liu Song Dynasty*.)

Confucius dreamt that a red whirlwind arose by a gate of three sophora trees in Fengpei. He called Yan Hui and Zixia to come and observe it. They saw a red snake change into gold, on which was inscribed the graphs *mao, jin,* and *dao.* It was a sign of the rise of the future Emperor Gaozu in Fengpei. (From Prince Yi of Xiangdong, *Master of the Golden Tower*.)

[*The graphs mao* 卯, *jin* 金, *and dao* 刀 *combine to form the graph liu* 劉, *surname of Liu Bang, later Emperor Gaozu of the Western Han.*—RES]

11. During the time of the Yellow Emperor, there was a star as great as a rainbow which fell down to the Flowery Island. Nüjie dreamt that she received it. Her thoughts were stimulated, and she subsequently gave birth to Shaohao. (From *Annals of the Thearchs and Kings*.)

12. Taisi dreamt that catalpa trees from the Zhou courtyard changed into pines, junipers, and oaks. (From *Documents of the Zhou Dynasty*.)

13. When Yi Yin was born, his mother dreamt that someone told her, "When water issues forth from the mortar, you should flee east." The next morning, his mother observed that water had issued forth from the mortar, so she fled more than three miles eastward. When she looked back at her village, it lay completely submerged under deep water. (From Wang Chong, *Judicious Discussions*.)

14. The mother of Confucius, Zhengzai, dreamt that the divine Black Emperor sent an emissary who ordered her to set forth, saying, "You will give birth in Kongsang." When she awoke, she felt stimulated. Later, she gave birth to Confucius in Kongsang. (From *A Chart of the Life of Confucius*.)

On the eve of Confucius's birth, two green dragons soared around in the sky and descended into the bedroom beside Zhengzai. Because of this, she dreamed about the green dragons, and Confucius was born. There were also such events as a goddess offering dew, five elders assembled in the courtyard, and a *qilin*-beast spitting forth jade writing. (From *Records from the Treasure Cabinet*.)

15. At the end of the Han dynasty, He Liang and others composed apocrypha, saying that these served as a woof to explain the classics, which were like a warp. The "Treatise on Arts and Literature" in *History of the Western Han Dynasty* states that the schools of "minor narratives" originated with the *baiguan,* the officials in charge of collecting stories. The commentator Ruchun said that the graph *bai* means small kernels of rice, and this refers to the trifling words they gather.

16. King Wen asked King Wu, "What have you dreamt?" King Wu replied, "I dreamt that the supreme god Di added nine years to my life." King Wen said, "I am destined to live to a hundred and you to ninety. I shall give you three years of my life." King Wen died at ninety-seven and King Wu died at ninety-three. (From "The Eldest Prince of King Wen" in *The Book of Ritual*.)

17. Confucius said, "The other night, I dreamt that I was sitting peacefully between two pillars in a hall." (From *"Tan Gong"* in *The Book of Ritual*.)

18. Zichan of Zheng was invited to Jin where Duke Ping of Jin had been ill for a long time. Han Xuanzi said, "Our lord has already been lying ill for three months. Recently, he dreamt of a yellow bear that entered the door of his residence. What kind of demon is this?" Zichan replied, "In the past, Yao sacrificed to Gun at Feather Mountain, and Gun's spirit changed into a yellow bear that entered Feather Abyss. This was actually where the altar of the Xia was, and three dynasties have continued to sacrifice to him there. Jin is now the leader of the alliance among the states, but is it possible that it has not yet sacrificed to Gun?" Han Xuanzi then performed a sacrifice at the Xia altar, and Duke Ping's illness abated. (From *Zuo's Narratives*.)

Duke Jing of Song had no sons and adopted De and Qi, the sons of Gongsun Zhou. He brought them up in the palace but did not establish either as his heir. After Duke Jing died, the governor of the capital established Qi as the heir. De dreamt that that Qi was sleeping outside the Lu Gate with his head facing north and that he, De, had become birds that assembled on top of Qi. Their beaks were over the south gate and their tails over the Paulownia Gate. De said, "This is a fine dream—I will certainly become the heir." Before long, the six chief ministers decided to establish De, who would become known as Duke Zhao of Song. The interpretation of his dream had stated that a head facing northward was a symbolic image of death. The eastern gate of Song is called the Lu Gate and the Paulownia Gate is the northern one. To sleep outside the eastern gate is a symbol of losing control of the state. That De transformed into birds that gathered on top of Qi's body meant that he would step into Qi's position. (From *Zuo's Narratives*.)

19. Lü Qi dreamt that he had shot at the moon and struck it, but when returning he got stuck in the mud. The interpretation stated that the royal Zhou surname Ji denoted the sun while the moon meant a foreign surname, certainly indicating the King of Chu. Shooting at the moon and hitting it, then becoming stuck in the mud while returning means certain death. During a battle, Lü shot and hit King Gong of Chu in the eye. (From *Zuo's Narratives*.)

Earl Sheng dreamt that he had crossed the Huan River where someone gave him jade and pearls, which he ate. When he cried, his tears became jade and pearls that overflowed onto his body. Upon awakening, he was afraid and dared not have the dream interpreted. (From *Zuo's Narratives*.)

20. After King Ling of Chu had the Terrace of Manifest Splendor completed, he wished to dedicate it together with the other nobles. Duke Zhao of Lu was about to proceed there when he dreamt of his ancestor, Duke Xiang. Xin Shen said, "Your Highness should not go. When Duke Xiang was about to go to Chu, he dreamt of his royal ancestor the Duke of Zhou and then went. Now, Duke Xiang is just your direct ancestor. You should not go." Zifu Huibo said, "You may go. Duke Xiang had never been to Chu; therefore, his ancestor the Duke of Zhou showed him the way. And he did indeed go to Chu. Now your ancestor Duke Xiang will show you the way, so why should you not go?" In the third month of that year, Duke Zhao went to Chu. (From *Zuo's Narratives*.)

Duke Yuan of Song was about to go to Jin when he dreamt that Crown Prince Luan had ascended the throne in the ancestral temple and that he and the former ruler Duke Ping were wearing court robes, assisting Luan. The next day,

Duke Yuan told this to the six chief ministers. He then went forth and died at Quji. (From *Zuo's Narratives*.)

21. Duke Wen of Jin dreamt that the ruler of Chu had pinned him to the ground and was sucking out his brains. The duke was terrified by this, but Zifan said, "This is auspicious. Our side was facing upward to receive the support of heaven while Chu was facing downward to acknowledge its crimes. Moreover, your brains would soften their resolve." When the battle of Chengpu occurred, the forces of Chu were scattered. (From *Zuo's Narratives*.)

Duke Zhuang of Wei had killed Hun Liangfu. He dreamt that he had gone to his Northern Palace and saw someone who had ascended the Kunwu Observatory. The man was facing north with his long hair unbound and scolding the duke. "I have climbed up Kunwu, where unbroken melon vines grow. I am Hun Liangfu, and I cry out to heaven because of your ingratitude." Duke Zhuang personally performed a divination with milfoil stalks, and Xu Mishe interpreted it. But Xu was afraid to speak the truth. Even though the duke offered him a fief, he refused and fled. In the eleventh month of that year during the winter, Duke Zhuang was killed by the Jishi tribe. (From *Zuo's Narratives*.)

22. The consort of Duke Xiang of Wei did not produce a son, but his favorite Zhou'e gave birth to Mengzhi. Kong Zhengchu dreamt that Kangshu said to him, "Establish Yuan as the heir, and I will have your great-grandson Yu and the historian-astrologer Shi Gou assist him." Shi Chao also dreamt that Kangshu told him, "I will command your son Gou and the great-grandson of Kong Zhengchu, Yu, to assist Yuan." Shi Chao went to see Kong Chengzi and told him about the dreams, both of which were in accord. However, Yuan had not yet been born. Later, Zhou'e gave birth to another son who was named Yuan. Since Mengzhi's foot was damaged, and he was unable to walk well, Kong Chengzi divined the matter using milfoil stalks. Consequently Yuan was established as Duke Ling. (From *Zuo's Narratives*.) According to a commentary, Zhengchu was the name of Kong Chengzi.

Duke Xiang of Wei had a low-ranking concubine whom he favored and who became pregnant. She dreamt that someone said to her, "I am Kangshu. Your son will certainly inherit the state of Wei, and you should name him Yuan." The concubine thought this was strange and asked Kong Chengzi about it. He said, "Kangshu is the ancestor of the house of Wei." When she gave birth, it was a son. He was named Yuan, who became Duke Ling. (From *Historical Records*.) In the thirty-first year of the reign of Duke Xi of Lu [629 BCE], Duke Cheng of Wei also dreamt of Kangshu. Refer to the text of *Zuo's Narratives* for details as they will not be recorded here.

Duke Wen of Zheng had a low-ranking concubine named Yanji. She dreamt that an emissary from heaven gave her a *lan*-flower, saying "I am Boshu, your ancestor, and this will be your son, for the *lan* is the most fragrant flower in the state." Subsequently, Duke Wen noticed her, gave her a *lan*-flower and favored her. Yanji said to him, "I am unworthy, but if I have had the good fortune to conceive a child, others may refuse to believe he is legitimate. May I use the *lan*-flower as proof?" The duke replied, "Agreed." She gave birth to the future Duke Mu, who was named Lan. (From *Zuo's Narratives*.)

23. The men of Song surrounded the state of Cao. Previously, a man of Cao

had dreamt that a group of nobles had assembled in the sacrificial hall of the altar to the earth god and were plotting the destruction of Cao. Among them, Caoshu Zhenduo suggested that they await Gongsun Qiang, and they all agreed. The next day, a search was made for a Gongsun Qiang, but no such person was found in Cao. The man who had had the dream told his son, "After I die, if you ever hear that a Gongsun Qiang is in charge of the government, you must flee the state." Later, Boyang of Cao assumed the throne. He loved to go hunting and shoot birds. A commoner of Cao, Gongsun Qiang, was good at shooting birds and shot a white goose that he presented to the court. Moreover, he was able to discuss hunting strategies. Boyang was pleased with him and consulted him about government affairs. He grew even more pleased with him and appointed him overseer of the city walls with official responsibilities. The son of the dreamer then left the state. Boyang followed Gongsun Qiang's strategies to expand his power by breaking his alliance with Jin and invading Song. When Song attacked Cao, the state of Jin did not come to its aid, and Cao was destroyed. Boyang and Gongsun Qiang were both taken back to Song as prisoners. (From *Zuo's Narratives*.)

The men of Zheng were all frightened by the demonic activities of Boyou. Someone dreamt that Boyou was roaming about wearing his armor and saying, "On the day *renzi*, I will kill Dai. The next year, on the day *renyin*, I will also kill Duan." When the day *renzi* arrived, Si Dai died, and on *renyin*, Gongsun Duan died. The people of the state were even more terrified. Zichan of Zheng then established Gongsun Xie, the son of Zikong, and Liangzhi, the son of Boyou. Thereafter, Boyou ceased his demonic activities. (From *Zuo's Narratives*.)

24. Zhao Dun dreamt that Shu Dai was grasping hold of his waist and sobbing in great despair. After a while, he laughed, clapping his hands and singing. Zhao performed a divination that indicated that it was an omen of an interruption in the family line, but that later, things would be fine. Shi Yuan, the historian-astrologer of Zhao, interpreted this saying, "This dream is extremely bad for either you or your son." Indeed, they subsequently suffered at the hands of Tu Angu. (From *Historical Records*.)

Xun Yan was about to attack the state of Qi when he dreamt that he was involved in a legal dispute with Duke Li of Jin and lost. The duke struck him with a dagger and his head fell off in front of him. He knelt down and put it back on. Holding up his head with both hands, he then ran off and saw the spirit-medium Wu Gao of Gengyang. A few days later, he met Wu Gao on the road and told him about the dream. It was the same as Wu's. Wu said, "You are certain to die within a year, but if there is war in the east, you can satisfy your ambitions." Xun prayed to the Yellow River by submerging an offering of a jade. Then, he assembled the feudal nobles and attacked Qi. The Qi army fled, but in spring of the following year, Xun died from malignant ulcers. (From *Zuo's Narratives*.)

25. Wei Ke of Jin defeated the Qin army at Fushi. He captured Du Hui, a man of Qin who possessed great strength. Previously, Wei Wuzi, who was named Chou, had a beloved concubine who had not produced any sons. When Wei Wuzi fell ill, he commanded his son, Wei Ke, "You must marry her." But as his illness grew more serious, he said, "You must bury her with me." After Wei Wuzi died, Wei Ke followed the father's first command and married her. At the battle at Fushi,

Wei Ke saw an old man who was tying grass together in order to trap Du Hui. Du Hui stumbled into this, fell down, and was thus captured by Wei Ke. That night, Wei Ke dreamt that the old man who had tied the grass said, "I am the father of the woman whom you have married. Since you followed the first command of your father, I have done this to repay you." (From *Zuo's Narratives*.)

The Jin army reached the Marquis of Qi and fought him at An. The Qi army was defeated and fled in disarray. Previously, the commander Han Jue dreamt that his father Ziyu [late Spring and Autumn period] said to him, "Avoid the right- and left-hand sides." Therefore, Han placed himself in the middle of the army when he pursued the Marquis of Qi. The marquis had heard that Han Jue was a noble man, so he shot at the soldiers on the right and left, felling them while Han Jue alone was spared. (From *Zuo's Narratives*.)

26. Shusun Muzi fled to Qi to avoid the difficulties at Qiaoru. When he got to Gengzong, he met a woman and slept with her. When Muzi arrived in Qi, he married a woman from the prime minister's family, and she gave birth to Mengbing and Zhongren. He dreamt that heaven was pressing down on him and that he was unable to overcome it. Then, he looked and saw a dark-skinned man with a hunchback, deep-set eyes, and a snout. He called to him, "Ox, help me!" and so he was able to prevail. Later, the people of Lu summoned Muzi back and established him as a government minister. The woman of Gengzong presented him with a pheasant, and her son followed behind Muzi holding the pheasant. It was none other than the man he had dreamt of. Moreover, his name was Niu [Ox]. So Muzi appointed him as his assistant official and called him Assistant Niu. When Assistant Niu grew up, he was put in charge of Muzi's household affairs. Later, Assistant Niu slandered Mengbing and caused him to be killed and Zhongren to be expelled. When Muzi fell ill, Assistant Niu starved him until he died. The divination of the dream had stated that when heaven is pressing one down it means that a ruler will bestow favor on him. But, Heaven should not be overcome, for to overcome heaven is unlucky. (From *Zuo's Narratives*.)

Meng Xizi met Duke Zhuang of Zhu and swore an alliance with him at Jinxiang. A man of Quanqiu had a daughter who dreamt that she used her bed curtains to cover the ancestral temple of the Meng family, so she ran off to join Meng Xizi. He sent her home as his concubine to assist his principal wife, Weishi, and she subsequently gave birth to Yizi and Nangong Jingshu. (From *Zuo's Narratives*.)

27. On the day *xinhai*, the first in the twelfth lunar month of the thirty-first year of Duke Zhao of Lu's reign [510 BCE], there was a solar eclipse. That night, Zhao Jianzi dreamt of a naked youth who started to sing and dance about. The next morning, he sought an interpretation of the dream from the historian-astrologer Shi Mo, telling him, "I have had this dream, and now there has been an eclipse of the sun. What can this mean?" Shi Mo replied, "Six years from this month, the state of Wu will invade Ying, the Chu capital, but in the end they will not be able to achieve victory. They will enter Ying on the day *gengchen* when the sun and moon are located in the tail of the constellation Green Dragon. On the day *gengwu*, the sun will begin to be obliterated. But since the agent "fire" overcomes the agent "metal," they will not be able to achieve final victory. (From *Zuo's Narratives*.)

Duke Jing of Jin dreamt of a great demon whose unbound hair reached down to the ground. The demon beat his chest and danced about saying, "You have killed my grandsons. This violates what is right, and I have demanded justice from the supreme god Di!" He destroyed the outer gate of the palace and the doors to the residential quarters as he came in. The duke was terrified and went into his bedchamber, but the demon broke through this door as well. Then the duke awakened. He summoned the spirit-medium from Sangtian who repeated to him exactly what he had dreamt. When the duke asked its meaning, the reply was, "You will not live to eat the millet from the new harvest." The duke fell gravely ill and requested a doctor from Qin. The ruler of Qin dispatched a doctor, but ordered him to travel slowly. Before the doctor could arrive, the duke dreamt that the illness had become two boys, one of whom said, "He is a good doctor, and I am afraid that he will harm us." The other said, "Let's hide between the heart and the diaphragm. What can he do to us there?" The doctor arrived and said, "The illness lies between the heart and the diaphragm—I am unable to treat it." The duke had the farmers present the newly harvested millet. He summoned the spirit-medium from Sangtian to show it to him; then he was going to kill him. But just as he was about to eat it, he had to go to the privy, which he fell into and died. (From *Zuo's Narratives*.)

Zhao Ying had sexual relations with Zhao Zhuangji. She was the wife of Zhao Shuo and thus the wife of Zhao Ying's nephew. In spring of the following year, Zhao Ying's elder brothers Yuan and Ping exiled him to Qi. Zhao Ying had dreamt that an emissary from heaven said to him, "Offer a sacrifice to me, and I will grant you blessings." He sent someone to ask Shi Zhenbo about this, and Shi replied, "I do not understand it." Later, Shi Zhenbo told his own followers, "The gods bring blessings to the humane and calamities to the wicked. To behave wickedly and yet not be punished for it can be counted as a blessing. Even if he were to offer a sacrifice, would he be able to avoid exile?" Zhao Ying sacrificed to the celestial emissary, but the next day, he was exiled. (From *Zuo's Narratives*.)

The state of Chu was at war with Jin. Prime Minister Ziyu of Chu [d. 632 BCE] had a hat with carnelian ornaments and chin straps ornamented with jade that he had not yet worn. Before the battle, he dreamt that Hebo, God of the Yellow River, said to him, "Give the hat to me, and I will grant you the territory of Mengzhu." (From *Zuo's Narratives*.)

28. When Duke Ping of Jin fell ill, Duke Jian of Zheng sent Zichan of Zheng to visit Jin and inquire after his illness. Zichan said, "When King Wu's wife Yijiang was pregnant with Taishu, she dreamt that the supreme god Di said to her, 'I command that your son be given Yu as his personal name and that he be granted the fief of Tang, which will be placed under the control of the lunar lodging Triaster. Furthermore, I will multiply his descendants.' When the child was born, he had markings on his palm that spelled out the graph *yu*, so he was given this as his personal name. Later, King Cheng destroyed Tang and enfeoffed Yu there. This is also how Triaster became the ruling asterism of the state of Jin." When Duke Ping heard Zichan's explanation, he exclaimed, "You are truly a nobleman who possesses a universal knowledge of things!" (From *Zuo's Narratives*.)

29. Confucius said, "You are still following the narrow knowledge of your own mind."

30. While King Gaozong of the Shang was respectfully and silently pondering the Way, he dreamt that the supreme god Di provided him with an excellent assistant. He then carefully described the man's appearance and had an exact portrait made so that the man could be searched for throughout the world. Fu Yue, who was a builder in Fuyan, was found to resemble the picture and as a result was made a minister within the king's inner circle. (From "The Charge to Yue" in *Documents of the Shang Dynasty*.)

King Gaozong dreamt one night that he had obtained a sage to assist him whose name was Yue. He looked among his entire group of officials and functionaries, but none resembled Yue. Therefore, he had all his other officials search for him outside the court. They found him in Fuyan, and he was elevated to the position of a government minister. (From *Historical Records*.)

31. See part I, chapter 4.

32. The poem "The Beck" in "Lesser Odes" in *The Book of Songs* says:

I slept, then awakened
And had my dream interpreted.
"What was your auspicious dream?"
"It was of black bears and brown ones,
Of vipers and other snakes."
The explicator interpreted it:
"Black bears and brown bears—
Auspicious signs of the birth of sons.
Vipers and other snakes—
Auspicious signs of the birth of daughters."

The poem "No Sheep?" in "Lesser Odes" in *The Book of Songs* says:

The herdsman then dreamt
Of locusts turning into fish
Of flags with tortoises and snakes becoming flags with birds.
The explicator interpreted it:
"'Locusts turning into fish'
Means a year of abundant harvests.
'Flags with tortoises and snakes becoming flags with birds'
Means the members of your house will multiply."

"The Beck" is about King Xuan's inspection of his palace, and "No Sheep?" is about the inspection of his herds. (From the short prefaces to these poems in *The Book of Songs*.) According to Mr. Chen's commentary, the king inspected his palace after it was completed, so it was the sovereign's dream that was interpreted as auspicious. After the herding was finished and inspected, it was the dream of the herdsman that was transcribed as auspicious.

33. Both "The Beck" and "No Sheep?" were interpreted by the official explicator. Zhu Xi said that the explicator was subordinate to the grand diviner and that both were officials who interpreted dreams. Kong Yingda said that Duke Wen of Jin's dream in *Zuo's Narratives* was interpreted by Zifan of Zheng, so it was not necessary to employ an official interpreter.

34. "I summoned the elders and asked them to interpret my dreams." (From

"The First Month" in "Lesser Odes" in *The Book of Songs*.) Zhu Shan commented that the elders elucidate what is morally correct while the dream interpreters elucidate auspicious or inauspicious meanings. The state relied upon the elders to rectify the slander at court.

35. The graph 䏒, pronounced "*nan*," means words spoken while sleeping. (From *Ocean of Rhymes*.)

CHAPTER 6

The Sage
聖人

"The sage does not have dreams"—this saying is empty and deceptive.[1] Anyone who lacks dreams must belong to a group that has withered bodies and ashen minds. No sleeping, no awakening, no birth, no extinction—these are heterodox teachings.[2] There was no sage greater than Confucius. In the prime of life, he dreamt of seeing the Duke of Zhou, and when he was about to die, he dreamt of sitting peacefully between two pillars. When did he ever discuss strange phenomena? A newborn is hardly ten days old when he is able to fall soundly asleep. He refuses his mother's milk and isn't even startled awake while being carried along. He may appear happy and laugh or look annoyed and express anger. If disturbed, he may even cry. This is called "dream laughter" or "dream cries." When he is gently called to, it becomes apparent that he has not been awake. This infant had not received any stimuli, so how did his happiness or anger arise? They came from his dreams. His *qi*-energy infused these emotions, and his spirit directed them.[3] The mind of a sage is no different from that of an infant.[4] Entrusting his spirit to the numinous depot so that he smoothly inhales yin and exhales yang does not mean that he does not have any dreams. It merely means that he does not have confusing dreams that would disturb his awareness.[5] Therefore, when Yang Zhu said that the events from the time of the five emperors seem like those in waking consciousness or like those in dreams, was he not, sadly, on the wrong track?[6]

NOTES

1. The sage does not think or deliberate, and he makes no future plans or strategies. He does not dream when asleep and is without worries when awake.

His spirit is pure and his *hun*-soul never tires. (From the *Master Zhuang*.) The perfected gentlemen of antiquity were unaware of their selves when awake and did not dream when asleep. (From the *Master Lie*.) The so-called perfected gentleman is someone whose nature is in accord with the Way. He does not dream when asleep, and his intelligence does not start sprouting. His *po*-soul is unshaken and his *hun*-soul does not take flight. (From the *Master of Huainan*.)

2. His body was like a withered tree and his mind was like dead ashes. (From the *Master Zhuang*.) No birth, no death, no defilement, and no purity. (From a Buddhist sutra.)

3. The compound *youran* 逌然 means a happy appearance, and the graph 寤, pronounced "*hu*," means being disturbed while asleep, as when a child cries out in his dreams. (From *Ocean of Chapters According to the Five Sounds*.) The body is the house of the life-force, and *qi*-energy is what the life-force infuses. Spirit is what controls the life-force. Why can man look and clearly see, listen and clearly hear, distinguish black from white, discriminate between beauty and ugliness, separate similarity from difference, and illuminate right from wrong? It is because he is infused with *qi*-energy, and this is guided by his spirit. (From the *Master of Huainan*.) What the mind responds to and understands are simply universal patterns. Just as in dreaming while asleep, there are only these universal patterns at work. (Master Cheng.)

4. The great man is someone who has not lost the mind he had as an infant. (From the *Mencius*.)

5. The sage entrusts his spirit to the numinous depot and returns to the harmony of all things . . . By inhaling yin and exhaling yang, all things are harmoniously blended. (From the *Master of Huainan*.) The five emotions of the sage are the same as those of other people, so how can he can be without dreams? (Kong Yingda's commentary to "Tan Gong" in *The Book of Ritual*.) When the mind falls asleep, it dreams, and so is never inactive. What is spoken of as its quiescence refers to not allowing dreams and disturbances to upset its awareness of things. This is what is meant by quiescence. (From the *Master Xun*.)

6. The events of remote antiquity have completely disappeared, those of the time of the two sovereigns have been preserved or have vanished, the events of the five emperors are like those in waking consciousness or like dreams while those of the three kings are either concealed or clearly manifest. (Yang Zhu.)

CHAPTER 7

The Six Types of Dreams
六夢

The six types of dreams result from the encounters of the spirit; the eight kinds of waking consciousness result from the contacts of the body. The six types of dreams are: 1) normal dreams; 2) nightmares; (3) dreams about waking thoughts; (4) dreams about waking statements; (5) happy dreams; (6) fearful dreams. These six are the categories used for interpretation.[1] The eight kinds of waking consciousness are: 1) consciousness of events; 2) consciousness of actions; 3) consciousness of gain; 4) consciousness of loss; 5) consciousness of sorrow; 6) consciousness of joy; 7) consciousness of birth; 8) consciousness of death. These eight are the categories for verifying waking consciousness.[2] Body and spirit influence each other; dreams and waking consciousness both have their origins; the true mechanism of natural transformation blends everything together without the slightest separation. Therefore, the interpreter of dreams utilizes the seasonal time, observes the conjunctions of heaven and earth, distinguishes the yin and yang qualities of atmospheric vapors, and investigates the sun, moon, stars, and asterisms when determining the meaning of a dream.[3] There are portents classified according to the five agents, and these portents are further governed by the various deputies of the five agents.[4] When the five agents are applied to correlate all phenomena, the heavenly branches and earthly stems are used to mark their movements. When calendrical calculations reveal orderly progressions, the seasons of the year are seen to transpire.[5] Therefore, one must examine the divisions of the year into equinoxes and the arrival of the solstices as well as the positions of "establishment" and "suppression."[6] Carefully investigate the situations of "regulating," "attacking," "protecting," "dutiful," and "monopolizing," as well as the conditions of "king" and "minister," "death," "good fortune," and "imprisonment."[7] One must also inquire into the approaches to the celestial lodgings[8] and the paths of the five planets as they move through such transformations as "harmony," "dispersing," "invading," "defending," "encroaching," "passing by," "fighting," "pressing," "comets," "meteors," "flying," and "flowing,"[9] as well as anomalous phenomena such as the sun and moon's "full eclipse," "partial eclipse," "halo," "arrival," "*bei*-shape," "jade-ring shape," "hugging," "earrings," and "male and female rainbows."[10] Moreover, these transformations and anomalous phenomena can be distinguished as "hidden," "manifest," "early," "late," "expanded," "reduced," "heavy," and "light." One should carefully "unravel the threads of silk" and "cut along the cracks in the jade."[11] Then, the full extent of the six types of dreams and the rhythms of the eight kinds of waking consciousness can be determined.[12]

NOTES

1. "Normal dreams" do not result from any particular influences. The dreamer is in an ordinary, peaceful state and dreams on his own. "Nightmares" result from having been frightened. "Dreams about waking thoughts" result from what was pondered when awake. "Dreams about waking statements" result from what was said when awake. "Happy dreams" result from being happy, while "fearful dreams" result from being fearful. (From *Commentary on The Government Organization of the Zhou*.)

2. There are eight categories for verifying waking consciousness and six categories for interpreting dreams. (From the *Master Lie*.)

3. "Seasonal time" refers to the four seasons in any given year. The conjunctions of heaven and earth and the yin and yang qualities of atmospheric vapors differ from year to year. "Sun, moon, stars, and asterisms" refers to the movements of the sun and moon and the locations of the asterisms in the sky. (From *Commentary on The Government Organization of the Zhou*.)

4. These agents are metal, wood, water, fire, and earth. Each agent possesses subordinate deputies.

5. The ten heavenly stems are: *jia* and *yi* [wood]; *bing* and *ding* [fire]; *wu* and *ji* [earth]; *geng* and *xin* [metal]; *ren* and *gui* [water]. The twelve earthly stems are: *hai* and *zi* [water]; *yin* and *mao* [wood]; *si* and *wu* [fire]; *shen* and *you* [metal]; *chen*, *xu*, *chou*, and *wei* [earth].

6. This statement means observing the conjunctions of heaven and earth. The equinoctial middle of the spring and autumn seasons are each denoted as "divisions." Division means half; that is, one-half of ninety days. On the days marked as the division within the spring and autumn seasons, the sun leaves the earthly stem *mao* and moves into *you*. During the day, it follows a path above the earth; at night, it follows a path below the earth. In both cases, the distance covered measures 180 degrees, one-half of the whole. Therefore, the length of day and

night are each the same. The solstitial middle of the winter and summer seasons are each labeled as "arrivals." The summer arrival is when yang reaches its ultimate state, which is when yin energy commences its journey toward its ultimate state. The sun arrives at its farthest position north and lasts for the longest time during the day, casting its shortest shadow. Therefore, this is called the "summer arrival." The winter arrival occurs when yin reaches its ultimate state, which is when yang energy begins to journey toward its ultimate state. The sun arrives at its farthest position south and lasts for the shortest time during the day, casting its longest shadow. Therefore, this is called the "winter arrival."

The positions of "establishment" and "suppression" refer to the conjunction of the sun's position in the sky with the signs of the horary cycle. The location "established" by the stars in the handle of the Northern Dipper is called the "yang establishment." In the first lunar month, it is designated by the earthly branch *yin,* in the second month by *mao,* and in the third month by *chen.* This follows a forward sequence. The station of the sun just before these locations is called the "yin establishment." In the first month, it is designated by the earthly stem *xu,* in the second month by *you,* and in the third month by *shen.* This follows a reverse sequence. The yin establishment is the same as the "lunar suppression," which "suppresses" its opposite. In the first lunar month this is designated by *chen,* in the second month by *mao,* and in the third month by *yin.* This also follows a reverse sequence. In the fourth month yang is "established" in *si* but is "destroyed" in *hai,* while yin is "established" in *wei* but is "destroyed" in the celestial stem *gui.* This is what is known as "yang destroys yin and yin destroys yang" so that when the fourth month is designated by cyclical graphs *guihai* or when the tenth month is designated by *dingsi,* both these cases indicate a conjunction of yin and yang.

7. These refer to distinguishing the rival energies of yin and yang. When a heavenly branch overcomes an earthly stem, this is called "regulating." When an earthly stem overcomes a heavenly branch, this is called "attacking." When a heavenly branch gives birth to an earthly stem, this is called "protecting." When an earthly stem gives birth to a heavenly branch, it is called "dutiful." When a branch and a stem are of comparable force and in harmony, this is called "monopolizing."

The "king" overcomes "death" and the "minister" overcomes "imprisonment." Therefore, in spring, the agent "wood" acts as the king, "fire" acts as the minister, "earth" functions as death, "water" functions as good fortune, and "metal" functions as imprisonment. In summer, "fire" acts as the king, "earth" acts as the minister, "metal" functions as death, "wood" functions as good fortune, and "water" functions as imprisonment. In autumn, "metal" acts as the king, "water" acts as the minister, "wood" functions as death, "earth" functions as good fortune, and "fire" functions as imprisonment. In winter, "water" acts as the king, "wood" acts as the minister, "fire" functions as death, "metal" functions as good fortune, and "earth" functions as imprisonment. (From *Apocrypha to the Spring and Autumn Annals.*)

8. From here on, the discussion refers to the sun, moon, stars, and asterisms, and to their approaches to their celestial lodgings. For example, in the first lunar month, the sun's orbit passes through the asterism Beak, and this position

is denoted by the earthly stem *hai*. In the second month, the sun's orbit descends into the asterism Harvester, and this position is denoted by *xu,* and so forth. The sun's orbit passes through the celestial lodgings in a cycle denoted by the earthly stems. It takes seven years to complete one cycle.

9. The changes in the five planets are as follows: when two share the same celestial lodging, it is called "harmony." When they change into evil planets, it is called "dispersing." When a planet's light forms a point and extends outward, it is called "invading." When a planet is located in its own proper asterism, it is called "defending." When planets threaten each other as they pass, it is called "encroaching." Simply proceeding is called "passing by." When they collide with one another it is called "fighting." When they crowd one another, it is called "pressing." A comet is known as a "sweeping star." A shooting star is also a kind of comet. When the point of light extends in a single direction, it is generally called a "comet," but when points of light extend in all four directions, it is called a "shooting star." A "flying star" is a meteor. When it moves upward in the sky, it is called "flying." When it descends, it is called "flowing." There are five different names for flying stars and eight different names for flowing stars. For more details, see *Treatise on Astronomy in an Era of National Revival.*

10. When the sun and moon lose all their light it is called a "full eclipse." (Meng Kang.) When vapors pressure them, it is called a "full eclipse," but when their light is only partly destroyed, it is called a "partial eclipse." (Wei Zhao.) "Halo" refers to vapors along the edge of the sun. "Arrival" means the point at which the solar eclipse is about to begin. Just before this, it undergoes a change and becomes dark. "*Bei*-shape" refers to shapes resembling the graph *bei*. "Jade ring" refers to shapes resembling the jade ring called "*jue*." "Hugging" indicates vapors that move toward the sun. "Earrings" indicate dark spots on the sun. The graph 玉, pronounced "*nie,*" indicates rainbows. The male rainbows are called *nie* and the female ones, *ni.*

11. In interpreting dreams, one must investigate all the clues. It is just like unwinding the individual threads from a cocoon in order to manufacture silk and carving jade by following along the cracks in the stone.

12. The auspiciousness or inauspiciousness of the six types of dreams and the eight kinds of consciousness can only be determined through confirmations by astronomical phenomena. This is the "lofty principle" behind the method of consulting the ten halos mentioned in *The Government Organization of the Zhou.* The *History of the Western Han Dynasty* says that the technique of investigating the five planets is indeed ancient. If it can be used to interpret the destiny of the state, then it can also be used to interpret the significance of events. If it can be used to interpret the significance of events, then it can also be used to interpret the destiny of people.

CHAPTER 8

The Ancient Methods of Interpretation
古法

Ever since the ancient methods disappeared, there has been no definite way to fully interpret dreams. For emperors and kings have dreams proper to them, sages and worthies have dreams proper to them, and workers and servants have dreams proper to them. Whether these indicate failure or success, poverty or abundance, every dream derives from the nature of the particular person. If an evil person has an auspicious dream, it will still have evil consequences for him, and he will not be able to enjoy its auspiciousness.[1] If a good person has an inauspicious dream, it will still have auspicious consequences for him, and he will be able to avoid its negativity.[2] Therefore, there are five kinds of dreams that should not be interpreted, and there are five kinds of interpretations that cannot be confirmed. A dream that occurs when the spirit and *hun*-soul are not in a stable condition should not be interpreted.[3] One that occurs when thoughts are disordered should not be interpreted.[4] One that is recognized as dangerous when awake should not be interpreted.[5] One that has been interrupted because the person was startled awake and panicked should not be interpreted.[6] One that has been completed but half forgotten upon awakening should not be interpreted.[7] If the interpreter is unclear about the origins of the dream, then his interpretation will not be confirmed.[8] If he is not technically proficient, then his interpretation will not be confirmed.[9] If he does not possess complete sincerity, then his interpretation will not be confirmed.[10] If he disregards the broad fundamentals and only utilizes petty methods, then his interpretation will not be confirmed.[11] If he harbors doubts about two different possibilities, then his interpretation will not be confirmed.[12] Therefore, one must have undergone a "great awakening" before one can interpret this "great

The Ancient Methods of Interpretation   85

dream."[13] Otherwise, one's own waking consciousness is nothing but a dream.[14] Those who have undergone this great awakening are able to recognize distinctions in the Great Cosmic Ancestor, comprehend heaven and earth, follow the principles of nature, and devote attention to the forms of things.[15] How can anyone simply speak of employing "cunning words" or "experience in examining cases"?[16]

NOTES

1. As in the case of Zhao Ying's dream of an emissary from heaven [see I:5n27].
2. As in the case of Dong Feng's avoiding the negative result of the affair involving a pillow and a bath [see II:10n17].
3. In considering the meaning of a dream interpretation, the former kings were strictly aware of their position at the border of heaven and the human world, so they conducted such matters in great secrecy. (Fu Guang.) Alas, the ancient methods of interpretation have not been transmitted. Later generations of people have been unable to govern their emotions and natures. Their conduct during the day is muddled, deluded, ignorant, and confused. They are lacking in self-awareness. Thus, what appears in their dreams is chaotic, perverse, and evil—by no means that which flows in accordance with the *qi*-energy of heaven and earth. Even if there were omens that could be used for confirmation, they would be incongruent and barely intelligible, so that one must wait for the consequences to appear before realizing what the dream meant. Even if the ancient methods had been preserved, it still might not be possible to completely interpret such dreams.
4. If a dream is perverse, it is because of perverse thoughts during the day. If a dream is reckless, it is because of reckless thoughts during the day. (From *Collected Essentials about the Six Categories of Graphs*.)
5. Such as when Earl Sheng realized upon awakening that his dream indicated danger, and when he later tried to force an auspicious interpretation.
    Earl Sheng dreamt that he was crossing the Huan River. He ate pieces of jade and pearls, and this caused him to cry and then sing. When he awoke, he was frightened and dared not have the dream interpreted. Later, when he was assisting the duke in an attack on the state of Zheng and arrived at Lishen, he had it interpreted, saying, "I was afraid of dying; therefore, I did not dare have it interpreted. But now, three years have passed and a multitude of supporters is following me—no harm will come from it." On the evening after he had it interpreted, Earl Sheng died. (From *Zuo's Narratives*.) Du Yu commented that *Zuo's Narratives* was warning against seeking multiple interpretations of a dream.
6. The graph *han* 撼 means "to be disturbed and awakened by someone" while the graph 㾓, pronounced *ping*, means "to become panicked." In such cases, the content of the dream remains incomplete.
7. A dream that has ended yet whose beginning or end has been forgotten upon awakening is not a complete dream.

8. A dream has an origin. If the interpreter can comprehend it, he can identify with heaven, earth, people, and things in the dream.

9. The art of dream interpretation must be practiced in a professional manner to produce results that are confirmed.

10. If the degree of his sincerity does not enable him to understand spirits and ghosts, then he should not interpret dreams.

11. Distinguishing between the calamity of a dangerous situation and the happiness of an auspicious situation marks the art of the sage who understands destiny. When the Way is in a state of disorder, calamities are caused by inferior men. They possess a forced understanding of the Way that destroys the larger view in favor of petty details and disregards what lies in the distance to focus on the immediate. This destroys the art of the Way and makes comprehension difficult. (From "Treatise on Arts and Literature" in *History of the Western Han Dynasty*.)

12. As in the case of Huang Fanchuo's interpretations of An Lushan's bizarre dreams.

After An Lushan rebelled, Huang Fanchuo was captured by the rebels. An Lushan had dreamt that his gown and sleeves had grown until they reached down to the steps of the imperial dais. Huang replied that it meant An would rule the empire by employing a policy of nonintervention in the government. An Lushan then dreamt that the window lattices in the palace were upside down. Huang replied that the lattices *[ge]* meant overthrowing *[ge]* the old order and following a new one. Later, An Lushan was defeated. When Emperor Xuanzong [r. 712–756] returned to the capital from Shu, he interrogated Huang, who replied, "Your humble minister interpreted An Lushan's dreams knowing that he would not succeed." Xuanzong asked, "How did you know that?" Huang answered, "When his sleeves grew long, I knew he would not be able to grasp hold of his goal, and when the window frames in the palace were upside down, I wondered how this barbarian could ever handle them." The emperor laughed and pardoned him. (From *Mr. Liu's Accounts of Past Events*.)

13. When he is dreaming, he does not know that he is dreaming and may even interpret his own dream while still dreaming. He only realizes it was a dream after he awakens. Moreover, he may have a great awakening and then understand that this is all a great dream. Yet, stupid people think they have awakened as they busily fuss over petty matters—how obtuse they are! (From the *Master Zhuang*.)

14. Yan Hui asked Confucius, "When Mengsun Cai's mother died, he carried out her funeral without expressing any sorrow, yet he is regarded throughout the state of Lu as having behaved well during the ceremonies. I, for one, find this quite strange." Confucius replied, "You and I have not yet awakened from this dream. Moreover, you may dream you are a bird that soars into the sky or a fish that dives among the depths, but how do I know if you, who are telling me about this now, are awake or dreaming?" (From the *Master Zhuang*.)

In the Land of Gumang, the people sleep for a long time and wake up once every fifty days. They consider what they do in their dreams as real and what they see when awake as false. In the Land of the Middle, the people alternate sleeping with waking. They consider what they do when awake as real and what they see in their dreams as false. In the Land of Fuluo, the people are awake for a long time and do not sleep. Mr. Yin of Zhou ran a large estate. Among his workers was someone who would dream at night of being the ruler of a state whose happiness was beyond compare. Yet Mr. Yin would dream at night that he had become a slave who was ordered about to do every kind of task while suffering no end of beatings. A friend of Mr. Yin said to him, "This alternation of suffering and ease is the way a man's fortune constantly balances itself. How can you expect to enjoy only ease when both awake and dreaming?" (From the *Master Lie*.)

If you wanted to distinguish waking from dreaming, then there was only the Yellow Emperor and Confucius who could do so. But, now, there is no Yellow Emperor or Confucius, so who can tell the difference? (From the *Master Lie*.)

15. The Yellow Emperor was able to recognize distinctions in the Great Cosmic Ancestor, comprehend heaven and earth, follow the nine principles of nature, devote attention to the nine forms of things, marking proper divisions and maintaining interconnectedness so that all things and people became organized coherently. (From the *Master of Huainan*.)

16. Zhang Wuzi said to Ju Quezi, "Both Confucius and you are dreaming. And, when I say you are dreaming, I, too, am dreaming. People will call these 'cunning words.'" (From the *Master Zhuang*.)

Suo Dan was skilled at interpreting dreams. Governor Yin Dan sought from him a book on dream interpretation. So Dan replied, "I formerly attended the National University where I studied with an old gentleman who was knowledgeable about everything. He also concealed his name and seemed to be something of a recluse. I asked this old gentleman about the art of dream interpretation, and he spoke of it based on his own experience in examining cases—there are really no books about this." (From *History of the Jin Dynasty*.)

CHAPTER 9

Auspicious Events
吉事

Auspicious events contain good omens. Through interpreting these events, the future can be known. Consultations were held regarding the king's dreams during the final month of winter as recorded in *The Government Organization of the Zhou*.[1] Then auspicious dreams were presented to the court in order to glorify the king. The king bowed and received them, recognizing the importance of the good omens. The chapters "Awakening in Cheng," "Historical Records," "The Cautions of King Wen," and "The Cautions of King Wu" in the *Zhou Dynasty Documents Recovered from a Tomb* all contain dreams that were publicly announced.[2] Thus were dreams instrumental in deciding such great matters as the heavenly mandate and the succession to the throne. Interpretations of dreams can also be altered as in cases of nightmares that are the result of the influence of sickness or demons. Nightmares are expelled in the final month of winter by casting out any ominous signs found throughout the four directions.[3] Then the *fangxiangshi* spirit-medium carries out the protocols of the *nuo* exorcism.[4] The god Boqi is recorded in *History of the Eastern Han Dynasty*.[5] The *yiyu*-bird is recorded in *The Guideways Through Mountains and Seas*.[6] An incantation against the god of night is recorded in *Miscellaneous Morsels from Youyang*.[7] Therefore, such practices from the past as displaying the god Yulei, peach-wood sticks, reed ropes, and images of tigers are still used to cast out inauspicious omens and expel nightmares.[8]

NOTES

1. The graph 聘 *[pin]* means "to consult." Dreams contain events that are good omens. Their interpretation can indicate auspiciousness or inauspicious-

ness based on correlations with the positions of the sun, moon, stars, and asterisms. In the last month of winter, the sun finishes its passage through its stations, and the stars complete their cycle through the sky. Numerological calculations reach their end. Therefore, presents of silk are sent forth inviting experts to the court who are consulted regarding the king's dreams. If the dreams are auspicious, it is regarded as cause for celebration, and so on. (From the commentary to "The Diviner of Dreams" in *The Government Organization of the Zhou*.)

2. Taisi dreamt that brambles were growing wildly in the courtyard of the Shang dynasty palace and that Crown Prince Fa planted catalpa trees in the empty spaces that turned into pines, junipers, and oaks. When she awoke, she told this to King Wen. King Wen then summoned Crown Prince Fa and had this interpreted in the Hall of Light. The king and Crown Prince Fa together expressed their reverence toward this auspicious dream, and received the great mandate of the Shang from the Supreme God of Heaven. (From "The Awakening in Cheng" in *Zhou Dynasty Documents Recovered from a Tomb*.)

In the first month of the year, the king was in the royal domain of Zhou. Just before dawn, he summoned the three dukes and Rongfu, the historian-astronomer of the left, telling them, "Upon awakening, I felt I had been frightened by a past event." Therefore, the important lessons of past events were selected, and these were explained to him by Rongfu on the first and fifteenth day of the month. (From "Historical Records" in *Zhou Dynasty Documents Recovered from a Tomb*.)

King Wen described his dream and feared that his dynasty would come to an end. On the day *gengchen*, he summoned Crown Prince Fa and said, "Show respect for this! There are many changes occurring among the people and things of the world. What directions are the people pursuing that are not beneficial? Alas! Show respect for this! Summon the responsible officials. Night and day, never forget this. Be a guide to the people." (From "The Cautions of King Wen" in *Zhou Dynasty Documents Recovered from a Tomb*.)

In the fourth month of the twelfth year, King Wu described his dream. On the day *bingchen*, he had the royal genealogy, the protocols for the sacrifice at the suburban altar, and the "Opening" and "Harmonizing" texts brought out and commanded Dan, the Duke of Zhou, to establish the successor to the throne. He conferred upon his young son Song the insignia and the dynastic statutes. The king said, "Alas! Show respect for this!" He then summoned and established his young son, saying, "Truly, you must ceaselessly exert yourself night and day." (From "The Cautions of King Wu" in *Zhou Dynasty Documents Recovered from a Tomb*.)

3. "The Diviner of Dreams" chapter in *The Government Organization of the Zhou* states that *meng* are cast off in the four directions in order to *zeng* nightmares. The commentary states that the graph 萌 *[meng]* means "ominous signs" and the graph 贈 *[zeng]* means "to expel." The entire phrase means that when a dream is not auspicious, inauspicious omens are sought throughout the four directions and cast out so as to expel the nightmares and insure that they do not have any effect.

Heaven warns the Son of Heaven and the nobles by means of demons. It warns the scholars by means of nightmares. In this way, demons do not overcome good government and nightmares do not overcome good behavior. (From *A Garden of Stories*.)

When the Son of Heaven has a nightmare, he should cultivate the Way; when a nobleman has a nightmare, he should improve the government; when a scholar has a nightmare, he should cultivate his person. (From Jia Yi, *New Writings*.)

4. The *nuo* exorcism is ordered to expel all forms of pestilence. (From "The Diviner of Dreams" in *The Government Organization of the Zhou*.) The *fangxiangshi* spirit-medium leads one hundred subordinates to carry out the seasonal *nuo* exorcism. (From "Summer Officials" in *The Government Organization of the Zhou*.) Zheng Xuan commented that the *nuo* exorcism to expel nightmares is carried out during the last month of winter. This is because in the last month of winter, the sun passes through the two lunar lodgings, Barrens and Roof. Barrens and Roof contain *qi*-energy emanating from tombs during the four seasons. Demons rely on these to emerge from the yin world and bring harm to people. Therefore, the proper official is ordered to carry out the grand *nuo* ceremony in order to exorcise them.

5. During the Eastern Han dynasty, a grand *nuo* exorcism was held ten days before the *la* sacrifice in the last month of winter; this was called "expelling pestilence." One hundred and twenty boys among the eunuch attendants served as acolytes wearing red turbans and black gowns with tight sleeves while carrying large drums. They acted as *fangxiangshi* spirit-mediums who, with the help of the twelve beasts, expelled evil demons from the palace. Eunuch performers together with the acolytes chanted, "Boqi, consume all nightmares," and so forth. (From *The Encyclopedic History of Institutions*.)

6. At Mount Yiwang there is a bird whose form resembles a crow, and it has three heads and a large tail. It is skilled at laughing and is called the "*yiyu*." Wearing a part of it against the body protects against nightmares, and it can guard against evil forces. (From *The Guideways Through Mountains and Seas*.)

7. There is an incantation to the god of night that can keep nightmares away. It goes "*poshan poyandi*." (Duan Chengshi.) For more details, see *A Continuation of A Record of Manifold Things*.

8. *The Guideways Through Mountains and Seas* states that in the Eastern Sea is Mount Dusuo. On its summit is a giant peach tree that coils about for three thousand *li*. On its northeast side is the Gateway of Demons through which myriad demons come and go. There are two gods named Shentu and Yulei. They investigate and arrest the demons that harm people, tying them up with ropes made from reeds and feeding them to tigers. Therefore, the Yellow Emperor made images of these gods. After the *nuo* exorcism is over, peach-wood sticks were affixed to the doorways along with painted images of Yulei, reed ropes, and a tiger. According to Han dynasty regulations, peach-wood sticks, images of the god Yulei, and stalks of reeds were to be placed at the residences of all the officials. Moreover, reed lances and peach-wood branches were presented to the highest government ministers.

CHAPTER 10

Influences and Abnormal Conditions

How many really understand the causes of the nine kinds of dreams resulting from influences that produce abnormal conditions?[1] The first is called "overabundance of *qi*-energy," the second, "deficiency of *qi*-energy," the third, "lodging of evil energy," the fourth, "physical obstructions," the fifth, "overflow of emotions," the sixth, "direct correspondence," the seventh, "symbolic correspondence," the eighth, "extreme opposite," and the ninth, "demons."

What is meant by "overabundance of *qi*-energy?" If yin energy is overabundant, one dreams of crossing a great river in fear; if yang energy is overabundant, one dreams of being burned in a great fire. If there is an overabundance of both yin and yang, one dreams of killing each other. If there is an overabundance in the upper part of the body, one dreams of flying; if there is an overabundance in the lower part of the body, one dreams of falling. If famished, one dreams of obtaining food; if satiated, one dreams of providing food for others. If there is an over-abundance of *qi*-energy in the liver, one dreams about being angry. If it is in the lungs, one dreams of being afraid, of weeping and flying about. If it is in the heart, one dreams of feeling happy and laughing, and of feeling apprehensive and fearful. If it is in the spleen, one dreams of singing and music, and of feeling too heavy to move. If it is in the kidneys, one dreams that one's waist and spine have separated from each other. If one's body contains many short parasites, one dreams of a crowd gathering; if one's body contains many long parasites, one dreams of people attacking and destroying each other. Such are dreams that derive from an overabundance of *qi*-energy, and this category can be extended to include further examples.[2]

What is meant by "deficiency of *qi*-energy"? Deficient *qi*-energy in the lungs causes a person to dream about white things. One may visualize someone being decapitated whose blood splatters about. However, if the deficiency occurs during a time period correlated with the lungs, then one dreams of armies fighting. Deficiency in the kidneys causes a person to dream of sinking in a boat and drowning. However, if this occurs during a time period correlated with the kidneys, then one dreams of hiding underwater as if one is afraid. Deficiency in the liver causes dreams of the fragrance of mushrooms or of grass and plants growing. However, if this occurs during a time period correlated with the liver, then one dreams of hiding under a tree and not daring to come out. Deficiency in the heart causes dreams of rescue from a fire, or of thunder and lightning. However, if this occurs during a time period correlated with the heart, then one dreams of a raging fire. Deficiency in the spleen causes dreams about not having enough to eat and drink. However, if this occurs during a time period correlated with the spleen, then one dreams of building a wall or roof. These are all dreams caused by deficiency of *qi*-energy, and this category can be extended to include further examples.[3]

What is meant by "lodging of evil energy"? When syncopic energy resides in the heart, one dreams of hills and mountains, and of smoke and fire. If it resides in the lungs, one dreams of fluttering about and of seeing unusual objects made of gold and iron. If it resides in the liver, one dreams of mountain forests and trees. If it resides in the spleen, one dreams of hills and great marshes, and of damaged homes, wind, and rain. If it resides in the kidneys, one dreams of approaching a deep chasm, and of sinking underwater and remaining there. If it resides in the bladder, one dreams of traveling. If it resides in the stomach, one dreams of eating and drinking. If it resides in the large intestine, one dreams of fields and countryside. If it resides in the small intestine, one dreams of a cluster of towns and thoroughfares. If it resides in the gallbladder, one dreams of conflict and litigation and of boasting. If it resides in the vagina, one dreams of receiving someone in the inner apartments. If it resides in the neck, one dreams of decapitation. If it resides in the shin, one dreams of walking yet being unable to go forward and of dwelling in a deep pit or storage cellar. If it resides in the buttocks, one dreams of performing courteous bows and greetings. If it resides in the placenta, one dreams of urinating and defecating. These are all dreams caused by the lodging of evil energy, and this category can be extended to include further examples.[4]

What is meant by "physical obstructions"? When something is lodged in the mouth, one dreams of struggling to speak yet remaining dumb. If the feet are restrained, one dreams of struggling to walk while lame. If the head hits the pillow, one dreams of ascending to great heights and then falling. If one sleeps on ropes like those used to bind a prisoner, one dreams of poisonous snakes. If one sleeps on brightly colored clothes, one dreams of tigers and leopards. If one's hair is tangled up with the twigs of a tree, one dreams of hanging upside down. These are all dreams due to physical obstructions, and this category can be extended to include further examples.[5]

What is meant by "overflow of emotions"? If excessively happy, one dreams of things opening up. If excessively angry, one dreams of things closing. If excessively fearful, one dreams of hiding. If excessively anxious, one dreams of blame. If excessively sad, one dreams of rescue. If excessively resentful, one dreams of scolding someone. If excessively frightened, one dreams of insanity. These are all dreams caused by the overflow of emotions, and this category can be extended to include further examples.

What is meant by dreams of "direct correspondence"? One dreams of the ruler and later actually sees him. Or, one dreams of a certain person and later actually sees him.[6] Someone dreamt of a deer and later caught one.[7] Someone dreamt of obtaining grain and then actually obtained it.[8] Someone dreamt of an assassin and then apprehended one.[9] Someone dreamt of being taught the autumn-driving technique and then was taught it.[10] These are all dreams of direct correspondence, and this category can be extended to include further examples.

What is meant by dreams of "symbolic correspondence"? When about to take up an official post *[guan]*, one dreams of a coffin *[guan]*, and when about to obtain money, one dreams of filth.[11] When about to become prominent, one dreams of ascending heights, and when it is about to rain *[yu]*, one dreams of fish *[yu]*.[12] When about to eat, one dreams of calling a dog. When about to suffer bereavement, one dreams of wearing white. When about to receive imperial favor, one dreams of wearing an embroidered robe. When strategies fail, one dreams of thorny bushes and mud. These are all dreams of symbolic correspondence, and this category can be extended to include further examples.

What is meant by dreams of the "extreme opposite"? When there is a banquet celebrating the marriage of a relative, one dreams of sobbing. When sobbing, involved in arguments or litigation, one dreams of singing and dancing.[13] When cold, one dreams of warmth; when famished, one dreams of eating one's fill; when ill, one dreams of a doctor.[14] When mourning for one's parents, one dreams of wearing red clothes. When celebrating a happy occasion, one dreams of wearing sackcloth and mourning clothes. These are all dreams of the extreme opposite, and this category can be extended to include further examples.

What is meant by "demonic presences"? Death-dealing demons attach themselves to people as disastrous influences.[15] Ghosts of people with grievances will seek revenge against those responsible.[16] They appear in dreams because the thoughts of the dreamer are filled with doubts and his spirit and *qi*-energy are in a state of confusion. Then, demons take advantage of these weaknesses to let loose their strange forms of retribution. Thus do calamities and disasters arise, and it becomes difficult to pray for blessings and well-being. Examples are when Duke Wen of Jin was imprisoned by the Earl of Qin, and after the Prince of Yan was banished to Fangzhou.[17] This is what is meant by dreams caused by demonic presences, and this category can be extended to include further examples.

Although these nine kinds of dreams differ, the method used for interpreting them is the same. Some elements may be similar, but their meanings are actually different while others may seem different but their meanings are the same—one cannot depend on fixed rules. However, Wang Fu's "A Classification of Dreams" offers a fairly complete discussion regarding their auspicious or inauspicious significance.[18]

NOTES

1. Those who do not understand how influences produce altered conditions are perplexed about the causes of such events when they occur. Those who do understand how these conditions arise can know their causes and will not be confounded. Then, the body's sufficiencies or deficiencies and its growth or decline can be brought into accord with the balance between heaven and earth; in this way it can properly respond to all kinds of things. (From the *Master Lie*.)

2. There are fifteen kinds of dreams caused by an overabundance of *qi*-energy. See the chapter, "Dreams Caused by Excessive and Perverse Energies" in *The Yellow Emperor's Book of the Spiritual Pivot*, as well as "Discussion on the Importance of Detecting the Subtle Vigor of the Pulse" in *The Yellow Emperor's Inner Canon of Medicine*. However, *The Book of the Spiritual Pivot* does not discuss the two kinds of dreams caused by short and long parasites, and *The Inner Canon of Medicine* does not discuss the three kinds of dreams involving the heart, spleen, and kidneys.

When yin energy is strong, one dreams of crossing a great river in fear; when yang energy is strong, one dreams of passing through a great fire and getting burned. When both yin and yang energies are strong, one dreams of sparing life and also of killing. When satiated, one dreams of giving away food; when famished, one dreams of obtaining food. (From the *Master Lie*.)

3. There are ten kinds of dreams caused by deficiency of *qi*-energy in the five *zang*-organs. See "Discussion on Diagnosing Overabundance and Deficiency of *Qi*-Energy" in *The Inner Canon of Medicine*. These are probably caused by an excess of yang energy and deficiency of yin energy.

4. For fifteen dreams caused by syncopic energy attacking internally, see *The Book of the Spiritual Pivot*. *The Inner Canon of Medicine* says that a lesser yin syncope can cause one to forget one's dreams.

Those suffering from dizziness will dream about rising upward while those suffering from depression will dream of sinking. (From the *Master Lie*.)

5. If one sleeps on top of a belt, one will dream of a snake. If a flying bird snatches strands of one's hair, one will dream of flying. (From the *Master Lie*.)

6. Men also have dreams of direct correspondence, as when one dreams of a certain person and the next day actually sees him. Or, one dreams of the ruler and the next day actually sees him. However, if one dreams of a certain person and the ruler but does not actually see them, then, the fact that they are not seen indicates that they belong to the category of symbolic images. (From Wang Chong, *Judicious Discussions*.)

7. A man of Zheng was gathering firewood in the countryside when he suddenly came across a frightened deer. He moved toward it, struck it, and killed it. He quickly hid the dead deer in a ditch and covered it with brush, fearing that someone would see it. The man was overjoyed with his success, but he soon forgot where he had hidden it. Later, he had a dream about the event. As he was walking along the road, he recounted the story out loud; a bystander heard what he said and, based on his words, found the deer and took it. The bystander then returned home and told his wife, "A woodcutter dreamt of catching a deer but forgot where he had left it. Now I have found it, so his dream must have been true!" The wife replied, "On the other hand, could it be that you have dreamt that there was a woodcutter who caught a deer? Was there really a woodcutter at all? Since you have truly obtained the deer, isn't your own dream the true one?" The husband said, "Since I have evidently obtained the deer, does it really matter if it is his dream or mine?" However, the woodcutter could not stop thinking about having lost the deer after he returned home. That night, he had a true dream about the place where he had hidden it, and he also dreamt of the person who had taken it. The next day, he searched and found the man based on his dream and consequently disputed the matter with him in court before a judge. The judge said, "If, originally, you had actually caught the deer, then you have wrongly attributed it to a dream. But, if you actually only dreamt of catching the deer, you are wrong to state that really happened. This man truly took your deer, and yet he disputes your right to it; his wife further says that he only recognized a man and a deer in a dream, not that someone had caught a deer. Evidently, this deer exists, so please divide it in two." When this affair was reported to the ruler of Zheng, the ruler said, "So! Is the judge now going to dream that he divided the deer between the two men?" When the ruler reported this to the prime minister, the prime minister said, "I cannot distinguish between what is a dream and what isn't." (From the *Master Lie*.)

8. See the commentary to Liu Hao's dream about grain by a fence in the chapter, "Plants and Trees" [II:18n17].

9. Zhu Youzi, Prince Kang of the Later Liang dynasty, had eyes with double pupils and thought so highly of himself that he felt he deserved to be emperor. In the first year of the Zhenming era [915], he sent an assassin to the bedchamber of the Last Emperor of the Later Liang. The Last Emperor had just fallen asleep and was dreaming that an assassin was harming him when he suddenly awoke. He heard the sword on his bed emit a clanging sound and jumped up, pulled out the sword, and said, "Is this a revolt?" Then he searched his bedchamber and found the assassin, whom he personally killed. (From *History of the Five Dynasties*.)

10. Yi Ru had been studying the art of the charioteer for three years but had not yet mastered it. One night, he dreamt that he was taught the autumn-driving technique by his teacher. The next day, he went to pay a formal visit to his teacher, who called him over and said, "Today, I will teach you the autumn-driving technique." Yi Ru retreated, faced north, bowed, and said, "Last night, I dreamt that I was taught this," and he recounted the dream to his teacher. What he had dreamt about was indeed the autumn-driving technique. (From *The Compendium of Mr. Lü*.)

11. Someone asked Yin Hao why one may dream of a coffin when going to take up office and of manure when about to receive money. Yin replied that an official position is basically corrupting; therefore, someone who is taking up office may dream of a corpse. Money is basically manure; therefore, someone about to receive money may dream of filth. These words became famous among his contemporaries. (From *History of the Jin Dynasty*.)

12. When the sky is about to become obscured, one dreams of water; when it is about to clear up, one dreams of fire. (From *A Garden of Stories*.)

13. He who dreams of drinking wine will find himself sobbing the next day while he who dreams of sobbing will enjoy hunting the next day. (From the *Master Zhuang*.) He who dreams of drinking wine will later feel anxious while he who dreams of singers and dancers will later sob. (From the *Master Lie*.)

14. When the sky is about to become overcast, one dreams of fire; when one is about to fall ill, one dreams of eating. (From the *Master Lie*.) A person who is freezing dreams of clothing, a famished person dreams of eating. (From a Buddhist text.) A starving person suddenly dreams of a pot of rice splitting open; but all anxieties vanish as he eats his fill in a dream. (From a poem by Su Shi.) A famished person often dreams of eating his fill and a sick person often dreams of a doctor. (Huang Shangu.)

15. In *Zuo's Narratives*, when Boyou of Zheng became a demon, Zichan of Zheng said, "Things that possess a great amount of vigorous essence have strong *hun*- and *po*-souls. Even the souls of commoners who have died violent deaths can attach themselves to the living as demons. Since Boyou had held power for three generations and then died violently, isn't it appropriate that he should have become a demon?"

16. During an era of peace, things do not become demons, but the ghosts of people with grievances will take revenge against those responsible. (From *Bo and Kong's Encyclopedia*.)

17. After the Earl of Qin imprisoned Duke Wen of Jin, he said that he was visited by dreams caused by demons. (From *Zuo's Narratives*.) After Prince Zhong of Yan was banished to Fangzhou, he had many dreams caused by demons. (From Sima Guang, *The Comprehensive Mirror*.)

18. The chapter "A Classification of Dreams" in *Discussions from a Gentleman in Hiding* by Wang Fu [ca. 90–165] states that there are dreams of direct correspondence, symbolic dreams, dreams caused by a fixation, imaginative dreams, dreams based on status, dreams in response to stimuli, seasonal dreams, contrary dreams, dreams caused by illness, and dreams based on the dreamer's nature. In the past, when King Wu's consort Yijiang was pregnant with Taishu, she dreamt that the supreme god Di told her, "I command that your son be given Yu as his personal name and that he will be granted the fief of Tang." When the child was born, he had markings on his palm that spelled out the graph *yu,* and so he was given this as his personal name. Later, King Cheng destroyed Tang and enfeoffed Yu there. This is an example of a direct dream. *The Book of Songs* states that, "Black bears and brown bears are auspicious signs of sons." This is an example of a symbolic dream. Confucius would often think about the Duke of Zhou and then dream about him at night. These were dreams caused by a fixation. When a person thinks about something, he may dream of it as when he is filled with anxiety and dreams about what he fears. This is a dream based on thoughts. Now, an event dreamt about by a high-ranking person may be auspicious, but if dreamt about by a lowly person, it may prove disastrous. If dreamt by a noble man, it may indicate honor, but if dreamt by a petty man, it may indicate disgrace. These are dreams based on social status. Dreaming when it is overcast and rainy causes one to feel weary and confused, while dreaming during a hot drought causes one to feel in turmoil. Dreaming during severe cold weather causes one to feel plaintive and depressed. Dreaming when strong winds are blowing causes one to imagine being blown about. These are dreams based on responses to stimuli. In spring, one dreams of birth and growth, in summer, of things at their peak and most glorious, in fall and winter, of harvesting and storing away. These are dreams based on the season. Just before the battle of Chengpu, Duke Wen of Jin dreamt that the prime minister of Chu had forced him to the ground and was sucking out his brains. He was revolted by it yet won a great victory in the battle. This is a contrary dream. During a yin illness, one will dream of cold while during a yang illness, one will dream of heat. An illness caused by internal factors results in dreams of chaos while one caused by external factors results in dreams of expansion. Among the many kinds of diseases, some produce dreams of disintegration, others of accumulation. These are all dreams caused by illness. People's minds, emotions, likes, and dislikes are different. Some will consider something to be auspicious; others will regard it as a misfortune. In interpreting dreams, one should examine each in connection with the dreamer's own self. These are dreams based on a person's individual nature.

Therefore, an earlier dream that is exactly like the events that follow is called "direct." A dream with elements that can be compared or correlated with what follows is called "symbolic." A dream based on concentrated thoughts and a focused spirit is called "caused by a fixation." Events in a dream at night that are based on thoughts during the day may first appear auspicious, then suddenly seem to indicate misfortune. Any judgments about their good or evil significance are not reliable. This is what is called "dreams based on thoughts." If influenced by the dreamer's high-rank or lowliness, worthiness or stupidity, male or female gender, older or younger age, such dreams are called "based on status." If influenced by wind, rain, cold, or heat, such dreams are called "based on stimuli." If influenced by the correlative functioning of "king" or "minister" within the cycle of the five agents, such dreams are called "based on the season." Dreams where yin reaches its height and yet are auspicious, or where yang reaches its height and yet indicate misfortune, are called "contrary." Dreams that are scrutinized when examining a person's illness are called dreams "caused by illness." Dreams where a person's mind, emotions, likes, and dislikes are later confirmed in actual events are called "based on individual nature."

This is a general summary of the ten kinds of dreams identified in dream interpretation. Yet most of those who pronounce dreams as auspicious or as indicating misfortune lose sight of these categories. Could it be that waking hours are yang in nature and sleeping is yin so that the operations of yin and yang are reversed during these two periods? Still, this does not seem like a very thorough explanation. If someone dreams of an auspicious event and consequently feels happy, then it is truly auspicious. If someone dreams of a misfortune and consequently feels anxious and fearful, then it is truly a misfortune. This is what is meant by dreaming of birth and growth in spring and summer, and dreaming of death and sorrow in autumn and winter. In investigating dreams, symbolic images of purity, cleanliness, and a wholesome freshness, of a solid appearance and healthy body, of fine, flourishing bamboo and trees, of newly constructed mansions, vessels, and utensils, of things properly arranged, open and pervading, gloriously bright, tenderly harmonious, of success and prosperity—all these are auspicious signs of happiness and of plans that will come to fruition. Symbolic images of filth, stench, pollution, and impurity, of corruption, decay, and desiccation, of things overturned, odd, and perverse, of nauseating smells, of things closed up, blocked, hidden, and in darkness, of coming apart, falling down or declining—all these indicate that plans will not succeed and all affairs will fail. Demons and strange phenomenon and hateful, disgusting events are all indications of anxiety and sorrow. Painted images of embryos, false engravings and inlays as well as empty clay pots all indicate cheating and deception. Actors, jesters, dancers, as well as children's toys all indicate looking and laughing. These constitute most of such cases.

Some dreams seem obvious yet do not yield a valid interpretation. Others seem very abstruse yet are followed by confirmations. Why is this so? I would say it is because these dreams are not fully investigated and the wrong nomenclature is applied out of ignorance. Therefore, one cannot place trust in them when determining the proper action in an affair. Even when people directly discuss a plan for a certain matter, there are still some things that do not follow smoothly. How much truer is this if confusing and bewildering dreams are relied on? And yet, why should this necessarily be so? Only those dreams stimulated by an absolutely sincere force or those that are communications from divine spirit are worthy of being interpreted. Therefore, when a gentleman has an uncharacteristically strange dream, it is not necessarily absurd, for there must be some reason for it.

When a petty man has an uncharacteristically strange dream, it doesn't mean glory, for there must be some secret mechanism at work. Now, a night's dream may involve many shifts and transformations with a hundred different things appearing one after another. If the dreamer cannot fully narrate everything that happened, the interpreter may not be able to explain it accurately. This is not due to the fault of the interpreter but to the errors of the dreamer. Or, it may be that the details of the dream have been fully scrutinized yet the interpreter is unable to apply the appropriate analytical categories that would provide insight into it. Consequently, the dream fails to result in a valid confirmation. This is not a defect of the dream manuals but because the interpreter's explanation is faulty. Therefore, the difficulty in interpreting dreams is due to the difficulty in correctly consulting the dream manuals under these conditions. Dream interpretation requires scrutinizing the reasons underlying a dream's transformations and scrutinizing its prognostications. Internally, one should examine the dreamer's emotions and intentions and externally, the operation of the correlative factors of "king" and "minister." Then the signs of auspiciousness or misfortune can be observed. If an auspicious meaning appears and a person cultivates his virtuous power, he will certainly receive blessings, but if an auspicious meaning appears and a person behaves licentiously, what might have been blessings will turn into calamity. If an evil meaning appears and a person behaves arrogantly, he will certainly suffer calamity, but if an evil meaning appears and a person maintains a vigilant and fearful attitude, what might have been calamitous will turn into blessings. Therefore, although his consort Taisi had an auspicious dream, King Wen did not dare to feel pleased about it. Instead, he first offered sacrifices to all the gods and then had it interpreted in the Hall of Light, whereupon he bowed in thanks for such an auspicious dream. He closely investigated his own behavior with a vigilant and fearful attitude and regarded this joyous event with anxiety. As a consequence, he was able to achieve auspicious results and came to possess the entire world. The Duke of Guo dreamt that the god Rushou bestowed some land on him, and he considered this auspicious. The historian-astrologer Shi Yin ordered that the entire state celebrate this dream. But, because the duke rejoiced at what he should have felt anxious about, it resulted in misfortune, and he lost his fief. *The Book of Changes* says that internal and external events should cause one to be on guard and realize the possibility of anxiety and calamity. In connection with this, whenever a strange dream occurs and causes one to feel disturbed, one should not inquire whether it is good or bad. Instead, one should maintain a fearful attitude and engage in examining oneself. If one faces the dream with a virtuous attitude, one can meet with an auspicious outcome.

PART II
The Outer Chapters
外篇

CHAPTER I

Heaven
天者

Heaven is the ancestor of all things and occupies the most exalted position. Thus, one speaks of the "Son of Heaven" as the son of the Supreme God of Heaven.[1] Formerly, Cui Lingyun dreamt that Xiao Daocheng was the nineteenth son of the Supreme God of Heaven, and Sun Fengbo also dreamt that Xiao ascended to heaven riding a dragon.[2] But this ruler of the Southern Qi dynasty was a superfluous figure. Even though he received the mandate from heaven above, he still brought about chaos and disrupted the unity of the cosmos. Did he really occupy the position of a legitimate ruler? Similarly, Emperor Wen of the Western Han dreamt that a yellow-helmeted gentleman pushed him upward toward heaven.[3] Emperor Shenzong of the Northern Song dreamt that someone lifted him upward toward heaven.[4] Emperor Guangwu of the Eastern Han dreamt that he was riding on a red dragon upward toward heaven and consequently, Feng Yi and all the other generals urged him to ascend the throne.[5] Zhao Ruyu dreamt that he ascended to heaven while carrying a white dragon on his back, and consequently Emperor Lizong of the Southern Song wore a white robe when he ascended the throne.[6] But these four emperors were all virtuous rulers of the Han and Song dynasties. Empress Hexi, formerly Mistress Deng, dreamt that she rubbed heaven with her hand. She was then elevated at court and produced an heir to carry on the Han dynasty sacrifices.[7] Yet how could these compare with the mother of Yuwen Tai, who dreamt of ascending toward heaven with her son in her arms, but stopped before she reached it. Tao Hongjing's mother dreamt that she herself ascended to heaven, but that she would have no more descendants and that the family line would be extinguished.[8] Or, consider the case of Liu Muzhi's dream of ascending to heaven in boats joined together. He finally was appointed to the position of vice director of the Department of State Affairs.⁹ Han Zhigui dreamt that he held up heaven with both hands on two occasions, and he served two sovereigns as a minister.¹⁰ Tao Kan and Xue Andu dreamt of visiting the gates of heaven, and both rose to high positions of military authority.¹¹ Duke Mu of Qin and Zhao Jianzi dreamt that they had arrived at the residence of the supreme god Di. In both cases this was a sign that their descendants would prosper.¹² Shusun Muzi dreamt that someone helped him to defeat heaven, but in the end he suffered the strange catastrophe of starving to death.¹³ Wu Shihuo dreamt that the emperor rode on him up to heaven, which later led to his being granted a false title.¹⁴ Furthermore, a minor official of Jin dreamt that he bore Duke Jing up to heaven on his back. Later, he bore the dead duke out of the privy and wound up entombed with him as a human sacrifice.¹⁵ Xu Yang of the Han dreamt that he had gone up to heaven and encountered the anger of the supreme god Di, yet he then achieved merit, and everything came to a good end.¹⁶ He Zhizhang of the Tang dreamt that he went up to heaven and traveled throughout the residence of the supreme god Di, but he only requested permission to become a Daoist priest.¹⁷ Alas! Such different interpretations can result from auspicious or ominous dreams!

NOTES

1. He whose virtue resembles heaven and earth is called "the emperor." Heaven supports him and considers him as its son, so he is called "Son of Heaven." (From *Luxuriant Dew of the Spring and Autumn Annals*.)

2. Cui Lingyun of Qinghe was serving as an upper-level adjutant when he dreamt that the Most Exalted in Heaven said to him, "Xiao Daocheng is my nineteenth son, and I have already granted him the position of Son of Heaven." From the time of the three emperors and the five sovereigns down to the Qi dynasty, there have been nineteen men who have received this mandate. (From *History of the Southern Qi Dynasty*.)

In the seventh year of the Taishi era [471] of the Liu Song dynasty, Emperor Ming dispatched the governor of Huainan, Sun Fengbo, to Huaiyin to oversee the New Year's audience of officials. Sun shared a room with Xiao Daocheng and dreamt that Xiao ascended to heaven riding a dragon. Sun tried to grasp hold of the dragon's leg from below but could not. When he awoke, Sun told Xiao, "Someone will arise in Yanzhou who will protect the people, but I will not live to see it." (From *History of the Southern Qi Dynasty*.)

Emperor Gaozu of the Qi dreamt that he ascended to heaven riding a green dragon where he traveled westward chasing the sun. (From *Grand History*.)

3. Deng Tong rose from washing a boat to become a yellow-helmeted gen-

tleman. Emperor Wen dreamt that he wanted to ascend to heaven and could not, but a yellow-helmeted gentleman pushed him upward to heaven. He looked at his clothes and noticed that the gentleman was wearing his shirt and belt on backward. After he awoke, he went over to the docks and saw that Deng Tong was wearing his shirt on backward just like in his dream. He summoned Deng to ask his name and was quite pleased with him. (From *History of the Western Han Dynasty.*)

4. When Emperor Shenzong of the Northern Song was young, he attended Emperor Yingzong and dwelled in the Palace of Blessings and Tranquility where he once dreamt that someone lifted him up to heaven. (From *History of the Song Dynasty.*)

5. Emperor Guangwu summoned Feng Yi and said, "I dreamt that I rode on a dragon upward to heaven. When I awoke, I realized that my heart was trembling with fear." Feng Yi bowed and congratulated him saying, "Thus is heaven's mandate expressed through the spirit. That your heart was trembling with fear indicates that you possess the vigilant and serious nature of a king." Consequently, he and all the other generals agreed after discussion that he should ascend the throne. (From *History of the Eastern Han Dynasty from the Dongguan Pavilion.*)

Emperor Guangwu of the Han had dreamt that he rode on a red dragon upward to heaven and subsequently ascended the throne in Luoyang. (From *History of the Liu Song Dynasty.*)

6. Zhao Ruyu dreamt that he received the bronze tripod of King Tang of the Shang from Emperor Xiaozong of the Southern Song and that he ascended to heaven carrying a white dragon on his back. This was confirmed when soon afterward Prince Jia ascended the throne as Emperor Lizong wearing a white robe. (From *History of the Song Dynasty.*)

7. Empress Hexi, wife of Emperor He of the Eastern Han, once dreamt that she climbed up a stairway and rubbed heaven with her hand. Heaven was vast, pure blue, and smooth like a stalactite. The empress looked up and sucked it. She consulted a dream interpreter who said, "Yao dreamt that he had pulled himself upward toward heaven where he stopped, and King Tang dreamt that he reached heaven and licked it. These were both extraordinary dreams." Afterward, she was admitted into the palace and subsequently raised to her noble position. (From *History of the Liu Song Dynasty.*)

8. Mistress Wang, mother of Yuwen Tai, later Emperor Taizu of the Later Zhou, dreamt that she ascended toward heaven with her son in her arms. She had almost reached it when she stopped. (From *History of the Northern Zhou Dynasty.*) The mother of Tao Hongjing dreamt of a green dragon without a tail and that she herself ascended to heaven. Indeed, Tao Hongjing did not marry and had no sons. (From *History of the Chen Dynasty.*)

9. Liu Muzhi dreamt that he ascended to heaven on a vessel constructed from two boats joined together with a decorated canopy placed on top. There was an old woman who interpreted it, saying, "You will certainly occupy a senior position in the Department of State Affairs." After she finished speaking, she disappeared. Later, he became a vice director there. (From *A Garden of Strange Events.*)

10. Han Qi, whose courtesy name was Zhigui, was serving as magistrate of Qinzhou when he fell ill and dreamt that he held up heaven with his hands on

two occasions. Later, he indeed served Emperor Yingzong while the latter was still a prince and assisted Emperor Shenzong in the Eastern Palace. (From *Notes Compiled While Weary from Traveling*.)

11. Tao Kan dreamt that he grew eight wings and flew up to heaven where he saw nine gateways. He had already passed through eight of them and was unable to enter the ninth when a gatekeeper struck him with a staff, causing him to fall down to earth and break his left wing. When he awoke, his left armpit still hurt. (From *History of the Jin Dynasty*.)

When Xue Andu was campaigning in the Guan-Shan area, he reached Jiukou where he dreamt that he looked up at the sky and saw the gates of heaven opening up. He related this to his close officials who said that dreaming of the gates of heaven opening up is a symbolic image of a dynastic revival. (From *History of the Liu Song Dynasty*.)

12. Duke Mu of Qin dreamt that he had arrived at the residence of the supreme god Di. He observed a performance of "The Boundless Music of the Center of Heaven." Di bestowed a patent of nobility on him, and Qin subsequently flourished. (From *Historical Records*.)

Zhao Jianzi fell ill and was unable to recognize anyone for five days. The grand masters were all frightened. The physician Bian Que said, "His pulse is regular so why are you so surprised? Formerly, Duke Mu of Qin was also like this. The duke did not awaken for seven days, and when he did, he told Gongsun Zhi and Ziyu [fl. late 6th-early 5th cent. BCE], 'I went to the residence of the supreme god Di and it was thoroughly enjoyable.' Gongsun Zhi wrote this down and stored it away. Now the ruler's illness is the same as Duke Mu's." After two and a half days, Zhao Jianzi awoke and said to his grand masters, "I went to the residence of the supreme god Di and it was thoroughly enjoyable. I traveled together with all the gods to where 'The Boundless Music of the Center of Heaven' was played. A bear approached, and Di ordered me to shoot it. After this bear died, another kind of bear approached. Again I shot at it, and it died. Di was happy and bestowed on me two square bamboo containers, each with accoutrements. I saw a boy standing beside Di. Di entrusted a dog of the Di people to me and said, 'When your son has grown to manhood, give this dog to him. I have born in mind the achievements of Shun, so I will betroth his descendant Meng Yao to your descendant in the tenth generation.'" Dong Anyu wrote this down and stored it away. One day, Zhao Jianzi went out and encountered someone blocking his path who said to him, "When you were ill, your humble servant was standing beside the supreme god Di." Zhao replied, "Yes, that's right." The man said, "Di commanded you to shoot the bears, and they both died." Zhao said, "What was the reason for this?" The man replied, "The state of Jin will face a grave crisis, so Di ordered you to kill two officials—the bears were their ancestors." Zhao said, "Di bestowed upon me two square bamboo containers with accoutrements. Why was this?" The man replied, "Your son will conquer two states in the northern land of Di, and these will belong to his posterity." Zhao said, "I saw a boy standing beside Di, and Di gave me a dog of the Di people. Why was this?" The man replied, "The boy was your son, and the dog was the ancestor of the state of Dai. Your son will possess Dai. Your descendant will alter the protocols of the government and adopt foreign dress, annexing two states belonging to the Di people. Zhao asked the man's name, but the man then disappeared. Zhao then wrote all this down and stored it away. After Zhao Jianzi died, his son Xiangzi was enthroned. He killed the king of Dai using trickery and annexed his territory. In the tenth generation, King Wuling married Meng Yao and took over the state of Zhongshan, annexing land containing foreign tribes. Later, he adopted foreign dress. The people of his state civilized these peoples. It was all just like the dream of Zhao Jianzi. (From *Historical Records*.)

Zhao Jianzi had dreamt that he ascended to heaven and saw a man standing beside the supreme god Di. Later, when Zhao went out, he encountered someone blocking the road, who was the person he had seen in his dream standing beside Di. Therefore, some expressed the opinion that this was a sign of the future glory of the state of Zhao. (From Wang Chong, *Judicious Discussions*.)

13. For an explanation of this, see the commentary to Muzi's encountering the woman from Gengzong in the chapter, "The Disciple of Emptiness" [I:5n26].

14. Wu Shihuo enjoyed forming useful connections. The future Emperor Gaozu of the Tang was at one point commander in the Fen-Jin area and stayed at his home. As a result, Wu entered his employ. He participated in the capture of the capital and was made commandery duke of Taiyuan. Wu said that he once dreamt that the emperor rode on him up to heaven. The emperor laughed and said, "You are just trying to flatter me." During the Yonghui era [650–655], Emperor Gaozong took Wu's second daughter as his empress and bestowed the title of "Duke of Zhou" on Wu. During the Xianheng era [670–673], he was posthumously given the additional title of "Commandery Prince of Taiyuan" and became an attendant spirit receiving sacrifices at the ancestral temple of Emperor Gaozu. During the reign of Empress Wu [r. 690–705] seven temples of the Wu Clan were established, and he was raised to the status of an emperor, but during the Xiantian era [712], an imperial order eliminated this false title. (From *Old History of the Tang Dynasty*.)

15. Duke Jing fell into the privy and died. That morning, a minor official had dreamt that he had borne Duke Jing up to heaven on his back, but by midday, he was carrying the duke out of the privy. Subsequently, he was entombed with him as a human sacrifice. (From *Zuo's Narratives*.)

16. Formerly, there was a Hongque Reservoir in Runan. During the reign of Emperor Cheng of the Western Han, Zhai Fangjin memorialized that it be destroyed. During the Jianwu era [25–55 CE], Governor Deng Chen wanted to restore it. He heard that Xu Yang understood waterways, so he summoned Xu to discuss the matter. Xu intended to discourage the idea. That night, Xu dreamt that he went up to heaven where the supreme god Di angrily said, "Why are you trying to destroy my deep waters where dragons bathe and eliminate the benefits they bring to the people?" Yang awoke and told this to Deng Chen. A lake more than four hundred *li* in area was created which the common people were able to enjoy. (From *History of the Eastern Han Dynasty*.)

17. When He Zhizhang fell ill, he dreamt that he traveled to the residence of the supreme god Di. Several days later, he awoke and requested permission to become a Daoist priest, choosing to retire to his hometown. (From *Bo and Kong's Encyclopedia*.)

CHAPTER 2

Sun and Moon
日月

The sun and moon are signs of extremely exalted position.¹ In the past, the mother of Emperor Wu of the Western Han dreamt that a goddess gave her the sun.² And the mothers who became pregnant and gave birth to the emperors Taizong, Zhenzong, Renzong, and Ningzong of the Song all dreamt of the sun. Either they received the sun under the gowns covering their bodies, or they received the sun from a god who bestowed it on them, or the sun fell down and they caught hold of it with their hands, or the sun pressed down on them and they grasped hold of it with the front of their gowns.³ This is also the case with lesser figures such as usurpers and rulers of the barbarian Yi and Di peoples. For example, there was Sun Quan, who established the state of Wu,⁴ Liu Yuan, who proclaimed himself "king of the Han,"⁵ the Tuoba clan, who inaugurated the Northern Wei dynasty,⁶ and the Yelü clan, who established the Liao dynasty.⁷ In all of these cases, there were auspicious signs of dreams about the sun. Did not these men dominate entire regions and rule all the people there? The justice of their government and the nobility of their positions certainly corresponded to the symbolic image of the sun. How excellent the words of Duke Ling of Wei were when he said, "He who dreams about the ruler dreams of seeing the sun." For, dreaming about the God of the Stove cannot indicate him.⁸ Because Duke Jing of Qi dreamt of battling two suns and suffering defeat, someone realized how he could recover from his illness.⁹ Because of a dream that the sun circled about a military camp, it became known that Emperor Ming of the Jin had arrived there.¹⁰ Emperor Wu of the Chen dreamt that gods clothed in vermillion offered him the sun in their hands and that he ingested it.¹¹ Emperor Xuanzong of the Tang dreamt that a soldier in crimson trousers carried him on his back out of a well.¹² For the same reason, Emperor Wen of the Wei and Emperor Shizu of the Chen both dreamt that the sun fell to earth and that they took one of its three pieces into their bodies. It was a sign that they would not be able to unify the entire land.¹³

Now, the sun is the vigorous essence of pure yang, so those who draw close to it will become prominent.¹⁴ Cheng Li dreamt that he stood upright while holding the sun with both hands. Consequently, his name was changed to Yu [sunshine]. Mistress Gui dreamt that she was facing the sunrise and named her son Yang [sunrise].¹⁵ The mother of Tao Hongjing dreamt that the vigorous essence of the sun entered her body; consequently, Tao Hongjing became famous for his mastery of the techniques for achieving transcendence.¹⁶ The mother of Yang Huan dreamt that light from the sun struck her body; consequently, Yang Huan achieved high rank because of his literary compositions.¹⁷ Jia Yinlin dreamt that the sun fell on his head; consequently, he rose to the position of judicial investigator.¹⁸ Fan Yingling dreamt that suns had shone on his house; consequently, he became a vice minister.¹⁹ Yang Yan dreamt that he had climbed up a mountain where he held up the sun with both hands; consequently, he advanced to enter the Secretariat.²⁰ Zheng Guang dreamt that he drove a fast carriage that carried the sun; consequently, he attained the position of military commissioner.²¹ The governor of Hailing dreamt that he supported the sun with his body and soon was managing the confidential affairs of the government.²² The magistrate of Feiru dreamt that some people used an ox to pull out the sun, and finally he was appointed a cavalier attendant-in-ordinary. Were these not confirmations that they would draw closer to the sovereign?²³ Likewise, Mao Zhenfu dreamt that he had swallowed the sun and that his stomach felt hot. Some might have said that this was a sign of exalted position. However, the interpreter only acknowledged that Mao would become a salt official during the Chiwu era [238–250], no doubt because he possessed the complete method for comprehending dreams.²⁴

Then there is the moon, which is preeminent among all things that are yin in nature.²⁵ It, too, serves as an emissary of heaven.²⁶ Lü Qi dreamt that he had shot at the moon and, consequently, the army of Chu was defeated. For the king of the Zhou dynasty was symbolized by the sun and Chu by the moon.²⁷ In both the birth of the future Empress Xiaoyuan of the Han dynasty and the births of the daughters of Empress Lou of the Northern Qi dynasty, there were dreams of the moon entering the mother's body. Indeed, they all assumed the rank of empress or consort.²⁸ In the cases of Sun Ce and Xiao Yi, their mothers both had dreams of the moon. Sun Ce became king of Wu and set up his capital in the eastern Jiang area while Xiao Yi became emperor of the Liang dynasty and established his line in eastern Xiang. Yet their dynasties were neither long lasting nor far reaching. How could they have avoided the natural cycle of waxing and waning?[29] In his youth, Kan Ze dreamt of seeing his name in the moon; in the case of Fan Chunren, there was a dream when he was about to be born that a child fell down into the moon. It is certainly fitting that their glorious reputations have been passed down through later generations.[30]

NOTES

1. King Wen of the Zhou dreamt that the sun and moon illuminated his body. (From *Annals of the Thearchs and Kings*.)

2. Empress Xiaojing, formerly Mistress Wang, was the mother of Emperor Wu. Previously, when Emperor Jing was crown prince, the then Lady Wang dreamt that the sun had entered her body and told this to the crown prince. The crown prince replied, "This is a sign of exalted position." (From *History of the Western Han Dynasty*.) Mr. Wang commented that Lady Wang dreamt that a goddess held the sun in both hands and gave it to her. She swallowed it and consequently became pregnant, giving birth to Emperor Wu.

3. Empress Zhaoxian, formerly Mistress Du, was the mother of Emperor Taizong of the Northern Song. She dreamt that a god held the sun in both hands and bestowed it on her. Subsequently she became pregnant and gave birth to the emperor in her chamber in the Junyi Palace. (From *History of the Song Dynasty*.)

Emperor Taizong's Consort Xian, formerly Mistress Li, dreamt that the round sun pressed down on her and that she grasped hold of it with the front part of her gown. Its brilliance illuminated her entire body and so frightened her that she awoke. Later, she gave birth to Emperor Zhenzong. (From *History of the Song Dynasty*.)

Empress Zhangyi, mother of Emperor Renzong of the Northern Song, dreamt that there were two suns in the sky, one of which fell down. She caught hold of it with the front part of her gown. (From *History of the Song Dynasty*.)

Emperor Ningzong of the Southern Song was the second son of Emperor Guangzong. His mother was Empress Ciyi, formerly Mistress Li. When Guangzong was still Prince Gong, she dreamt that the sun had fallen into her courtyard and that she caught hold of it with her hands. After a while, she became pregnant and gave birth to the future Emperor Ningzong in the princely mansion. (From *History of the Song Dynasty*.)

4. When the wife of Sun Jian was pregnant with Sun Quan, she dreamt that the sun had entered her body. She told this to Sun Jian, who said, "This is a sign of exalted position. My descendants will rise in the world," (from *History of the Liu Song Dynasty*).

5. The wife of Liu Bao, Mistress Huting, prayed for a son at Dragon Gate.

Suddenly, a huge fish came to the place where sacrifices were held, and, after a long time, left. That night, she dreamt that the fish she had seen during the day had transformed into a person. In his left hand he held something that looked like half a chicken's egg. Its brilliance was extraordinary. He gave it to Mistress Huting and said, "This is the vigorous essence of the sun. If you swallow it, you will produce a noble son." She awoke and told this to Liu Bao who said, "This is an extremely auspicious sign." Subsequently she gave birth to Liu Yuan. (From *History of the Jin Dynasty*.)

The mother of Liu Cong, Mistress Zhang [fl. late 3rd cent.], dreamt that the sun entered her body. She awoke and told Liu Yuan who said, "This is an extremely auspicious sign." She was pregnant for fifteen months before giving birth to Liu Cong. (From *History of the Jin Dynasty*.)

6. Empress He, mother of Emperor Taizu of the Northern Wei, dreamt that the sun emerged from her bedchamber. She awoke and saw a brilliant light pass from her window into the sky. Immediately, she felt stimulated and later, on the seventh day of the seventh lunar month, she gave birth to Emperor Taizu north of Canhe Slope. (From *History of the Northern Wei Dynasty*.)

Empress Gao, mother of Emperor Shizong of the Northern Wei, dreamt that she was being chased by the sun and hid under a bed. The sun transformed into a dragon and wound itself around her in several coils. She awoke with fright. Later, she became pregnant and gave birth to the emperor in the Pingcheng Palace. (From *History of the Northern Wei Dynasty*.)

When Empress Gao of the Northern Wei dynasty was young, she dreamt that she was standing in a hall when the light of the sun shone on her through the window. It was brilliant and hot. She fled from it toward the east and toward the west, but the light continued to shine its rays on her. This repeated itself for several nights. The empress felt this was very strange, so she told her father Gao Yang [n.d.]. He asked a man from Liaodong, Min Zong, about this, and Min said, "This is an unusual sign. It means an exalted position beyond words. The sun is the virtue of a ruler and the symbolic image of emperors and kings. If the sun shone on your daughter's body, then it must mean that she has been granted a most favorable destiny." Later, Empress Gao indeed entered the palace where she gave birth to Emperor Shizong and Prince Guangping. (From *History of the Northern Wei Dynasty*.)

7. Mistress Xiao was the mother of Yelü Yi, Emperor Taizu of the Liao. She dreamt that the sun had fallen into her body. She became pregnant and gave birth to Yi. (From *History of the Jin [Jurchen] Dynasty*.)

8. Duke Ling of Wei made Yong Yi and Mi Zixia his confidants. The two men took complete control of the Duke's authority and kept his high officials in the dark. Then Tu Zhen told the duke, "The other day I dreamt I saw Your Excellency." The duke replied, "What kind of dream did you have?" Tu replied, "I dreamt I saw the God of the Stove." The duke became angry and said, "I have heard that when one dreams of a ruler, one dreams about the sun. Now, you have dreamt about the God of the Stove and said it indicated me. Why is this?" Tu answered, "The sun illuminates everything under heaven, and nothing can be kept in the dark. But this is not so in the case of the stove. Someone may light a fire in the front but someone standing behind may not see it. I fear that some

people may be lighting a fire in front of you; therefore, I dreamt about the God of the Stove." (From *Intrigues of the Warring States*.)

9. Duke Jing of Qi dreamt one night of battling two suns and suffering defeat. When Master Yan attended him at court, the duke told him, "This was my dream, so I must be fated to die." Master Yan replied, "Let us summon the dream interpreter." When the interpreter arrived, Master Yan met him at the gate and told him the reason for being summoned. He had the interpreter say to the duke, "Your illness is yin and the sun is yang. A single yin cannot defeat two yang, so you will recover from your illness." After three days, the duke's illness abated. (From *Remarks While at Leisure from Watering the Fields*.)

10. When Wang Dun rebelled, the emperor personally went forth to spy on Wang's army. That night, Wang dreamt that the sun circled around his military camp. He awoke and realized what had happened, saying, "The yellow-whiskered boy of the Xianbei tribe has come." The emperor's mother came from the Xianbei tribe. Wang urgently sent men out after him, but they could not catch him. (From *History of the Jin Dynasty*.)

11. Chen Baxian, Emperor Wu of the Chen, once visited Yixing and stayed with the Xu family. At night, he dreamt that heaven opened up for several dozen feet and four gods clothed in vermillion appeared offering him the sun in their hands. They ordered Emperor Wu to open his mouth and ingest it. When he awoke, his stomach still felt hot. (From *History of the Chen Dynasty*.)

12. Emperor Xuanzong of the Tang [r. 712–756] dreamt that he had fallen into a well and that a soldier wearing crimson trousers carried him out on his back. The next day he sent men to search for the soldier throughout the palace gardens and found Ma Xian wearing crimson trousers. He was taken to see His Majesty who asked, "What did you dream about last night?" He replied, "I dreamt that I carried the sun on my back out of a well and went up to heaven." His Majesty scrutinized him closely. Ma's appearance resembled the person in the dream, so the emperor bestowed 50,000 cash on him. (From *A Record of a Purposeful Mind*.)

13. When Emperor Wen of the Wei was a prince, he dreamt that the sun fell to earth and broke into three pieces. He obtained one of these and took it into his body. (From *Collected Conversations*.)

Emperor Shizu of the Chen dreamt of two suns battling each other, one large and one small. The larger one lost its brilliance and fell to earth. Its color was a pure yellow, and it was as large as a dipper. Shizu took one of the three pieces into which it had broken and took it into his body. (From *History of the Chen Dynasty*.)

14. The sun possesses all five colors and is the vigorous essence of pure yang. It is a symbolic image of the virtue of a noble man. (From the *Master Shi*.)

15. Cheng Li dreamt that he had climbed up Mount Tai and stood upright while holding the sun with both hands. He told this to Emperor Taizu, who added the graph for sun 日 on top of that for Li 立, thereby changing Cheng's name to Yu 昱 [sunshine]. (From *History of the Wei Dynasty*.)

Gui Yang, whose courtesy name was Yanwen, was from Bianliang. His mother Mistress Yang dreamt that just before he was born, she was facing the sunrise over East Mountain. Above were faint clouds that came and covered her. Therefore, she named him Yang [sunrise]. He became a metropolitan graduate in the first year of the Zhishun era [1330], but later was captured by the Henan rebel Fan Meng. In the end, he was not harmed and rose to the position of minister of the Ministry of Rites. (From *History of the Yuan Dynasty*.)

16. Tao Hongjing's mother had dreamt that the vigorous essence of the sun had entered her body before he was born. (From *The Bookcase of the Clouds*.)

17. The mother of Yang Huan dreamt that a ray of sunlight from the southeast struck her body and that a divinity beside her gave her a brush. Not long afterward, Yang Huan was born. His father gave him the name Huan [bright talent] and the courtesy name Huanran [radiant] because he regarded the dream as symbolizing future literary brilliance. (From *History of the Yuan Dynasty*.)

18. Jia Yinlin submitted a memorial stating, "Your humble official once dreamt that the sun fell down and that I supported it with my head." The emperor replied, "Does this not refer to Us?" Therefore, he appointed Jia judicial investigator of the capital. (From *Bo and Kong's Encyclopedia*.)

19. Fan Yingling, whose courtesy name was Qisou, was from Fengcheng. While he was still in the womb, his grandfather dreamt that double suns shone into the courtyard. He became a metropolitan graduate in the first year of the Kaixi era [1205] and later rose to the position of vice minister of the Court of Judicial Review. (From *History of the Song Dynasty*.)

20. Yang Yan of the Tang dynasty dreamt that he climbed up a mountain and observed the sun whose light was glorious. He held it up with his left and right hands. Later, he rose to the position of grand councilor. (From *Records from the Grand Hall*.)

21. At the end of the Huichang era [841–846], Zheng Guang dreamt that he drove a large carriage that carried the sun and moon. He reached the middle of a crossroads where their brilliance illuminated the six directions. After he awoke, he had the dream interpreted, and the interpreter told him, "You will quickly rise to an exalted position." Within a month, Emperor Xuanzong [r. 846–859] ascended the throne and Zheng Guang, who had raised a militia, became general of the guards and later rose to military commissioner of Pinglu. (From *Old History of the Tang Dynasty*.)

22. When the future Emperor Shizu was governor of Hailing, he dreamt that the sun fell down onto his body, and soon thereafter, he was summoned back to the capital to manage the confidential affairs of the government. (From *The Taiping Miscellany*.)

23. During the Northern Wei dynasty, Lü Ying served as magistrate of Feiru and dreamt that the sun fell down into the water at Huangshan, where he was living. The local people tried to use an ox-drawn cart to pull it out but couldn't. However, Ying embraced it and carried it back. Later, he attained the position of cavalier attendant-in-ordinary. (From *Exceptional Dreams*.)

24. During the illegitimate Wu dynasty, Mao Zhenfu repeatedly served as a district magistrate. When he went to take the official examinations in Guangling, he dreamt that he swallowed the sun. Upon awakening, his stomach still felt hot. He asked Attendant Censor Yang Tingshi about this. Yang said, "This dream signifies greatness, but you are not capable of such responsibility. Based on what you have said, you will only become a salt official during the Chiwu era [238–

250]." Yang's words indeed turned out to be true. (From *A Record of Inquests into Spirits*.)

25. The moon is preeminent among all things that are yin in nature. It is the symbolic image of imperial consorts, high officials, and nobles. (From *History of the Western Han Dynasty*.) Government ministers and servicemen are like the moon. (From *The Documents of Antiquity*.)

26. The sun and moon are the emissaries of heaven. (From the *Master of Huainan*.)

27. For an explanation, refer to the commentary on Lü Qi shooting at the moon in the chapter, "The Disciple of Emptiness" [I:5n19].

28. Empress Xiaoyuan was the aunt of Wang Mang. Her father was Wang Jin and her mother was Mistress Li. Mistress Li dreamt that the moon entered her body and then gave birth to the empress. (From *History of the Western Han Dynasty*.)

Empress Lou gave birth to two daughters, and both times she dreamt that the moon entered her body. The daughters became empresses during the Northern and Eastern Wei dynasties. (From *History of the Northern Qi Dynasty*.)

29. The wife of Sun Jian of Wu dreamt that the moon had entered her body when she first became pregnant with their son Ce. (From *History of the Liu Song Dynasty*.)

Emperor Wu of the Liang dreamt that a monk blind in one eye and holding an incense burner was reborn in the royal palace. Soon afterward, an imperial concubine attended the emperor, and he favored her. The imperial concubine dreamt that the moon had descended into her body, and she subsequently became pregnant. On the day *dingsi* in the eighth lunar month of the seventh year of the Tianjian era [508], the future Emperor Shizu was born. He was indeed blind in one eye. (From *History of the Liang Dynasty*.)

30. At thirteen years of age, Kan Ze dreamt that he saw the graphs of his name emblazoned in the moon. (From *Biographies of Eminent Worthies of the Past from Guiji*.)

On the night before Fan Chunren was born, his mother Mistress Li dreamt that a child fell into the moon and that she caught hold of him in her sleeves. After she awoke, she gave birth to Fan. (From *History of the Song Dynasty*.)

CHAPTER 3

Thunder and Rain
雷雨

Thunder, rain, stars, lightning, clouds, violent winds, fire, ice, and clear and dark skies are all symbolic images of heaven. Wind and thunder indicate commands, rain indicates benefits from a superior, while auspicious stars, colorful clouds, lightning, and fire indicate literary brilliance. Ice melting indicates marriage. The reasons behind these are subtle indeed. During the Northern Qi dynasty, Dou Tai's mother dreamt that thunder and lightning dazzled her eyes and, consequently, she gave birth to him.[1] The mother of Zong Ze dreamt that thunder and lightning illuminated her body and, consequently, she gave birth to him.[2] He who dreamt of wearing a hat in the rain did not enjoy a glorious destiny, but he who dreamt of encountering thunder while on a river consequently ruled over a district a hundred *li* in extent.[3]

As for stars, they are exceptional forms of primal *qi*-energy.[4] How could they be symbolic images of commoners? Thus, the Northern Dipper indicates the position of a minister. When scholars dream of it, this means they will achieve the highest ranks in the official examinations.[5] The star Changgeng formed a harmonious correlation with Academician Li.[6] The star Old Man responded to Grand Master of Remonstrance Zang.[7] The mother of Huang Kang dreamt that she swallowed a star; consequently, Kang became renowned during the Song dynasty.[8] The mother of Huang Jin dreamt that a star entered her body; consequently, he enjoyed a notable career during the Yuan dynasty.[9] Gao Huan of the Northern Qi dynasty walked among the stars, and Wu Qiao of the Southern Tang possessed a name that matched that of a star.[10] From this, one can understand that dreams of stars coming into contact with the body are auspicious, while stars falling down into the countryside are unlucky.

Fire is also the vigorous essence of yang. Violent winds are explosive *qi*-energies. Earl Zhi dreamt that a brilliant fire appeared in the states of Qin and Chu. Confucius dreamt that a red whirlwind arose in the commandery of Fengpei.[11] Colorful clouds that transformed into *feng*-birds were an auspicious sign of the birth of Xu Ling.[12] Speaking to someone from on top of firm ice was a fortunate omen that Linghu Ce would serve as a matchmaker.[13] A colorful rainbow soaring to heaven confirmed that Li Xiong would usurp a royal title.[14] A malevolent whirlwind blew down a house, and someone uttered sighs of regret that King Jie of the Xia was about to be destroyed.[15] When a piece of cloud entered his mouth, someone knew that his literary reputation would flourish.[16] It was predicted that enemies in the north would cause a calamity after clouds obscured the stars.[17] Zhang Zhuo dreamt that auspicious clouds covered his body; consequently, he earned first-place for his essays in the official examinations.[18] The mother of Cui Shaoxuan dreamt that a book was bestowed on her at the edge of an azure cloud; consequently, she gave birth to a daughter who became a transcendent.[19] The dreams of Wen Qian, who prayed for clear weather, of Xu Fen, who prayed for snow, and of Daxi Wu, who asked for rain,[20] were all effective because of their absolute sincerity, so that above and below were able to communicate. This is, moreover, a regular cosmic pattern and should hardly cause astonishment.

NOTES

1. During the Northern Qi Dynasty, the mother of Dou Tai dreamt that violent winds and thunder arose. It appeared as if it would rain, so she stepped out into the courtyard to observe the weather: lightning dazzled her eyes as a torrent of rain drenched her. When she awoke, she was sweating with fright. She subsequently became pregnant, but was unable to give birth when the time arrived. She was terribly afraid, but a spirit-medium said, "If you soak your skirt as you cross a river, you will have an easy delivery." So, she went to a river and saw someone who told her, "You are about to give birth to a son who will attain an exalted position. You should alter your residence so that you face southward." After Dou Tai's mother followed these instructions, she soon gave birth to Dou Tai. (From *History of the Northern Dynasties*.)

2. Mistress Liu was the mother of Zong Ze, whose courtesy name was Rulin. She dreamt of immense thunder and lightning from heaven that illuminated her body. The next day, Zong Ze was born. (From the *History of the Song Dynasty*.)

3. Editor Wang and Administrative Assistant Xu both wished to become district magistrates. Wang dreamt that he was walking along in the rain while wearing a hat. Xu dreamt that he was surrounded by a clap of thunder as he was traveling on a river. They consulted Ye Guangyuan, and Ye said, "Wang will not obtain

such an office because walking in the rain while wearing a hat means that he will not be drenched by benefits from above. Xu will obtain it because a river *[jiang]* implies a river bank *[pu]*." Subsequently, Xu became magistrate of Jiangpu. (From *A Record of Inner Light*.)

4. Stars are exceptional forms of primal *qi*-energy. (From *Events from the Epoch of the Three Sovereigns and Five Thearchs*.)

5. When Yuan Guo was about to take the examinations, he dreamt that he stood beneath the Northern Dipper. Consequently, he placed seventh among the successful candidates. (From *Random Notes*.)

6. The mother of Li Bo dreamt about the star Changgeng, so when he was born, she named him in accordance with it. (From *Old History of the Tang Dynasty*.)

7. When Grand Master of Remonstrance Zang was young, he once dreamt that his father summoned him into the courtyard and pointed up to the sky saying, "There is the star Old Man." He looked up and indeed saw a yellow star that was bright and glistening. Therefore, he worshipped it by offering a sacrifice. After Zang awoke, he changed his name to Bing because the star was leaving the phase denoted as *bing* and entering the phase *ding*. He also took the courtesy name Mengshou [dreaming of longevity]. (From *Leisurely Reading*.)

8. Huang Kang's courtesy name was Jichen. His mother dreamt that a star descended toward her body. She caught it with both hands and swallowed it. Afterward, she became pregnant. (From *History of the Song Dynasty*.)

9. Huang Jin's courtesy name was Jinqing. His mother Mistress Zhang [fl. early 14th cent.] dreamt that a giant star descended into her body. She subsequently became pregnant and gave birth to him after twenty-four months. (From *History of the Yuan Dynasty*.)

10. Emperor Gaozu of the Northern Qi dynasty was surnamed Gao and posthumously named Huan. He once dreamt that he was walking among a multitude of stars. (From *History of the Northern Dynasties*.)

Wu Qiao lived during the Southern Tang dynasty. He studied hard despite the poverty of his family. There was a Buddhist priest who dreamt of a great star and that someone said to him, "I *[wu]* am the star Qiao." After he awoke, he sought out Wu Qiao and offered him support. Later, Wu was ranked first among the metropolitan graduates and served as court gentleman for evaluations. (From *Exquisite Words on the Origins of Surnames*.)

11. After Earl Zhi was defeated, he dreamt that a fire appeared in the west, so he fled to Qin. He then dreamt that a fire appeared in the south, so he fled to Chu. (From *Trifling Conversations*.) For the red whirlwind, see the commentary on a red vapor and the three sophora trees in the chapter, "The Disciple of Emptiness" [I:5n10].

12. Mistress Zang, the mother of Xu Ling, dreamt that multicolored clouds transformed into *feng*-birds who gathered on her left shoulder. Consequently, she gave birth to Xu Ling. (From *History of the Chen Dynasty*.) See the commentary on a celestial *qilin*-beast in the chapter, "The *Feng* and Other Birds" [II:14n5].

13. Suo Dan, whose courtesy name was Shuche, was skilled at interpreting dreams. Linghu Ce dreamt that he was standing on the ice and talking to some-

one underneath it. Suo Dan said, "'On top of the ice' indicates yang and 'beneath the ice' indicates yin. It refers to a matter involving male and female. If a scholar wishes to take a wife, it should be before the ice melts. This indicates a marriage. Your standing on the ice and talking to someone underneath symbolizes yang talking to yin, an indication of matchmaking. You will act as a matchmaker for someone." Soon afterward, Governor Tian Bao asked Linghu Ce to arrange a match between Tian's son and the daughter of a local man, Mr. Zhang. They were married in the second month of spring. (From *History of the Jin Dynasty*.)

14. The elder son of Li Te was named Ying and his younger son was named Xiong. Their mother Mistress Luo dreamt that two rainbows rose up to heaven, but one of them broke in the middle. Mistress Luo said, "It seems that of my two sons, the elder will die, but the younger will attain a very exalted position." Indeed, Li Xiong became king of Shu. (From Chang Qu, *Record of the Lands South of Mount Hua*.)

15. For an explanation, see the commentary to the dreams of a malevolent whirlwind and a great bolt of lightning in the chapter, "The Disciple of Emptiness" [I:5n7].

16. When Zhang Jiong was young, he experienced difficulties as a poet and was unable to achieve any success. He dreamt that a multicolored cloud descended from the sky and that he grabbed a piece and swallowed it. From then on, he was able to master the art of poetry. (From *Elegant Chats from a Commandery Studio*.)

17. For an explanation, see the commentary to the statement that the graph for "sophora" *[huai]* is composed of the elements "tree" *[mu]* and "ghost" *[gui]* in the chapter, "Written Graphs" [II:10n2].

18. When Zhang Zhuo was competing for the metropolitan graduate degree, he went to Huaizhou where he dreamt that auspicious clouds covered his body. That same year, his essays earned him first-place in the examinations. (From *The Taiping Miscellany*.)

19. Cui Shaoxuan was the youngest daughter of Cui Gong, prefect of Fenzhou. Her mother dreamt that a divinity dressed in raw silk rode on a red dragon, holding a purple book that he bestowed on her at the edge of an azure cloud. Thereafter, she was pregnant for fourteen months before giving birth to Cui Shaoxuan. (From *The Taiping Miscellany*.)

20. Wen Qian's courtesy name was Zhongru. The local magistrate was filled with anxiety when heavy rains destroyed the economy of the people. Wen Qian had been appointed an administrator in the local revenue section and received instructions to hold a fast. At night, he dreamt that an elderly, white-haired man said to him, "Why have you delayed in coming here?" Wen Qian told all this to the magistrate who replied, "In the past, Yu the Great dreamt of an emissary from the Cang River. Your dream is comparable." Indeed, the skies cleared on the following day. (From *Biographies of Eminent Elders of the Past from Changsha*.)

When Xu Fen was magistrate of Caizhou, he once prayed for snow. At night, he dreamt that an emissary told him that the snow had already arrived. The dreams of his family members were similar, and the next day, there was a heavy snowfall. (From *Exquisite Words on the Origins of Surnames*.)

Daxi Wu of the Later Zhou dynasty held the title of grand guardian while serving as prefect of Tongzhou. At the time, there was a drought, so he sacrificed at the temple at Mount Hua. Pulling himself up with the help of vines, he ascended the mountain, slept on the grass, and dreamt that someone dressed in white grasped hold of his hands to console him. Daxi Wu awoke frightened, but the next morning, there was a timely rain. (From *Exquisite Words on the Origins of Surnames*.)

CHAPTER 4

Mountains and Rivers
山川

Mountains, rivers, roads, soil, and rocks all belong to the category of earth. Wang Chong said in his *Judicious Discussions* that mountains, hills, towers, and terraces are symbolic images of official position. When someone dreams of ascending mountains and hills, or climbing up towers and terraces, he will soon obtain an official position. These words can be trusted. Peaks and palace pavilions are signs of exalted rank. Rivers, seas, and waves are indications of wealth. Therefore, after Liu Muzhi dreamt of the sea and a beautiful peak, he was summoned to serve in office.[1] Li Xuzhong dreamt that Mount Tai split open; consequently, he passed away.[2] Xue Chu dreamt that Zhang Liang hung silk threads on a mountain.[3] Xie Feng dreamt that Zheng You drowned while fighting over money.[4] Emperor Xuanzong of the Tang dreamt that he traveled to a well at Mount Qian.[5] Emperor Shizu of the Southern Qi dynasty dreamt that he walked in the field of King Wen of the Zhou.[6] Emperor Wu of the Western Han dreamt that he had climbed Mount Song.[7] Emperor Wen of the Sui dreamt that he encountered a flood.[8] A Song dynasty ruler dreamt that the Yellow River dried up.[9] A Liang dynasty ruler dreamt that the water in the ditches beside the fields was deep.[10] Zheng Xie dreamt that he met a functionary and bathed in a pool.[11] Zhang Min dreamt that he was searching for a friend and lost his way.[12] Xie Lingyun dreamt of the cave at Mount Mao.[13] Zhao Xiangjing dreamt of a river lined with willows.[14] Sun Zanming dreamt that he bathed in a hot spring.[15] Deng Shizai dreamt that he was contemplating a mountain and a stream.[16] She who dreamt of picking up the vigorous essence of a chime-stone gave birth to a fine son.[17] He who dreamt of washing in the West River attained excellence in his writings.[18] A dream of hills suddenly arising confirmed a rocky road ahead.[19] A dream

Mountains and Rivers 121

that the Central Plains became smooth in the end was confirmed when the world was pacified.[20] There was a dream that a pagoda was presented by the edge of the sea as a monk uttered astonishing words.[21] There was a dream that the land in the southeast tilted, so it was difficult to pacify the Jiangzuo region.[22] And yet, wasn't Yao's dream that he ascended a mountain riding a dragon a sign that he would occupy the throne?[23] When Emperor Taizu of the Ming dreamt that flowing water reached his feet, wasn't this a sign of military success along the border?[24]

As for dreams of towers, terraces, and cities, their significances differ. Emperor Ming of the Eastern Han dreamt that a golden man walked into his palace.[25] Emperor Xuanzong of the Tang dreamt that he traveled and met transcendents in the Moon Palace.[26] Wang Su dreamt that he visited the Jade Capital.[27] Niu Yi dreamt of arriving at a mansion in heaven.[28] Gentleman for Closing Court Fang dreamt about the Jade Flower Palace.[29] Wang Pingfu dreamt about the Palace of the Divine Fungus.[30] Cai Junmo dreamt that he was lying down in a watchtower.[31] Shen Yu dreamt of the graphs "House of Mr. Fan."[32] The ancestor of Fan Yingling dreamt that double suns shone upon his house.[33] The mother of Zhang Meng dreamt that she wore a seal of office and ascended a tower.[34] Duke Zhuang of Wei dreamt that he had arrived at the Kunwu Observatory.[35] Emperor Shizu of the Southern Qi dynasty dreamt that he walked up the stairs to the Hall of the Great Ultimate.[36] Fu Youyi dreamt that he ascended to the Hall of Benevolent Dew.[37] Xun Boyu dreamt that he climbed atop the city walls of Guangling.[38] Cui Yuanzong dreamt that he went to Lüxin Ward.[39] Ding Yuanzhen dreamt that he visited the Yellow Ox Temple.[40] And, then there was the case of Shi Manqing who dreamt that he had become the ruler of the Hibiscus City.[41] Ouyang Zhongchun became Lord of the Changbai Mountains.[42] Jiang Ji's son became a section manager at Mount Tai.[43] The elder Zhao became a city god in Lizhou.[44] Emperor Xuanzong erected a palace for the investigation commissioner from the nine heavens.[45] Lu Ji administered nine prefectures from Yangming Superior Prefecture.[46] Cui Wan'an's household offered prayers to the Lord of the Earth for Cui's recovery from illness.[47] Xu Jing begot a son who became a village god.[48] And, there are many other dreams that are so strange and outlandish that they cannot be thoroughly investigated.

NOTES

1. Liu Muzhi dreamt that he was sailing on the ocean with Emperor Wu of the Liu Song dynasty when they encountered strong winds. He looked down and

saw that two white dragons were carrying the boat between them so that they soon arrived at a mountain. The mountain's peak was tall and beautiful, and Liu was overjoyed. After Emperor Wu conquered the capital, Liu Muzhi was summoned to become an assistant magistrate of a prefecture. (From *History of the Chen Dynasty*.)

2. Just before Li Xuzhong fell ill, he told his friend Han Yu, "I dreamt that Mount Tai had split open and that a red and yellow substance like gold flowed out." Someone said that this is what is called the "great return." After Li died, Han Yu consulted a dream interpreter who said, "The mountain symbolizes the trigram *Gen:* 'Keeping Still,' which also indicates the back of the body. 'Splitting open and flowing out' is a symbolic image of ulcers. The 'great return' meant that he would pass away." (From "Epitaph for Li Xuzong" in *Collected Works of Han Changli*.)

3. Xue Chu dreamt that Zhang Liang hung silk threads on a mountain. After he awoke, he told this to Zhang, who had the dream interpreted. He was told, "The components meaning 'silk threads on a mountain' form the graph *you.* Doesn't this mean that you will become an official in Youzhou?" Within a year, Zhang Liang became the prefect of Youzhou. (From *History of the Northern Wei Dynasty*.)

4. Xie Feng and Zheng You were good friends. Xie unexpectedly dreamt that Zheng was fighting with someone over money and drowned, and that he then provided Zheng with a coffin. Xie suddenly awakened and immediately went over to Zheng's house and told him everything. Zheng You said, "Yesterday, I dreamt that I was fighting with someone over money and fell into the privy and died. You provided me with a coffin." It was just like the previous dream. (From *In Search of the Supernatural*.)

5. The Well of Our Dream is located at Mount Qian within the Palace of the Pure Source. Emperor Xuanzong of the Tang [r. 712–756] once dreamt that he had traveled here, and because of this he bestowed the name. (From *The Comprehensive Gazetteer*.)

6. Emperor Shizu dreamt that someone indicated to him that the place where he was walking was called "The Field of King Wen." (From *History of the Southern Qi Dynasty*.)

7. Emperor Wu dreamt one night that he had ascended Mount Song together with Li Shaojun. When they reached halfway up the mountain, an emissary in an embroidered robe rode down out of the clouds on a dragon, holding a document. He said, "The Lord Taiyi summons you." When the emperor awoke, he told this to his most intimate officials, saying, "According to Our dream, Li Shaojun will soon depart from Us." (From *An Unofficial Biography of Emperor Wu of the Western Han*.)

8. Emperor Wen of the Sui dreamt that floodwater had inundated the city. He was repelled by this dream and consequently moved the capital to Daxing. An interpreter said, "'Floodwater' *[hongshui]* is the name of the future Emperor Gaozu of the Tang." (From *Excellent Stories of the Sui and Tang Dynasties*.)

9. A Song dynasty ruler fell ill and dreamt one night that the waters of the Yellow River dried up. His countenance was filled with anxiety, for he regarded the dragon as symbolizing the monarch. That there was no water in the Yellow

River meant that the dragons would no longer possess their underwater residences. At that time, a dream interpreter said, "When the graph for 'river' 河 loses the component meaning 'water' 氵, it becomes the graph meaning 'to be able to' 可. Your Majesty will be able to recover from your illness." The emperor was delighted, and his illness indeed subsided. (From *Ocean of Jade.*)

10. Cao Wu was able to recognize talent in people. In the beginning when the future Emperor Wu of the Liang was in Xiangyang, only Cao Wu treated him generously. Cao said to him, "Your Excellency will certainly attain an exalted position, but I shall not live to see it. Now I would like to entrust my young sons to you." At that time, Emperor Wu was encamped and short of funds. He borrowed the sum of 170,000 from Cao Wu. But when Emperor Wu ascended the throne, he forgot about these kindnesses. In the second year of the Tianjian era [503], Emperor Wu suddenly dreamt that he was walking along in the ditches below the field paths where the water was so deep on both sides that it seemed bottomless. He was feeling terribly afraid when, suddenly, he saw Cao Wu approach. Cao carried the emperor on his back so he could pass through the area and said, "Your Excellency is the ruler of the world now, but have you forgotten my words when I entrusted my sons to you? They are now cold and hungry. You might return the 170,000 I previously lent you in the form of a residence in the city." Emperor Wu awoke and had one of his scribes send the money as a repayment, and he gave them a residence in the city. The sons Shicheng and Shizong both received official positions. (From *History of the Chen Dynasty.*)

11. Before Zheng Xie rose to an exalted position, he fell ill during an epidemic. He dreamt that he arrived in a place resembling a palace where a functionary welcomed him most respectfully. Zheng told the functionary, "I would like to take a cool bath." The functionary replied, "It has already been prepared for you, sir." He was led to a small pool whose tiled walls were made of brilliant jade and whose water was shimmering. Zheng sat down on the tiles and bathed his body. Suddenly, he saw that scales were growing on both his arms, and when he looked at his reflection in the water, he saw that there were already horns on his head. Frightened, he immediately got out. The functionary said, "This is the Pool of the Jade Dragon. What a pity that you did not immerse yourself in the middle of it, for then you would have become a prime minister." Then, Zheng awoke. Later, he passed the official examinations and wrote a poem with the lines, "A clap of thunder arose from the earth; it was, after all, Mr. White Dragon." (From the "Biography of Zheng Xie of the Palace Gate.")

12. During the period of the Six Feudal States [ca. 240–221 BCE], Zhang Min and Gao Hui were friends. They often thought of each other but were unable to meet. Zhang then went in search of him in a dream, but halfway along the road, he lost his way. (From the *Master Hanfei.*)

13. "One night while traveling I dreamt that I saw a cave at Mount Mao at Chuling southeast of the capital. In the morning, I obtained one of the *Cave Scriptures,* which recorded information about Mount Luofu. It stated that Mount Mao stands at the entrance to Lake Dongting, from where one can reach Mount Luofu to the south. This accorded with what I had seen in my dream. Thus, I was moved to write 'Rhapsody on Mount Luofu.'" (From "Preface to Rhapsody on Mount Luofu" by Xie Lingyun.)

14. When Zhao Xiangjing entered a certain protectorate, he said to two administrative assistants there, "A mile or two ahead there should be a river; beneath the willows along the river should be an official standing in shabby clothes." It turned out to be exactly as he had said. The two assistants asked him how he knew and Zhao replied, "I dreamt about this journey some thirty years ago." (From *A Record of the Excellent Conversations of Liu Binke*.)

15. Sun Zanming served as prefect of Fuzhou. Previously, while commandery defender of Wujiang during the reign of King Wusu of Wu-Yue, he dreamt that he was bathing in a hot spring. At this point, he was proceeding toward Fuzhou and just before arriving saw a waterfall along the route. Sun asked an aide about this and was told, "This is a hot spring." Then, he understood his earlier dream and wanted to draw some of the water from it to bathe in. But the aide said, "The water is not very good right here. It is much better in Fuzhou." When he arrived at the official residence, Sun quickly had water taken from the spring there and bathed in it. (From *Complete History of the Wu-Yue Dynasty*.)

16. Deng Ai of Wei, whose courtesy name was Shizai, was attacking Shu when he dreamt that he was sitting on top of a mountain where a stream was flowing. He consulted Yuan Shao about this, and Yuan said, "A stream atop a mountain signifies difficulty. Benefit lies in proceeding southwest, where you will gain success, but not toward the northeast, where the road becomes difficult. If you take the latter route, you will certainly conquer Shu, but would you be able to return alive?" (From *History of the Three Kingdoms*.)

17. The mother of Gao Lin performed the spring bathing ritual in the Si River. She saw a stone in it that was brilliant and glistening, so she picked it up and returned home. That night, she dreamt that someone in a formal hat and gown resembling a transcendent said to her, "The stone that you picked up and brought home is the vigorous essence of a chime-stone that appears to float in the water. If you preserve it, you will certainly give birth to a fine son." The mother awoke with fright and was soaked in sweat. Shortly thereafter, she became pregnant and later gave birth to a son. Therefore, she named him Lin [gem] and his courtesy name was Jimin [jade-like fourth son]. (From *History of the Northern Zhou Dynasty*.)

18. Wang Renyu dreamt that his stomach and intestines had been cut open and that he washed them in the waters of the West River. There, he saw that the sand and stones all resembled ancient graphs, so he drank from the water. The quality of his literary imagination grew. Consequently, he titled an anthology of his poems *Collected Works from West River*. (From *History of the Five Dynasties*.)

19. When Kong Ji set forth with his army, he dreamt that he was walking along the road toward the Xuanyang Gate. When he looked ahead, he saw that hills had arisen everywhere. After awakening, he secretly told this to someone saying, "The hills are a symbolic image that things will not go smoothly. The city of Jiankang will probably be difficult to conquer." (From *History of the Southern Dynasties*.)

20. During the Datong era [535–545], Emperor Gaozu of the Liang dreamt that the Central Plains 中原 [Zhongyuan] region had become flat, and the entire court proclaimed this an auspicious sign. The next morning, he told this to Zhu Yi who said, "The form of the graph *zhong* 中 [central] is composed of an inte-

rior square □ *[neifang* 內方*]* and the graph *yi* 一 [one], which sounds like 'the country will finally be unified' *[nei fang yi* 內方一*].*" In the second year of the Taiqing era [548], Hou Jing indeed surrendered. (From *History of the Liang Dynasty.*)

21. The Xiling Pagoda in Yangzhou was extremely tall. When Liu Yinzhi, a poet from Huainan, was traveling in Mingzhou, he dreamt that he seemed to be floating on the sea and saw the Buddhist priest Huaixin on the third story of the pagoda. Huaixin said to him, "I am escorting this pagoda to the Eastern Sea and will return in ten days." Liu went back to Yangzhou and immediately called on Huaixin, who said to him, "Do you remember when we met on the sea?" Liu clearly understood what he meant and made a note of the incident. Several days later, the Xiling Pagoda was destroyed in a fire. (From *Accounts of Unique and Strange Things.*)

22. When Fu Jian [r. 357–385] was about to campaign against the south, he dreamt that an entire city was filled with vegetables *[cai]*, and that the land tilted to the southeast. His empress said, "When there is a lot of food *[cai]* served, it becomes 'difficult to judge which dish is best' *[nan wei jiang,* a homonym for "there will be difficulties for a general"]. 'Land tilting toward the southeast' means it will be impossible for you to pacify the Jiangzuo region." (From *The Taiping Miscellany.*)

23. Refer to the commentary on the dream about riding a dragon in the chapter, "The Disciple of Emptiness" [I:5n3].

24. In the fourth lunar month of the twenty-first year of the Hongwu era [May-June, 1388], Lan Yu and others led a northern expedition and reached the Qulü River. They received the surrender of Grand Councilor Awanzhu and others and took numerous prisoners. The Ming army advanced to occupy the area, and Lan Yu dreamt that his spirit proceeded along a southern route. There was no water, and the soldiers became extremely thirsty. They reached a small mountain where suddenly there was a sound like an explosion, and they found that four springs were spouting forth. The soldiers and horses were rescued from their difficulty, and the excess water formed a stream. Previously, His Majesty had dreamt of a small mountain in the northwest corner of the palace where springs spouted forth, their water reaching his feet before stopping. The springs sprouting forth in Lan Yu's dream accorded with the ones in the emperor's dream. (From *Comprehensive Annals of the Ming Dynasty.*)

25. For an explanation, see the commentary to Emperor Ming's dream of a golden man more than ten feet tall in the chapter, "Gods and Strange Things" [II:12n8].

26. Emperor Xuanzong [r. 712–756] dreamt that he traveled to the Moon Palace where transcendents played "The Music of Supreme Purity." It was so fluid and sonorous, so clear and refined that it was unlike anything heard in the human world. When he woke, he wrote down the melody for the jade flute and named it "The Music of the Swirling Purple Clouds." (From *Reliable Accounts of the Kaiyuan and Tianbao Eras.*)

27. Wang Su was an edict attendant who once dreamt that he had arrived at the yellow gate towers of the Jade Capital. There, someone in a purple robe and emerald green hat said, "I am an attendant gentleman of the eastern gate. You, sir, are an attendant gentleman of the western gate." In the past, his memorials

to the emperor were widely criticized. He thought about his dream of the Jade Capital in his later years and wrote a poem:

> Hidden in the azure void is the White Jade Capital.
> In a dream, my soul flew inside its golden walls.
> When shall I stroll there again beyond the smoke and mist?
> Green Lad, the god with white teeth, has already swept the hall for me.

(From *Chats on Past and Contemporary Poetry*.)

28. The metropolitan graduate Niu Yi dreamt that he arrived at a mansion in heaven where a functionary said, "This is the Palace of Many Jades." He saw a white jade stele with vermillion graphs inside a hall there. It was covered with crimson silk gauze. The large graphs read, "Register of Celestial Transcendents in the Central Continent." This was followed by several thousand names of which he could only recognize Lü Yijian, Li Di, and Yu Jing. An old friend of his, Lü Zhen, was an official here. Niu asked him, "Are all the government ministers in this generation transcendents?" The answer given was, "Seven or eight out of ten of them are." (From Li Chuo, *True Stories from a Government Minister*.)

29. Gentleman for Closing Court Fang of Putian was seriously ill but still conscious. He dreamt that he had arrived at the Jade Flower Palace. A Daoist said, "You, sir, possessed virtue that went unrecognized so the supreme god Di has summoned you the White Jade Tower. Di had read your composition when your literary ability was tested and was very pleased, so you were appointed attendant gentleman of the Jade Flower Palace. But, because you committed a transgression, you were exiled to the mortal world below. Before long, you should be able to return here." (From *Yijian's Accounts*.)

30. When Wang Pingfu was serving at court, he dreamt one night that he arrived at a hall built across the water whose sign read, "Palace of the Divine Fungus." Someone was about to invite Wang in, saying, "I wish to escort him inside," but someone else across the water stopped him, saying, "The proper time has not arrived. We shall welcome him on another day." Wang suddenly awoke just as the bell in the palace sounded. He was always proud of his poetic skills and wrote,

> I flew in a skiff across myriad acres of waves
> To a palace with pipes and flutes named "Divine Fungus."
> The calligraphy on the sign seemed not of the human world.
> When the bell struck in the Palace of Everlasting Joy,
> I awoke from my dream.

Four years later, Wang died. (From *Jottings from the East Belvedere*.)

31. Cai Junmo was serving as prefect of Fuzhou when he became so ill that he could not attend to affairs for many days. Every night, he would dream that he was lying down on top of the drum in the city watchtower. After he recovered from his illness, he asked his administrative assistant why the third watch had not been struck for days. He was told that there had been a giant snake coiled on top of the drum for several nights, and the master drummer was afraid to approach it. Cai then realized that he was a snake demon. (From *A Record of Events from the Eastern Studio*.)

32. Shen Yu [451–509] served in the household of Xiao Ziliang, the Prince of Jingling. Previously, he had become good friends with Fan Yun. At the end of the Southern Qi dynasty, he once stayed at Fan's house and dreamt that he was sitting on top of a roof beam. He looked up to see the graphs "House of Mr. Fan" in the sky. Later, Shen told this to Emperor Gaozu of the Liang dynasty, who said, "If Fan Yun can avoid death, it will confirm this dream." (From *History of the Liang Dynasty*.)

33. See the commentary containing the phrase "rose to the position of vice minister of the Court of Judicial Review" in the chapter, "Sun and Moon" [II:2n19].

34. Zhang Huan served as governor of Wuwei. While his wife was pregnant, she dreamt that she wore Zhang Huan's official seal, climbed up a tower, and boldly sang out. A dream interpreter was consulted who said, "You will certainly give birth to a son who will come back to this place and who will end his life in this tower." Subsequently, she gave birth to Zhang Meng, who became governor of Wuwei during the Jian'an era [196–219]. After he killed Regional Inspector Handan Shang, he found himself in desperate straits when surrounded by soldiers of the regional army. Ashamed that he might be arrested, he climbed up the tower and immolated himself. His death was just as the interpretation predicted. (From *Encyclopedia for Literary Composition*.)

35. See the commentary to Duke Zhuang's dream about Hun Liangfu in the chapter, "The Disciple of Emptiness" [I:5n21].

36. When the future Emperor Shizu was in Xiangyang, he dreamt that he wore sandals of hemp and walked up the stairs of the Hall of the Great Ultimate. Yu Wen said, "Sandals are correlated with the agent 'wood,' and the graph for 'hemp' 桑 contains four elements shaped like 'ten' 十 plus two dots." After reaching the age of forty-two, Emperor Shizu ascended the throne. (From *History of the Southern Qi Dynasty*.)

37. Fu Youyi dreamt that he ascended to the Hall of Benevolent Dew and told this to a confidant. Someone reported that he intended to revolt. Fu was imprisoned and then committed suicide. (From *Bo and Kong's Encyclopedia*.)

38. When the future Emperor Gao of the Southern Qi was still in Huainan, Xun Boyu was ordered to return to Guangling. He dreamt that he climbed up the southern tower atop the city walls of Guangling. There he found two youths dressed in black, who told him, "The grass is growing tall and straight. People are competing with one another to become the emperor." Xun looked down and saw that there was grass growing on the heads of all the people below the walls. (From *History of the Southern Qi Dynasty*.)

39. When Cui Yuanzong was about to take a wife, he dreamt that someone told him, "This woman is not meant to be your wife. Your wife has just been born today." In his dream Cui followed him to the Lüxin Ward in the Eastern Capital where a woman had just given birth to a daughter. Cui awoke but believed none of this. The woman he was then negotiating for to be his wife did indeed die violently. Later, at the age of thirty-eight, he married the younger sister of Prefectural Governor Wei Zhi. She was nineteen years old, and when Cui investigated, he found that she had the same birth date as the child in his dream. (From *The Divine Matchmaker's New Book*.)

40. Ding Yuanzhen once dreamt that he and I arrived at a temple. When we exited the gate, we saw a horse with one ear. Later, Ding and I were both exiled, and we made our way up the Yangzi Gorges where we visited the Yellow Ox Temple. It was just like Ding's dream, for outside the gate we saw a clay horse that was missing one ear. We looked at each other in great astonishment. (From *Ouyang Xiu's Remarks on Poetry.*)

41. Shi Manqing had died, and someone dreamt that Shi said to him, "I have become a transcendent and rule over the Hibiscus City." After speaking, he flew off on a dark mule. (From *Ouyang Xiu's Remarks on Poetry.*)

42. Ouyang Xiu's son Zhongchun once told Su Shi, "I dreamt that a Daoist informed me, 'I am conveying the command of the supreme god Di appointing you Lord of the Changbai Mountains. What a glorious honor this is.'" One year later, Zhongchun died. (From *A Commentary on Su Dongpo's Poems.*)

43. Jiang Ji's courtesy name was Zitong. His wife dreamt that his dead son said, "At present, I have merely been made a section manager at Mount Tai, and I cannot begin to describe my anxiety and suffering. Now, west of the temple is a professional singer, Sun Ke, who is destined to become the magistrate of Mount Tai after he dies. I would like you to ask him to appoint me to a more enjoyable position. Jiang Ji paid a call on Sun Ke and told him the reason for it. Sun agreed to the request. More than a month later, the wife dreamt that her son said, "I have been given the position of overseer." (From *Bo and Kong's Encyclopedia.*)

44. Zhao Rujian was prefect of Lizhou. During the fifth lunar month of the year *jiaxu* during the Xianchun era [June–July 1274], he suddenly told his second son, "In life I am the prefect here, so in death why shouldn't I become the city god?" When asked how he knew this, he replied, "Last night I found this out in a dream." Indeed, a few days later, the elder Zhao passed away. (From *A Record of Ghosts and Other Strange Things.*)

45. During the Kaiyuan era [713–741] of the Tang, Emperor Xuanzong dreamt that a divinity in vermillion robes and a golden hat visited him and said, "I am the investigating commissioner from the nine heavens come to inspect and administer justice in the mortal world. I wish to have an earthly palace prepared for me on the northwest of Mount Lu. There is a supply of wood and a stone foundation there already. All that is required is the labor to construct it." After the emperor awoke, he sent a commissioner to examine the northwest of the mountain and, indeed, there was a foundation on the site. Several thousand giant trees suddenly arrived along the river. They were sufficient to build the halls, pavilions, loggias, and roofs. Upon completion of the construction, the commissioner dreamt that the divinity told him, "Ochre, white, vermillion, and green pigments lie in the earth north of the temple." When they dug there, it was just as he had said. (From *Records from the Grand Hall.*)

46. When Lu Ji was vice commissioner in Huainan, he was good friends with Li Chengsi. In the ninth lunar month of the year *yichou* [October 905], Lu dreamt that someone sent a mounted escort to summon him. They stopped about a mile west of the Temple of Great Illumination, arriving at a large official building whose sign read, "Yangming Superior Prefecture." After entering the gate and proceeding west, they then turned east toward a large gate. Lu dismounted and entered a chamber. A functionary led him to the foot of steps leading to a dais.

Inside the doorway stood two functionaries dressed in green who set up a table. On the table was a document which someone wearing a purple robe and holding a tablet of authority took and proclaimed: "Lu Ji will serve as a vice director in Yangming Superior Prefecture from where he is to act as director-in-chief of nine prefectures. Next year on the seventeenth day of the ninth month [Oct. 7, 906], you are to assume your duties in this superior prefecture." Then, he had the mounted escort take Lu back home. Suddenly, Lu awoke, and he told this to others. On the sixteenth day of the ninth month of the following year [Oct. 6, 906], Li Chengsi came to visit him, and Lu said, "It has already been arranged in the superior prefecture. Tomorrow I must set forth." Li asked him, "Could there be demons near you?" Lu answered, "You and I have a karmic connection. Someday we will be neighbors." The next day, Lu died and was buried at Caiman Bay. Li Chengsi later served as prefect of Chuzhou. When he died, he was buried north of Lu Ji's grave. (From *A Record of Inquests into Spirits*.)

47. When Cui Wan'an was serving as vice minister of the National Treasury in Jiangnan, he was sent to Guangling on official duties and was continuously ill from hemorrhaging of the spleen. Members of his family prayed for him at the Temple of the Lord of the Earth. Cui dreamt that a woman wearing pearl earrings, pearl sandals, and five layers of clothes all studded with pearls told him, "You should make pills with birthwort root, cardamom, and the flesh of dates. Eat twenty-nine of these with food and drink." He did as she said, and he recovered from his illness. (From *A Record of Inquests into Spirits*.)

48. At the beginning of the Xianhe era [326–334] of the Jin dynasty, Xu Jing was traveling far from home. He dreamt that he slept with his wife, who became pregnant with a son destined to become a spirit-medium and, after death, an earth god. The next year, his wife indeed gave birth. Subsequently, things were just as the dream had foretold. (From *The Taiping Miscellany*.)

CHAPTER 5

Forms and Appearances
形貌

Forms and appearances, as well as sounds, may appear as signs in dreams, but their ultimate meanings vary. The *Master Zhuang* says, "Someone who dreams of crying may go on to enjoy hunting the next day." The *Master Lie* says, "Someone who dreams of singing and dancing may wind up crying." *The Book of the Long-Willow Method* says, "Those who dream of praising others may actually wish to make a request for themselves." Thus, happiness and sadness are interdependent, for the mechanism of *qi*-energy follows its own twists and turns. By recognizing this, one can comprehend other similar instances. In antiquity, a nobleman of Jin dreamt that the prime minister of Chu was sucking out his brains.[1] Zheng Zhuo dreamt that Huang Kan spit something into his mouth.[2] Liu Zhilin dreamt that he would become a governor with one arm.[3] Rectifier Zhang dreamt that he became a pregnant woman.[4] Yang Xiong dreamt that he spit out his five *zang*-organs.[5] Zhang Shentong dreamt that he grew an ear.[6] Wei Yan dreamt that he had grown a horn on his head.[7] Zheng Xie dreamt that he grew fish-scales on his arms.[8] Zheng Xuan dreamt that a dagger pierced his heart, and Yin Zhizhang as a youth also dreamt that someone chiseled a hole into his heart.[9] Ding Gu dreamt that a pine tree grew forth from his stomach and Zhang Zhihe's mother also dreamt that a maple tree grew forth from her stomach.[10] Duke Jing of Qi dreamt of someone who was dark-complexioned and short.[11] Li Linfu dreamt about someone who had a light complexion and a beard.[12] Feng Deming dreamt that his lungs and liver had been changed.[13] Wang Renyu dreamt that he washed his intestines and stomach.[14] Empress Zhangjing dreamt that a god pierced her side with a sword.[15] The mother of Sun Jian dreamt that her intestines wound themselves around a gate in Wu.[16] Jia Bizhi dreamt that someone changed his head.[17] Sima Yi dreamt that the emperor used his thighs as a pillow.[18] Wang Chu'na had his chest cut open and received a giant mirror into it.[19] Wu Yuanzhao dreamt that his stomach was washed clean and that he received a divine talisman.[20] Shen Yue dreamt that his tongue was cut off, and a spirit-medium described the dream to him exactly.[21] A Southern Tang dynasty ruler dreamt that he was decapitated; subsequently, the succession of the crown prince proceeded smoothly.[22] Emperor Shizu of the Southern Qi dynasty dreamt about growing hair all over his body; subsequently, he assumed the throne.[23] The wife of Zhang Jing'er dreamt that her entire body was burning hot; subsequently, her husband was executed.[24] Scholar Tao dreamt that he had exchanged his eyes for those of demons, so he never attained a high position.[25] Governor Li had a dream that his head transformed into a tiger's; consequently, he was ennobled.[26] Someone dreamt that he had been given a beard, and he became a grand councilor.[27] Someone dreamt that somebody else selected another nose for him, and he finished his career as a bureau director.[28] Li Guang dreamt that his mind was suffering.[29] Liu Dan dreamt that he lost his hair.[30] King Zhao of the Zhou dreamt that someone rubbed his chest.[31] Emperor Wen of the Sui dreamt that he only possessed a single fist.[32] Mi Yuanzong dreamt that his wife had black marks on her face.[33] Song Luo's wife dreamt that the Buddha's hand was like a mat.[34] Doulu Rong's wife dreamt of someone dripping blood, and she avoided the chaos of war.[35] Gu Cong dreamt about his mother's genitals, and his life was preserved.[36] There was a dream of blackened buttocks, and thus it was known that the future Duke Cheng of Jin had received a mandate from a celestial god.[37] Because of a dream about pubic hair, it became known that Li Fan would achieve power in Lower Qi.[38] One can further gather from this type of dream that when a divine intelligence exercises pivotal control, no human effort can alter it.

NOTES

1. See the commentary to Duke Wen of Jin's dream of the prime minister of Chu in the chapter, "The Disciple of Emptiness" [1:5n21].

2. Zheng Zhuo as a youth dreamt that he met Huang Kan on the road. Huang said to him, "Young Master Zheng, open your mouth." Huang then inserted medicine into Zheng's mouth. From then on, Zheng made great strides in understanding the moral principles of Confucian philosophy. (From *History of the Chen Dynasty.*)

3. When Liu Zhilin was in Jingfu, he stayed in the government house in the

southern part of the commandery where he unexpectedly dreamt that the former governor Yuan Tuan told him, "You will later become a governor with one arm and will reside here." Later, Liu did indeed lose his arm and subsequently administered this commandery. (From *History of the Liang Dynasty*.)

4. When Rectifier Zhang fell seriously ill, he dreamt that he was pregnant, which appalled him. Ye Guangyuan told him, "Your illness will abate, and you will recover on the day *renchen*. The graphs for *renchen* 壬辰 with the element for 'woman' 女 added means 'pregnant' (*renshen* 妊娠), which is a great blessing." Zhang did indeed recover on the day *renchen*. (From *A Record of Inner Light*.)

5. Yang Xiong responded to the summons of Emperor Cheng of the Western Han and composed the "Rhapsody on the Sweet Spring." He felt tired and lay down, dreaming that his five *zang*-organs spilled out onto the ground. Using his hands, he put them back inside himself. But, when he awoke, he felt short of breath and consequently fell ill, dying a year later. (From Huan Tan, *New Discussions*.)

After Yang Xiong wrote a rhapsody, there was a story that he dreamt about his innards, and after Cao Zhi wrote a piece, there was talk about his stomach turning over. Their words had overburdened their spirits. (From the *Master of the Golden Tower*.)

6. Zhang Shentong of Yanzhou dreamt that he grew another ear on his head. When he awoke, he felt an itch and, indeed, he had grown another ear. People at that time called him the "Triple-Ear Scholar." (From *The Taiping Miscellany*.) For details of this incident, see the commentary in chapter 16 of *Trifling Discussions of Su Dongpo's Poetry* by Zhang Junfang.

7. When Zhuge Liang was leaving the mouth of North Valley, Wei Yan led the vanguard. They proceeded more than three miles from Zhuge's camp when Wei dreamt that he grew a horn on his head. He consulted the dream interpreter Zhao Zhi. However, Zhao deceived him by saying, "A *qilin*-beast has a horn, but he does not use it. This symbolizes that the rebels will destroy themselves without your having to engage in battle." After leaving Wei, Zhao told others, "The graph for 'horn' 角 is comprised of the graph 'sword' 刀 on top of the graph 'to use' 用. A sword used over one's head is an extremely unlucky sign." (From *History of the Three Kingdoms*.)

8. See the commentary to Zheng Xie's dream of meeting a functionary and bathing in the chapter, "Mountains and Streams" [II:4n11].

9. Zheng Xuan had been studying with Ma Rong for three years but had not yet gained any recognition. Ma Rong felt disdain toward him and sent him away. Zheng passed by a tree and fell asleep under it. He dreamt that an old man cut open his heart with a knife, saying, "Now you can really study." Thereupon, Zheng decided to return and subsequently became a great Confucian scholar.

When Yin Zhizhang was a youth, he had not yet mastered anything. He dreamt that someone took a giant chisel and pierced his heart as if internally administering a dose of medicine. He was startled awake and felt that his mind and thoughts had expanded, becoming more profound. Subsequently, he thoroughly understood the *Six Classics*. (From *Old History of the Tang Dynasty*.)

10. Ding Gu dreamt that a pine tree grew forth from his stomach. He told

someone, "The graph for 'pine' 松 is composed of the graphs for 'eighteen' 十八 and 'duke' 公. I will become a duke eighteen years from now." Subsequently, it turned out just as he had dreamed. (From *A Record of Wu*.)

The mother of Zhang Zhihe dreamt that a maple tree grew forth from her stomach. Subsequently, she gave birth to Zhihe. (From *Old History of the Tang Dynasty*.)

11. When Duke Jing of Qi attacked Song, he passed by Mount Tai and dreamt that two men were angry with him. The duke said they were spirits sent by Jiang Taigong. However, Master Yan said, "These were King Tang and Yi Yin," and he described their appearances: Tang had a fair complexion and a full beard, while Yi Yin was dark-complexioned and short. It accorded with the dream. However, Duke Jing did not listen to the warning and proceeded with the campaign anyway. Indeed, his army wound up being destroyed. (From *A Record of Manifold Things*.)

12. Li Linfu dreamt of someone who had a light complexion and a beard. The man was threatening him when Li awoke. He searched for someone with this appearance and found that Pei Kuan resembled the man in his dream. He said, "Pei intends to supplant me," and he joined with Li Shi's faction to drive out Pei. Later, Yang Guozhong supplanted Li, and it was said that he resembled Pei Kuan. (From *Old History of the Tang Dynasty*.)

13. Feng Jun, whose courtesy name was Deming, was a native of Qiantang. When he was eighteen years of age, he dreamt that the supreme god Di sent a god to change his organs, who told him, "You will have an excellent destiny." After he awoke, he suddenly found that he had attained a new level of mental clarity and intelligence. Feng ceased studying the art of literature, yet, from this point on, his writings conveyed great understanding. He could predict both good fortune and calamities. Though he never left his house, others sometimes saw him appear along the waterways. During the Yuanyou era [1086–1093], a boat crossing the Yangzi River encountered strong winds. Suddenly he was seen among the clouds. Feng announced his name whereupon the violent waves immediately subsided. In the eleventh lunar month of the third year of the Daguan era [November-December, 1109], he suddenly told someone, "The supreme god Di has appointed me to control the waves on the river." He died without illness at the age of thirty-six. In the twentieth year of the Shaoxing era [1150], a placard in his honor was bestowed by the court at the Temple of Peaceful River Crossings. In the year *gengshen* of the Qingyuan era [1200], he was canonized as Duke of Spiritual Aid, and during the Shaoding era [1228–1233], he was further elevated, becoming King of Meritorious Bravery. (From *Gazetteer of Hangzhou*.)

14. See the commentary to the dream about washing in the waters of the West River in the chapter, "Mountains and Streams" [II:4n18].

15. When the future Emperor Suzong of the Tang was living as crown prince in the Eastern Palace, the future Empress Zhangjing suddenly fell asleep and did not awaken for a long time. Afterward, the crown prince asked her about this, and she replied, "I dreamt that a god came down to me. Suddenly, a sword pierced my side and entered my body. It was unbearable." When observed by candlelight, a faint line was found there. Subsequently, she gave birth to the future Emperor Daizong. (From "Biographies of Empresses and Consorts" in *New His-*

tory of the Tang Dynasty.) The *Record of Inner Light* describes this event in more detail.

16. After the mother of Sun Jian gave birth to him, she dreamt that her intestines left her body and wound themselves around the Changmen Gate in Wu. She told this to a neighboring mother, who declared this to be an auspicious sign. (From *History of the Liu Song Dynasty.*)

17. Jia Bizhi of Hedong served as adjutant of the superior prefecture of Langye during the Yixi era [405–418]. He dreamt one night of a man whose face was covered with acne, with long side-burns, a big nose, and twitching eyes. The man asked, "I like your appearance. Could we exchange heads?" Jia agreed to the exchange in his dream. The next morning when he got up, he was unaware of what had happened, but everyone else ran from him in fright. Jia sat down and explained what had happened. Afterward, he was able to laugh with just half of his face. He could hold brushes in both hands and both feet and also in his mouth, then write using all them at once. The language and meaning of each piece were excellent. This was quite extraordinary. In all other things, though, he remained similar to the way he was before. (From *A Record of Ghosts and the Living.*)

18. When Sima Yi arrived in Xiangping, he dreamt that the emperor used his thighs as a pillow and said, "Look at my face." When Sima looked down at him, the emperor's appearance seemed different than usual. Sima was appalled by this dream. Later, he was summoned to the court and quickly admitted into the imperial bedchamber in the Palace of Excellent Blessings. He approached the emperor's bed with tears in his eyes as he inquired about his illness. The Son of Heaven grasped Sima's hand and, looking at the Prince of Qi, said "Entrust him with affairs after I am gone." (From *History of the Jin Dynasty.*)

19. Wang Chu'na was from Luoyang. He dreamt of someone holding a giant mirror with shining stars and asterisms in its center. His belly was cut open, and he received the mirror into his body. Wang awoke dripping with sweat. After more than a month, he continued to feel a pain in his chest. But, as a result of this, he studied astronomy and astrology and gained a deep understanding of their principles. (From *History of the Five Dynasties.*)

20. Wu Yuanzhao was from Xiaoshan. One night he dreamt that a god told him, "You were originally a divine jade maiden who committed a crime and was temporarily banished to the human world. You may cease consuming food." When he awoke, he no longer wanted to eat anything, but his mother forced him. Then he dreamt that the god told him angrily, "You have disobeyed my prohibition." The god cut open Wu's stomach and washed it clean. As a result, Wu received the techniques of the Numinous Treasure School of Daoism. From then on, he used talismans in water to cure people of their illnesses, and these were immediately effective. Wu finally cast off his bodily form in the eleventh year of the Shaoxing era [1141]. (From *The Comprehensive Gazetteer.*)

21. Shen Yue dreamt that Emperor He of the Southern Qi dynasty cut off his tongue with a sword. He consulted a spirit-medium, who described the dream exactly. Shen was terrified and died soon after. (From *History of the Liang Dynasty.*)

22. When the Last Emperor of the Southern Tang dynasty was going to abdicate, it was Zhou Zong who formally proposed it. The emperor said, "I dreamt at night that someone decapitated me with a sword." Zhou bowed and con-

gratulated him, saying "Now is the time to enthrone the heir-apparent." A few days later, the emperor abdicated. (From *History of the Five Dynasties*.)

23. The future Emperor Shizu of the Southern Qi dynasty, also known as Emperor Wu, dreamt at the age of thirteen that his entire body was covered with hair and that the hair on his head grew down to his feet. (From *History of the Southern Qi Dynasty*.)

24. The wife of Zhang Jing'er said to him, "In the past I dreamt that my hands were as hot as fire, and then you became the administrator of Nanyang Commandery. During the Yuanhui era [473–476], I dreamt that half my body was hot, and then you became magistrate of Xiangyang. Now, I have further dreamt that my entire body was hot." A eunuch heard what she had said and reported it to Emperor Shizu of the Southern Qi. A few days later, Zhang Jing'er was executed. (From *History of the Southern Qi Dynasty*.)

25. When Tao Gu was young he dreamt that several functionaries told him, "We can offer you talismans to change your eyes." The functionaries demanded one hundred thousand in cash to change the first eye, but Tao refused. Then they said, "Fifty thousand to change the second eye," but he refused again. The functionaries said, "We will change your 'third eye,'" and they inserted two pills into his eyes. When he awoke, his eyes had changed to a deep green. Later a physiognomist told him, "What a noble face you have, but what a pity that you have a pair of demon's eyes. You will never attain a high position." (From *A Record of Collected Strange Events*.)

26. Li Shengmei was a governor during the Tang dynasty. He dreamt that his head turned into a tiger's head. When he awoke, he was most unhappy about it. His wife asked, "Did you dream that your head turned into a tiger's head?" "How did you know?" he replied. His wife said, "Last night, I dreamt that I was looking in the mirror and my head was that of a tiger's. I am quite happy about it because the ruler is a dragon and his officials are tigers. It is certain that you will be ennobled." Ten days later, Li was summoned to court to become grand councilor of the right and both husband and wife were ennobled. (From *Transmissions of Unique Events*.)

27. Zhou Bida was held personally responsible for a fire in an official storage house. He was relieved of his office and exiled. On his way there, he bid farewell to his father-in-law. Just before Zhou arrived, his father-in-law had dreamt that someone said to him, "Sweep away the snow and prepare to welcome a chief councilor." At that time, Zhou dreamt that he arrived someplace where a voice issued forth from a palace, saying, "His appearance is crude so give him an imperial beard." When he awoke, his cheeks itched, for he had grown a beautiful beard. Later on, he did become a grand councilor. At the time, none of the physiognomists were able to recognize that he would occupy an exalted position. But later, he would stroke his beard and say, "This is an imperial beard." (From *History of the Song Dynasty*.) It is also said that Lü Mengzheng dreamt that a god added a beard to his face.

28. Director Xu dreamt that a god carrying a bamboo basket filed with human noses looked at him and said, "Your body and face are not too weak, but your nose is crooked and small." He cut it off, then picked another one out of the basket and changed it. The god laughed, "How about the nose of a bureau

director?" After more than a month, Xu's nose grew straight and well-shaped. He held various offices finishing up as a bureau director. (From *A Record of Collected Strange Events*.)

29. During the Tianbao era [550–559] of the Northern Qi dynasty under Emperor Wenxuan, Attendant Censor Li Guang diligently sought to obtain a universal knowledge of things and became an attendant censor. One night, he dreamt that someone emerged from his body and told him, "You have overworked your mind, which is suffering. Now I am leaving you." Li fell ill and died soon after. (From *Past and Present Records about the Five Agents from the Tang Dynasty*.)

30. When Liu Dan, the Prince of Jingling, was in Guangling, he took a nap during the day and dreamt that someone told him, "You must get rid of your hair, Your Excellency." When he awoke, his hair had already fallen out. (From *A Continuation of Accounts of Strange Events*.)

31. King Zhao of the Zhou dreamt that someone in a feathered robe bestowed upon him the technique for achieving the highest form of a transcendent being. Then, he used his finger to make a mark over the king's heart, which instantly split open. The king was startled awake, and he had a pain in his heart for ten days. Unexpectedly, he saw the one he had dreamt of arrive, take out medicine from a tiny green pouch, and rub it on his chest. The king subsequently recovered from his illness. (From *Wang Zinian's Recovered Records*.)

32. Before Emperor Wen of the Sui attained nobility, he often traveled by boat on the Yangzi River. One night, he moored his boat among the reeds and dreamt that he no longer possessed his left hand. He felt appalled by this after he awoke. Later, he went ashore and visited a hut where an old monk lived. The future emperor told the monk his dream. The monk rose and bowed, saying, "He who lacks a left hand is a 'single fist' [*duquan*, a homophone for 'sole power']. You will become the Son of Heaven." After the emperor ascended the throne, he rebuilt the hut into the Temple of the Auspicious Sign. It is located ten miles downstream from the city of Wuchang. (*Accounts of Unique and Strange Things*.)

33. The daughter of Zhu Zhongwu became the wife of Mi Yuanzong. She died in childbirth at home. It was a local custom to mark the faces of those who died in childbirth with black dots, but her mother could not bear to do such a thing. So Zhu secretly added the black dots himself when no one was looking. Mi was then serving as the assistant magistrate of Shixin district. He dreamt that his wife had come into his bed, and he clearly saw that there were black dots on her freshly powdered face. (From *In Search of the Supernatural*.)

34. Mistress Fei, the wife of Song Luo, never tired of reciting *The Lotus Sutra*. Later, she fell seriously ill and dreamt that the Buddha stuck his hand through the window and that it resembled a mat to sit on. Soon after, Mistress Fei recovered from her illness. (From *Narrations of Strange Events*.)

35. At the beginning of the Shangyuan era [760–761], Doulu Rong was serving as administrative aide in Wenzhou when he died. His wife was the daughter of the Princess of Jinhe. At the beginning of the Baoying era [762–763], Yuan Chao, a bandit from the mountains in Linhai, attacked and captured Taizhou. The daughter of the princess dreamt that someone with unbound hair who was dripping blood said, "Chaos will break out in Wenzhou. You should quickly leave." The princess then moved her residence to Wuzhou, but when Wuzhou

fell, she fled without her possessions just as the dream had foretold. (From *An Extensive Record of Anomalies*.)

36. When Gu Cong served as a rectifier of omissions, he committed a crime for which he was arrested and sent to prison. The magnitude of his crime warranted the death penalty. He dreamt that he saw his mother's genitals, which terrified him even more. At the time, there was a skillful interpreter of dreams who congratulated him, saying, "You will be pardoned." When asked how he knew this, he replied, "Madam's genitals were your pathway to life. That you have once again seen the pathway to life is why I am offering congratulations." The next day, Vice Director of the Chancellery Xue Ji memorialized the throne that he be pardoned, and, later on, Gu rose to the position of grand councilor. (From *An Extensive Record of Anomalies*.)

37. Duke Xiang of Shan said, "I heard that when Duke Cheng of Jin was born, there was a dream that a god made a mark in black on his buttocks to indicate that he would rule over the state of Jin. This is how heaven revealed its mandate." (From *Conversations of Zhou*.)

38. Li Fan, whose courtesy name was Shize, was from Fanyang. He once dreamt that his pubic hair was brushing against his ankles, and, one day, he spoke of this to someone. At that time, there was an interpreter of dreams in Qi who said, "He will attain power in Lower Qi [*qixia*, a homophone for 'below the navel']". Li Fan consequently became regional inspector of Qingzhou. (From *History of the Northern Wei Dynasty*.)

CHAPTER 6

Food and Clothing
食衣

Food and clothing are necessities of life. In the past, He Dian dreamt that he swallowed a pill, and his illness was cured.[1] A Southern Qi dynasty empress dreamt that consuming two bottles of sesame porridge caused a wet nurse's milk to flow.[2] Han Yu dreamt that he swallowed a volume containing seal-script graphs written in cinnabar ink.[3] Yu Fan dreamt that he had swallowed three lines of a hexagram from *The Book of Changes*.[4] Zhang Jiong dreamt that he swallowed a multicolored cloud.[5] Li Zhi's mother dreamt that she had swallowed a written talisman from eight transcendents.[6] The Daoist priest Zhao dreamt that he swallowed a green cypress leaf.[7] Vice Minister Feng dreamt that he swallowed a purple lotus blossom.[8] Liu Zan dreamt that he spit out a golden turtle.[9] Shao Yong's mother dreamt that she used jade chopsticks.[10] Hou Hongshi dreamt that he drank water from the Yellow River.[11] Wang Renyu dreamt that he drank from the West River.[12] Zhang Ruming dreamt that he had ingested the Southern Star.[13] Emperor Xuanzong of the Tang dreamt that he ate wisteria blossoms.[14] Xiahou Xin dreamt of a divine herb that could cure his mother's illness.[15] Chen Yizhong dreamt that rhubarb could cure an epidemic.[16] Jiang Fou dreamt about drinking from the spring of the Wisdom Eye.[17] Qiu Jie dreamt that he had eaten poison from raw vegetables.[18] Metropolitan Graduate Xie's fame as a poet spread widely after he dreamt that he swallowed pearls.[19] Emperor Xizong of the Tang dreamt that he had swallowed *The Book of Chess* and immediately mastered the principles of the game.[20] Liu Jingxuan dreamt that he had swallowed some earth and considered it fortunate, while Emperor Taizong of the Liang dreamt that he had swallowed some earth, and it proved to be inauspicious. How could a single reason explain both

Food and Clothing

these dreams?[21] In the case of the birth of the divine Yu of the Xia dynasty, his mother Xiuji dreamt that she had swallowed *yiyi*-barley.[22] When Emperor Taizu of our own Ming dynasty was conceived, Empress Dowager Chen dreamt that she had swallowed a medicinal pill.[23] Thus did the pure essences of yin and yang energies conjoin in the bodies of these sagely mothers from two different dynasties. Historical records have passed down these glorious moments, transmitting these radiant events from past to present. Ordinary dreams can hardly compare with these.

There are also dreams about clothing worthy of interpretation. Suo Chong dreamt of a prisoner who had taken off his clothes.[24] Chen Zun dreamt of a boy pulling at his sleeve.[25] Emperor Wu of the Western Han dreamt of an emissary in an embroidered robe.[26] Minister of State Wang dreamt of a young boy with tufted hair dressed in green.[27] Empress Zhangyi dreamt that someone in a feather robe came down through the window.[28] Emperor Shizu of the Qi dreamt of wearing hemp sandals while walking in the palace.[29] General Liu dreamt that a sleeping mat was bestowed on him as a gift.[30] Vice Censor-in-Chief Dou dreamt about a garment that covered his arms and legs.[31] Fei Xuan dreamt of an embroidered robe of high rank in a well and returned with honor to his hometown.[32] Tuoba Shun suffered harm after he dreamt that he had removed his cap and lay down on the ground.[33] A dream of images drawn with a brush along the edges of a garment was a verifiable sign of ascending the imperial throne of the Southern Qi dynasty.[34] A dream of the sun entering under a skirt was an auspicious sign of the birth of the future Last Emperor of the Northern Qi dynasty.[35] Deng You dreamt that his sack was cut up by the waterside, and later he assumed the office of governor of Ruyin.[36] Dao Gai dreamt that a hat was doffed to the Prince of Xiangdong, and he received an appointment as administrator in Guiji.[37] Yue Yanzhen dreamt that he was walking along carrying his shoes, and it was indeed a warning to beware of soldiers.[38] Wang Yuanshu dreamt that he led someone wearing a purple robe into the imperial palace, and the dream was later confirmed by Duke Jing.[39] Li Guyan dreamt that he was wearing the ceremonial robe of a grand councilor.[40] Liu Shenyi dreamt that he received the crimson robe of a filial son.[41] The mother of Xue Xia dreamt of a chest containing an embroidered robe and consequently gave birth to a vice director of the palace library.[42] A divine mother dreamt that celestial beings in vermillion robes filled the sky and consequently gave birth to a son who became the Lord of Fates.[43] As for the dream of Fang Xiaoru's father, in which someone in a red robe knelt and informed him that a deadline had been suspended,[44] and the dream of Mr. Pei, in which someone in an embroidered robe bowed and thanked him for his virtuous act of kindness,[45] both were cases of snakes and pheasants changing their shape so that calamity or good fortune could be repaid.

NOTES

1. When He Dian was young, he suffered from thirst and dysentery that lasted for a number of years without relief. Later, after he sponsored a lecture at the Temple of the Stone Buddha in Wu, he dreamt one night that an adept of the Way gave him a handful of pills, which he swallowed while still dreaming. After this, he was cured. Some maintained that this event was a response to the pure virtue that he had accumulated. (From *History of the Liang Dynasty*.)

2. Empress Chen gave birth to the future Emperor Taizu of the Southern Qi. When he was two years old, his wet nurse ceased producing milk. The empress dreamt that someone gave the wet nurse two bottles of sesame porridge. When the empress awoke, the wet nurse's milk was flowing in abundance. (From *History of the Southern Qi Dynasty*.)

3. When Han Yu was young, he dreamt that someone gave him a volume containing seal-script graphs written in cinnabar ink. The man forced him to swallow it while someone else standing beside him clapped his hands and laughed. When Han later awoke, he felt as if he were choking on something in his stomach. Later, he met Meng Jiao, who was none other than the man laughing beside him in the dream. (From *Biographies of Extraordinary People*.)

Han Yu often said that when he was young, he dreamt that someone gave him a volume containing seal-script graphs written in cinnabar ink to swallow. Later, he felt as if he were choking on something in his stomach. He was able to write down from memory one or two of the graphs, and their forms were unlike any writing by humans. (From *A Record of Longcheng*.)

4. Yu Fan created a method for interpreting *The Book of Changes*. In a memorial to the throne announcing this, he stated, "Commandery Chief Chen Tao dreamt that your humble official and a Daoist were casting the six lines of a hexagram when the Daoist took three of the lines and served these to me as a drink. I swallowed it completely, and the Daoist said, 'The Way of *The Book of Changes* lies in heaven, so three lines are sufficient.'" (From *History of the Wu Dynasty*.)

5. For an explanation, see the commentary to the dream of a cloud entering his mouth in the chapter, "Thunder and Rain" [II:3n16].

6. Mistress Zhang [fl. mid-10th cent.], mother of Li Zhi, once dreamt that eight transcendents descended from heaven and gave her a written talisman that they had her swallow. When she awoke, she felt that there was something in her body, and before long she gave birth to Li Zhi. (From *History of the Song Dynasty*.)

7. Zhao Ziran was from Fanchang. When young, he suffered from a serious illness. His father brought him to the Temple of the Green Lotus Blossom where he entrusted his son to become a Daoist priest. Later, Zhao dreamt of an old

man who told him his surname was Yin and led him up a high mountain where he said, "You possess Daoist *qi*-energy, so I will teach you the method of avoiding the consumption of grains." Then, he took a green cypress leaf and had Zhao swallow it. After Zhao awoke, he no longer ate food. More than a year later, he again dreamt that he met the old man, who taught him several hundred seal-style graphs. When he awoke, he was able to write them all down from memory and showed them to others. No one could understand them, and some said that they were not seal-style graphs at all but sacred Daoist talismans. Emperor Taizong of the Northern Song summoned Zhao to court and questioned him, bestowing upon Zhao the robes of a Daoist priest. (From *History of the Song Dynasty*.)

8. When Feng Yuan was seven and studying *The Book of Changes*, his mother dreamt one night that an extraordinary person gave a purple lotus to Yuan and had him swallow it. Then he said, "Later, you will certainly achieve exalted rank and recognition." Yuan indeed rose to become vice minister of the Ministry of Revenue. (From *History of the Song Dynasty*.)

9. During the Five Dynasties, Liu Zan, who was slow-witted when it came to literary imagination, prayed to the heavenly bodies for talent. He dreamt one night that he swallowed a little golden turtle. After that, he found that he possessed a great deal of literary imagination. Then, he dreamt one day that he spit out the golden turtle into the water. He died not long afterward. (From *Casual Chats of a Herd-Boy*.)

10. Shao Yong's mother was Mistress Li [fl. early 11th cent.]. Her mother-in-law was Mistress Zhang, who treated her so harshly that one night she wanted to kill herself. Mistress Li dreamt that a god ordered her to eat a bowl of porridge with jade chopsticks and told her, "Do not kill yourself, for you will give birth to a fine son." Later, she gave birth to Shao Yong.

11. During the Five Dynasties, Hou Hongshi at the age of thirteen or fourteen was once asleep under the eave of a roof. There was a heavy rain, and a rainbow extended from the Yellow River into his mouth. After a long while, it disappeared. When he awoke, his mother asked him whether he had had a dream, and he replied, "I just dreamt that I had entered the Yellow River, drank from its waters, and returned home full." Several months later, a monk came to the door. Hou's mother called her son and asked the monk to examine his physiognomy. The monk said, "This is the outer rainbow ring of a dragon. He will certainly become an eminent official." In the third year of the Tongguang era [925], Hou assisted Crown Prince Xingsheng in recovering Shu and served as military commissioner of Kuizhou. (From *A Record of Cautionary Examples*.)

12. For an explanation, see the commentary to the dream about washing in the water of the West River in the chapter, "Mountains and Rivers" [II:4n18].

13. Zhang Ruming displayed filial piety in serving his parents. His grief at their funerals caused him to become so thin and weak that he would often stumble and fall while walking. He dreamt that his father taught him the method of ingesting the Southern Star. It proved effective, and others said that it was a response to his filial piety. (From *A Collection of Strange Tales*.)

14. When the future Emperor Xuanzong of the Tang [r. 712–756] was still comparatively insignificant, he visited the home of Cui Rizhi, the magistrate of Luoyang. Cui was having a meal prepared for his guest, but it was not yet ready,

so Xuanzong took a nap. Meanwhile, a wisteria vine in the courtyard was just beginning to bloom, and Cui saw a giant snake eating the blossoms. He was about to approach it with some trepidation when it disappeared. After Xuanzong awoke, he said, "I felt extremely hungry, so I dreamt that I ate wisteria blossoms until I was quite full." Cui then realized that this was a sign of a future emperor. (From *A Supplemental History*.)

15. Xiahou Xin was extremely filial by nature. When his mother fell ill and could not be cured by the physicians, he dreamt that his father told him, "Your mother cannot be cured by ordinary medicine. The Supreme God of Heaven has taken pity because of your filial piety and has bestowed a divine herb located on a branch of the mulberry tree behind the house. You should go yourself and take it." After awakening, Xiahou went to look for it and indeed found the herb. He administered it to his mother, who subsequently recovered. (From *Exquisite Words on the Origins of Surnames*.)

16. Chen Yizhong dreamt that someone told him, "This year an epidemic sent down by heaven will spread widely, and half the population will die. Those who eat rhubarb will survive." Later, a plague ran wild and, indeed, those who consumed rhubarb did not die. (From *History of the Song Dynasty*.)

17. As a youth, Jiang Fou, whose courtesy name was Hanjie, was filial by nature. When his father, Jiang Qian, suffered from an eye disease, Jiang Fou attended him for an entire month and had no time to even change his clothes. One night, he dreamt that a monk said, "Those who suffer from an eye disease will be cured if they drink from the water of the Wisdom Eye." After Jiang Fou awoke, he told this to others, but no one could explain what it meant. Jiang Fou's third uncle, Jiang Lu, was on friendly terms with Buddhist Master Zhizhe of the Cottage Temple, so he paid him a call. Master Zhizhe said, "*The Sutra of the Buddha of Measureless Life* says that the Wisdom Eye can see the true state of things and can guide one to cross over to the shore of enlightenment." Based on what Master Zhizhe had said, Jiang Qian gave up his house and converted it into a temple which was named "Temple of the Wisdom Eye." During the construction, an old well was tapped whose water was unusually clear and pure. Following his son's dream, Jiang Qian drew forth some of its water to bathe his eyes and also used it to brew some medicine. Subsequently, his illness was cured. (From *History of the Southern Dynasties*.)

18. Qiu Jie was from Wucheng and lost his mother at the age of fourteen. He refused to eat any tasty, cooked vegetables. After more than a year, he fell ill. He dreamt that his mother said to him, "Death is but a parting. Why should you suffer so much over it? In the raw vegetables you ate was poison from a toad. In front of my memorial bier are three pills which you should take." Qiu awoke, startled, and indeed found a bottle there with medicine inside. After taking it, he expelled several liters of tadpoles. The Qiu family treasured this bottle for generations, but in the seventh year of the Daming era [463] it was destroyed in a fire. (From *Transcriptions of Historical Events*.)

19. Metropolitan Graduate Xie E's family lived in Nankang, where there was a stream in front of his house. When Xie was a child, he once dreamt that he was bathing in the stream. Someone gave him a vessel full of pearls saying, "If you swallow these, you will become brilliant." Xie figured that he couldn't swal-

low the larger ones, so he swallowed more than sixty of the smaller ones. When he grew older, he was skilled in poetry. Metropolitan Graduate Pei Yue selected more than sixty of his pieces for an anthology, and they became widely known. (From *A Record of Inquests into Spirits*.)

20. Emperor Xizong of the Tang succeeded to the throne after having been the Prince of Jin. He was young and highly capable, but he had never learned how to play chess. One night, he dreamt that someone gave him *The Book of Chess* in three chapters, which he burned and swallowed. Upon awakening, he summoned others to observe him playing a match. Every move made by the emperor surpassed their expectations. (From *Additional Records*.)

21. Liu Jingxuan dreamt that he had formed some earth into a pill and swallowed it. When he awoke, he felt happy and said, "' Pill' *[wan]* is pronounced like 'regularly' *[huan]*. By regularly swallowing some earth, I shall recover my homeland." (From *History of the Southern Dynasties*.)

Emperor Taizong of the Liang had been imprisoned for a long time when he dreamt one night that he swallowed some earth. Later he was killed and, in fact, earth was found in his mouth. (From *History of the Liang Dynasty*.)

22. Xiuji, the wife of Gun, observed a comet invading the asterism Mane. She dreamt that she encountered it and was stimulated by it. She also dreamt that she had swallowed a divine pearl like a kernel of *yiyi*-barley. Her body split open, and Yu the Great was born. (From *Annals of the Thearchs and Kings*).

23. Empress Dowager Chen, the mother of Emperor Taizu of the Ming, dreamt of a god in vermillion robes who was holding an ivory tablet of high rank. He offered her medicine in the form of a pill that glowed brilliantly. She swallowed it and upon awakening sensed that an unusual fragrance had suffused her body. Subsequently, she became pregnant. (From *A Record of the Founding Destiny of the Ming Dynasty*.)

Heaven feels sympathetic toward benevolent ancestors. When it came to Empress Chen, she enjoyed a dream where she consumed medicine. Upon awakening, she smelled the fragrance of orchids. Emperor Taizu had descended from heaven just at this very moment. (From Sang Yue, "Rhapsody on the Two Capitals.")

24. Suo Chong dreamt of a captive who had removed his upper garments when he came to see him. Suo Chong asked Suo Dan about this, and Suo Dan replied, "If the upper part of the graph *lu* 虜 [captive] is taken off, this leaves the lower part, which is the graph *nan* 男 [son]. Captives belong to the yin category, so your wife will give birth to a son. In the end, it was just as he said. (From *History of the Jin Dynasty*.)

25. Qin Guangheng was from E. The local custom was to drown sons at birth if there already were too many and poverty prevented the raising of any more. When Qin was born, his uncle Chen Zun dreamt that a boy was pulling at his sleeve. Chen remembered that his elder sister was pregnant. He hurried over and saw that the child had already been put in a basin filled with water, so Chen saved him and raised him. Later, Qin became a legal administrator in Anzhou. (From *Annals of Chu*.)

26. For an explanation, see the commentary to Emperor Wu's dream of climbing Mount Song in the chapter, "Mountains and Rivers" [II:4n7].

27. His Excellency, the future Minister of State Wang, was working at the headquarters of Qiao Commandery in the year *bingshen* [996] when thousands of families fled from their homes. He memorialized the throne about providing the people with grain seed and fodder for their oxen, and the court agreed. One night when he was staying at an official way-station, he dreamt that someone was calling him, so he went out to greet him. He saw someone wearing a purple cord and holding an ivory tablet of high rank. The man resembled a governor and presented Wang with a young boy with tufted hair dressed in green, saying, "Because you were concerned for the common people, the supreme god Di was pleased and presents you with this boy, who is a suitable son for a prime minister." Wang accepted the child and then woke up. That same night, his wife also experienced auspicious signs and became pregnant. Later, she indeed gave birth to a son, and he was named Qingzhi [blessed]. He often spoke about matters in heaven. In the year *renzi* during the Xiangfu era [1012], he told his parents, "The Lady of the Upper Monad commanded me to serve as a divine Jade Boy as long as my father has not yet received the seal of a minister. When he does, I shall leave." A few days later, His Excellency became minister of state, and after a month, Qingzhi died. (From *An Unofficial Record from Mount Xiang*.)

28. Empress Zhangyi, formerly Mistress Li and the mother of the future Emperor Renzong, dreamt that someone barefoot in a feather robe descended through the window. Subsequently, she became pregnant with Emperor Renzong. (From *History of the Song Dynasty*.)

29. For an explanation, see the commentary on the dream about walking in the Hall of the Great Ultimate in the chapter, "Mountains and Rivers" [II:4n36].

30. During the Liang dynasty, Liu Shilong was general-in-chief and his son Qingyuan also served as general of campaigns against barbarians. Liu Qingyuan's son, Liu Jin, succeeded to his father's position. Liu Qingyuan once told Liu Jin, "I previously dreamt that a sleeping mat was bestowed on me as a gift by my father, the general-in-chief. Afterward, I became a high minister. Now, I have dreamt that a sleeping mat was bestowed on you. You will certainly bring glory to our ancestors." (From *History of the Southern Dynasties*.)

31. During the Tang dynasty, Dou Shen served as Vice Censor-in-Chief. He had dreamt that Emperor Dezong bestowed on him an embroidered, short-sleeved shirt. Dou said, "A short-sleeve shirt is for the 'upper arms and thighs' [i.e., an official aiding the ruler]." Several days later, he indeed rose to high rank. (From *A Record of Mist and Flowers*.)

32. When Fei Xuan went to take the official examinations, he dreamt of an embroidered robe of high rank in a well. Upon awakening, he felt happy and said, "It means that I shall pass the examinations and travel back to my hometown [*xiangjing*, literally, 'the well in my hometown'] with a high rank." (From *Conversations of a Guest in a Thatched Pavilion*.)

33. For an explanation, see the commentary to the dream containing an analysis of the graph *huai* [sophora] to mean "a ghost beside a tree" in the chapter, "Written Graphs" [II:10n2].

34. When the future Emperor Shizu of the Southern Qi was in Yingzhou, he dreamt that someone flew down from heaven. The man had a brush stuck in his hair and drew images along both edges of Shizu's upper garment. Then, with-

out speaking, he departed. Yu Wen said, "The images depict the imperial symbols of a mountain dragon and a multicolored pheasant." (From *History of the Southern Dynasties*.)

35. Mistress Hu, the mother of the Last Emperor of the Northern Qi dynasty, dreamt that she was sitting in a jade basin in the sea when the sun entered under her skirt. Subsequently, she became pregnant and gave birth to the future Last Emperor. (From *History of the Northern Dynasties*.)

36. Deng You dreamt that he was walking along the edge of the water when he saw a woman and a ferocious beast come up from behind him and tear off his leather belt-pouch containing a seal of office. A dream interpreter said, "The element for 'water' 氵 placed beside that for 'woman' 女 is the graph pronounced *ru* 汝. Tearing off the pouch means 'a new beast becomes the leader,' for 'beast' [*shou*] is a homophone for 'leader' [*shou*]. You will either become governor [*shou*] of Ru'nan or Ruyin." Indeed, Deng became governor of Ruyin. (From *History of the Jin Dynasty*.)

37. Dao Gai, whose courtesy name was Maoguan, served during the Liang dynasty as secretariat receptionist, vice director in the Secretariat and concurrently in the Ministry of Personnel. When Prince Yi of Xiangdong was governor of Guiji, he made Dao administrator of light chariots. Dao had once dreamt that Emperor Wu of the Liang looked over all his sons and doffed his cap to the Prince of Xiangdong. Later, the Prince of Xiangdong indeed succeeded to the throne as Emperor Yuan. (From *History of the Southern Dynasties*.)

38. Yue Yanzhen once dreamt that he had resigned from office and was walking along carrying his shoes [*dailü*, a homophone for "leading an army"]. When he awoke, he said, "Is this not a god telling me that a subordinate general will rebel against me?" Indeed, a revolt soon broke out in the army, and before long he was killed. (From *Bo and Kong's Encyclopedia*.)

39. Wang Zhu's courtesy name was Yuanshu. According to *A Record of Mr. Wang's Conversations*, he said, "When I began to serve as an official for ceremonials, I dreamt that I entered the imperial palace garden leading a man wearing a purple robe. We reached the rear garden where we saw His Majesty. After a year, Duke Jing received the purple robe of high rank. I was then chamberlain for ceremonials and led him into the imperial garden. The path we followed was exactly as I had seen it in the dream." (From *History of the Song Dynasty*.)

40. Li Guyan dreamt that he was wearing Song Jing's robe. At the beginning of the Changqing era [821–824] when Emperor Muzong of the Tang was to sacrifice at the altar to heaven, Li was serving as left reminder in the Chancellery. According to the longstanding regulations, remonstrance officials were supposed to accompany the emperor in performing such rituals, and the chamberlain for ceremonials issued a formal robe to each participant. The one that Li wore bore the inscription, "The Robe of Left Rectifier of Omissions in the Chancellery Song Jing." (From *A Continuation of A Record of Fates*.)

41. Liu Tan, whose original name was Shenyi, dreamt that a filial son led him to a sandalwood tree and ordered him to climb it, saying, "Quickly climb it, sir." He climbed it whereupon the filial son pulled forth a crimson robe from his body and ordered Liu to put it on. After Liu awoke, he changed his name to Tan [sandalwood]. In less than a year, the governor of Shu commandery invited Case Re-

viewer Du Guang to become his deputy and recommended him to become an auxiliary palace censor. A crimson robe was bestowed upon him by imperial command. However, Du was forced to observe the period of mourning for a parent and could not assume the position. He therefore recommended Liu Tan to the governor. Upon the governor's recommendation, Liu was appointed to the same position as Du Guang. Du also gave him the newly issued crimson robe of office, which indeed accorded with Liu's dream. (From *Collected Stories from Jade Stream*.)

42. Xue Xia was from Tianshui. When his mother was pregnant with him, she dreamt that someone gave her a chest containing an embroidered robe and said, "Madam will certainly give birth to a wise and virtuous son whom the emperor will rely on." Mother Xue wrote down what she had dreamt. Xue Xia was born, and by the time he reached twenty, his talent and abilities exceeded those of other men. Emperor Wen of the Wei dynasty had endless discussions with him all day long for his literary style was elegant, perceptive, and extraordinary. His responses to questions easily flowed forth without the slightest hindrance. The emperor said, "In the past, Gongsun Long was praised as a master of disputation, but he was pedantic, absurd, weird, and irresponsible. Now, your statements never stray from the words of the sages, and truly the likes of Ziyou and Zigong could not surpass you. If Confucius himself were alive today in Wei, you would be admitted into his household as a disciple." The emperor presented a book to Xue that he had written, and inscribed upon it, "To the scholar admitted into the household." His rank reached that of vice director of the Palace Library. The emperor took off one of his imperial robes and presented it to him, which confirmed the dream of Xue's mother. (From *Wang Zinian's Recovered Records*.)

43. The family of the god Lord of Fates had embraced Daoism for generations. His mother dreamt that celestial beings dressed in vermillion robes filled the sky, each one more than ten feet tall. Their banners covered her dwelling and a golden light illuminated her body. As a result, she became pregnant and subsequently gave birth to the Lord of Fates. As a youth he was highly intelligent, studying together with Tang Yuanhuan. When he was fifteen or sixteen years of age, he left home in search of the secret of longevity and subsequently obtained the technique for becoming a transcendent. (From *Recovered Biographies of Transcendents*.)

44. For an explanation, see the commentary to the dream of Fang Xiaoru's father about burning a snake in the chapter, "Reward and Retribution" [II:19n24].

45. Pei Anzu was resting beneath a tree on a hot day when a bird of prey chased after a pheasant. The pheasant panicked and hurled itself at the bird, only to collide with the tree and die. Pei felt compassion for it and moved its body to a shady spot. He patiently looked after it for a long while. Then it revived, whereupon he released it. That night, he unexpectedly dreamt that a gentleman impressively dressed in an embroidered robe with a round collar bowed down to him twice. Pei thought this was odd and asked the reason for it whereupon the man said, "I am grateful that you released me yesterday, so I have come to thank you for your virtuous act of kindness." Everyone who heard about this considered it a strange event. (From *History of the Sui Dynasty*.)

CHAPTER 7

Utensils and Things
器物

Utensils and things can appear in dreams. There is clear evidence of this from the past as when King Tang of the Shang dreamt of someone carrying a bronze tripod on his back.[1] Liu Mian dreamt that someone gave him candles.[2] Tao Kan dreamt that a commander gave him armor.[3] Emperor Wu of the Wei dreamt that three horses ate from the same trough.[4] A crown prince of the Liang dynasty dreamt that he played chess and lost.[5] Empress Wu of the Tang dreamt that she played the dice game doublesixes and was defeated.[6] The mother of Zhang Meng dreamt of wearing an official seal from her belt in a tower.[7] The mother of Li Bo dreamt that she obtained a chess piece outside her house.[8] Liu Xie dreamt that he was holding a vermillion-lacquered ritual vessel.[9] Wang Mao dreamt that a musical set of bells and chimes fell down.[10] Qian Gongzhi dreamt about silver cups used as divining blocks.[11] Zhang Zhan dreamt of cooking food in a stone mortar.[12] Wang Jun dreamt that four knives were suspended.[13] Xu Pu dreamt that he received six keys.[14] Liu Rengong dreamt that a Buddhist banner emerged from his fingertip.[15] Shen Qingzhi dreamt that an honor guard went into the privy.[16] The mother of Tao Hongjing dreamt that an incense burner descended into her room, a sign that he would become a transcendent.[17] The mother of Ren Fang dreamt about a multicolored canopy with bells suspended, an auspicious sign that Ren would achieve renown.[18] There was a dream of a woman holding a giant sieve as she walked in the sky, which was a sign of destruction to come in Jinling.[19] There was a dream of a divinity holding up a scale to weigh the world, and thus it was known that a lady of bright countenance would wield power.[20] The mother of Dao Jing dreamt that a mirror was placed in her body; consequently, she gave birth to a son.[21] Mr. Wang dreamt that there was a mirror in his stomach and that he gained an understanding of technical knowledge.[22] Pei Yuanzhi dreamt that he drew a bow and shot at a dog; consequently, he earned the highest examination degree.[23] Hun Tian dreamt that he carried a bow along with him to sea and achieved success.[24] There was a dream of cries of greetings by the ceremonial guard; consequently, Emperor Xuanzong of the Tang assumed the throne.[25] There was a dream of a crimson curtain swirling about; subsequently, Yin Xi was born.[26] There was a dream of Daoists holding up traveling insignia and other banners; subsequently, Li Su, Duke of Liangwu, died in the Temple of the Celestial Palace.[27] There was a dream that a young monk was holding a banner and Vice Censor-in-Chief Xue died in office.[28] Moreover, there are cases of boats and carriages appearing in dreams whose meanings differ. Zheng Guang dreamt about a carriage carrying the sun and moon.[29] Liu Muzhi dreamt of a decorated parasol on a boat.[30] Shen Bo dreamt that his boat capsized while crossing a river where the river divided into two courses.[31] Wang Xingxiu dreamt that while he was on a boat crossing a river, the boat split in two.[32] Xie An dreamt of riding in the carriage of Huan Wen.[33] Du Ling dreamt of a warship that defeated Hou Jing.[34] These are instances of boats and carriages appearing in dreams. Beyond these, are not all useful objects beneficial to ordinary people considered utensils and other things? Yet, only sages can invent utensils and recognize the importance of cosmic images, while noble men, for their part, value preserving the past so as to know the future.

NOTES

1. King Tang of the Shang dreamt that someone carrying a bronze tripod on his back and holding a wooden sacrificial stand was facing him and laughing. Later, he obtained the services of Yi Yin, who indeed arrived and met Tang carrying a tripod and holding a sacrificial stand. (From *Annals of the Thearchs and Kings*.)

2. Liu Mian initially served as a minor military officer in Zhongwu. He participated in a campaign against rebels in Huaixi and was so severely injured by the enemy that he lay down in the grass. It grew dark and he did not know the way back, so, in a confused state, he fell asleep. He dreamt that someone gave him a pair of candles saying, "You, sir, are on the brink of achieving an exalted position. You shall not suffer harm on this journey and can use these to return." When he awoke, he saw two brilliant lights in front of him. (From *Old History of the Tang Dynasty*.)

3. When Tao Kan was in Guangzhou, he dreamt that a commander gave him a suit of armor. Administrator Chen Xie interpreted it, saying, "'Commander'

Utensils and Things

[sima] is the surname of the imperial family while the armor is an object that affords protection. You, sir, will be promoted." Tao indeed became general of Pingnan. (From *History of the Jin Dynasty.*)

4. Emperor Wu of the Wei was suspicious of Sima [literally, "in charge of horses"] Yi and his sons, and he often dreamt of three horses eating from the same trough *[cao]*. He was very leery of this and summoned the future emperors Wen and Ming to tell them about it. The latter said, "You have adequate precautions for your security, so do not be overly concerned about such matters." Emperor Wu agreed. But later, the Wei imperial family [surnamed Cao] was destroyed and the dynasty changed because of the Sima family, just as the dream indicated. (From *A Record of Ghosts and the Living.*)

5. Emperor Taizong of the Liang was originally enfeoffed as the Prince of Jin'an. In the third year of the Datong era [529], he was summoned to the court, but before he arrived, Crown Prince Zhaoming told his close advisors, "I dreamt that I was playing chess with the Prince of Jin'an and lost, so I gave him an ornamental sword. Doesn't this mean that the prince will be raised higher when he returns to the court?" In the fourth lunar month of that year, Crown Prince Zhaoming died, and in the fifth month, the Prince of Jin'an was raised to the position of crown prince. (From *History of the Liang Dynasty.*)

6. Empress Wu [r. 690–705] summoned Di Renjie to court and told him, "We have dreamt several times of playing the dice game double-sixes and losing. What can this mean?" Di Renjie and Wang Fangqing both replied, "'To lose at double-sixes' means that you are 'without a son' [*wuzi*, a homophone for 'no dice']." The empress immediately understood and that very day recalled her demoted son, the Prince of Luling, welcoming him as the heir apparent. (From *Old History of the Tang Dynasty.*)

7. For an explanation, see the commentary to the dream of wearing an official seal and climbing a tower in the chapter, "Mountains and Rivers" [I:4n34].

8. The mother of Li Bo dreamt of two Daoist priests playing chess outside her house. She went to watch, and one of them took a chess piece and gave it to her. Subsequently, she gave birth to Li Bo. (From *A Continuation of A Garden of Strange Events*).

9. Liu Xie, who authored *The Literary Mind and the Carving of Dragons*, stated in his preface, "When I was a little more than thirty, I once dreamt at night that I was holding a vermillion-lacquered ritual vessel and followed Confucius southward." (From *History of the Liang Dynasty.*)

10. Wang Mao was given a set of bells and chimes suspended from a frame as a gift by Emperor Wu of the Liang for his achievements in helping to establish the dynasty. When Wang was in Jiangzhou, he dreamt that the bells and chimes had fallen down from the frame by themselves for no apparent reason. After he awoke, he ordered a musical performance and, indeed, the chimes and bells fell down. He was appalled by this and, quite suddenly, fell ill and died. (From *History of the Liang Dynasty.*)

11. An Bing, whose courtesy name was Ziwen, was from Guang'an. In the fourth year of the Kaixi era [1208], Wu Xi usurped power, establishing his own officials, changing the name of the era, and declaring himself a loyal official of the Jin dynasty. Gentleman for Attendance Qian Gongzhi dreamt that Wu Xi

was praying to the gods in a temple using silver cups as divining blocks. After he cast them on the ground, a god appeared and said to Wu Xi, "Why have any doubts? An Bing has already been ordered to handle all subsequent matters." After Qian Gongzhi awakened, he felt that this incident was quite strange and spoke of it to Wu Xi, who appointed An Bing to be a grand councilor and administrator. An Bing then secretly conspired with Yang Juyuan, Li Haoyi, and others to execute Wu Xi. (From *History of the Song Dynasty*.)

12. Zhang Zhan was on his way home after traveling when one night he unexpectedly dreamt that he was cooking in a stone mortar. He sought out one Scholar Wang [n.d.] of Jianghuai to explain it, and Wang said, "You will not see your wife when you return, for to cook in a stone mortar means, 'there is no wife' [*wu fu*]." This was probably based on the homophony between the graphs *fu* [cauldron] and *fu* [wife]. (From *Miscellaneous Morsels from Youyang*.)

13. When Wang Jun was serving in a commandery, he dreamt that four knives were suspended from the rafters. Wang was appalled by this dream, but his subordinate Assistant Magistrate Li Yi bowed and congratulated him, saying, "Three graphs for 'knife' 刀 compose the graph for 'region' 州 while the fourth knife you saw means an additional [*yi* 益] one. Your Excellency will administer Yizhou 益州!" Soon, it turned out exactly as predicted. (From *History of the Jin Dynasty*.)

14. When Xu Pu had just arrived in the capital for the official examinations, he dreamt that he went to a place like the present-day Pavilion of the Depths of Literature. Inside there were three elders who gave him six keys. Xu became an official and successively served in the editorial service in the household of the heir apparent, in the left and right secretariats of the heir apparent, as supervisor of the household of the heir apparent, and as a minister-envoy before finally rising to the Grand Secretariat. Indeed, he held six offices. (From *Collected Trifles from the Studio of Honesty*.)

15. When Liu Rengong occupied a humble position, he dreamt that a Buddhist banner flew forth from his fingertip. Someone said, "You, sir, will certainly achieve an exalted position with banner insignia when you are forty-nine." Indeed, things turned out as predicted. (From *Trifling Words from Beimeng*.)

16. Shen Qingzhi once dreamt that he led the honor guard bearing the imperial insignia into a privy. He was appalled by the vulgar image of the privy, but at that time an expert interpreter of dreams told him, "You, sir, will enjoy great wealth and exalted position. However, it will not be soon." When asked the reason for this, the interpreter replied, "The honor guard, of course, signifies wealth and position while what enters the privy could be said to denote under 'a future emperor' [*houdi*, a homophone for 'rear end']. Thus, I know that such wealth and position will not be achieved in this lifetime." (From *History of the Chen Dynasty*.)

17. Tao Hongjing's courtesy name was Tongming. His mother dreamt that two celestial beings holding an incense burner came to her room. Soon afterward, she became pregnant and gave birth to Tao. (From *History of the Liang Dynasty*.) When Tao Hongjing was born, his mother dreamt that the vigorous essence of the sun was in her body and that two celestial beings holding a golden incense burner descended into her room. (From *The Bookcase of the Clouds*.)

18. Ren Fang's courtesy name was Yansheng. His mother Mistress Pei dreamt of a multicolored banner with bells suspended from its four corners. One of the bells fell down into her body. She subsequently became pregnant and gave birth to Ren Fang. At eight years of age, he could compose literary pieces, and he attained the position of palace aide to the censor-in-chief. (From *History of the Liang Dynasty*.)

19. When the imperial army attacked Jinling and the city was about to fall, someone dreamt of a woman walking in the sky with a giant sieve who was sifting things that fell down all over like beans. When these hit the ground, they all became people. The dreamer asked what this meant and was told, "These are people who are destined to die in the calamity." Then, he saw a noble man in formal hat and gown descending to earth and was told, "This is His Lordship Xu." When the dreamer awoke, he learned that Xu had died in the besieged city. Later, Wang Pingfu in his "A Poem Rhyming With the Graph for 'Sieve'" referred to this when he wrote, "At that time, Mr. Xu was skilled in literature and calligraphy; during the siege someone dreamt that he fell from the sky through a sieve." (From *Chats on Poetry from the Western Capital*.)

20. The imperial concubine Lady of Bright Countenance Shangguan was named Wan'er. When her mother, Mistress Zheng, had just become pregnant, she dreamt of a divinity holding up a large scale who said, "Use this to weigh the affairs of the world." More than a month after Wan'er was born, her mother teased her, "Aren't you the one who will weigh the affairs of the world?" and the baby suddenly gurgled in agreement. Later, the imperial concubine wielded political power in the government in exact accordance with the dream. (From *Old History of the Tang Dynasty*.)

21. Dao Jing's courtesy name was Yuanzhao [perfectly illuminating], and he was the son of Dao Gai. His mother dreamt that there was a mirror in her body so, after he was born, she named him Jing [mirror]. (From *History of the Southern Dynasties*.)

22. For an explanation, see the commentary to Wang Chu'na's dream about his stomach being opened up in the chapter, "Forms and Appearances" [II:5n19].

23. When Pei Yuanzhi became a presented scholar, he dreamt that a dog emerged from a hole, so he drew a bow and shot at it. However, his arrow traveled at a slant, and he considered this a bad omen. He dreamt that a god explained it to him thus, "The graph *gou* 苟 [a homophone for 'dog' 狗] is like the top portion of the graph *di* 第 [the highest examination degree, i.e., presented scholar], the graph *gong* 弓 [bow] forms the body of *di*, and the arrow forms its vertical stroke. With the addition of a slanted stroke, this completes the graph *di*." Indeed, Pei obtained the highest examination degree [*jidi* 及第]. (From *Collected Records from Court and Countryside*.)

24. Originally, there was a female ruler in Funan whose name was Liu Ye. A man from the Land of Mofu named Hun Tian liked to be of service to a certain god. He dreamt one night that the god bestowed a bow on him and told him to board a merchant ship going to sea. Hun Tian awoke and went to the temple where he found a bow at the foot of a sacred tree. He boarded a large ship going to sea and the god sent forth a whirlwind, ordering him to go to Funan. Liu Ye wanted to capture Hun Tian. He shot at her with his divine bow, and his ar-

row pierced her boat straight through. Liu Ye was terrified and submitted to him. Thus, Hun Tian became king of Funan. (From *Biographies of Foreigners*.)

25. The son of Minister Lu Zhenyou was a Buddhist monk, but during the Huichang era [841–846] many monks were defrocked and ordered to return to their families. Because of hereditary privilege, the son was appointed to serve as adjutant in the establishment of Prince Guang. One night, he dreamt of soldiers stationed in every direction. There were a thousand chariots and ten thousand cavalry whose flags and banners blocked out the sun and moon and who wore finely embroidered clothes. They formed a ceremonial guard on all four sides. From among this army came shouts welcoming Prince Guang, which startled the dreamer awake. Indeed, Prince Guang assumed the throne and became Emperor Xuanzong of the Tang. [r. 846–859]. (From *Records from the Grand Hall*.)

26. Yin Xi was a grand master of the Zhou dynasty. His mother dreamt while taking a nap that a crimson curtain descended from heaven and wrapped itself around her body. She saw an elder who told her, "Mother, swallow it." After she awoke, she felt a strange taste in her mouth. When she gave birth to Yin Xi, a pair of lights as bright as the sun flew over to her side, and the entire room was illuminated. (From *The Private History of the Guardian of the City Gate*.)

27. Li Su, Duke of Liangwu and son of Li Shuxun, had captured Cai and destroyed Yun. In autumn of the first year of the Changqing era [821], after serving as military commissioner of Weibo, the vice director of the left of the Department of State Affairs, and manager of affairs, he was summoned to return to the capital. Shi Jiwu, a general attached to his office, was already in Luoyang as the duke was about to enter the city. Shi dreamt that he was leading the duke's procession as they crossed the Celestial Ferry Bridge. There were eight Daoists riding on horses holding up crimson traveling insignia and other banners. Shi's lead horseman yelled at them to get out of the way, but they replied, "We have come to welcome a transcendent. We didn't realize that he is a grand councilor." One of the Daoists said to Shi Jiwu, "Take note of my poem and convey it to His Excellency." The poem went,

> You urge your horses to line up by golden palace towers.
> You ride in a chariot that becomes a raft floating toward heaven.
> Why bother to yearn for fleeting fame?
> Soar higher to enter the mists and clouds.

Three days later, the Duke of Liangwu indeed crossed the Celestial Ferry Bridge led by Shi Jiwu. Then the duke stopped to rest at the Temple of the Celestial Palace. He died more than a month later. (From *A Continuation of A Record of Strange Things*.)

28. Vice Censor-in-Chief Xue Cuncheng went from the Censorate to became a supervising secretary at the end of the Yuanhe era [806–820] and then returned to serve as a vice censor-in-chief. An official at the censorate dreamt that several dozen young monks holding jeweled banners told him, "The vice censor-in-chief was originally an arhat who was banished to the mortal world. His term of fifty years is now fulfilled and we have come to welcome him back." Before long, Xue died, having just turned fifty. (From *Collected Records from Court and Countryside*.)

29. For an explanation, see the commentary to Zheng Guang's dream in the chapter, "Sun and Moon" [II:2n21].

30. For an explanation, see the commentary to the dream of ascending to heaven on two boats joined together in the chapter, "Heaven" [II:1n9].

31. Shen Bo sought to become a district magistrate. One night, he dreamt that he was crossing a river on his way home when his boat capsized. The river's course divided *[fenshui]*—westward the water was clear while eastward it was muddy. He then made his way following the eastward course. Shen asked a friend about this, who replied, "You will soon receive the magistracy of Fenshui District." Ten days later, this prediction was indeed fulfilled. Shen went to thank his friend, and the friend advised him, "In government, it is proper to behave with clarity. Following a muddy course will not bode well." Later, Shen was dismissed because of his excessive actions [*lan*; also meaning "a river overflowing"]. (From *A Record of Inner Light*.)

32. Wang Cong of Yiyang and his two younger brothers all died in Guilin. In the fourth year of the Kaiyuan era [716], Wang Xingxiu, the son of Wang Cong, requested permission to take charge of the coffins for burial. When he arrived, he found they were unsealed. The person with whom he discussed this told him it was because the bodies had not been found. Wang Xingxiu spread his mat out on the ground and prayed for guidance. That night, he dreamt that the Wangs were on a boat *[zhou]* that had split into two parts. He then went into the countryside and saw an islet *[zhou]* to the east that was divided in two at the middle, whereupon he suddenly understood. After digging there, he was indeed able to recover the bodies. (From *Old History of the Tang Dynasty*.)

33. When Hsieh An fell seriously ill, he told someone who was close to him, "In the past, when Huan Wen was alive, I often felt threatened. Suddenly, I had a dream that I was riding in his carriage for more than five miles until it stopped. Riding in Huan Wen's carriage meant that I would take over his position." (From *History of the Jin Dynasty*.)

34. When Emperor Wu of the Chen attacked the Dalei River, the military officer Du Ling dreamt that Zhou Heshen, the Lord of the Leichi River, proclaimed himself "Generalissimo of Conquest." Zhou was sailing in a vermillion vessel and wore armor. He said that he was off to defeat Hou Jing; he then returned in an instant, announcing, "I have already killed Hou Jing." And, indeed, Hou Jing's troops were defeated. (From *History of the Chen Dynasty*.)

CHAPTER 8

Valuables and Goods
財貨

Dreams of valuables and goods involve such things as pearls, jade, cash, and silk. Some who dreamt of excrement, filth, trees, and rocks gained valuables and goods while many who dreamt of pearls, jade, cash, and silk enjoyed glory and renown. In the past, the mother of Yue Shi dreamt of a multicolored pearl.[1] The mother of a Buddhist ancestor dreamt of two pearls.[2] The mother of Xi Shi dreamt that a pearl struck her body.[3] The mother of Kou Jian dreamt of a pearl put in her mouth.[4] Mistress Huan of the Southern Qi dynasty dreamt that she ate a jade crown.[5] Mistress Hu of the Northern Qi dynasty dreamt that she was sitting in a jade basin.[6] The mother of Shao Yong dreamt that she used jade chopsticks.[7] The mother of Zhang Dexiang dreamt of obtaining a jade statue.[8] In the case of Chief Councilor Zhang Yue, there was a dream of a jade swallow when he was born.[9] Director Li Chao dreamt of a jade fish and then died.[10] Lu Yanxu dreamt of a woman whose mirror he took.[11] Yan Zhi dreamt of a woman who presented him with money.[12] The mother of Fan Mai dreamt of a gold mat; consequently, she gave birth to a son.[13] An emperor of the Later Jin dynasty dreamt of a jade basin and continued to occupy the throne.[14] A ruler of the Liang dynasty dreamt that he had borrowed money from Cao Wu.[15] Xie Feng dreamt that Zheng You fought over money.[16] After dreaming that the Director of Destinies would lend him ten million in cash, a poor scholar suddenly became rich.[17] Some dreamt that a divinity traded one million cash and their eldest sons suddenly died.[18] Emperor Wen of the Wei dreamt of grinding down a coin.[19] Zhang Huan dreamt of a pile of ceremonial tablets of official rank.[20] Shen Hongxian dreamt that he had received two bolts of silk, which indicated that the length of his life had been determined.[21] Jiang Yan dreamt that he had returned several feet of embroidered silk; consequently, his literary reputation declined.[22] These are just typical examples as there are many dreams about valuables and goods.

NOTES

1. Yue Shi was from Yihuang. His mother dreamt that an extraordinary person gave her a multicolored pearl, and consequently she gave birth to Yue Shi. He exerted himself in study and achieved a mastery of literature. During the Southern Tang dynasty, he was ranked as number one in the presented scholar examination, and under the Song, he again scored in the top rank in the examinations. Yue Shi wrote *Gazetteer of the World during the Taiping Era*. (From *History of the Song Dynasty*.)

2. The mother of the Twenty-Fourth Buddhist Patriarch dreamt that she swallowed two pearls. An arhat said, "You are destined to give birth to two children." One became the Twenty-Fourth Buddhist Patriarch and the other became a nun. (From a Buddhist text.)

3. The mother of Xi Shi dreamt that a brilliant pearl struck her body. She felt stimulated by it and became pregnant. (From *Famous Chats from the Bureau of Writers*.)

4. Kou Jian's courtesy name was Cigong; he was from Linru. His mother dreamt that a god gave her a pearl, which she swallowed. She became pregnant, subsequently giving birth to Kou Jian, who became a metropolitan graduate. (From *History of the Song Dynasty*.)

5. Mistress Huan, the mother of Empress Liu of the Southern Qi, dreamt that she swallowed a jade crown. She became pregnant, later giving birth to the future empress. (From *History of the Southern Qi Dynasty*.)

6. For an explanation, see the commentary to the dream about the sun entering her skirt in the chapter, "Food and Clothing" [II:6n35].

7. For an explanation, see the commentary to the mother of Shao Yong's dream of using jade chopsticks in the chapter, "Food and Clothing" [II:6n10].

8. Zhang Dexiang's [*dexiang* means "obtaining a statue"] courtesy name was Xiyan. When his mother was pregnant with him, she dreamt that she climbed a mountain and met a god who gave her a jade statue. (From *History of the Song Dynasty*.)

9. The mother of Zhang Yue dreamt that a jade swallow flew into her body. Because of this, she became pregnant and gave birth to Zhang. Later, he became a chief councilor. Therefore, someone composed the line, "a flying swallow entered her body." (From *Events of the Kaiyuan Era*.)

10. During the Zhenyuan era [785–804] of the Tang, Li Chao, the director of the Bureau of Merit Titles, returned to his residence and dreamt that two men dressed in yellow shirts led him to a place where someone said, "It is not yet time. The jade fish must first descend." Later, Li was on the Longwei Road when he came across a jade fish. He toyed with it on his way home and several days later he died. (From *Casual Chats from Army Headquarters*.)

11. The privy of Lu Yanxu, the director of granaries of Xuzhou, filled up with

water during torrential summer rains. Suddenly, the water drained, so Lu sent someone to inspect it. One could see an ancient vault with an earthenware coffin at the bottom. Inside was a woman more than twenty years old whose body was pure white, intact, and lightweight. Her nails were five or six inches long, and she wore more than ten gold hairpins. The funerary inscription stated, "This is a person from the Qin dynasty. A thousand years from now, it is fated that the tomb will be opened by Lu Yanxu. Keeping it sealed will bring blessings, but opening it will invite evil." There was also a mirror decorated with gold flowers. When Lu held it up to reflect the sun, the flowers resembled golden wheels. So Lu took the mirror and dozens of other objects before closing up the tomb. That night, he dreamt that the woman appeared with an angry expression as she said to him, "Why did you take my favorite things?" A year later, Lu died. (From *An Extensive Record of Anomalies*.)

12. When Yan Zhi was young, his father served as an administrator in Mizhou, and Yan accompanied him when he took up his position. He dreamt that a girl about fifteen or sixteen with a beautiful appearance came to make love to him. No sooner did he fall asleep then he would dream of her. Later, he dreamt that she came to bid him farewell, saying, "I am the daughter of the former administrator. I died and my coffin now lies in the southeast of the city. Tomorrow, they will come to bury me. Now I am going to present you with hundreds in cash." After saying this, she placed the money beneath where he was sleeping. When Yan awoke, he looked there and found hundreds in paper money. (From *An Extensive Record of Anomalies*.)

13. In Linyi, people consider purple refined gold as the highest grade and popularly call it "Yang Mai's gold." The mother of Fan Mai dreamt that someone spread out a mat made of Yang Mai's gold for her to use to give birth to a son. When the son was born, the mat shone brilliantly. Later, she actually gave birth to a son and named him Mai. He later became King of Linyi. (From *A Record of Linyi*.)

14. At the end of the year *jiachen* in the Kaiyun era [944], the Later Jin emperor sent an imperial commissioner to the Office of the Palace to consult the academicians, announcing, "We dreamt at night of a jade basin which contained a jade pillow and a jade belt, both with engraved inscriptions. They glistened and were delightful. What kind of omen is this?" In response, Recipient of Edicts Li Shenyi memorialized, "Jade is the treasure of an emperor, the belt is a favorable sign of swearing oaths of alliance and of military achievements, and the basin is a symbol of maintaining control of the ritual vessels of the state. This is an auspicious dream." (From *Casual Conversations from the Jade Hall*.)

15. For an explanation, see the commentary to the dream about deep water beside a field in the chapter "Mountains and Rivers" [II:4n10].

16. For an explanation, see the commentary to the dream about fighting over money and drowning in the chapter, "Mountains and Rivers" [II:4n4].

17. Zhou Chou was poor, and he had to keep on farming into the nighttime. After falling asleep, he dreamt that the Supreme God of Heaven came and took pity on him. The Director of Destinies examined Zhou's record and reported that this person has the physiognomy of a poor man but that his situation would not continue beyond the present. He noted that there is a Zhang Juzi on record

who will possess ten million in cash but who has not yet been born, and he requested that this money be lent to Zhou. The Supreme God replied, "Excellent." (From Gan Bao, *In Search of the Supernatural*.)

18. Wang Yue, the eldest son of Wang Dao, died. Previously, Wang Dao had dreamt that someone had purchased Yue for a million cash. Wang Dao secretly offered up prayers, but soon afterward, he obtained a million in cash dug up from the earth. The thought of this appalled him. Wang Yue took to bed with an illness and soon died. (From *History of the Jin Dynasty*.)

Grand Councilor Mao Hong dreamt that someone wanted to buy his eldest son Zhangru for one million cash. Later, he excavated a vault with money in it to the exact amount of a million cash. Zhangru died, although he was not ill. (From *A Record of Ghosts and the Living*.)

The eldest son of a grand councilor was bought with money dug up from the earth. (From *Bo and Kong's Encyclopedia*.)

19. Emperor Wen of the Wei dynasty dreamt of grinding down the design *[wen]* on a coin, but this only caused it to shine more brilliantly. He asked Zhou Xuan about this, and Zhou replied, "This is a matter within Your Majesty's family. Even though you may wish to act, the empress dowager will not hear of it." (From a commentary to *History of the Three Kingdoms*.)

[*Emperor Wen was jealous of his younger brother, Cao Zhi, who was skilled in literature* (wen). *He wished to punish him, but their mother opposed it.*—RES]

20. When Zhang Dexiang was born, his father Zhang Huan dreamt that ceremonial tablets of official rank were piled as high as a mountain in the courtyard of their house. (From *History of the Song Dynasty*.)

21. Shen Qingzhi, whose courtesy name was Hongxian, was eighty years old when he dreamt that someone gave him two bolts of silk saying, "This silk will suffice for the rest of your life." When Shen awoke, he told this to someone who said, "Venerable Sir, you will not live beyond this year. Two bolts of silk measure eighty feet. To 'suffice for the rest of your life' means that there is no more beyond this number." (From *History of the Southern Dynasties*.)

22. Jiang Yan, whose courtesy name was Wentong, served as magistrate of Xuancheng. He retired and was returning home when his boat moored at the island where the Temple of the Buddhist Soul stood. At night he dreamt that someone who identified himself as Zhang Jingyang said to him, "Could you return the bolt of brocade that I previously gave you?" Jiang felt inside his body and found several feet of it, which he gave to him. Zhang said with annoyance, "Why have you cut it up and practically used it all?" He turned to Qiu Chi and said, "Since these few remaining feet are useless, I shall give it to you." After that, the quality of Jiang's writing declined. (From *History of the Qi Dynasty*.)

CHAPTER 9

Brush and Ink
筆墨

Brush and ink also belong to the category of utensils and things. However, literati and talented scholars rely on them to express their emotions. Traces of the past and unusual stories require them in order to be transmitted far and wide. They are but slight objects, yet great indeed are their merit and utility. Therefore, it can be said that they deserve a special chapter. In the past, a king of Wu dreamt that a mark was made with a brush on his forehead.[1] A future ruler of the Southern Qi dynasty dreamt that marks were made with a brush on his clothing.[2] The drafter Li Qiao dreamt of two brushes, which was the same as Ma Yisun's dream.[3] In the cases of Fan Zhi and He Ning, there were dreams of multicolored brushes, which did not differ from Jiang Yan's dream.[4] Huang Yuan dreamt that he had received a brush soaked with ink from Confucius.[5] Ji Shaoyu dreamt that he received a carved green jade brush from Lu Chui.[6] Shortly before Yang Huan was born, his mother dreamt that a god gave her a brush and that a brilliant light struck the side of her body.[7] When Li Bo was young, he dreamt of flowers sprouting from his brush; consequently, his fame spread throughout the world.[8] Wang Xun dreamt of a brush as large as a roof rafter.[9] Wang Bo dreamt of an ink cake in the shape of a ball that filled his sleeve.[10] These were all auspicious signs.

As for dreams about poems, rhapsodies, and songs, the results that confirmed these were quite diverse. Thus, King Wuling of Zhao dreamt of a song by a virgin.[11] Sima Xiangru dreamt of writing "Rhapsody on the Great Man."[12] Linghu Chi dreamt of a conversation about a paulownia-wood hammer.[13] Xun Boyu dreamt about the saying that the grass is growing tall and straight.[14] Xiao Guan dreamt that he wrote a poem about a wintry morning.[15] Young Mr. Xing dreamt that he heard the

"Springtime Melody."[16] Xu Hun dreamt that he changed a line of poetry about Xu Feiqiong.[17] Su Shi dreamt of writing a palindrome poem.[18] Di Zundu's dream led to his writing "The Beautiful City."[19] Li He dreamt that he wrote "Record of the Jade Tower."[20] Suo Sui dreamt of inscriptions on a letter envelope.[21] Du Mu dreamt that he wrote "a sunbeam."[22] Tang Yin dreamt about the graphs *zong lü*; subsequently, he would lament his short lifespan.[23] Wang Bo dreamt of a discussion about the Great Ultimate; consequently, he wrote on the principles of *The Book of Changes*.[24] Cai Shaoxia dreamt that he was a scribe in the Secretariat of Multicolored Clouds who wrote out an inscription for a stele.[25] Shan Xuanqing, the Perfected Gentleman of Ziyang, wrote an inscription about a palace.[26] Scholar Wang dreamt that he wrote a song of lamentation for Xi Shi.[27] "Husband" Shen dreamt that he wrote a piece to be engraved at the tomb of a princess of Qin.[28] Guo Renbiao dreamt that a Daoist inscribed a sheet of paper.[29] Shangguan Wei dreamt that Emperor Yang yearned for his books.[30] Su Jian dreamt that his wife cut off a piece of writing paper.[31] Wei Jian dreamt that his beautiful concubine composed a poem matching his.[32] Zhang Xinggong dreamt that a friend wrote a poem to him.[33] Li Zhongyun dreamt that his departed brother intoned a poem for him.[34] As for the lines about the weeping toad and cassia fragrance in the poem about the auspiciousness of ascending to heaven,[35] the buzzing cicadas and the blossoming sophora tree in Sun Qiao's "Essay on the Double Seventh Festival,"[36] the line "along the pond grows spring grass" that resulted from Mr. Xie's thoughts about his younger cousin,[37] and the line "my *hun*-soul has crossed the Great River," which a wife composed at home and sent to her husband[38]—all of these came from dreams. And were not the collected poems of Editor Hu[39] and the score for a *qin*-zither composed by Zheng Shuzu the results of things transmitted in dreams? [40]

NOTES

1. Gao Yang [529–559] dreamt that someone used a brush to make a mark on his forehead. Wang Tanzhe congratulated him, "Your Highness will rule as emperor." Previously, Sun Quan, King of Wu [r. 222–252], also had a dream like this. Moreover, Xiong Xun similarly interpreted Sun's dream. (From *History of the Northern Qi Dynasty*.)

2. For an explanation, see the commentary to the dream about such images confirming becoming emperor in the chapter, "Food and Clothing" [II:6n34].

3. Li Qiao's courtesy name was Jushan. When he was a boy, he dreamt that someone gave him two brushes. After this, he was able to write literary compo-

sitions. By the age of fifteen, he understood the *Five Classics* and was praised by Xue Yuanqi. At twenty, he became a presented scholar and served as a drafter in the *Feng*-Bird Hall. (From *The Valley Embroidered with Myriad Flowers*.)

Ma Yisun lived during the Later Tang dynasty and served as a gentleman for service in Hezhong. On his way to the palace, he spent the night at an inspection station. There was a pond there beside which was a Temple of the Inspector God. He dreamt that a god presented him with two brushes, one small and one large. When Ma became a grand councilor and administered affairs in the Secretariat, a functionary provided him with two brushes whose sizes were just as in the dream. (From *Biographies of Officials according to Historical Period*.)

4. Fan Zhi's courtesy name was Wensu. The night before he was born, his mother dreamt that a god gave her a multicolored brush. At the age of nine, he could compose literary pieces. Later he became a metropolitan graduate and grand councilor. He was enfeoffed as Duke of Lu. (From *History of the Song Dynasty*.)

When He Ning was seventeen, he obtained the classicist degree and went to the capital. He unexpectedly had a dream that someone gave him a multicolored brush and told him, "You will be able to pass the presented scholar examination while still young." From then on, his talent and thoughts became even more keen and vigorous. He was nineteen when he passed the examination. (From *A Continuation of The Treasury of Rhymes*.)

Jiang Yan, whose courtesy name was Wentong, dreamt of a multicolored brush. From then on, his literary style underwent a daily renewal. Later, he dreamt that someone who identified himself as Guo Pu took back the brush. After that, he was unable to write a beautiful line of poetry, and others said that he had exhausted his talent. (From *History of the Southern Qi Dynasty*.)

5. Huang Yuan's courtesy name was Tiansou, and he was from Putian. On the eighth day of the fifth lunar month in the second year of the Baoqing era [June 4, 1226] of the Song dynasty, he took a nap and dreamt that a god was sitting in the niche of a shrine. When he looked more carefully, he discovered it was a statue of Confucius seated in a relaxed position. He quickly bowed to it again and again. The god said, "Since you have come before me, I shall give you two brushes." Huang received them and bowed once more. The god said, "Do not bow any more." So he withdrew and put one of the brushes inside his clothes close to his chest. They were about three inches in circumference and soaked with ink. He put the other inside his sleeve and asked the god for instructions. Suddenly, a boy appeared requesting a poem. Then Huang woke up and consequently composed "A Record of a Dream of Brushes." (From *Collected Works of Siru*.)

6. Ji Shaoyu, whose courtesy name was Youyang, once dreamt that Lu Chui gave him a carved green jade brush saying, "I consider this eminently useful. You, sir, should choose the finest thoughts to express with it." Because of this, Ji made great strides in his literary writings. When Wang Sengru read them, he praised them. (From *History of the Liang Dynasty*.)

7. For an explanation, see the commentary to the dream about sunlight striking her body in the chapter, "Sun and Moon" [II:2n17].

8. When Li Bo was young, he dreamt that flowers sprouted from the tip of his brush. Afterward, the results of his genius were so abundant and surpassing that his fame spread throughout the world. (From *Old History of the Tang Dynasty*.)

9. Wang Xun was an administrator under Huan Wen. Once, he dreamt that someone had given him a brush as large as a roof rafter. When he awoke, he said, "This must be a brush for writing on an important occasion." Soon afterward, Emperor Wu died. The funerary announcement and the proclamation of posthumous titles were both drafted by Wang. (From *History of the Jin Dynasty*.)

10. Wang Bo [ca. 650–ca. 676] once dreamt that someone gave him an ink cake in the shape of a ball that filled his sleeve. After this, he made great strides in literary composition every day. (From *Miscellaneous Morsels from Youyang*.)

11. When King Wuling of Zhao was visiting Daling, he dreamt that a virgin performed a song while playing the *se*-zither. It went,

A beautiful woman—how dazzling she is.
Her face as voluptuous as a trumpet vine.
Oh Fate! Oh Fate!
Why has no one ever won [*ying*] my heart?

On another day, the king was drinking wine and enjoying music when he spoke about his dream in some detail and said that he wished he could actually see this woman. Wu Guang heard this and, urged by his wife, presented their daughter Ying Mengyao. She was much favored by the king and became Queen Hui. (From *Historical Records*.)

12. When Sima Xiangru was going to submit a rhapsody to the court, he didn't quite know what to write about. He dreamt that an old man with yellow whiskers told him, "You can write a rhapsody about being a great man." Sima then wrote "Rhapsody on the Great Man" and submitted it. He received four bolts of silk brocade as an imperial gift. (From *Conversations by a Fishing Jetty*.)

13. The Last Emperor of the Western Liang dynasty was named Xin, his courtesy name was Shiye while his childhood name was Tongchui [paulownia-wood hammer]. Linghu Chi, an elder from Dunhuang, dreamt that a white-haired gentleman told him, "A south wind is stirring. It will blow through the tall trees. A foreign paulownia-wood hammer [*tongchui*] can't serve as the hub of a wheel." After speaking thus, he disappeared. It was at this time that the Last Emperor died. (From *History of the Jin Dynasty*.)

14. For an explanation, see the commentary to the dream about climbing to the tower on the city wall of Guangling in the chapter, "Mountains and Rivers" [II:4n38].

15. Xiao Guan was from Xinyu. He dreamt that a palace lady dressed in green invited him to the residence of the emperor where he wrote a lyric on the wintry morning in the palace. The words possessed a pure sensuousness that people compared to Li He of the Tang. (From *History of the Song Dynasty*.)

When Xiao Guan was young, he dreamt that he went to a palace where the women were like goddesses and transcendents. Someone gave him paper saying, "This is 'ripples' stationery. Could we trouble you to write a lyric about the wintry morning?" He was given a brush and immediately composed:

The palace's twelve lofty gate-towers
  conceal green-clad ladies.
From gaping "lion-spouts" flows wine
  with its heavy, spiced fragrance,

> Trickling through "thirsty-crow" tubes
>   in intermittent streams.
> As the dispenser's pulley begins to turn,
>   the red jade liquid splashes.
> Little scent remains from time-marking incense
>   and lotus-shaped candles have burned down.
> On a clepsydra, five dragons all spew forth
>   an overflow of cold water.
> Unattended ladies wear fish-shaped pendants
>   dangling from red sashes
> As they stand on tiptoes gazing toward
>   the sunrise in far-away Fusang.
> A half-disk rises over surface ripples
>   and crimsoned duckweed in the lake.
> They turn to look back beyond the ridge of the roof
>   at a sky filled with colorful clouds.
> But now, courtiers with scabbards clanging
>   descend from heaven above.
> Their mighty swords and lofty hats
>   throng the audience hall.

A transcendent said, "Your poem contains many unusual phrases. Someday, you will certainly achieve exalted rank." During the Dazhong xiangfu era [1008–1016], he became a presented scholar in the same group as Cai Qi. (From *Chats on Past and Contemporary Poetry*.)

16. The son of Xing Feng dreamt that a woman sang and danced the "Springtime Melody." It went:

> When it's springtime in the mortal world,
>   the light rain of the second month mixes with the dust.
> But, when the dance of spring is over,
>   the winds of autumn stir
> And sorrow overwhelms those in the mortal world
>   whose hair has turned white.

(From *A Record of Strange Things Heard*.)

17. The poet Xu Hun once dreamt that he climbed up a mountain to a palace among the clouds, where someone said, "This is Mount Kunlun." Then, he entered and saw a number of people drinking wine. They invited him to join them, and it was not until night fell that the banqueting ended. He wrote a poem which went:

> In the morning I went to the Yao-stone Terrace,
>   where the dew and atmosphere are pure.
> Among those who were seated,
>   Xu Feiqiong stood out.
> My passions have not been severed,
>   my worldly karma remains.
> For ten *li* as I descended the mountain,
>   the moon was aglow, but in vain.

Another day he again dreamt of arriving at this place where Xu Feiqiong said to him, "Why did you reveal my name to the mortal world?" Xu Hun immediately changed the line "Among those who were seated . . ." to "Celestial breezes waft the sounds of my pacing through the void." Xu Feiqiong replied, "Excellent." (From Zhong Rong, *Critical Rankings of Poets*.) [*This source is incorrect. The anecdote appears in* Poems and Their Events *by Meng Qi.—RES*]

18. After a heavy snowfall cleared, I dreamt that someone made tea by boiling the snow and that a beauty was asked to sing as she served it to me. I wrote a palindrome poem in the dream, and when I awoke, I remembered a line from it that went, "A confusion of camellia blossoms were spit onto a viridian blouse." It was based on the story of Zhao Feiyan spitting out blossoms. (From "Author's Introduction" in *Collected Poems of Su Dongpo*.)

19. Di Zundu loved to compose literature in the ancient-style. He especially appreciated the poetry of Du Fu and once wrote an encomium to a collection of his works. One night, he dreamt he saw Du Fu intoning a poem that was unknown to the world. When Di awoke, he still remembered about ten words and finished the poem himself as "The Beautiful City." Several months afterward, he died. (From *History of the Song Dynasty*.)

20. Li He's courtesy name was Changji. He dreamt that someone riding a red dragon and holding a placard summoned him, saying, "The Supreme God of Heaven has just completed the White Jade Tower, and you, sir, are invited to write a commemorative record of it." Li had no choice but to follow him, and he subsequently died. (From *Old History of the Tang Dynasty*.)

The mother of Li He of the Tang dreamt that he said to her, "The supreme god Di has recently moved his capital to the Cinnabar Garden and built the White Yao-stone Palace. I have been summoned to write a record commemorating it. He also built the Hall of the Condensed Void and has had a certain someone of my generation compose music for it." (From *Records from the Grand Hall*.)

21. Suo Sui dreamt that there were two envelopes from East Commandery addressed to him. The larger one had deteriorated. The smaller one bore inscriptions. One of these was written on the front or "chest" [*xiong*] and the other was written on the reverse or "back" [*bei*]. He took this to mean that there would be a death notice [*xiongbei*]. At that time, Suo's father was in East Commandery. Three days later, a notice of his death arrived. (From *History of the Jin Dynasty*.)

22. Du Mu dreamt that someone told him, "Your destiny has come to an end." He then dreamt that he wrote out the graphs for "a brilliant sunbeam." Someone said, "The sunbeam has passed through a crack," [an idiom for the brevity of human life]. Shortly thereafter, Du Mu died. (From *Old History of the Tang Dynasty*.)

23. Tang Yin's courtesy name was Ziwei. He placed first in the provincial examinations in Yingtian. However, he fell victim to slander and lost his status as a scholar. Tang left the Wu area and traveled to the Min area where he visited the Temple of the Nine Transcendents and prayed for a dream. He dreamt that someone showed him the two graphs *zhong lü* [the sixth of the twelve ritual pitch pipes and a symbol of the exhaustion of yang energy]. When he returned, he told the dream to others, but no one could understand it. One day, he went to Wang Ao's house and saw an inscription on the wall of a lyric to the tune of "Fragrance Fills the Courtyard" by Su Shi, which contained the graphs *zhong lü*. Tang Yin was surprised and said, "This is what I saw in my dream." He attempted to in-

tone the lyric, which contained the line, "The better part of a half-century has passed, but sorrows will be few in the days to come." Tang Yin indeed died at the age of fifty-three. (From *Long Conversations by Thunder Lake*.)

24. Wang Bo [ca. 650–ca. 676] often discussed *The Book of Changes*. He dreamt that someone told him, "*The Changes* contain the Great Ultimate. You, sir, should make an effort to ponder this." After he awoke, he began to write about *The Changes* and completed several chapters containing his insights. But, when he reached the hexagram *Jin*: "Progress," he fell ill and died. (From *Old History of the Tang Dynasty*.)

25. Cai Shaoxia dreamt that someone had him compose a text for a stele. It read in short, "Formerly I rode in noble carriages decorated with fish-skins. Now I walk on the tips of the clouds. I travel lofty roads through the void where the wheels of my elegant carriage trace spirals." At the end was the inscription, "Written by the Scribe of the Secretariat of Multicolored Clouds, Cai Shaoxia." (From *Biographies of Divine Transcendents*.)

26. During the Tang dynasty, there was a person who dreamt that he had written a commemorative inscription for the New Palace that stated, "Written by Shan Xuanqing, the Perfected Gentleman of Ziyang." It read in short, "Its excellent virtue maintains the constancy of the western foothills; its source replenishes the eastern lake. Majestic, noble, and opulent indeed is the New Palace." (From *Extensive Records*.)

27. Yao He told Shen Yazhi, "My friend Scholar Wang dreamt at the beginning of the Yuanhe era [806–820] that he had traveled to Wu to serve Fuchai, the King of Wu [r. 495–477 BCE]. He heard the royal carriage emerge from the army camp to the sounds of flutes and drums. It was said that they were burying the king's favorite, Xi Shi. The king was mourning her and ordered his literary retainers to compose songs of lamentation. Scholar Wang responded to the command by writing,

> Westward, I gaze toward the palace gate
>   of the King of Wu.
> Graphs styled like clouds and *feng*-birds
>   grace the memorial plaques.
> The array of pearl-studded tents
>   forms a meandering river.
> A plot has been chosen
>   to bury the "golden-hairpin" beauty.
> Filling the route
>   are plants red with weeping.
> The altar with green jade steps
>   is three levels high.
> The spring breeze
>   has no place to go
> For sadness and loneliness
>   overwhelm our hearts.

The king was extremely pleased with it. After he awoke, Scholar Wang was able to write down the entire incident. (From *An Extensive Record of Anomalies*.)

28. Shen Yazhi dreamt that he became the husband of Nongyu, the young

daughter of the Duke of Qin. The princess died, so he wrote a song of lamentation in response to a command that went:

> Weeping, I bury a single red flower,
>   together in life, we are parted by death.
> Her golden hairpins lie fallen among fragrant plants,
>   perfumed embroidery infuses the spring breeze.
> The place where the sounds of a flute were heard
>   is the tall tower in the bright moon.
> Snowflakes fall on the night of the Cold Meal Festival,
>   and the Greenery Palace is tightly locked up.

(From *Bo and Kong's Encyclopedia*.)

At the beginning of the Taihe era [827–835], Shen Yazhi went to Bin. He left the city of Chang'an and stayed at a residence in Tuoquan where he dreamt that Duke Mu of Qin said to him, "I have a beloved daughter whom I wish to give to you as a wife." One year later, the princess suddenly died. The duke was inconsolable with grief and had Shen compose her epitaph. Shen was only able to remember the commemorative poem which went:

> The wind weeps among the white willows,
>   sedge grows over the stone-lined well.
> Random blossoms cover the ground,
>   a springtime scene with balmy mist.
> Bejeweled, sorrowful, powered, thin—
>   she no longer wears fine silk gauze.
> Deep, deep, is the buried jade—
>   what must her longings be like?

(From "A Record of a Strange Dream.")

29. Guo Renbiao was a subofficial functionary in the Secretariat of the Heir Apparent of the illegitimate Wu dynasty. While ill he dreamt of a Daoist in a purple robe with golden medallions who came into the reception hall of his house following behind a young boy. Guo therefore asked him when he might recover from his illness. The Daoist's expression became fierce as he replied, "It will grow worse." No sooner had Guo awakened then his illness worsened. Several days later, he again dreamt that the same Daoist as before had arrived. He kowtowed and humbly expressed his gratitude. After a while, the Daoist relented and took out a piece of paper on which he wrote:

> Ponder well the whirlwinds and violent storms.
> The crane gazes toward its nest and unfurls its wings to fly.
> The principles of my Way can be relied on.
> Herein are the calculations of all destinies.
> If you cannot utilize these, what else can you do?

Guo, still dreaming, didn't understand what he meant. But as soon as he awoke, he found his illness had subsided (from *A Record of Inquests into Spirits*).

30. In the fourth year of the Wude era [621] of the Tang dynasty after the Eastern Capital was pacified, the New Books in Precious Cases Collection in the Hall for Perusing Literature, amounting to some eight thousand volumes, was

going to be shipped to the capital. Shangguan Wei dreamt that the late Emperor Yang of the Sui dynasty said to him, "Why are you suddenly taking my books to the capital?" At that time, Grand Treasurer Song Zungui was having the books shipped to the capital on board a large vessel when a strong wind blew across the river, capsizing and sinking the ship. Shangguan Wei again dreamt of Emperor Yang who gleefully told him, "Now, I have my books back!" The emperor had loved to read books almost daily, and the New Books in Precious Cases Collection had been his private imperial library during the Daye era [605–617]. (From *Recovered Records from the Daye Era*.)

31. Su Jian had passed the official examinations and was returning to Wu. He passed through Tongzhou where he visited the towered pavilion in the district of Dengcheng. After having drunk a great deal, he dreamt that his wife had taken out a sheet of red stationery from his writing box, cut off a piece, and wrote a poem that went:

> The waters of Chu are calm as a mirror.
> White birds fly around in circles.
> How grand must be the city of Jinling.
> Once there, you've not a single thought of returning.

Su also cut off a piece of writing paper from Shu and composed a poem. It went:

> Returning to Wu, I proceeded east
>   and visited Dengcheng.
> The pure breezes at the tower
>   half revived me when drunk.
> I imagine by the time I arrive home,
>   spring will be coming to an end
> And blossoms on a thousand crabapple trees
>   will all have withered and fallen.

After writing this poem, he put them both under his sleeping mat. He also saw his wife flogging Xiaoqing, the concubine he had brought along with him. After he had awakened, he found the poems under his sleeping mat, and when he looked in his writing box, he found that some of the red stationery had been cut off. Xiaoqing died after a sudden illness, and by the time he had returned home, his wife had already died. It happened on the very day that he had visited Dengcheng. (From *A Record of Unusual Things Heard*.)

32. Wei Jian had a beautiful concubine who clutched her heart and died. Wei was desolate with grief and composed a poem which went:

> The precious sword became a dragon
>   and returned to the viridian depths.
> The daughters of Yao followed the sun
>   to the Yellow Springs below.
> I down a cup of wine
>   to escape the springtime breeze.
> In solitude beside the library window,
>   I lament sleeping alone.

That night he dreamt that his concubine wrote a poem in response:

> The spring rain drizzles,
>   obscuring the sky.
> Outside every household,
>   willows form a haze.
> Now, I am heartbroken,
>   and I weep in vain.
> We'll be happy when we meet again
>   in some future year.

Wei felt depressed all day long. Later, he dreamt again of his concubine who said, "Soon, we'll see each other." Indeed, he then died. (From *A Record of Romances*.)

33. Zhang Xinggong was the son of the magistrate of Zhijiang, Zhang Ting [fl. early 9th cent.]. Zhang Ting died, and Zhang Xinggong lived on in Zhijiang. He dreamt that Zhang Chui wrote a poem to him that went:

> Misery, and then more misery.
> This hall in autumn looks a hundred years old.
> Alone, I find myself far, far away,
> Passing the Cold Meal Festival in the wilds.

Zhang Xinggong was startled awake. Several days later, he died. (From *Miscellaneous Morsels from Youyang*.)

34. Investigating Censor Li Shuji and his elder brother Li Zhongyun had both earned the presented scholar degree. Li Shuji died during the Dali era [766–779]. More than a year later, both his brother-in-law and Li Zhongyun dreamt that they saw Shuji, who still felt a deep attachment to them. But when Li Shuji spoke to Zhongyun, his tone and appearance became despondent, saying, "The living and dead are cut off from each other. There is no possibility of a happy meeting except that we shall be together again after one hundred years." He recited a poem that went:

> Suddenly, I parted from you before my time.
> In the dark world below, my sorrows never end.
> Though Chang'an is not far away,
> No letter can ever get through.

Several years later, Li Zhongyun also died. (From *An Extensive Record of Anomalies*.)

35. Li He wrote a poem about a dream of ascending to heaven which went:

> The moon's old hare and shivering toad
>   weep forth the blue sky.
> Its towering palace opens slightly
>   to reveal walls aglow with white light.
> A jade wheel, it rolls across the dew,
>   moistening its halo
> As I meet a transcendent wearing *luan*-bird pendants
>   on a path through fragrant cassia.

(From *Bo and Kong's Encyclopedia*.)

36. Sun Qiao, whose courtesy name was Kezhi, wrote "Essay on the Double Seventh Festival" which went, "When the morning watch is struck and horses

and carriages race about, that is when I go to bed carefree. I lie down and sleep, breathing deeply, snoring as I dream of returning to my hometown. Sophora blossoms fill the courtyard along with the buzz of the singing cicadas." (From *New History of the Tang Dynasty*.)

37. Xie Lingyun was from Guiji and was the grandson of Xie Xuan. He used to compose poems together with his younger cousin Xie Huilian, and every one contained excellent lines. Once, when his cousin was not there, he tried to come up with a line but could not succeed. That night, he dreamt about Huilian and suddenly came up with "along the pond grows spring grass; the garden is transformed by singing birds," which he considered the result of spiritual assistance. (From *Chats on Past and Contemporary Poetry*.)

38. There was a student who married and then went off to the National University. A long time passed and still he had not returned home. One night, he dreamt that he had gone home and saw his wife writing a poem by candlelight that went:

> Beyond counting are the days spent longing for you.
> Know that my thoughts have become confused.
> While dreaming, my *hun*-soul feared no danger
> As it flew westward across the Great River.

After the student awoke, he thought this was strange and wrote down the poem. Later, a letter from home arrived with a poem by his wife. It was just like the one in his dream, and the letter was written the very day on which he had the dream of returning home. (From *A Record of Collected Strange Events*.)

39. Scholar Hu earned his living from editing books. He lived near White Duckweed Island next to an old tomb. Every time he drank some tea, he would always offer some at the tomb. Unexpectedly, he dreamt of a person who said, "My name is Liu. In life, I was skilled at poetry and enjoyed drinking tea. I am grateful for your offerings of tea, but I have nothing with which to repay you. So I would like to teach you something about writing poems." Scholar Hu declined, saying that he lacked the ability for poetry. Liu insisted, saying, "Just set your mind on expressing something, and you will master it." Scholar Hu then studied the art of poetry with him and people at that time spoke of "the poems of Editor Hu." Liu was probably Liu Yun. (From *A Compendium on Tea*.)

40. Zheng Shuzu, whose courtesy name was Gongwen, was from Kaifeng. He could play the *qin*-zither and composed "Sounds of the Dragon in Ten Pieces," saying, "I once dreamt that someone was playing it on the zither and wrote it down after I awoke." People at the time considered it marvelous. (From *History of the Northern Qi Dynasty*.)

CHAPTER 10

Written Graphs
字畫

Written graphs have undergone many changes, and the forms of later ages are not the same as the ancient script of Cang Jie. Nevertheless, interpreting dreams by analyzing graphs has often yielded results, as when the graph for "pine" 松 was analyzed into "eighteen" 十八 and "duke" 公,[1] and "sophora" 槐 was analyzed into "ghost" 鬼 beside a "tree" 木.[2] When "earth" 土 was removed from "dirt" 垢, it became the graph *hou* 后.[3] When a "captive" 虜 removed his clothes, he became a "son" 男.[4] A "goat" 羊 without its horns and tail became a "king" 王,[5] and a dot placed on the forehead of a "king" 王 became a "ruler" 主.[6] A "tree" 木 breaking into "heaven" 天 became "not" 未.[7] A "river" 河 without "water" 氵 became "possible" 可.[8] A wolf eating a "foot" 腳 became "retreat" 卻.[9] A "man" 人 who climbs up a "mountain" 山 became "unlucky" 凶.[10] Three "knives" 刀 combined to form "region" 州.[11] Two "mountains" 山 combined to form "exit" 出.[12] "Slice" 片 and "dog" 犬 together made "examination essay" 狀.[13] "To lose" 失 and "grain" 禾 together made "official salary" 秩.[14] A "carriage" 車 from which meat is hung meant "decapitation" 斬.[15] When an arrow shoots a "dog" 狗, it becomes an "official mansion" 第.[16] Fu Rong realized that Feng Chang had murdered the wife of Dong Feng.[17] Li Gongzuo understood that Shen Chun had murdered the husband of Xie Xiao'e.[18] A dream that the Jin dynasty was exhausted anticipated a realization about the words "prosperity and brilliance."[19] The wife of Zeng Chongfan realized before she was a bride that her husband's surname would include the graphs for "field" 田 and "sun" 日.[20] Cui Shi was seated at the foot of a dais listening to a Buddhist sermon when he saw himself in a mirror.[21] Li Ling carried grass on his head and entered water while holding knives.[22] Regional Inspector

169

Liu was short seven thousand bundles of firewood.[23] The graphs for "ninety" 九十 were written for Vice Minister Meng.[24] As for "man" 人 and "inner" 內 forming "meat" 肉,[25] "fire" 火 and "army" 軍 forming the graph *hui* 煇,[26] "silk threads" 絲 and "mountain" 山 forming the graph *you* 幽,[27] both "elder brother" 昆 and "all" 皆 containing the graph *bi* 比,[28] "horn" 角 composed of "to use" 用 beneath "knife" 刀,[29] *ru* 汝 composed of "water" 氵 beside "woman" 女,[30] *zhen* 甄 composed of "earth" 土, "west" 西, and "tile" 瓦,[31] "to hear" 聞 composed of an "ear" 耳 inside a "door" 門,[32] and the dreams about the graphs *su* 蘇, "brambles" 棘, "cinnabar" 丹, "hill" 丘, and "eight" 八: these were all later confirmed. How can one say that fate is not predetermined?[33]

NOTES

1. For an explanation, see the commentary to the dream about a pine tree growing forth from someone's stomach in the chapter, "Forms and Appearances" [II:5n10].

2. Tuoba Shun of the Northern Wei was killed by Xianyu Kangnu, a guardian of the imperial tombs. Originally, when the future Emperor Zhuang was still Prince Changle, Tuoba Shun dreamt that black clouds moved from the northwest directly toward the southeast. They collided with the sun and moon, which were both destroyed, and all the stars were obscured. Heaven and earth became dark. After a short time, the clouds dispersed and a sun appeared. The southwest corner of the sky became especially bright. It was said that this was the sun of Prince Changle. Then, Tuoba Shun saw the future Emperor Zhuang enter the palace through the Gate of Heaven and ascend to the Hall of the Great Ultimate. There were many cries of "May you live ten thousand years!" All the officials were dressed in court robes as they stood in audience before the emperor. Only Tuoba Shun removed his cap and gown and lay down beneath a sophora tree along the west side of a corridor in the Department of Scholarly Counselors. After awakening, he told Yuan Huiye about the dream and said, "My dream last night was not a good one." After narrating the dream, he then proceeded to interpret it, saying "Black clouds are a kind of evil *qi*-energy, and black is the color of the north. In the end, an enemy will come from the north and spread chaos throughout the capital. They will kill those in the two palaces and destroy the entire government. The sun is a symbolic image of the sovereign, and the moon of the empress, while the stars are the officials. Doesn't this mean that a calamity will befall the capital? Xie, Prince of Pengcheng, is known throughout the world for his culture and virtue. I have just dreamt that his son became the son of heaven, which is a reward for the prince's accumulated virtue. This is certainly natural. I only regret that he will not possess the throne for long. The sun rising from the southwest means that according to calendrical calculation, his reign will only last three years. I only regret that I shall not live to see it. As for my lying down under the sophora tree, the graph for 'sophora' is composed of the graph for

'ghost' next to that for 'tree.' I shall be among the ghosts. Moreover, doesn't taking off my cap and gown mean that I will die? Still, after I am gone, I shall be posthumously raised to the highest rank as one of the 'three dukes.'" Later, it indeed turned out as he had said. (From *History of the Northern Dynasties*.)

The Prince of Guangling dreamt that he was wearing royal robes and standing beside a sophora tree. Tang Yuanshen said, "The Prince will die. The graph for 'sophora' contains the element for 'ghost' next to that for 'tree.'" It indeed turned out to be so. (From an unofficial history.)

3. For an explanation, see the commentary to the dream about Feng Hou and Li Mu in the chapter, "The Disciple of Emptiness" [I:5n2].

4. For an explanation, see the commentary to the dream about a captive taking off his clothes in the chapter, "Food and Clothing" [II:6n24].

5. The Duke of Pei began as a neighborhood head. He dreamt that he chased a goat and pulled out its horns and tail. The interpretation stated that the graph for "goat" without its horns and tail is the graph for "king." According to another account, it was the future Emperor Guangwu of the Eastern Han who had this dream. (From *Unworldly Chats*.)

6. For an explanation, see the commentary regarding the King of Wu's [r. 222–252] dream about a brush in the chapter, "Brush and Ink" [II:9n1].

7. When Wang Dun was planning to rebel, he dreamt of a tree that grew upward and broke into heaven. The interpretation stated, "This forms the graph 'not.' It means you should not make such a move." (From *History of the Jin Dynasty*.)

8. For an explanation, see the commentary to the dream about the water of the Yellow River drying up in the chapter, "Mountains and Rivers" [II:4n9].

9. Zhang Miao, an official in the personnel evaluation section of a commandery, received an ad hoc assignment and was about to proceed to a certain region. At night, he dreamt of a wolf eating a foot. Suo Dan interpreted the dream saying, "If the element 'flesh' 月 is eaten from the graph 'foot,' it becomes 'retreat.'" It happened that the eastern barbarians had risen in revolt, so Zhang did not travel any further. (From *History of the Jin Dynasty*.)

10. Zhang Zhai, an assistant magistrate of a commandery, dreamt that he rode a horse up a mountain and circled a house three times. All he could see were pines and junipers, and he was unable to locate the door. Suo Dan interpreted it, saying, "'Horse' is associated with the trigram *Li:* 'Clinging.' *Li* is correlated with the agent 'fire' *[huo],* which has the same sound as 'disaster' *[huo].* When the graph for 'man' climbs up that for 'mountain,' it becomes the graph 'unlucky.' Seeing only pines and junipers symbolizes the gate to a tomb. Not to be able to find the door indicates that there is no door. 'Circling three times around' symbolizes three years. In three years, a great disaster will befall you." Indeed, Zhang plotted a rebellion and was executed. (From *History of the Jin Dynasty*.)

11. For an explanation, see the commentary to the dream about four suspended knives in the chapter, "Utensils and Things" [II:7n13].

12. Yang Wenguang was trapped in Liuzhou by the Man barbarians for one hundred days. He dreamt one night of fleeing to two mountains. A dream interpreter explained, "Two 'mountains' combine to form the graph for 'exit.'" The next day, Yang was able to escape. (From *Annals of the Song Dynasty*.)

13. Ten days before Liang Hao attended the official examinations, he dreamt

that someone gave him a slice of dog meat. Liang was not pleased by this and asked a dream interpreter, who analyzed it. "The graphs for 'slice' and 'dog' combine to form 'examination essay' *[zhuang]*." Indeed, he wrote the top-ranked essay to become the principal graduate *[zhuangyuan]*. (From *A Garden of Strange Events*.)

14. When Cai Mao was in Guanghan, he dreamt that he was sitting in a great hall. On the top of the roof were three ears of grain. Cai jumped up and grabbed the one in the middle, but then he lost it. He asked the recorder Guo He about this, and Guo replied, "The great hall is a symbolic image of the palace. 'Grain on the top of the roof' means a large official salary. Taking the middle ear of grain refers to a government position in the Central Pavilion. As for the graphs, when 'grain' is combined with 'to lose,' it forms 'official salary.'" Within a month, Cai's dream was confirmed. (From *History of the Eastern Han Dynasty*.)

15. Yi Xiong dreamt one night of riding in a carriage from which meat was hung alongside. He interpreted it himself, saying "Meat must have 'tendons' 筋 *[jin]*, and this graph has the same sound as *jin* 斤 [catty; a unit of weight]. The graph 'carriage' with 'catty' alongside becomes 'decapitation.' It means I will be killed!" Later, he was decapitated by Wang Dun. (From *History of the Jin Dynasty*.)

16. For an explanation, see the commentary to the dream about drawing a bow and shooting a dog in the chapter, "Utensils and Things" [II:7n23].

17. Dong Feng, a man from the capital, spent three years traveling in pursuit of learning before returning home. On his way back, he stopped at the home of his wife's family where she was staying, and that very evening, his wife was murdered by a thief. Her elder brother suspected that Dong had killed her, so he had Dong arrested and brought a lawsuit against him. Dong was severely beaten and falsely confessed to killing his wife. But when Fu Rong investigated the case, he felt there was something strange about it. He asked Dong, "In your travels, were there any strange occurrences and were any divinations performed?" Dong replied, "Originally, as I was about to depart, I dreamt of riding a horse southward across a river. Then, the horse turned around and crossed it northward. And then, it crossed the river from north to south again. The horse stopped in the middle of the river and would not move no matter how much I whipped it. When I looked down, I saw that there were two suns in the water. The one to the left of the horse was white and moist, the one to its right was black and dry. When I awoke, I felt my heart beating with fear and considered this an unlucky omen. On the night of my return, I had the same dream and asked a diviner about it. He said, "You will suffer imprisonment and a lawsuit. Keep away from 'three pillows,' and avoid 'three baths.'" When I arrived at the house, my wife prepared a bath for me and at night provided a new pillow. Though I remembered the words of the diviner, I did not follow them. My wife bathed herself, slept on the new pillow, and then died." Fu Rong said, "Now I understand. In *The Book of Changes,* the trigram *Kan*: 'The Abysmal' is correlated with the agent 'water' while the horse is a correlative of the trigram *Li*: 'Clinging.' When you dreamt that you rode a horse southward across a river, then went north, and then south again, it indicates the progression from *Kan* to *Li* whereby all three lines of *Kan* undergo transformation into their opposites to become the trigram *Li. Li* represents the middle daughter while *Kan* represents the middle son. The two suns

Written Graphs 173

are symbolic images indicating two husbands. *Kan* also represents a judge. The judge interrogates the husband, for the wife died by bleeding to death. *Kan* contains two yin lines and one yang line while *Li* contains two yang lines and one yin line. They perfectly mirror each other when their lines change places. When the trigram *Li* is below and *Kan* is above, it forms the hexagram *Jiji*: 'After Completion.' King Wen encountered it. He was imprisoned in Jiangli and survived by behaving properly. Had he not done so, he would have died. As for the wet sun to the horse's left, wetness means water. The element for 'water' 氵 on the left and the graph for 'horse' 馬 on the right is the graph *feng* 馮 while the graphs for two suns 日 combined form *chang* 昌. Feng Chang 馮昌 is the one who killed her!" Thus, the case was reopened for further investigation. Feng Chang was arrested and interrogated, whereupon he immediately confessed, "I plotted with Dong Feng's wife to kill him. We arranged to use a bath and a new pillow as signs. Later, we were careless, and I killed his wife by mistake." (From *History of the Jin Dynasty*.)

18. The wife of Duan Juzhen was originally surnamed Xie; her personal name was Xiao'e. Both Duan and Xiao'e's father were merchants who traveled through eastern China, and both were killed by robbers. Xiao'e dreamt that her father told her, "I was killed by a monkey in a carriage and by grass east of the gate." She also dreamt that her husband told her, "I was killed by walking through grain and by a husband for a day." She asked all her relatives about this, but no one understood it. However, Li Gongzuo of Longxi discovered its meaning by interpreting the dream as a riddle: "The 'monkey' in the 'carriage' 車 is the graph *shen* 申 [a heavenly stem, correlated with the monkey]. The graphs for 'door' 門 and 'east' 東 along with the element for 'grass' ⁺⁺ form the graph *lan* 蘭. 'Walking through grain' is to penetrate a 'field' 田, which is also the graph *shen* 申. 'A husband for a single day' 一日夫 *[yi ri fu]* forms *chun* 春. The one who killed your father is Shen Lan 申蘭 and the one who killed your husband is Shen Chun 申春." Xiao'e sought to find them based on this interpretation. It turned out the Shens were notorious robbers and desperados. Xiao'e changed her clothes and impersonated a man, mixing with servants in order to search for them. After more than a year, she found Shen Lan in Jiangzhou and Shen Chun in Dushupu. Shen Lan and Shen Chun were elder and younger cousins. Xiao'e hired herself out as a servant in Shen Lan's house, working diligently until he gradually came to rely upon her. Xiao'e saw the clothing and household items that he had stolen from Duan and Xie. Thus, she was even more convinced that her dream was beyond doubt. She waited until both Shen Lan and Shen Chun were drunk, then drew a sword and decapitated Shen Lan. Then, she quickly called the neighbors to arrest Shen Chun, revealing for the first time her own situation. Regional Inspector Zhang Xi praised Xie Xiao'e for her ardent devotion. (From *Old History of the Tang Dynasty*.)

19. Emperor Xiaowu of the Jin was posthumously named Yao [luminous]; his courtesy name was Changming [prosperity and brilliance]. Originally, Emperor Jianwen had dreamt that the Jin dynasty was about to exhaust its prosperity and brilliance. But, while pregnant with the future Emperor Xiaowu, the future Empress Dowager Li dreamt that a god told her, "You will give birth to a son and should name him Chang [prosperity]." When she gave birth, the east

had just become brilliant *[ming]*, so he was given the courtesy name Changming. Emperor Jianwen then shed copious tears. (From *History of the Jin Dynasty*.)

20. The wife of Zeng Chongfan had been betrothed to several different men, but in each case the groom suddenly died on the eve of the wedding. One night, she dreamt that someone told her, "The one with deer horns on the head of a field 田 and a brilliant sun 日 as the field's tail will be your husband." She realized what this meant when she later married Mr. Zeng 曾. (From *Random Notes from the Western Capital*.)

21. During the Tang dynasty, Assistant Director of the Right Lu Cangyong and Secretariat Director Cui Shi were both banished to Lingnan. They reached Jingzhou, where Cui dreamt that he was seated beneath the dais listening to a Buddhist sermon when he saw himself in a mirror. He asked the dream interpreter Zhang You about it, and Zhang You told Assistant Director Lu, "Mr. Cui is in great danger. Dreaming of being seated at the foot of a dais and listening to a Buddhist sermon means that sounds are coming down from on high. The graph for 'mirror' 鏡 *[jing]* is composed of the elements 'metal' 金 beside 'finished' 竟 *[jing]*. His life will be finished today!" Soon afterward, an imperial order from a censor arrived, and Cui committed suicide. (From *The Taiping Miscellany*.)

22. Li Ling of Jiangnan had grown old and no longer had any ambitions to be an official. He built a house for himself west of the Temple of the Dharma Clouds in Guangling where he planned to live for the rest of his life. Li once dreamt that he tied up a bunch of grass, put it on top of his head, bit hold of a knife, and held a knife in each hand as he entered the water and proceeded to walk. Li thought this was terribly strange. Shortly thereafter, Sun Ru conquered Guangling, and one of his generals, Li Qiong, quartered soldiers in the Temple of the Dharma Clouds. The general himself stayed at Li Ling's home for some time and treated him as a father. When Ma Yin occupied Hunan, Li Qiong became surveillance commissioner and employed Li Ling as magistrate of Lipu 荔浦 whose graphs confirmed the dream about "grass" ⁺⁺ on top, three "knives" 刀, and entering "water" 氵. (From *A Record of Inquests into Spirits*.)

23. When Gentleman of the National Treasury Wei Zhengguan was attending the official examinations, he once went to Ruzhou. Regional Inspector Liu Ling retained him and appointed him an administrative assistant for military affairs. Liu once dreamt that someone submitted a report that there was a shortage of 7,700 bundles of kindling. He sought out Wei to explain the dream, and Wei said, "'Kindling' is 'firewood' [*xin;* the expression 'the firewood has been consumed' indicates death]. You, sir, have not much longer to live." More than a month later, Liu died of an illness. Wei conducted an official accounting of government funds and supplies and only found that there was a shortage of 7,700 bundles of kindling. As he was consulting the records, he realized the meaning of Liu's earlier dream. (From *Miscellaneous Morsels from Youyang*.)

24. Meng Dechong, vice minister of the Court of the Imperial Clan in Shu, was the son of Yiye, Prince of Yan. He was unrestrained, haughty, and boastful. Meng used to bring courtesans along with him when carrying out his duties in the Imperial Ancestral Temple. One night, he dreamt that an old man upbraided him. Furthermore, the man took a brush from a table and suddenly ordered Meng to open the palm of his hand on which he wrote in large graphs "ninety" before

Written Graphs 175

Meng awakened. The next day, Meng discussed this incident with his retainers saying, "When this old man criticized me, he was expressing his compassion for me. When he wrote 'ninety,' it meant that he was granting me a long life of ninety years." One of his retainers, Feng Lian, joked about this by saying, "The graphs for 'nine' 九 and 'ten' 十 compose the cursive form of the graph for 'death' 卒. You, Vice Minister, will surely die." And, in less than ten days, Meng did indeed die. (From *Leisure Notes from a Country Man*.)

25. Song Jue dreamt of someone in the palace wearing red clothes while Song himself was rapidly beating him with two staves. Suo Dan said, "A 'man' added to the graph 'inner' [i.e., the palace] is the graph for 'meat.' Meat is red in color. The two staves are symbols of chopsticks. The rapid beating indicates eating one's fill of meat [i.e., attaining high rank]." Later events indeed confirmed this. (From *History of the Jin Dynasty*.)

26. An official in the secretariat dreamt of a fiery volcano and an army, and that someone surnamed Liu would become the principal graduate in the official examinations. The next year, a Liu Hui 劉煇 did indeed become the principal graduate. (From *A Record of Events from the Eastern Studio*.)

27. For an explanation, see the commentary to the dream about hanging silken threads on a mountain in the chapter, "Mountains and Rivers" [II:4n3].

28. Du Mu sought an official appointment from the prime minister but without success. He dreamt that someone told him:

After spring, before the arrival of fall—
the feet of "elder brother"
and the head of "all."

Indeed, he was made vice director of the Bureau of Review 比部 *[bibu]*. (From *A Record of Strange Events*.)

29. For an explanation, see the commentary to the dream about horns growing from the head in the chapter, "Forms and Appearances" [II:5n7].

30. For an explanation, see the commentary to the dream about tearing off a pouch beside a river in the chapter, "Food and Clothing" [II:6n36].

31. Zou Zhan, whose courtesy name was Runfu, dreamt that someone identifying himself as Zhen Shuzhong 甄舒仲 bowed down to him and sought reburial. When Zou awoke, he thought about the dream and said, "The name is a combination of "west" 西, "earth" 土, "tile" 瓦, "middle" 中, and "man" 亻. He then found the body and reburied it. He dreamt again that Zhen bowed and thanked him. (From *History of the Jin Dynasty*.)

32. Wei Reng and Li Guinian both passed the examinations at the same time. Wei had dreamt that he was to become an attendant gentleman and that he sent someone to spy at the Bureau of Civil Appointments who listened by pressing his ear against a door. Li had dreamt that someone brought news that he would become a vice magistrate of a district. The next day, they interpreted these dreams together and felt that pressing an "ear" against a "door" forms the graph "to hear" and that they would be 'hearing glad tidings' 聞喜 *[wenxi]*." Wei did indeed become commandant of Wenxi 聞喜 District and Li did indeed become the vice magistrate of Qi District. Later, Wei was demoted to commandant of Huanggang in Qi'an Commandery. After receiving the order, he was trying to estimate

the distance he had to travel when he dreamt that he had picked up a strand of rope. Li interpreted it, saying "The graph for 'strand' 毛 is composed of 'one thousand' 千 above 'seven' 七. You will have to travel one thousand seven hundred *li*," and it was just as he said. (From *A Record of Fates*.)

33. Gao Jidi was from Suzhou in Wu. One night he dreamt of someone who grasped his hand, wrote the graph "*su*" on it, and then said, "You will be killed." Gao became suspicious as a result of this, and he refused to have contact with anyone surnamed "Su." When the government office of the prefectural government of Suzhou was relocated, a watchdog official falsely accused the prefect of treason. The prefect was arrested and condemned. Because Gao had authored a congratulatory "Essay on Raising the Roofbeams of the Prefectural Hall," he was also publicly executed. (From *Chats on Poetry from Rongtang*.)

Wang Zijin was an expert at interpreting dreams. Someone dreamt about brambles and Wang said, "The graph for 'brambles' 棘 is a doubling of the graph for 'thorn' 束. 'Thorn' repeated 束束 means 'an infernal chattering' and is how ghosts summon a person's *hun*-soul." The man, indeed, died. (From *Miscellaneous Morsels from Youyang*.)

Editing Clerk for the Heir Apparent Zhou Yanhan of Jiangnan was fond of practicing Daoist alchemy. He dreamt that a god gave him a scroll whose text was composed of lines of seven graphs each. He could only remember the last line which went, "The companion of the purple beard will be cinnabar 丹砂 *[dansha]*." When Zhou awoke, he was delighted, for he considered that he would certainly obtain the alchemical effects of cinnabar to induce transcendence. Later, he served in Jianye where he died and was buried beside the tomb of Emperor Dadi of Wu. He left no wives or sons, only a boy servant named "Dan" 丹 [cinnabar]. (From *The Taiping Miscellany*.)

Fu Jian [r. 357–385] decided to banish Murong Chui. Palace Attendant Quan Yi remonstrated against this, but Fu would not listen. Quan then dispatched brave troops along the main roads to attack Murong. That night, Murong dreamt that the road he was traveling on had come to an end. He looked and saw eight graves beside the tomb of Confucius. When he awoke, he was appalled by this dream and summoned a dream interpreter who said, "The road's end means that your way is exhausted and you should not proceed. The personal name of Confucius was Qiu 丘 and those canonized as his attendant spirits numbered eight 八. These two graphs together form the graph for 'soldiers' 兵. The roads are lined with soldiers hiding in ambush." Murong proceeded along another road, but he was captured by Quan's soldiers hiding there. (From *A Continuation of the History of the Jin Dynasty*.)

CHAPTER 11

The Official Examinations
科甲

The highest rankings in the official examinations have always been presaged by auspicious signs. In the past, Sun Wu dreamt that he stepped on top of a pile of wood.[1] Yuan Guo dreamt that he was standing under the Northern Dipper.[2] Li Di dreamt that his moustache was shaved off.[3] Zeng Jiong dreamt about an extra ear.[4] Xu Yan dreamt that he had been decapitated.[5] Liu Hang dreamt that his head fell off.[6] Yang Tong dreamt that a future principal graduate presented his calling card identifying himself as the "Dragon-Headed Mountain Dweller."[7] An official of the Secretariat dreamt of a principal graduate named Liu, whose personal name was identified by combining graphs from the words "fiery volcano" and "army."[8] Wang Fu dreamt that music was being played to welcome the arrival of a principal graduate.[9] Zhang Fu dreamt that he passed the examinations ahead of a principal graduate.[10] Ma Xixian dreamt that the examination question was about the "Divine Raft."[11] Qin Shaoyou dreamt about the burial of a coffin.[12] Lin Rongzu changed his name to Wen and placed first in the provincial examinations.[13] Sun Guan changed his personal name to Bian and placed third in the metropolitan examinations.[14] Peng Shi and Yue Zheng passed the examinations as exemplars, and, in both cases, it was predicted in the dreams of local officials.[15] Wang Ao and Qian Fu became principal graduates, and both confirmed the dream of the examiner.[16] Wang Wenbo dreamt that Xiong Yi and Liu Zhu passed the examinations.[17] Ding Xianxu dreamt of the linked names Long Qi and Luo Qi.[18] Song Yue changed his personal named to Yan and scored among the top ranks in the metropolitan examination.[19] Doulu Zhezhen changed his personal name to Zhu and passed on his fourth attempt.[20] Wei Ci dreamt that the top candidate was Li Guyan.[21]

Fan Xi dreamt that the head of the list would be Wang Zhengqing.[22] Yang Jingzhi dreamt of the surname Puyang.[23] Huangfu Hong dreamt about the goddess Stone Matron.[24] A Song ruler dreamt there were vegetables as high as the base of the palace hall when he was examining scholars.[25] Shen Hui, who scored as the top graduate, dreamt that he had ridden on the back of a *peng*-bird.[26]

These were all outstanding talents in the examinations, so there were certainly prior indications of their success. Furthermore, isn't the glory of exalted rank preordained? Thus, when Wang Yanbo entered the Temple of the Yangzi River, a shaman-supplicant knew he would obtain a high-ranking position.[27] When Pei Xuanzhen visited the Temple of Mount Hua, an old man announced to him that he would attain an exalted rank.[28] Before Zhang Wenyi became a grand councilor, a temple monk received indications of this.[29] When Lü Yijian gained power, this was also foreseen by the prefect of Haozhou.[30] Wang Bo dreamt that he sat on the left-hand side of Vice Director Du.[31] Pan Jie dreamt that he was standing to the east of Zhao Ziqin.[32] Gao Yuanyu of Xiangzhou and Shang Lingjun of Hengyang dreamt that someone was calling them.[33] "Vice Director He" and "Vice Minister Zhu" were heard in dreams when demons spoke.[34] Cao Que dreamt of becoming a monk, but it was Grand Councilor Du who retired from office.[35] Emperor Xuanzong of the Tang dreamt of a filial son and Wei Jiansu was able to gain power.[36] Zhang Yi dreamt that Ren Tiao received an imperial appointment.[37] Xi Zhi dreamt that a functionary's document was stained with ink.[38] Xu Xianzhi dreamt that his father told him that he would achieve an exalted position.[39] Liu Muzhi dreamt that a defense commander unexpectedly greeted him.[40] Shen Yu was promoted to be an official of the fifth rank.[41] Xing Tao found it difficult to obtain the document of appointment to the Bureau of Waterways and Irrigation.[42] Within ten days, Aide Xue was appointed as a bandit-suppression commissioner.[43] Warlord Wang held power as a general and a minister throughout his life.[44] Chen Anping was reassigned to a position in the Eastern Capital.[45] Li Fuguo's official salary was terminated.[46] The mother of Hua Song dreamt that he would become metropolitan commandant.[47] Yang Li dreamt that his sovereign was a celestial worthy.[48] As for Emperor Wen of the Chen, who dreamt of Zhang Zhaoda, and Emperor Shenzong of the Northern Song, who dreamt of Feng Jing,[49] were these any different from the dreams of King Gaozong of the Shang, who dreamt of Fu Yue, and Emperor Chengzu of the Ming, who dreamt of Zhou Zhou?[50] These were all cases of spiritual encounters between sovereign and minister which revealed unusual indications of the future. However, Liu Yuxi's so-called dream of a journey to meet a divinity and Liu Zongyuan's so-called dream of drawing close to the imperial countenance were nothing but literary flatteries.[51]

NOTES

1. Sun Wu dreamt that he stepped on top of a pile of several hundred pieces of wood. He said, "I will certainly become the principal graduate, for I stand atop of all this timber [*cai*, which also means 'talent']." Before long, it indeed turned out to be so. (From *Gathered Talks*.)

2. When Yuan Guo began to take the examinations, he dreamt that he was standing under the Northern Dipper and, indeed, he passed as the seventh-highest candidate. (From *The Newly Expanded Treasury of Rhymes*.)
[*The Northern Dipper contains seven stars.*—RES]

3. Li Di, also known as Li Wending, had a fine moustache [*zi*] and whiskers. The night before the palace examination, he dreamt that someone had shaved them off completely. Li was appalled by this dream, but an interpreter said, "You, sir, will become the principal graduate. This year, the top candidate from the provincial examinations is Liu Zi, but you have already 'replaced Zi' [*tizi*, a homophone for 'shaving off a moustache']." That year, he indeed became the principal graduate. (From *Random Notes from a Green Box of Knowledge*.)

4. When Zeng Jiong of Jiaxing attended the examinations, he dreamt of a boy who had grown another ear on the right. Suddenly, he observed that the boy lacked a pair of hands, so he considered this dream inauspicious. He asked his elder brother Zeng Zhui about this and Zhui said, "'Another ear' means the graph for 'another' 又 beside 'ear' 耳, which forms the graph 'to obtain' 取. A 'child' 子 without a pair of hands is the graph 'to end' 了. You will certainly 'end up obtaining' 取了 an official degree." Before long, it indeed turned out to be so. (From *Collected Trifles from the Studio of Honesty*.)

5. When Xu Yan was attending the examinations, he dreamt that a General Xu cut off his head and wrote a poem that went, "Before you were a flower on the top of a tree, now you will become bones in a grave." Xu Yan considered this inauspicious. The following year, Xu Shibang passed with the second highest score. (From *New Writings from Nanbu*.)
[*The surname Xu for both General Xu and Xu Shibang is different from Xu Yan's, though it is pronounced the same. The personal name Shibang (literally, "red list") could allude to the list of successful examination candidates.*—RES]

6. During the Tiansheng era [1023–1032], Liu Hang went to the provincial capital for the examinations. He dreamt that he had been beheaded by someone and was thoroughly appalled by this. But someone explained it, saying "You won't pass as the principal graduate, but you will be ranked second. Though your head was cut off, your neck was still preserved. Your surname, Liu 劉, and 'to preserve' 留 *[liu]* have the same sound. 'Neck' 項 *[xiang]* and your first name,

Hang 沆, belong to the same rhyme category." Indeed, he did pass as the second highest candidate. (From *Random Notes from a Green Box of Knowledge*.)

7. Yang Tong was friends with the future principal graduate Yang Tian. He dreamt that Yang Tian had presented his calling card identifying himself as the "Dragon-Headed Mountain Dweller." During the Qingli era [1041–1048], Yang Tian passed the official examinations and then died. Later, someone explained that "dragon-head" indicated a principal graduate, but "mountain dweller" meant "no official salary." (From *Comprehensive Record of Strange Things*.)

8. For an explanation, see the commentary to the dream about the graphs "fire" and "army" combining to form the graph *hui* in the chapter, "Written Graphs" [II:10n26].

9. On the twenty-second day of the fifth lunar month in the year *gengxu* of the Hongwu era [June 16, 1370], Controller-General of Linchuan [in Jiangxi] Wang Fu dreamt that music was being played in the city to welcome a principal graduate. Wang was surprised by this. On the twenty-fifth day [June 19], an emissary arrived and announced the summons of candidates for the official examinations. In the autumn of that year, Wu Bozong of Jiangxi, who had placed first in the Jiangxi provincial examination, also placed first in the palace examination. (From *The Collected Works of Song Jinglian*.)

10. Zhang Fu was from Songjiang. Before he had passed the examinations, he dreamt that someone told him, "You will pass the examinations ahead of the principal graduate." When he awoke and thought about it, he wondered how it was possible to pass ahead of the principal graduate. At the initial metropolitan examination in the year *dingwei*, the twenty-third year of the Chenghua era [1487], Zhang passed as number fifteen and Fei Hong of Qianshan was number sixteen. But in the end, it was Fei Hong who became the principal graduate of this class. Zhang reckoned that at the time of his dream, Fei Hong had not yet been born. (From *Collected Trifles from the Studio of Honesty*.)

11. Ma Xixian was from Huaiyuan and was a prefectural nominee who became a metropolitan graduate. The night before, he dreamt about the "Rhapsody on the Divine Raft" and, indeed, it appeared as a question on the examination. (From *The Comprehensive Gazetteer*.)

12. Qin Shaoyou dreamt of a coffin being taken *[fa]* to be buried and that it was the coffin of a Liu Fa. That year, Liu Fa placed first in the examinations. (From *The Collected Works of Su Dongpo*.)

[The symbol of a coffin (guan) *can signify official position based on a homophony with the word for "official"* (guan).—RES]

13. Lin Wen of Yongjia was born on the eight day of the eighth lunar month of the year *dingsi* during the Yanyou era [Sept. 13, 1317]. He was named Rongzu when he was three years old. Then, at the age of twelve, he changed it to Wen. Another ten years later in the year *renwu* of the Zhizheng era [1342], he placed first in the Jiangzhe provincial examination on the *Spring and Autumn Annals*. Dong Yi placed fourth, Dong Chaozong, fifth, and Zhu Gongqian, twenty-eighth. Lin Wen was appointed an instructor in the Fenghua prefectural school and assumed the position in the year *dinghai* [1347]. He met Dong Yi, who was also made an instructor and who was serving in Qingyuan. Dong said, "My grandfather once had an extraordinary dream that he recorded. It stated, 'On the sev-

enth day of the ninth lunar month in the year *dingsi* [Oct. 12, 1317], I dreamt that Lin Wen passed first in the examinations. Someone surnamed Zhu was included among the successful candidates. The fourth and fifth candidates were both surnamed Dong.'" The strangest thing about this dream was that Lin Wen was only a month old when it occurred. (From *The Collected Works of Song Jinglian.*)

14. The personal name of Military Affairs Commissioner Sun Bian was originally "Guan." While attending the examinations, he dreamt that he arrived at a government office. In the hall, a list of names had been copied down, and Sun looked through those succeeding in the metropolitan examinations without finding his. He happened to notice an empty space where the name of the third successful candidate should have been, and he wanted to fill in his own name. A voice out of thin air said, "This is not for Sun Guan but for Sun Bian." So, in the dream, he wrote "Sun Bian." After he awoke, he changed his personal name to Bian, and that year, he did indeed pass with the third highest rank. (From *Random Notes from a Green Box of Knowledge.*)

15. In the winter of the year *dingmao*, the twelfth year of the Zhengtong era [1447–1448], an official of Guangji district in Huguang province who was on his way to an imperial audience dreamt that he opened the list of successful candidates and found that Peng Shi had placed first in the examinations. When he arrived in the capital, he mentioned this to Zhang Duanben, a student at the National University from Guangji district, who visited Peng and told him about it. At this time, another official who was there for an imperial audience dreamt that the top candidate would be Yue Zheng. The following year, Yue Zheng placed first in the metropolitan examinations, and Peng Shi became the principal graduate after the palace examination, confirming both dreams. (From *Random Notes.*)

16. At the metropolitan examination in the year *yiwei*, the eleventh year of the Chenghua era [1475], Xu Pu and Qiu Jun served as the chief examiners. Xu dreamt that something resembling a turtle emerged from a large lake. It kowtowed upon climbing ashore, and there were three arrows embedded on its top. When the successful candidates were announced, Wang Ao [a homophone for *ao*, a turtle] was the principal graduate. Wang's home was in the Lake Tai area. Later, Xu recommended him to become an academician and again to become vice supervisor of the Household of the Heir Apparent. Together with his success in the metropolitan examinations, these confirmed the symbolism of the three arrows. Furthermore, at the metropolitan examinations in the year *gengxu*, the third year of the Hongzhi era [1490], Xu Pu and Wang Xie were the chief examiners. Xu dreamt that someone gave him a large coin *[qian]*. That year, Qian Fu became the principal graduate. (From *A Record of Stories.*)

17. Wang Zai, whose courtesy name was Wenbo, was from Fengxin. He dreamt that he went with Liu Zhu to the offices of the Jiangxi provincial government where he saw a list of the prefectural nominees who had became metropolitan graduates. When he examined it more closely, he found that ten vermillion placards were hung high up on which were graphs written in gold. However, the sunlight was shining so brightly that he could not read the names. Suddenly, a functionary said, "The first name is Xiong Yi of Nanchang. You are number six." Wang called to Liu, "Your name is also there but further below."

Wang awoke and told this to others, all of whom laughed at him. Eight years later, in the year *gengxu* of the Hongwu era [1378], the examinations were reinstituted. Of the forty candidates in the quota from Jiangxi, ten came from Nanchang, which exactly matched the number of vermillion placards. Xiong Yi had placed first, Wang Zai was sixth, and Liu Zhu was nineteenth. In the palace examination, Wang also placed sixth. (From *The Collected Works of Song Jinglian*.)

18. Before Ding Xianxu had passed the examinations, he dreamt that he was riding a dragon that was rising upward. When he turned to look back, he saw a camel behind him. Twenty years later when the results of the palace examination were announced, coming after Ding were Long Qi [literally, "a dragon arising"] and, next, Luo Qi [literally, "a camel arising"]. Thereupon, he realized the meaning of his dream. (From *An Unofficial History of Jiangnan*.)

19. The personal name of Song Yan was originally Yue 嶽 [sacred mountain]. Despite ten attempts, he was unable to succeed in the examinations. In the eleventh year of the Dazhong period [857] when he was about to obtain the necessary recommendation by his prefecture to compete in the capital, he dreamt that someone announced to him, "Licentiate Song, the graph of your personal name is topped by the element 'mountain' 山. There is no particular reason why you should bear this name. If you eliminated the 'mountain,' you ought to be able to succeed." After he awoke, he thought that he couldn't possibly take the name Yu 獄 [prison] that would result from eliminating "mountain," so he also dropped the two elements 犭and 犬 meaning "dog" and thus changed his name to Yan 言 [speech]. Indeed, he was ranked fourth among the successful candidates the following spring at the metropolitan examinations. (From *Friendly Discussions at Cloud Stream*.)

20. Doulu Zhu's personal name was originally Zhezhen. When young, he traveled to seek patronage in Quzhou. Prefect Zheng Shizhan was a generous patron to him and said, "It is not very fitting to have a personal name of two graphs together with a double surname. I will change it for you." Thereupon, he wrote out three graphs for "Shu," "Du," and "Zhu" [to aid] and gave them to him, saying "I am afraid that there may be others in the commandery who have the same name, so choose from these yourself." That night, Doulu dreamt that an old man told him, "Since the prefect himself has given you alternate names, you will succeed in passing the examinations on the fourth attempt, since four is an excellent number." He also said, "In twenty years time, you will administer this commandery." And, he also pointed to a spot and said, "You should build a pavilion right here." When Doulu awoke, he changed his name to Shu but failed the examinations. Then, he changed it to Du and again to Zhu [to aid] but still failed each time. Before the fourth attempt, he changed his name on his own to another graph pronounced Zhu [outstanding]. Indeed, twenty years later, he was the prefect of Quzhou and built the Pavilion of the Confirmed Dream on the spot he had dreamt about. (From *Recorded Stories*.)

21. In the sixth year of the Yuanhe era [811], Metropolitan Governor Wei Ci was serving as investigation commissioner of Wanling and assigned as a retainer in Fangwu. He dreamt that someone sent in his calling card with the name Li Guyan 李故言 on it. Then, someone said, "He will be the principle graduate next

The Official Examinations

year." Recently, at the beginning of the Yuanhe era [806–820], a Li Guyan 李顧言 had passed the examinations, so Wei felt surprised by this and said, "That Li's name contained a different graph *gu* 顧 from the one in the dream." In autumn during the eighth lunar month of this year [August–September], the local authorities selected recommendees for the metropolitan examinations. All the candidates sent in their name cards. One of these was similar to the name in the dream but the graph for *gu* 故 was written as 固. It was none other than the name of the present Western Commander Li Guyan 李固言. Wei told him, "You, sir, will certainly pass the examinations next year and place first among the candidates." That winter, Xu Mengrong, the vice minister of the Ministry of War, presided over the examinations, and Li Guyan 李固言 was indeed ranked at the head of the list.

22. Vice Director Fan Xi dreamt that he passed the examinations and that when the list of successful candidates was announced, Wang Zhengqing was ranked first. Altogether, the list contained twenty-six names. The following year, Fan attended the examinations and passed while Wang Zhengqing was indeed ranked first. The number of names on the list was also the same as in the dream. (From *A Record of Fates*.)

23. When Yang Dai, the son of Yang Jingzhi, was attending the examinations, Yang Jingzhi dreamt that the new list of successful candidates would number forty presented scholars and that his son's name was among them. Next to Yang Dai on the list was the surname Puyang. When Yang Jingzhi awoke, he was overjoyed. He visited the examination halls where there was a Puyang Yuan, who enjoyed a considerable reputation for his writings. However, Puyang Yuan suddenly died just before the exams were to take place. Yang Jingzhi said to himself that his dream must have been wrong. Yet, the following year, his son passed. When Yang Jingzhi went to the Temple of Benevolence, he saw that among the names listed were "Yang Dai of Hongnong" and "Wu Dang of Puyang," and these appeared just like in his dream. (From *Omitted History of the Tang Dynasty*.)

24. Huangfu Hong was going to attend the examination for metropolitan graduate and had been selected as a recommendee from Huazhou. But, he became drunk and behaved rudely toward the prefect of Huazhou, Qian Hui. Huangfu was expelled and went to Shaanzhou. When Huangfu heard that Qian had been transferred from his post in Huazhou to serve as administrator of the examinations, he knew that he would never pass and returned east. He had gone a short distance when one night he dreamt that the wet nurse employed by his late wife said, "Mr. Huangfu, why are you going back?" Huangfu told her that it was because of a quarrel with the presiding examiner. The wet nurse replied, "Mr. Huangfu, you should seek help from the goddess Stone Matron." She led him to a grassy spot north of his inn where he saw a broken stone statue. The wet nurse said, "Mr. Huangfu wishes to take the examinations. Matron, do you think he will pass or not?" The statue nodded and said, "He will." Then, Huangfu bowed down to thank her. The wet nurse escorted him back to the inn, and he awoke. He subsequently went to the city and attended the examinations. Qian intended to deal him a setback. When it came time to write down the list of successful candidates, he decided to change one of the names but couldn't decide

on an alternative. He told his subordinate, "Bring me another examination paper." When he opened it, it was none other than that of Huangfu Hong. Qian said, "This must be heaven's will." Huangfu passed and on his way back reached Shaanzhou where he sought out the statue of the Stone Matron and made a sacrifice to her. (From *A Supplemental History*.)

25. When Emperor Zhenzong of the Northern Song was examining scholars, he dreamt that there was an abundance of vegetables *[cai]* at the foot of the palace hall as high as *[qi]* the foundation. The person whom he ranked as number one turned out to be Cai Qi. (From *Past Events from the Eastern Studio*.)

26. When Shen Hui was on his way to attend the metropolitan examination and the road passed through Tianchang, he dreamt that he rode on the back of a *peng*-bird which soared upward on the wind. Because of this, he wrote "Rhapsody on the *Peng*-Bird" to record the event. During the Xuanhe era [1119–1125] of the Song dynasty, he indeed became the top graduate in the country. (From *A Biographical Encyclopedia according to Surnames*.)

27. When Wen Yanbo was young, he followed his father, who went to Shuzhou to serve in the regional headquarters. When he entered the Temple of the Yangzi River, the temple's supplicant treated him with considerable respect and moreover said, "Last night, I dreamt that the god ordered the temple be swept clean because a grand councilor would be arriving. Isn't it Your Honor who will be this grand councilor in the future?" Wen laughed and said, "It is not my ambition to be a grand councilor. If I just become the magistrate of Chengdu, I would feel obliged to help renovate this temple." During the Qingli era [1041–1048], Wen became prefect of Yizhou while serving as an auxiliary academician in the Bureau of Military Affairs. He was deeply moved when he visited the temple. While he was engaged in raising funds to renovate it, several thousand large trees floated down the Yangzi River and obstructed the water's flow. He collected these and used them for the renovation, which was successfully completed. (From *Mr. Shao's Records*.)

28. Pei Ji's courtesy name was Xuanzhen. During the Kaihuang era of the Sui dynasty [581–600], he was appointed to the palace guard of the left. Originally, his family suffered from poverty, so they moved to the capital. On his way there, Pei passed by the Temple of Mount Hua where he made an offering to the god under the moonlight. That night, he dreamt that an old man told him, "When your years surpass forty, you will attain an exalted position." Later, he gained a high position and held sway over his generation. (From *Old History of the Tang Dynasty*.)

29. When Zhang Wenyi was a community head, he would regularly visit the village temple when he went out of the city, and an old monk at the temple would come out and welcome him. Even when he arrived unannounced, the monk would always appear. Zhang found this strange and asked the reason for this. The monk said, "At night, I dream that the god of the mountain tells me that a certain grand councilor will be arriving." One day, Zhang went there again, but the monk did not appear. He later said, "Why did you not come out and welcome me?" and the monk apologized, saying, "The god did not inform me of your visit." Zhang thought this sounded absurd, so he had the monk ask the god directly about it. That night, the monk dreamt that the god told him, "This official mistakenly de-

cided a case involving the killing of an ox. The divine command has come down that he will not become a grand councilor." Zhang was shocked. But when he thought about it, indeed, there had been a case involving the killing of an ox. As a result, he altered his decision and the next day, went by the temple. The monk again came out to greet him saying, "Last night, the god of the mountain said, 'This official has been reinstated as a future grand councilor, and he should be coming by tomorrow. However, his longevity has been reduced.'" Later, Zhang served in the Secretariat on three occasions. (From *Mr. Wang's Record of Things Heard and Seen*.)

30. Yang Xun liked to sit and discuss Daoist books. He was serving as prefect of Haozhou when he dreamt that someone told him, "Grand Councilor Lü has arrived." Soon afterward, Lü Yijian came to serve as comptroller-general of the prefecture. Yang, therefore, treated him most generously. Later, Lü came to Yang's assistance when the latter was in political disgrace. Yang was able to attain an exalted position because of Lü's power. (From *History of the Song Dynasty*.)

31. When Wang Bo [759–830] was young, he was poor and living in Yangzhou. His only support came from a military official. When Vice Director Du was serving as a subordinate official in Huainan, Wang dreamt that he was sitting to the left of Du during the dragon-boat competition at the Midsummer Festival. The comptroller-generals were seated below them, and Wang's position was greater than Du's. Later, Wang became a grand councilor and served as salt and iron monopoly commissioner in Huainan. When he attended a banquet by the river, the scene was just like the one in his dream. (From *A Supplemental History*.)

32. Pan Jie stated that someone destined to become an official would certainly dream of it beforehand. He passed the examinations together with Zhao Ziqin. Both submitted their names to the government, but for a long time they were not given any official appointments. Later, Pan said, "I have already dreamt that an appointment will be issued soon." He dreamt that he and Zhao offered their thanks together in the palace. Pan walked in first and Zhao followed behind. When they arrived at the ritual position for offering thanks, Pan stood to the east and Zhao to the west as they looked at each other and laughed. Three days later, the official appointments were issued. Pan became a censor and Zhao, a reminder. The same day, they offered thanks. At the beginning, Pan was led in first and Zhao followed behind. Once inside the court, Pan stood to the east and Zhao to the west. The two men looked at each other and laughed just as in the dream. (From *A Record of Fates*.)

33. Gao Yuanyu, the military commissioner of Xiangyang, originally served as a vice director in the Bureau of Merit Titles and lived in the office compound of the Department of State Affairs. One day during a nap, he dreamt that someone told him, "In ten years you will be prefect of Xiangzhou." When he awoke, he thought to himself that this was strange and wrote it down on a hidden spot on a railing on the eastern side of his office. In the third year of the Dazhong era [849], he was given control of the Hannan region by the minister of the Ministry of Personnel. (From *Collected Records of Anomalies* [ca. 871].)

Shang Lingjun dreamt during the Yixi era [405–418] that someone came and tied him up. As the man was about to leave, Shang felt that his body and spirit were separating from each other. Then another person said, "Leave him be. Later, he will administer Hengyang. We are supposed to fetch him then." Later, he became the prefect of Hengyang and indeed died while in office. (From *A Garden of Strange Events*.)

34. He Zhiyong was the son of a merchant. When young, he loved to study and once accompanied his uncle. They moored their boat at Wankou where the uncle dreamt that night of a person resembling an official who was riding a horse followed by many servants. The official rode back and forth along the waterfront where he thoroughly inspected the number of boats and people there. Then, someone behind him shouted out, "Vice Director He is here!" This suddenly startled the uncle awake. He visited all the neighboring boats, but found no one surnamed He. So he moved his boat into the middle of the deep harbor. The next day, there were strong winds and the boats still moored where he was the day before all sank. Only the He family boat survived. The uncle told He Zhiyong, "Our family is poor and humble, and I am now old. 'Vice Director He' must be you. Take good care of yourself." Later, He Zhiyong became an administrative assistant for the military commissioner of Hunan. When Ma Yin, King of Chu, proclaimed himself emperor, he made He Zhiyong vice minister of the Ministry of Personnel and Hanlin academician. He Zhiyong told himself that he deserved to be a grand councilor. Later, Ma Xifan succeeded to the throne as King of Chu and discarded the imperial title while making He administrative assistant to a military commissioner and an acting vice director. He Zhiyong finally died in office. (From *A Record of Inquests into Spirits*.)

During the Former Shu dynasty ruled by the Wang family, there was a Vice Minister Zhu. He was poor and humble when young and was staying in an inn in Chengdu. There, he dreamt that someone knocked on his door looking for Vice Minister Zhu. He also dreamt that someone holding a scroll said, "Here is the vice minister." Zhu replied, "Zhu is my surname, but I am not a vice minister." The man showed him the scroll with the words, "Vice Minister Zhu." Following this, someone came leading a horse, which he handed over to Zhu. But, when Zhu looked at it closely, he saw that it was missing its front legs. Thereupon, he was frightened awake. After the king of Shu established his state, Zhu attained the position of vice minister of the Court of the Imperial Granaries. Later, he suffered from ulcers and lost both his legs up to his knees, dying on the fifth day of the fifth lunar month. The dream about the horse was confirmed. (From *Mr. Wang's Record of Things Heard and Seen*.)

35. Cao Que was just a supervisor in the Ministry of Revenue, but he had ambitions of becoming a grand councilor. It happened that he dreamt of shaving his head and becoming a monk. When he asked a dream interpreter about this, he was told, "Renouncing the world to become a monk is referred to as 'shaving one's head and crossing over' [*tidu* 剃度]. You, sir, will 'be appointed' [*tidu* 替度] a grand councilor." Later, Grand Councilor Du was demoted to the defense command in Jiangxi, and Cao indeed served 'instead of Du' [*ti Du* 替杜] as a grand councilor. (From *Trifling Words from Beimeng*.)

36. Emperor Xuanzong of the Tang [r. 712–756] dreamt that he was in the Bathing Pavilion and a filial son was assisting him. One day, he asked Gao Lishi

about this, and Gao replied, "A filial son wears white clothes when mourning. It must be Wei Jiansu [*jiansu,* a homophony for 'appearing in white']." The emperor agreed, and several days later, Wei was made a grand councilor. (From *An Extensive Record of Anomalies.*)

37. During the Dali era [766–779], Zhang Yi held the office of minister of the Ministry of Works and served as supervisor in the Ministry of Revenue. His recommendations were favorably received by the throne, and Emperor Daizong of the Tang personally agreed to his appointment as a grand councilor. However, weeks passed without any formal notification. Suddenly, Zhang dreamt that someone announced, "Ren Tiao 任調 has become a grand councilor." After awakening, he realized that there wasn't anyone by that name inside or outside the court. So he sought out an explanation of the dream, but no one understood it. His nephew Li Tongli congratulated him, saying, "You will certainly become a grand councilor. 'Ren tiao' is a double-phonic recombination of *rao tian* 饒甜 [abundant sweetness]. For abundant sweetness, nothing surpasses licorice root, which is the most 'precious medicinal herb' [*zhenyao* 珍藥] and a double-phonic recombination of these graphs conceals your name, uncle." Soon, an emissary on horseback came and announced an imperial summons, "Your Excellency is to become a manager of affairs. (From *Collected Records of Anomalies* [ca. 824].)

[A double-phonic recombination (fanyu 反語) *involves switching the initials and finals of two graphs twice:* ren+tiao = rao; tiao+ren = tian. *Through another double-phonic recombination,* zhen *and* yao *could signify "Zhang Yi" in Tang dynasty pronunciation.—RES]*

38. As a young man, Vice Minister Xi Zhi dreamt that he was having tea with more than twenty court officials. It was summertime, and he was quite thirsty. Soon, a heavyset and dark-complexioned functionary appeared with a ledger requesting that Xi affix his seal to it. Xi became angry. He pushed the desk away and said, "Begone!" The thick ink that had filled the ink stone stained the document and also the face of the functionary. This startled Xi awake. He wrote down the dream and stored it in a cloth-covered tube. Fifteen years later, when he was serving as vice minister of the Ministry of Personnel, he was attending an office tea party with directors in the same ministry when a heavyset and dark complexioned functionary appeared holding a ledger. Xi pushed the desk away and said, "Begone!" The desk fell over. The ink was splashed on the functionary's face and thoroughly stained the ledger. Then he understood the dream from years ago and together with the ministry directors retrieved the account he had written to show that the dream had been confirmed. There was not the slightest difference between the two events. (From *A Supplemental History.*)

39. Xu Xianzhi dreamt that his father told him, "You will achieve an exalted position if you avoid traveling on Vermillion Bird Street from now on." Later, Xu was traveling on this street and had gone halfway when he remembered the dream about his father, so he turned his horse around. Indeed, he became a grand councilor. (From *Records of Ghosts and the Living.*)

40. Liu Muzhi dreamt that someone calling himself "Defense Commander Liu" welcomed him. Liu awoke and said, "I will certainly die. Where else could there be a Defense Commander Liu right now?" Later, Liu Yu, the future Emperor Wu of the Liu Song dynasty, sent someone to welcome Liu Muzhi to join

him in making plans to establish a new dynasty. At that time, the future Emperor Wu was serving as a defense commander. (From *A Continuation of A Record of Strange Events*.)

41. Dai Zhou was on good terms with Prefectural Administrative Aid Shen Yu. Dai died in the seventh year of the Zhenguan era [791]. While in the prefecture in the eighth lunar month of the eighth year [August-September, 792], Shen dreamt that he was walking along a street in the southwest of the Righteous and Brave Precinct in the capital. There he met Dai, who said, "We were friends when I was alive, but I was unable to advance you to a higher rank. Now, you have merited promotion to the fifth rank on your own. The official document has already been approved by the appropriate celestial bureau, so I have come to bring you the announcement." Shen was indeed granted the fifth rank and became vice prefect of Wuzhou. (From *The Taiping Miscellany*.)

42. Chief of the Court of Judicial Review of Jiangnan Xing Tao dreamt in the year *guimao* that someone told him, "You, sir, will become prefect of Jingzhou." However, he became the magistrate of Jingxian district in Xuanzhou prefecture. After he had completed his term of office, he again dreamt that the same person told him, "Come spring, all the officials in the districts of Xuanzhou will be replaced, but no notice will arrive of any other position for you, sir." Xing was appalled by this dream. The following year, he retired. Xing was then recommended to become a vice director in the Bureau of Waterways and Irrigation. The document of appointment was sent down, but someone in charge lost it. A request was made for another copy, but it took twenty days to arrive. In the end, Xing died before assuming the office. (From *A Record of Inquests into Spirits*.)

43. Xue Jichang of the Tang dynasty was an aide in Jingzhou when he dreamt that a cat was crouching on a threshold *[xian]* with its head facing the outside. He asked the dream interpreter Zhang You about this, and Zhang said, "A cat that possesses its claws while crouching on a threshold indicates a military command *[kun,* which also means 'threshold'] on the frontier. You, sir, will be given a military assignment." Within ten days, Xue was appointed commander-in-chief of Hongzhou and bandit-suppression commissioner for Lingnan. (From *Collected Records from Court and Countryside*.)

44. Wang Yu, the commander of E during the illegitimate Wu dynasty, became a warlord while young when he joined the forces encircling Yingzhou. One night, he dreamt that a Daoist told him, "At dawn, meteors will fall to earth. If you can avoid them, you will become both a general and a government minister." The next day, all the forces attacked the city where rocks fell down like rain. Wang, wielding his sword, sought protection beside a wooden post as he conducted the battle. Suddenly, a large rock struck the post shattering half of his armor. However, Wang was uninjured and in the end rose to high office. (From *A Record of Inquests into Spirits*.)

45. When Chen Anping's term of office ended, he applied for another official position. He was with his fellow local, Li Xianyao, when he dreamt of raising silkworms in the twelfth lunar month. Li said, "Raising silkworms in the twelfth lunar month means 'silk threads in winter' *[dongsi]*. You will be reassigned to an office in the eastern capital *[dongsi]*." After several months, he was

indeed reassigned to the Ministry of Personnel there. (From *Collected Records from Court and Countryside*.)

46. Li Fuguo behaved without restraint as if there were no sovereign. Emperor Daizong of the Tang detested him. Consequently, the emperor dreamt that he had climbed up a tower from where he watched Gao Lishi lead several hundred armed cavalry. They used halberds to stab Li until blood flowed from his head and drenched the ground. Throughout all this, Li was singing and crying out. Then, he fled northward. The emperor sent an emissary to ask Gao Lishi about this, and Gao said, "This was the command of Emperor Xuanzong [r. 712–756]. Li Fuguo's official salary has been terminated." Emperor Daizong awoke but said nothing. When Li was killed by bandits, the emperor thought it strange and only then told his close advisors about his dream. (From *A Miscellany from Duyang*.)

47. Hua Song's family was humble and poor. His mother dreamt one night that two men came knocking on the door, saying, "The metropolitan commandant is here!" Hua indeed became metropolitan commandant. (From Xie Cheng, *History of the Eastern Han Dynasty*.)

48. Emperor Zhenzong of the Northern Song was originally named "Yuankan" and enfeoffed as Prince of Xiang. There was a prefectural graduate, Yang Li, who once dreamt that he arrived at a palatial hall where someone seated there said to him, "I am not your sovereign. The Celestial Worthy of Future Harmony is your sovereign, and you will attain an exalted position." He gave Yang certain instructions and ordered Yang to visit the Celestial Worthy. Yang later placed first among the presented scholars and became a record keeper in the establishment of the Prince of Xiang. When he visited the prince's residence, it was just like what he had seen in his dream. (From *An Outline of History*.)

49. Zhang Zhaoda was promoted for his achievements to defense commander and given the title of executive with honors equivalent to those accorded the three dukes. Originally, Emperor Wen of the Chen dynasty dreamt that Zhang had risen to become one of the three dukes. In the morning, he told Zhao about the dream. Around this time, Zhang attended a banquet where the emperor, flushed with wine, looked at him and said, "Do you remember Our dream? How shall We reward you?" Zhang replied, "My duty is to serve you like a dog or a horse and to act as your official with the utmost integrity. There is no need for any other reward." (From *History of the Chen Dynasty*.)

Feng Jing was from Jiangxia. He served as an academician in the Hall for Aid in Governance and was transferred to become prefect of Chengdu. Because Emperor Shenzong of the Northern Song felt that Wang Anshi had deceived him, he summoned Feng to the capital to serve in the Bureau of Military Affairs. But Feng did not take up the post on account of illness. The emperor called to his attendants in the middle of the night and said, "We just dreamt that Feng Jing had entered the court, which is a consolation to Our hopes." Consequently, he issued an imperial summons to Feng, "You are constantly in Our thoughts. Do not forget what was uttered after Our dream." (From *History of the Song Dynasty*.)

50. Zhou Zhou [boat] was from Yiyang. He was recognized as a man of tal-

ent during the Yongle era [1403–1424] and was made prefect of Jurong. When he was to attend an imperial audience, Emperor Chengzu of the Ming dreamt that a great boat was carrying a small boat on the Golden River. The next morning, the emperor noticed that among the assembled officials was someone named Zhou Zhou and considered him to be a confirmation of the dream. Consequently, Zhou was given an extraordinary promotion to chief minister of the Court of Judicial Review. (From *Gazetteer of Changsha*.)

51. Liu Yuxi wrote in his "Memorial Requesting a Court Audience," "Fearfully anxious with thoughts of the imperial palace gates, I dreamt of a journey to meet a divinity." Liu Zongyuan wrote in his "Memorial Requesting a Court Audience Composed for Vice Censor-in-Chief Cui," "The majesty of the emperor is but a foot away; indeed, it remains close whether I am awake or asleep. Like the luminous Milky Way, I gaze upward but cannot reach it."

CHAPTER 12

Gods and Strange Things
神怪

The sages and philosophers have stifled discussion of gods and strange creatures. However, *The Book of Changes* mentions demons under the hexagram *Kui:* "Opposition," *The Book of Songs* poeticizes an abundance of gods, and *The Book of Documents* records the ritual ceremonies for the six major gods, as well as distinguishing those for the five state sacrifices. This is because they are referring to the principles of actual things. They are not the kind of writings that are used to deceive the common people. In speaking of the encounters of *hun*-souls in dreams, it is difficult for some to avoid engaging in profound discussions that are nonetheless exaggerated and far-fetched. Still, dreams are clearly recorded in various books and histories, so how can one characterize all of them as insubstantial? In this chapter, I have gathered somewhat diverse examples. Still, they will suffice for observing that events are predestined and difficult to alter and that there are omens of things to come from which none can escape. Shouldn't these be scrutinized by the noble man who cultivates himself while awaiting his destiny?

In antiquity, Yao dreamt that the White Emperor granted him a son.[1] Yu of the Xia dynasty dreamt that a book was revealed to him at Green River.[2] Our own Emperor Taizu of the Ming dreamt that a divinity bestowed a robe on him.[3] Emperor Chengzu of the Ming dreamt that the God of the City rescued him.[4] These are dreams of sagely rulers which involved the change of dynasties. One cannot speak of them as merely dreams of gods and strange creatures. But as for the Duke of Guo, he dreamt of the god Rushou.[5] Zhao Ying dreamt of a celestial emissary and Ziyu dreamt of the God of the Yellow River.[6] The Qin emperor dreamt of the God of the Sea.[7] Emperor Ming of the Eastern Han dreamt of a golden man more than ten feet tall.[8] Liu Yao dreamt of golden men who faced eastward.[9] Fu Jian dreamt that a vermillion-robed emissary bestowed upon him the title of Generalissimo Racing Dragon.[10] Du Ling dreamt of the Lord of the Leichi River sailing in a vermillion vessel who called himself "Generalissimo of Conquest."[11] Zhang Chan's name was determined by divine writing.[12] Zhao Gai's name was changed because of a register written in gold.[13] Sun Bian filled in this name for the official examinations.[14] Zheng Quan's name was written on the doors of Cangzhou.[15] Qin Yan changed his name to what someone called him.[16] Cao Xi took a name identical with that of an ancient worthy.[17] Xie Fu dreamt of a mountain deity and was able to profit through him.[18] Xi Yu dreamt of a mountain god and was enfeoffed as a marquis.[19] Xu You dreamt of becoming the Lord of the Northern Dipper.[20] Emperor Xuanzong of the Tang dreamt that he had obtained a presented scholar from Mount Zhongnan.[21] A King of Chu dreamt that he encountered the goddess of Shaman Mountain.[22] Houji dreamt that he met the Nymph of the Luo River.[23] Tian Qianqiu dreamt about a white-haired old man and thus knew how to present the crown prince's grievance to the throne.[24] Liu Lingzhe dreamt of an old man dressed in yellow and was able to cure his mother's illness.[25] Xu Xiaosi dreamt that boys asked him to move the location of his bed, and he thereby avoided disaster.[26] Qiao Zhihong dreamt that a god came to bestow upon him an official post, and he suddenly died.[27] Cui Hao dreamt that he was fighting with a demon for a righteous cause and reformed the calendar.[28] Wang Yanshou dreamt that he had observed the transformations of demons and wrote "Rhapsody on a Dream."[29] A Jin dynasty emperor dreamt that the God of the Yellow River requested a horse.[30] Huan Huo dreamt that a mountain demon announced his departure to him.[31] Shi Pu dreamt that a god had come down from heaven and learned that the Chen family was destined to rise in the world.[32] Ziying dreamt that a god arrived from Shaqiu and learned that the world would erupt into chaos.[33] Zhao Xu dreamt that the Green Maiden became his spouse.[34] Xian Chao dreamt that the Jade Maiden became his wife.[35] There was a dream that assembled transcendents played music and transmitted the sounds of the "Purple Clouds."[36] There was also a dream that the asterisms were defending the frontier, which led to the discovery of statues in a cave.[37] And then, there was the dream of Lü Guang that Fu Yao had been killed.[38] Fan Shi dreamt that Zhang Yuanbo informed him of Zhang's death.[39] Huangfu Mi dreamt that Cao Shuang would be executed.[40] Tao Hongjing dreamt that Xiao Jian bid him farewell.[41] Emperor Gaozu of the Northern Wei dynasty dreamt that Ji Shao came to welcome him on his visit.[42] Lu Yuanming dreamt that Wang You presented him with a poem.[43] Jia Su dreamt that Shen Fushi announced that Jia could cease his activities.[44] Yu Ji dreamt that Chen Zhongxing conversed with him.[45] Shi Hu dreamt that Xuan Xian entrusted his son to him.[46] Zhang Jun dreamt about Ziyu and promoted his great-grandson.[47] Cai Mo dreamt that Zhang Jia had died of an illness.[48] Yang Wo dreamt that Xu Shan would visit from afar.[49] Wang Fengxian dreamt that his beloved son would return home.[50] Lu Xiufu dreamt that his friend died after becoming an official.[51] The mother of Zhuge Yuanchong dreamt that he met with disaster.[52] The commandant of Goushi District dreamt that Lu Shumin reported the calamity that had befallen him.[53] Emperor Taizong of the Tang dreamt of Wei Zheng and Du Ruhui.[54] Emperor Taizong of the Tang dreamt of Xue Shou and Yu Shinan.[55] These are cases of *hun*-souls who had not been wandering for long after death and who communicated through dreams.

There are also cases of eminent people of the past who, despite their remoteness, lodged themselves in the dreams of later people, such as when Duke Jing of Qi dreamt of Yi Yin.[56] Emperor Huan of the Eastern Han dynasty dreamt of Laozi.[57] Sun Hao of Wu dreamt of Huo Guang.[58] Emperor Gaozong of the Southern Song dreamt of Magistrate Cui.[59] Sima Kuo dreamt of Deng Ai.[60] Lü Meng dreamt of Fuxi and King Wen.[61] Son-in-law Li dreamt of Master Tian.[62] Emperor Xuanzong of the Tang dreamt of Sun Simiao.[63] Emperor Wu of the Western Han dreamt of Emperor Gaozu.[64] Huang Fan dreamt of the Lord of Guzhu.[65] Are these similar or not to Confucius's dream of the Duke of Zhou? As for the spirit of Confucius in heaven, Liu Xie, Zhang Zhichun, Huang Yuan, Huang Ze, Zheng Xuan, Qiao Zhou, and Qi Jixuan dreamt of having met him.[66]

Now, the line in the poem that goes, "Sacred mountains send down gods," no doubt also refers to the marvelous Way whereby the Mysterious Controller creates human life. Thus, Prince Rong dreamt of a god in a golden hat who came into his room before Emperor Lizong of the Southern Song was born.[67] Alanguohuo dreamt that a golden god rushed over to her bed and, consequently, she gave birth to an ancestor of the Yuan dynasty.[68] Mistress Yin dreamt that an old man granted her a son, and so she named the boy Rui [auspicious].[69] Liu Shu dreamt that a god on horseback brought him a son and named the boy Yin [piebald].[70] The mother of Gao Lin dreamt that a transcendent spoke to her, and she named her son Lin [gem].[71] The father of Liu Jun dreamt of a strange event and named his son Jun [extraordinary].[72] Gao Yan dreamt that a Daoist would be reborn as a human and named his son Li [ritual].[73] Ma

Congzheng dreamt that the father of his concubine came to thank him, so Ma named his son Juan [stream].[74] Both Zhao Kui and Yu Ji were in accord with dreams about Mount Heng, the Southern Marchmount.[75] In the case of Minister Ni Yue, his mother maintained that she had been stirred by the God of the Northern Marchmount.[76] One person dreamt about Deng Yu and gave birth to Fan Zuyu; another dreamt of Li Bo and gave birth to Guo Xiangzheng.[77] There was a dream about Xie Lingyun when Bian Hao was born; also a dream about Niu Sengru when Liu Hang was born.[78] There was a dream about Buddhist Master Jie and then Su Shi was born; also a dream of Perfected Lord Xu and then Song Xiang was born.[79] Although these dreams were recorded in texts, they are not sufficiently strange or unusual. However, when Yang Yi was born, the exuviae of a crane covered his body.[80] When Xue Xuan was born, his flesh was like crystal.[81] These are things that have seldom been heard of, past or present. How could they be explained by the heterodox theory of reincarnation?

NOTES

1. When Yao was the son of heaven, he dreamt at the end of autumn that the god White Emperor bestowed upon him a child with a small mouth. This child was Gao Tao. His mother said, "Originally, I climbed up a tall hill and sacrificed to the White Emperor. Above me appeared a cloud shaped like a tiger." She became pregnant and gave birth to Gao Tao. (From *A Profusion of Primal Qi and Ruling Mandates in The Spring and Autumn Annals*.)

2. For an explanation, see the commentary to Yu's dream about obtaining a book about the mountains in the chapter, "The Disciple of Emptiness" [I:5n5].

3. Emperor Taizu of the Ming dreamt of a vermillion terrace in the northwest sky with balustrades on all four sides, where two men resembling *vajra* guardians were standing. On the south side, several men wearing turbans were seated. In the middle stood three divinities, who resembled the Three Purities of Daoism. Many purple-robed transcendents bestowed a crimson robe on him. When he received it, he saw that the lining was multicolored and asked what it was. A Daoist said, "This is the robe of the Perfected Gentleman of Literary Culture. It is a sign that the Supreme God has bestowed the mandate of heaven on you." (From *Collected Policies and Achievements*.)

4. During the period that he was fighting for the throne, the future Emperor Chengzu of the Ming dreamt that he was battling against Ping An. He was about to be defeated when a stalwart man with a fine beard who was riding a white horse and carrying a large sword came from the northwest. In a loud voice, he said that he came to rescue His Majesty. Then, he struck at Ping An's horse, which immediately fell. Emperor Chengzu asked his name, and he replied, "Your humble official is the God of Xin District." When he awoke, the emperor thought

the dream strange. When he came to do battle with Ping An, Ping chased after Emperor Chengzu brandishing a long spear. Just as Ping was about to catch up with him, it happened that his horse stumbled and could not go on. Indeed, it was just like the dream. (From Chen Jian, *Comprehensive Annals of the Ming Dynasty.*)

5. The Duke of Guo dreamt that someone with a human face, white hair, and tiger's claws was holding an execution axe and standing in the western corner. The historian-astrologer Shi Yin said, "According to Your Excellency's description, this was Rushou, the god of punishments from heaven." (From *Conversations from the Feudal States.*)

6. For explanations, see the commentary to the dreams about a celestial emissary and the God of the Yellow River in the chapter, "The Disciple of Emptiness" [I:5n27].

7. The First Emperor of Qin dreamt that he was battling the God of the Sea, who resembled a human. He asked the erudite for interpreting dreams about this, and was told, "It is impossible to see the God of the Sea. He makes use of giant fish and dragons to communicate. Your Majesty has scrupulously carried out sacrifices, yet such an evil spirit has appeared. It is fitting that he should be exorcised so that good spirits can be summoned." The emperor then ordered men to enter the sea and capture a large fish, which was set up as bait. He personally took up a bow and arrow, waited for the giant fish to appear, and shot it. (From *Historical Records.*)

8. Emperor Ming dreamt of a golden man more than ten feet tall. A brilliant light shone from his head, and he could fly through the halls of the palace. The emperor asked his officials about this, and someone said, "In the west there is a god named 'Buddha' who is sixteen feet tall and gold in color." (From *History of the Eastern Han Dynasty.*)

9. In the third year of the Xianhe era [328], Liu Yao dreamt one night of three men with gold faces and cinnabar lips who were facing eastward but hesitated to move forward. They withdrew in silence. Liu bowed to them and followed after their footsteps. The next morning, he summoned his ministers and discussed this with them. All considered it an auspicious dream. Only Grand Astrologer Ren Yi said, "Three represents the total number of the ancient dynastic calendrical systems. East is the location of the trigram *Zhen:* 'Arousing.' It is the initial position of a king. Gold corresponds to the trigram *Dui:* 'Joyous,' which indicates things in decline. Cinnabar lips that do not speak mark the end of a matter. Hesitating, greeting yet withdrawing, symbolizes the Way of relinquishment. Bowing down indicates submitting to others, and following in their footsteps shows caution in not wanting to go beyond the borders. Moreover, the asterism Eastern Well governs the Qin region while the asterism Three Vehicles governs the Zhao region. The army of Qin will attack, and it will mean the death of a ruler along with the defeat of his army. Zhao will be defeated and lose its territory. At the most, it is but three years away, or at the soonest, in seven hundred days. The manifestation of this dream is not far off." Liu was terrified, and indeed, his dream was confirmed. (From *History of the Jin Dynasty.*)

10. When Fu Jian [r. 351–355] invaded the Guanzhong area, he dreamt that a celestial god sent an emissary in a vermillion robe and crimson hat who com-

manded him to appoint his younger cousin Fu Jian [r. 357–385] as Generalissimo Racing Dragon. The next day, Fu Jian [r. 351–355] erected an altar at Quwo where he formally granted his cousin the title, saying, "Your ancestor received this title in the past. Now, you are receiving this mandate from the gods." (From *History of the Jin Dynasty*.)

11. For an explanation, see the commentary to the dream about defeating Hou Jing in the chapter, "Utensils and Things" [II:7n34].

12. Zhang Chan, whose courtesy name was Dadian, was from Yongjia. While young, he was skilled at literary composition. When it came time to give him a personal name, his father dreamt that a god wrote a large graph, *chan* [to elucidate], and said, "Give your son this name." His father thought this was strange but consequently named him "Chan." (From *History of the Song Dynasty*.)

13. Zhao Gai, whose courtesy name was Shuping, was from Yucheng. Originally, his name was Yin [worshipping with reverence]. Once, he dreamt that a god had a register of names written in gold that contained Zhao Gai, so he subsequently changed his name to Gai [wooden grain leveler]. (From *History of the Song Dynasty*.)

14. For an explanation, see the commentary to the dream about Sun Guan changing his personal name to Bian in the chapter, "The Official Examinations" [II:11n14].

15. Military Commissioner Cheng Quan was originally named Zhigong [upholding courtesy]. He once dreamt that the government buildings in Cangzhou all had the graph *quan* [power] written on them, so he changed his personal name to Quan in response. After he entered the court, Censor Zheng Quan was appointed to replace him in Cangzhou. (From *Old History of the Tang Dynasty*.)

16. Qin Yan was originally named Li [erect], and he came from a military family. During the Qianfu era [874–879], he was put in shackles by bandits and sentenced to death. He dreamt that someone called out, "Qin Yan! Follow me out of here!" When he awoke, he saw that the shackles were broken, so he was able to flee. He then changed his name to Yan [man of talent and virtue]. (From "Biography of Gao Pian.")

17. Cao Yingshu's courtesy name was Xiuzhi. He was from Qiao District in Haozhou. Originally, he was named Xi. He once dreamt that he went to the government office and saw Ying Shu. When he awoke, he changed his name to Yingshu. (From *History of the Song Dynasty*.)

18. There is a Mount Niaodai in Zhuji District with many valuable purple stones on its heights. Few people knew about this. When Xie Fu traveled there, he dreamt that the god of the mountain said to him, "I shall help you to the amount of fifty thousand." In the morning, he saw that under the bed of his host was a stone of unusual color. When he asked where it came from, he was told that it came from the mountain. Xie then went to the mountain and unearthed more of the stones from which he derived much profit. (From Kong Lingfu, *A Record of Guiji*.)

19. Xi Yu was a palace attendant who served Emperor Guangwu of the Eastern Han as magistrate of Liqiu. Both the emperor and Xi dreamt of the God of Mount Suling. Later, Guangwu enfeoffed Xi as marquis of Xiangyang and had him construct a temple to the God of Mount Suling. Two stone deer were carved

and placed along the path to it, so the people called it the "Temple of the Deer Gate." (From *History of the Eastern Han Dynasty*.)

20. Xu You dreamt of an emissary dressed in black who presented him with six documents and said, "Your Excellency will become Lord of the Northern Dipper and Chen Kangbo will be assistant magistrate." As soon as he awoke, Chen Kangbo came to visit him. Xu told Chen about the dream, and Chen said, "I had been a Daoist master, but after I died I was reborn as a mere community head. It is fitting that I will now become assistant magistrate of the Northern Dipper." The following year, they both died on the same day. (From *A Records of Ghosts and the Living*.)

21. Emperor Xuanzong of the Tang [r. 712–756] took a nap and dreamt of the two demons, Emptiness and Waste. In anger, he called for a soldier, and suddenly a man appeared wearing a cap and gown. He caught the demons, cut them up, and then ate them. When asked his name, the man replied, "I am Presented Scholar Zhong Kui from Mount Zhongnan." (From *A Record of Festivals*.)

22. In the past, a former king [King Huai of Chu] once traveled to Gaotang, where he took a nap. He dreamt of a woman who said, "I am the daughter of Shaman Mountain and am at the service of guests at Gaotang. I learned that Your Majesty has traveled here to Gaotang, and I wish to share my bed and pillow with you." The king then favored her. When she was about to leave, she bid him farewell with a poem:

> I dwell on the southern slopes of Shaman Mountain
> Located beside Gaotang.
> In the morning, I am the moving clouds.
> In evening, I become the showering rain.
> Every morning and every evening,
> I can be found beneath South Terrace.

(From Song Yu, "Preface to Rhapsody on the Gaotang Shrine.")

23. Houji dreamt that he had sexual relations with the Nymph of the Luo River. (From *Liuchi duizhu*.)
[This source remains unidentified.–RES]

24. Tian Qianqiu presented the grievance of the crown prince to the throne, saying, "Your humble official dreamt that a white-haired old man told me to speak out." (From *History of the Western Han Dynasty*.)

25. Liu Lingzhe's courtesy name was Wenming. Once, when his mother had fallen ill, he prayed to the gods for her. He dreamt that an old man dressed in yellow said, "You should fetch bamboo shoots from South Mountain and feed these to her." After Liu awoke, he did as he was told, and her illness was cured. (From *History of the Southern Qi Dynasty*.)

26. When Xu Xiaosi was in the guard command of the heir apparent, he took a nap beside the northern wall in his quarters. He dreamt that two boys suddenly said to him, "Move your bed, sir." Xu was startled awake and heard a sound coming from the wall. He had moved about twenty feet away from it when the wall collapsed onto the bed. (From *History of the Chen Dynasty*.)

27. Qiao Zhizhong, whose courtesy name was Xisheng, was from Gaoyou. He was an edict attendant in the Hall for Treasuring Culture and became pre-

fect of Yunzhou. Qiao dreamt that a god bestowed upon him the title of commandant of cavalry. The next day, he told a guest about this, and while they were chatting and laughing, he died. (From *History of the Song Dynasty*.)

28. Cui Hao submitted "Memorial on Reforming the Calendar Based on the Five Yin-Stems" where he stated, "Your humble official was devoting his entire mind and thoughts to this matter, forgetting to eat and sleep. I then dreamt of struggling against a demon for a righteous cause and subsequently obtained important calculation techniques from the Duke of Zhou and Confucius." (From *History of the Sui Dynasty*.)

29. The "Rhapsody on a Dream" by Wang Yanshou of the Eastern Han Dynasty states, "One night I fell asleep and had an unusual dream. I closely observed the transformations of demons and strange creatures."

30. During the time of Emperor Ming of the Jin dynasty, someone who was going to present a horse to the emperor dreamt that the God of the Yellow River requested it. When he arrived at the court, it turned out that his dream was the same as the emperor's. The horse was promptly cast into the river as an offering to the god. Earlier, Grand Mentor Chu Bao also took a liking to this horse, but the emperor told him that it had already been given to the God of the Yellow River. After Chu died, a soldier saw him riding on this horse. (From Kong Yue, *Accounts of Anomalies*.)

31. The prefect of Jingzhou Huan Huo saw a man more than ten feet tall in the studio of his residence. He dreamt that the man said, "I am the god of Dragon Mountain and came here with evil intentions. But, since you are a firm and unwavering person, I shall willingly take my leave." (From *Investigations of Strange Events*.)

32. Before Chen Baxian achieved nobility, Shi Pu, the official on duty in the hall dreamt that a god in a vermillion robe bearing jade tablets descended from heaven. Written in gold on the tablets were the graphs, "The Chen family will rule for five generations and thirty-four years." When the Last Ruler of the Chen dynasty surrendered to the Sui dynasty, Shi Pu was still alive. (From *Accounts of Unique and Strange Things*.)

33. Ziying, the King of Qin, was sleeping in the Palace that Looks Out at the Distant Barbarians. One night, he dreamt of a god one hundred feet tall with magnificent hair. He was wearing jade slippers and riding in a cinnabar carriage pulled by vermillion horses. The god arrived at the palace and said that he wished to see Ziying, King of Qin. The gatekeeper admitted him and Ziying spoke with him. The god said, "I am an emissary from heaven who has come from Shaqiu [i.e., the place where Ziying will later die]. The world will erupt into chaos and those who act violently will be executed." (From *Wang Zinian's Recovered Records*.)

34. Zhao Xu of Tianshui was dwelling in Guangling when he dreamt of a girl dressed in green who was smiling seductively at him through the window. He continued to see her even after he awoke. Zhao thought this was definitely strange, so he prayed to her, asking, "Which deity are you?" Suddenly, he heard laughter from outside the window. He prayed to her again. Then, she said, "I am the Green Maiden of the Upper Realm." (From *A Record of Communications with the Other World*.)

35. Xian Chao, whose courtesy name was Yiqi, was an administrator retainer in Jibei Commandery during the Wei dynasty. During the Jiaping era [249–253], he dreamt one night of a goddess who followed him and became his wife. She called herself "Jade Maiden of Heaven." She was originally from Dong Commandery, surnamed Chenggong, and her courtesy name was Zhiqiong. While young, she had lost both her parents, and the Supreme God of Heaven took pity on her loneliness and suffering. He ordered that she descend into the human world and marry. (From *Collected Records of Transcendents.*)

36. Emperor Xuanzong of the Tang [r. 712–756] dreamt that more than ten transcendents descended on auspicious clouds and arrayed themselves in the courtyard. Each played a musical instrument that he was carrying, and their performance was clear and resounding. After it was finished, a transcendent came forward and asked, "Does Your Majesty know this piece? It is the 'Purple Cloud Music of Divine Transcendents.'" Xuanzong was delighted. Suddenly he woke up, but the lingering sounds were still in his ears. (From *Records from the Grand Hall.*)

37. While napping, Emperor Xuanzong of the Tang [r. 712–756] dreamt that twenty-seven transcendents said to him, "We are the twenty-eight asterisms. One of us is stationed on duty in the human world. We have been staying beneath Luo for three years to protect the borders of Your Majesty's empire and prevent any barbarians from invading the frontier." The emperor awoke and ordered emissaries to mount a search. In Luozhou District in Ningzhou they found a cave with twenty-seven stone statues. These were sent to the emperor, and sacrifices were held to them in the inner palace. (From *Stories of Encounters with Divine Transcendents.*)

38. Fu Yao, the local inspector of Zhangye, was investigating the administration of his subordinate districts when Yin Xing, the magistrate of Qiuchi, killed him and cast his body into an empty well. Fu Yao appeared to Lü Guang in a dream and said, "I was a lowly functionary in Zhangye Commandery and was investigating the various subordinate districts when I found Magistrate Yin Xing engaged in corruption and wastefulness. He feared that I would disclose this, so he killed me and cast my body into an empty well in Nantai. My clothing and appearance are like this . . ." Lü suddenly awakened, but he could still see Fu Yao, whose image only disappeared after a long while. He sent someone to recover the body, and it was just as in the dream. Lü angrily executed Yin Xing. (From *History of the Jin Dynasty.*)

39. Fan Shi, whose courtesy name was Juqing, was friends with Zhang Yuanbo. Fan served as an official in the labor section of a commandery. Later, he dreamt that Zhang appeared to him wearing a black hat with dangling hatstrings and called to him while walking, saying "I have died and will be buried on the appropriate date to proceed to the Yellow Springs for all eternity. Please do not forget me. Is it possible that you can hurry and arrive in time for my funeral?" Fan immediately rushed to get there. (From *History of the Eastern Han Dynasty.*)

40. Huangfu Mi of Anding dreamt that he had gone to Luoyang and was coming out of a temple when he saw a multitude of chariots and cavalry. They made offerings to the temple and said, "We will execute Generalissimo Cao

Shuang." Huangfu awoke and told someone of his dream. Later, it was indeed confirmed. (From *The Spring and Autumn Annals of Han and Jin*.)

41. Xiao Jian, Prince of Yidu, was obliged to leave the imperial palace at the age of ten. Tao Hongjing served as his reader-in-waiting for eight or nine years, so they often had contact with one another. When Xiao reached the age of eighteen, he died after drinking an herbal potion. At that time, Tao was dwelling in reclusion in the mountains. He suddenly dreamt that Xiao came to him and sadly bid him farewell, saying, "On such-and-such a day my life ended. But, as I have committed no sins, three years from now I will be reborn into a certain family." Tao tried to learn more but couldn't because such affairs of the underworld are kept secret. When Tao awoke, he wrote letters seeking the facts and left the capital to make further inquiries. Indeed, he found that his dream accorded with events, so he composed "Record of a Dream." (From *History of the Chen Dynasty*.)

42. Emperor Gaozu of the Northern Wei dreamt one night of an old man with white hair and whiskers who straightened out his cap and robes and bowed down to him along the left side of the road. His Majesty found this strange and asked him about it. The old man replied, "I am Attendant Gentleman Ji Shao of the Jin dynasty and have come to welcome you." When he awoke, the emperor told his close officials about this and ordered a search for Ji Shao's tomb, where a sacrifice was held. (From *History of the Northern Wei Dynasty*.)

43. Lu Yuanming, whose courtesy name was Youzhang, was good friends with Wang You of Yingchuan. He dreamt that Wang brought over some wine and bid him farewell, writing a poem to him. When day came, Lu remembered ten words from the poem:

> Now, after I take my leave of you,
> Neither fame nor fortune shall I further pursue.

Lu sighed and said, "Wang You never kept vulgar company, nor did he travel about seeking patronage. There must be some other reason behind this dream just now and for these lines afterward." Indeed, he learned three days later that Wang had died at the hands of rebellious soldiers. When he inquired about the actual date of Wang's death, it turned out to be on the night of the dream. (From *History of the Northern Wei Dynasty*.)

44. Jia Su was friends with Shen Fushi from his youth. Shen died first, and Jia once dreamt that Shen said, "You can cease your activities now." Jia awoke and sacrificed to Shen's spirit in his bedchamber. Then, he again dreamt of Shen, who said, "Since matters have reached their end, what more can you do?" Subsequently, Jia was executed. (From *Bo and Kong's Encyclopedia*.)

45. Chen Lü, whose courtesy name was Zhongxing, enjoyed a fine friendship with Yu Ji. One day, Yu dreamt that Chen toasted him, saying, "I often think of you, and I know that you have not forgotten me though we will no longer be able to meet." Not long afterward, Yu learned that Chen had died, and he mourned him deeply. (From *History of the Yuan Dynasty*.)

46. Five years after Xuan Xian died, Shi Hu dreamt that Xuan tearfully entrusted his son Xuan Fen to him. After Shi Hu awoke, he said, "This is beyond my understanding. Where is Xuan Fen now?" His close officials replied, "He is

the governor of Zhao Commandery." Therefore, Shi Hu had him promoted to chamberlain for law enforcement from where he rose to chamberlain for ceremonials. (From *History of the Later Zhao Dynasty.*)

47. Zhang Jun, King Wen of the Former Liang dynasty, dreamt of someone with white hair on his temples and white eyebrows who identified himself as Ziyu [n.d.] and said, "Affairs on earth are entrusted to your authority while affairs in the underworld are under mine." After the king awoke, he inquired about this and learned that there had been a marquis, Ziyu, who had already died. The king found Ziyu's great-grandson Liang and appointed him magistrate of Qilian. (From *A Record of Dunhuang.*)

48. Zhang Jia was related to Minister of Education Cai Mo. He was staying at Cai's house. When he did not return from a trip at the expected time, Cai dreamt while napping that Zhang told him, "I had just set out when I suddenly fell ill and died on such-and-such a day." When Cai awoke, he sent someone to retrace Zhang's steps to confirm this. Zhang had indeed died. (From *A Record of Ghosts and the Living.*)

49. Xu Shan, the illegitimate "secretariat drafter" in Jiangnan, was orphaned when young and lived in Yuzhang. When the Yang Wu dynasty conquered Yuzhang, Xu's younger sister was kidnapped by an army officer. So Xu traveled to the headquarters in Yangdu to accuse the officer. At that time, Yang Wo had just succeeded to his father's position as military governor and discipline was tight. For a year, he did not receive any commoners or itinerant advisors. But, when Xu had just reached Baisha, Yang Wo dreamt that someone told him, "A scholar from Jiangxi, Xu Shan, will arrive to see Your Excellency. He is now staying at an inn in Baisha. Xu is a fine man and Your Excellency should treat him generously." Yang Wo sent cavalry to welcome Xu and asked what it was he wished to say. After Xu explained in detail about the matter of his younger sister, Yang ordered that she be ransomed and returned to her home. (From *A Record of Inquests into Spirits.*)

50. Magistrate of Yongxing Wang Fengxian's son had died, and Wang dreamt that he had conversed with him in a dream as if he were alive. Wang asked if it were possible to travel from the other world, and his child replied, "On such-a-such a day, I will come home to visit the maidservant." After awakening, Wang asked the maidservant, who said, "Today, I dreamt that the young gentleman had come back." (From *A Record of Ghosts and the Living.*)

51. Presented Scholar Wang Yun was talented in literature. In the second year of the Huichang era [842], his friend Lu Xiufu dreamt that he had received an official appointment and went to a certain place where a servant stopped him. From behind a screen, he saw dozens of people like bound convicts. Among them was Wang Yun. Lu spoke to Wang, who tearfully said, "I recently received an official appointment but grew sick of the human world." Lu awoke. At that time, Wang had been living in Yangzhou. After seven days an obituary notice arrived indicating that Wang had died on the very day that Lu had had the dream. (From *Miscellaneous Morsels from Youyang.*)

52. Zhuge Fu of the Liu Song dynasty was serving as governor of Jiuzhen when he died from an illness. Only his eldest son, Yuanchong, had accompanied him when he assumed his post. Monk He coveted his property and, with the help

of an accomplice, pushed Zhuge Yuanchong into the water, where he drowned. Yuanchong's mother, Mistress Chen, was in Yangdu and dreamt that Yuanchong had returned. He informed her of the death of his father and provided her with the facts of how he himself had been killed. Mistress Chen had her first cousin Xu Daoli travel to investigate this. Indeed, it turned out to be true. The two felons were arrested and executed. (From *The Taiping Miscellany.*)

53. Lu Shumin was on his way to attend the examinations. He had set out early one day and was killed by bandits. Zheng Chu, the commandant of Goushi District dreamt that Lu appeared with unbound hair and dripping with blood to make an accusation that he had been killed by bandits. When Zheng asked for details, Lu said, "These bandits have not yet been caught. But they are bringing along a white ox whose left foot is lame. Please make a note of this ox. Next year on the first day of the eighth lunar month, the bandits will bring this ox to the Outer Western Gate of the city." Zheng awoke and issued an order to find the bandits, but they could not be apprehended. At the stated time, they did indeed bring along a white ox whose left foot was lame to the Outer Western Gate. They were arrested and readily confessed after interrogation. (From *The Taiping Miscellany.*)

54. When Wei Zheng fell seriously ill, Emperor Taizong of the Tang and the heir apparent both called on him at his residence. That evening, the emperor dreamt of Wei as he had normally been in life, but by the next day, Wei passed away. Furthermore, when Du Ruhui passed away, the emperor also dreamt of Du as he had normally been in life. (From *Old History of the Tang Dynasty.*)

55. Xue Shou had died. The Prince of Qin [Emperor Taizong of the Tang] assumed the throne and once dreamt of Xue as he had normally been in life. After Yu Shinan died, the emperor also dreamt that he was boldly addressing the throne as he had in life. (From *Old History of the Tang Dynasty.*)

56. For an explanation, see the commentary to the dream about a short, dark man in the chapter, "Forms and Appearances" [II:5n11].

57. Emperor Huan of the Eastern Han favored the book by Laozi. He dreamt one night that he met Laozi and consequently ordered that a Laozi Temple be built. (From *Biographies of Exalted Recluses.*)

58. The sacrifices at the Eminent and Loyal Temple are dedicated to Generalissimo Huo Guang of the Eastern Han. According to legend, when Sun Hao, the king of Wu, was ill, he dreamt that a god descended into his room and identified himself as Huo Guang. He asked that a temple be established to him by the salt pond at Golden Mountain in order to control floods. After the temple was built, the king recovered from his illness. During the Tianfu era [936–942] of the Later Jin dynasty, the King of Wu-Yue established the present temple here. Emperor Lizong of the Southern Song bestowed the placard "Eminent and Loyal." (From *Gazetteer of Hangzhou.*)

59. The sacrifices at the Eminent and Responsive Temple are dedicated to the late Mr. Cui of Cizhou. The departed's name was Ziyu. He served as the magistrate of Fuyang district in Cizhou prefecture during the Zhenguan era [627–649] of the Tang dynasty, and the people established the temple to sacrifice to him because of his extraordinary administration. During the Jingkang era [1126], Emperor Gaozong of the Southern Song lost his way while fleeing from the Jin dy-

nasty marauders. Suddenly, a white horse appeared and guided him so that by evening, he arrived at this temple. Drops of sweat were dripping down some of his ordinary horses, so he decided to sleep here underneath the eaves. He dreamt that Cui struck the ground with his staff, urging him to move on. The white horse led him further to Crooked Bridge Valley where he met Geng Nanzhong, who had come to welcome him. Suddenly, the white horse disappeared. (From *Gazetteer of Hangzhou*.)

60. In the New City at Jingkou was the Temple to Deng Ai, which had long fallen into disrepair. When Sima Kuo, Prince Qiao of the Jin dynasty, was commander-in-chief, he dreamt of someone who identified himself as Mr. Deng and who requested that his house be repaired. Sima Kuo consequently ordered that the temple be restored. (From *A Garden of Strange Events*.)

61. When Lü Meng, whose courtesy name was Ziming, came to the state of Wu, the king urged him to study. So he read extensively and consulted many learned texts, concentrating on *The Book of Changes*. Once, as a guest of Sun Ce, he drank too much wine and fell asleep. He awoke suddenly, startling the others who asked him what happened. Lü replied that he dreamt that he was discussing the trigrams and hexagrams with Fuxi, the Duke of Zhou, and King Wen. (From *Wang Zinian's Recovered Records*.)

62. Master Tian is the Great Transcendent of the Nine Flowers Cavern-Heaven. During the Yuanhe era [806–820], he lived in reclusion at Youting Village in Raozhou Prefecture. There, he taught youngsters in an elementary school. The prefect of Raozhou, Qi Tui, had a daughter, and he arranged for a scholar, Li, to become his son-in-law. After a few months, the daughter became pregnant, and Li went to Chang'an to take the official examinations. When she was about to give birth in the private quarters of the prefectural office, she dreamt that demons berated her for having polluted herself by eating meat. Qi Tui did not believe this, but after she gave birth, the demons caused her death. She was placed in a coffin that was stored beside the public road. The next year, Scholar Li passed the examinations and returned to Raozhou. One evening, he saw his wife in the countryside, and she told about the events that had transpired. Then she said, "If you go and seek help from Master Tian in Youting Village, I can be resurrected through his spiritual power." Scholar Li followed her instructions and sincerely implored Master Tian to intercede. His wife was indeed resurrected while Tian was never seen again. (From *Recovered Biographies of Transcendents*.)

63. When Emperor Xuanzong of the Tang [r. 712–756] was traveling in Shu, he dreamt that Sun Simiao requested some realgar from Wudu. So the emperor commanded an imperial commissioner to present more than ten pounds of realgar and escort it to the summit of Mount Emei. Before he had reached halfway up the mountain, the commissioner saw an old man in a turban and open shirt, attended by two boys in green clothes. The old man pointed to a flat stone and said, "You can place the medicine here where there is a memorial to be transcribed for the emperor." On the stone the commissioner observed more than one hundred vermillion graphs that disappeared as soon as he transcribed them. In an instant, a white vapor arose and everything suddenly vanished. (From *Bo and Kong's Encyclopedia*.)

64. After he returned from conducting the *feng* and *shan* sacrifices, His Majesty

Emperor Wu of the Western Han dreamt that Emperor Gaozu was in the Hall of Light, and all the officials also had this dream. Therefore, he sacrificed to Emperor Gaozu in the Hall of Light. (From *Precedents of Emperor Wu of the Western Han*.)

65. During the time of Emperor Ling of the Eastern Han, Governor of Liaoxi Huang Fan dreamt that a corpse floating on the sea said to him, "I am Lord of Guzhu, the younger brother of Boyi, and I beseech you for a proper burial." (From *A Record of Manifold Things*.)

66. Zhang Zhichun was the father of Zhang Kongsun, whose courtesy name was Mengfu [sign of the dream]. Zhang Zhichun served as an administrator in the Dongping Brigade. One night, he dreamt that he was visiting the Confucian Temple and that a fine fruit was bestowed upon him. Later, a son was born, and Zhang sought an appropriate name for him from the reigning Duke of the Sage's Descendants. The son was consequently named "Kongsun" or "descendant of Confucius." (From *History of the Yuan Dynasty*.)

Huang Ze, courtesy name Chuwang, dreamt that he met Confucius, but he considered it a chance occurrence. However, he then had a number of dreams about meeting him, and on the final occasion, he dreamt that Confucius gave him the *Six Classics,* which he had personally edited. The graphs seemed as if they had been newly written. From this time on, he felt deeply inspired. (From *History of the Yuan Dynasty*.)

Zheng Xuan dreamt that Confucius visited him and said, "Arise! Arise! This year is *chen* in the horary calendar and next year will be *si*." As soon as Zheng awoke, he prognosticated this and realized that his life was destined to end. A short while later, he fell ill and died. (From *A Continuation of the History of the Han Dynasty*.)

Qiao Zhou dreamt that he met Confucius. Qiao said, "In antiquity, Confucius died at the age of seventy-three. Now I am more than seventy, and I fear I will not escape the same fate." The following year, he died. (From *Bo and Kong's Encyclopedia*.)

Qi Jixuan, whose courtesy name was Baoding, was from Bohai. He composed commentaries to the *Six Classics* in which he often expressed his own ideas. When Qi was suffering from an illness, he dreamt that Confucius was so angry that he had made such exceedingly broad commentaries that he beat him and berated him. When Qi awoke, he burned his commentaries, and soon he recovered from his illness. (From *A Summary of the Canons of the Three Kingdoms*.)

For an explanation of Liu Xie's dream of Confucius, see the commentary to the dream about ritual vessels painted vermillion in the chapter, "Utensils and Things" [II:7n9]. For an explanation of Huang Yuan's dream of Confucius, see the commentary to the dream about a brush soaked with ink in the chapter, "Brush and Ink" [II:9n5].

67. Emperor Lizong of the Southern Song was the son of Prince Rong, and his mother was originally Mistress Quan. His Majesty was born at the princely residence in Hongqiao Village in Shanyin District. The night before, his father dreamt that a god in purple robes and a golden hat came to call on him. (From *History of the Song Dynasty*.)

68. Alanguohuo was the mother of Beiduanchaer, the tenth-generation ancestor of Emperor Taizu of the Yuan (Chingis Khan). She was dwelling alone and sleeping in her bed when she dreamt that a white light came down from heaven through her window. After entering her room, it changed into a golden god who rushed over to lay down with her in her bed. Alanguohuo was startled awake and, subsequently, she became pregnant, giving birth to a son, who was Beiduanchaer. (From *History of the Yuan Dynasty*.)

69. Mistress Yin, the mother of Tuoba Rui, was injured while pregnant with him. Later, she dreamt during a nap of an old man wearing a formal hat and gown who told her, "I will grant you a son. You need have no anxieties." She awoke and was secretly pleased by this. Before long, she gave birth to a son, whom she named Rui [auspicious]. His courtesy name was Tianci [granted by heaven]. (From *History of the Northern Wei Dynasty*.)

70. Liu Shu was the father of Liu Yin [cause], whose courtesy name was Mengji [auspicious dream]. At the age of forty, Liu Shu was still without a son when he dreamt that a god on horseback brought a boy to his house and told him, "Bring him up well." As soon as Liu awoke, a son was born whom he named Yin [piebald]. His courtesy name was Mengji [dreaming about a thoroughbred]. Later, Liu Yin changed his personal name and courtesy name. (From *History of the Yuan Dynasty*.)

71. For an explanation, see the commentary to the dream about the vigorous essence of a chime-stone in the chapter, "Mountains and Rivers" [II:4n17].

72. Liu Jun, whose courtesy name was Ziqi [unusual gentleman], was from Jiangling. His father was moved by a strange dream in which the graph *jun* [extraordinary] was written. That evening, a son was born, and he gave him this name. Liu Jun rose to become minister of the Ministry of War, and he was given the honorary title of junior mentor, and the posthumous name, Zhongmin [loyal and kindhearted]. (From *Annals of Chu*.)

73. Minister of Education Gao Yan of Huzhou dreamt that a Daoist who used a sword as a staff came over to where he was sleeping to say, "I have arrived to become your son and shall kill several thousand enemies." After Gao awoke, he thought this was strange. That same month, his wife became pregnant and gave birth at the expected time to Gao Li. (From *A Record of Inner Light*.)

74. Ma Juan was from Nanbu. Originally, his father Ma Congzheng had no son, so he purchased a concubine. Upon inquiring, he learned that both her parents had died and that she had sold herself to become a concubine in order to provide them with funerals. He did not blame her for her burden. Later, Ma dreamt that an old man thanked him, saying, "I am the father of your concubine and these things have become known in the highest heaven. Your family is to enjoy an unending stream *(juanjuan)* of wealth and nobility." When a son was born, Ma named him Juan (stream) after what had been said in the dream. The son became the top metropolitan graduate during the Yuanyou era [1086–1093]. (From *History of the Song Dynasty*.)

75. Zhao Kui's courtesy name was Nanzhong. His father Zhao Fang was commandant of Puqi. A neighbor had dreamt that the God of the Southern Marchmount had descended into Zhao Fang's house, and subsequently Zhao

Kui was born. He later held the rank of junior preceptor, was enfeoffed as duke of Jiguo, and given the posthumous name "Zhongjing" [loyal and tranquil]. (From *History of the Song Dynasty.*)

Yu Ji's [1272–1348] courtesy name was Bosheng. His father was Yu Ji [d. 1318] and his mother was Mistress Yang. She was the daughter of Yang Wenzhong, chancellor of the National University. During the Xianchun era [1265–1274], Yang Wenzhong was governing the Mount Heng area and had brought Yu Ji [d. 1318] along. Yu Ji still did not have a son, so he prayed to the Southern Marchmount. When Yu Ji [1272–1348] was about to be born, Yang Wenzhong arose in the morning, put on his official cap and robes, sat down, and fell asleep. He dreamt that a Daoist came before him. Accompanied by an entourage of soldiers, the Daoist announced, "The Perfected Gentleman of the Southern Marchmount has come to visit you." As soon as Yang Wenzhong awoke, he learned that a boy had been born to his son-in-law. Yang regarded this as a strange occurrence. (From *History of the Yuan Dynasty.*)

76. Ni Yue's father was named Qian. He served as minister of rites and was given the posthumous name Wenxi [cultured and cautious]. Ni Qian had sacrificed at the Northern Marchmount and prayed to its god. Ni Yue's mother, Mistress Yao, dreamt that a divinity in a scarlet robe entered her chamber. When she awoke, she gave birth to a son and considered that she had been stirred by the God of the Northern Marchmount. Therefore, she named her son Yue [marchmount]. He rose to the position of minister of personnel and was given the posthumous name Wenyi [cultured and brave]. (From *Collected Trifles from the Studio of Honesty.*)

77. The mother of Fan Zuyu dreamt that a man wearing golden armor came into her bedroom and said, "I am the former Han dynasty general Deng Yu." Fan Zuyu was born that very day, therefore, she named him Zuyu [venerating Deng Yu] and his courtesy name was Mengde [obtained by a dream]. Because a biography by Sima Guang had praised Deng Yu as "honest and sincere" *[duxing chunbei]*, Fan changed his courtesy name to Chunfu [sincere man]. (From *Biographies of the Fan Family.*)

Guo Xiangzheng's courtesy name was Gongfu; he was from Dangtu. His mother dreamt of Li Bo and then gave birth. Guo achieved a reputation for his poetry while still young. Mei Yaochen saw him and uttered praise, "With such innate talent, he is truly a reincarnation of Li Bo!" (From *History of the Song Dynasty.*)

78. Just before Bian Hao was born, his father dreamt that Xie Lingyun, the former governor of Yongjia, came to visit him and said that he wished to regard him as his father. When Bian Hao was born, the child bore a resemblance to the person in the dream. Later, he pacified Jianzhou and conquered Xiangtan, becoming known as "Bian the Arhat." (From *Pure Conversations from Yuhu.*)

On the mountain where the ancestors of Liu Hang had dwelled for generations was the Terrace where Niu Sengru Studied. Liu's mother dreamt that a man in a formal cap and gown said, "His Excellency Niu is arriving." Before long, she became pregnant and later gave birth to Liu Hang. (From *History of the Song Dynasty.*)

79. When Su Zhe was in Gaoan, he had the same dream as Buddhist Master Cong about welcoming Buddhist Master Jie. I, Su Shi, arrived there and said

that when I was eight or nine, I dreamt that I was a monk who traveled back and forth between home and Shaanxi. I also said that while my mother was pregnant with me, she dreamt of a monk who was emaciated and blind in one eye and who sought lodging for the night. Buddhist Master Cong was startled by this and said, "Jie of western Shaanxi had lost his sight in one eye." (From *Forest of Jottings*.)

Song Xiang's father Song Si served as an administrator in Jiujiang and prayed to Mount Lu together with his wife Mistress Zhong. He dreamt that a Daoist priest gave him a book and said, "This is a gift for your son." When he looked at it, he saw that it was the *Younger Dai's Book of Ritual*. Not long afterward, Song Xiang was born. One day, his father saw an image of the Perfected Lord Xu which was exactly like the person he encountered in his dream. (From *History of the Song Dynasty*.)

80. Yang Yi, whose courtesy name was Danian, was from Pucheng. His grandfather Yang Wenyi served as magistrate of Yushan during the Southern Tang dynasty. When Yang Yi was about to be born, Yang Wenyi dreamt that a Daoist priest who called himself the "Mountain Dweller with a Heart of Jade" came to visit him. Shortly afterward, Yang Yi was born. He had feathers more than a foot long that covered his entire body. After a month, they fell off. (From *History of the Song Dynasty*.)

Yang Yi's mother Mistress Zhang [fl. late 10th cent.] dreamt that a Daoist who called himself the Lord of Wuyi requested her aid in undergoing rebirth. When she gave birth to Yang Yi, he was a crane chick. The entire room was frightened by this and threw him into the river. However, her uncle said, "I have heard that the births of extraordinary men who appear between long intervals are always unusual." They ran to look for the chick and found a child within the exuviae of a crane. His body still had feathers, which fell off a month later. (From "A Preface to a Poem.")

81. Xue Xuan was from Hejin. His father, Xue Zhen, was an instructor in Yutian. Xue Xuan's mother Mistress Qi dreamt that a man dressed in purple robes visited her. Subsequently, she gave birth to Xue Xuan in her quarters at the school. When he was born, his flesh was like crystal, revealing all his five *zang*-organs. When his grandfather Xue Zhongyi heard the child cry out, he said, "He will certainly attain an exalted position." (From *Annals of Chu*.)

CHAPTER 13

Longevity and Destiny
壽命

Whether one's longevity and destiny are long or short is not something a wise man worries about. Still, time is always rushing by, so sages and worthies anxiously seek to understand the Way in order to cultivate themselves. In antiquity, the mother of King Wen dreamt that she would give birth to a son who would enjoy longevity and prosperity.[1] The mother of Yuwen Yonggui dreamt that she would give birth to a son who would enjoy longevity and nobility.[2] King Wu died at the age of ninety-three because King Wen considered their ages and gave him three more years of life.[3] The grandmother of Gong Mingzhi died at the age of eighty-two because her grandson prayed for five more years of life for her.[4] When Yang Danian reached the age of forty-seven, he died.[5] Liu Hongjing had twenty-five years added to his longevity and was never ill.[6] Li Zizhi dreamt that he was discussing the number of stalks used to cast the hexagrams of *The Book of Changes,* and his life ended at age forty-nine.[7] Chu Yanhui dreamt that he lost one of the yarrow stalks for casting the hexagrams, and his life ended at age forty-eight.[8] Shen Qingzhi dreamt of two bolts of silk.[9] Liu Zhiheng dreamt of two carp.[10] Wang Zijin interpreted a dream about brambles and knew it signified an untimely death.[11] Zhao Zhi interpreted a dream about a mulberry tree and determined the dreamer's lifespan.[12] Old Mr. Dou dreamt that his life had been extended by three dozen years.[13] Xu Pu dreamt of two *yu* graphs.[14] Zha Dao dreamt that he had increased his years by accumulating good deeds.[15] Zheng Xuan dreamt that the year in the horary calendar was *chen,* and this accorded with the prognostication.[16] Yan Ji's lifespan had not been completed and dreams about his return to life were confirmed.[17] Murong De's lifespan was about to come to an end, so he carried out his dream about the imperial succession.[18] Song Ying dreamt that his late wife came to bid him farewell.[19] The wife of Li Shaoyun dreamt that her husband departed tearfully.[20] Mr. Lou dreamt about the register of wealth and destiny.[21] Lü Yin dreamt about a judge in the underworld.[22] Bo Shi dreamt that a prefect welcomed him.[23] Wang Zhan dreamt that a functionary came to summon him.[24] These are cases where the destinies decreed by heaven cannot be altered, for a man's lifespan is preordained. Employing coffins and tombs are the prescribed practices for sending off the departed so that they can enjoy eternity. When these forms appear in dreams, they can also differ as to whether they are auspicious or unlucky. Thus, Zhao Liangqi dreamt of eleven coffins and attained an exalted rank in the secretariat.[25] Gao Shi dreamt of a coffin that was large and wide, and so he became a supervisor of the Household of the Heir Apparent.[26] After a dream that a coffin arrived in the hall of his residence, Mr. Li became a grand councilor.[27] After he dreamt that two coffins fell down from the sky, Suo Chong was twice promoted.[28] Yang Xiuzhi dreamt that he had climbed atop a tomb and pushed against a pillar there. He advanced in rank to become one of the three dukes.[29] But Zhu Zhaolin dreamt of a coffin that was not finished and failed the official examinations.[30] Zhou Pan dreamt that he was lecturing on the Way in a dark chamber and sighed that his life was over.[31] Li Yuanzhong dreamt that he entered his father's tomb holding a torch, but it was a sign that he would bring glory to his ancestors.[32] As for the deaths of Wen Xu and Li Deyu, both were able to obtain burial in their hometown by using dreams. Is this not because their *hun-* and *po-*souls had never been extinguished?[33]

NOTES

1. Tairen dreamt that she was stimulated to conceive by a tall man who told her, "Your son will enjoy longevity and prosperity." (From *Destinies Revealed by the Yellow River Diagram*.)
2. The mother of Yuwen Yonggui dreamt than an old man holding a baby boy gave him to her and said, "I give you this boy so that he may enjoy both longevity and nobility." After he was born, he was named Yonggui [eternally noble]. (From *A Summary of the Canons of the Three Kingdoms*.)
3. For an explanation, see the commentary to the dream about nine more years of life in the chapter, "The Disciple of Emptiness" [I:5n16].
4. When Gong Mingzhi was young he lost his parents and so was brought up by his grandmother, Mistress Li. She had said, "When I was young, I dreamt that a divine judge dressed in green robes said to me, 'You have been given seventy-seven years of life.'" During the Chongning era [1102–1107] under Emperor Huizong, she reached this age and, as expected, fell ill. Gong burnt incense and

prayed, "I wish to reduce my own years by five and add them to the longevity of my grandmother." Mistress Li indeed recovered from her illness, and she died at the age of eighty-two. (From *History of the Song Dynasty*.)

5. Yang Danian became a Hanlin academician at the age of thirty-seven. During a nap he dreamt that the Mountain Dweller with a Heart of Jade came to visit him and produced a document on which he wrote the graphs for "thirty-seven." Yang was shocked and said, "Is this not an indication of my lifespan? Is it permissible to add to it?" The Mountain Dweller used his brush to add a single stroke to make it read "forty-seven." When Yang reached this age, he did indeed die. (From *The Complete Book on Writing*.)

6. Liu Hongjing's courtesy name was Yuanpu. For generations, his family had dwelled in Huaifei and was wealthy. There was an expert in physiognomy who looked at him and said, "You, sir, will live only two or three more years." Liu used some money to purchase four maids from Weiyang for his daughter, who was going to be married. One of them was called Lansun and possessed unusual beauty. When he asked about her, he discovered that she was the daughter of a defeated general in the Huaixi rebellion. She had wandered here and there and had lost all contact with her family. Her mother's family was also surnamed Liu. Liu Hongjing took care of her as if she were his niece and married her off with a generous dowry. In the spring of the second year of the Changqing era [822], he dreamt of someone in green clothes holding a tablet of authority who bowed and said, "I am Lansun's father. I have been moved by your act of virtue, which is difficult to repay. Since your life is soon to end, I will make a request of the supreme god Di on your behalf." Three days later, Liu again dreamt of Lansun's father, who now appeared in purple robes holding an ivory tablet accompanied by very dignified attendants. He thanked Liu and said, "I made a request of Di on your behalf and permission was granted to extend your longevity by twenty-five years. Prosperity shall extend down to the third generation of your descendants, who will suffer no harm." Later, Liu again met the physiognomist, who said with surprise, "You must have secretly performed a good deed, for you will enjoy long life." (From *The Taiping Miscellany*.)

7. Li Shi's courtesy name was Zizhi, and he rose to the position of vice director in the Ministry of Personnel. He died at the age of forty-nine. He once dreamt that he was discussing the number of stalks used to cast the hexagrams of *The Book of Changes* [i.e., forty-nine]. When he awoke, he said, "My life will be over when I reach this number." (From *New History of the Tang Dynasty*.)

8. When Chu Yanhui was young, he fell seriously ill and dreamt that someone gave him a set of yarrow stalks used to cast the hexagrams of *The Book of Changes*. However, he then lost one of the stalks. At the age of forty-eight, he died in bed of an illness. (From *History of the Chen Dynasty*.)

9. For an explanation, see the commentary to the dream about his longevity being predetermined in the chapter, "Valuables and Goods" [II:8n21].

10. During the Liang dynasty, there was a governor of a commandery named Liu Zhiheng. He once dreamt of two men surnamed Li who begged him for their lives, but he did not understand what they meant. The next day was the second month of summer, and someone presented him with two carp *[li]*. Liu suddenly realized who they were and said, "They must be the ones who came to me in my

dream." Therefore, he set them free. That evening, he dreamt that they came again to thank him, saying, "Your longevity will be extended because of this." (From *History of the Southern Dynasties*.)

11. For an explanation, see the commentary to the dreams about the graph *su* and the graph for "brambles" in the chapter, "Written Graphs" [II:10n33].

12. He Zhi dreamt that a mulberry tree was growing in a well. Zhao Zhi interpreted it saying, "A mulberry is not something found in a well. The graph *sang* 桑 [mulberry] is composed of elements indicating four 'tens' 十 and an 'eight' 八. I fear your lifespan will not surpass this." He Zhi died at the age of forty-eight. (From *Biographies of Eminent Elders of the Past from Yidu*.) Ding Gu dreamt that a mulberry tree was growing in a well. (From *A Collection of Ivory Bodkins*.)

13. Dou Yujun was from Yuyang. His family was very wealthy. At the age of thirty, he was still without a son and dreamt that his late grandfather told him, "You will not have a son and your life will not be long. You should engage in charitable deeds as soon as possible." Dou Yujun agreed. Ten years later, he dreamt again of his grandfather, who told him, "Because of your secret acts of kindness, the Office of the Underworld has decided to extend your life for three dozen years and grant you five sons, each of whom will enjoy honor and renown." This story was recorded by Fan Zhongyan. (From *History of the Song Dynasty*.)

14. Xu Pu visited the Fan Zhongyan Temple where he decided to rest and took a nap. Suddenly, he dreamt that someone wearing a vermillion cap came to him saying, "Your lifespan still has two more *yu* 于." Xu pondered this after he awoke and thought that it meant "twenty years." He died twenty-two years later. No doubt, it was because the graph for *yu* contains the graphs "ten" 十 and "one" 一, two such graphs adding up to twenty-two. (From *Collected Trifles from the Studio of Honesty*.)

15. Zha Dao once dreamt of a god who said, "You should attain the position of regular chamberlain and have a lifespan of fifty-seven years. However, this has been extended to sixty-four years because of the good deeds you have accumulated." (From *History of the Song Dynasty*.)

16. For an explanation, see the commentary on Confucius's spirit in heaven in the chapter, "Gods and Strange Things" [II:12n66].

17. Yan Ji, the elder brother of Yan Han, fell ill during the Xianning era [275–279] and went to consult a physician. He died in the physician's house. His relatives collected the corpse, but when they carried out the funeral rites, the funeral banner kept getting caught in the trees and could not be disentangled. Upon returning home, his wife dreamt that Yan Ji told her, "I did not complete my full lifespan, so I am supposed to return to life. Hurry and open up my coffin." That night, his mother and others in the family also dreamt this. When the coffin was opened, there were indeed confirmations that he was alive. He had been clawing at the coffin from inside and his nails were all damaged. However, his breathing was quite faint. For months afterward, he was unable to communicate that he wanted to eat and drink. When he needed food or drink, he would make it known through dreams. In this way, he was nurtured for thirteen years, but he never set foot outside his house. (From *History of the Jin Dynasty*.)

18. Murong De welcomed Chao, the son of his elder brother, to the capital

Chang'an. That night, he dreamt that his father told him, "Since you have no sons, why not quickly establish Chao as crown prince? Otherwise, evil men may begin to plot against you." When he awoke, Murong De said to his wife, "The spirit of the former emperor has issued a command. It would appear from this dream that I am soon to die." Therefore, he established Chao as the imperial crown prince. Indeed, Murong De died during that very month. (From *History of the Jin Dynasty*.)

19. Mistress Deng was the wife of Song Ying of the Northern Wei dynasty. She had been dead for fifteen years when, without any warning, Song dreamt that she came and bowed before him, saying, "It has now been decided that I am to marry Gao Chong, so I have come to bid you farewell." She left in tears. Several days later, Gao Chong died. (From *Exceptional Dreams*.)

20. Li Shaoyun of Longxi was the son-in-law of Lu Junxu of Fanyang. By nature, he was fond of wine. One night, his wife dreamt that Li and over ten others together with courtesans had been arrested and that they were crying out tearfully as they were led away. She was startled awake. That night, Li Shaoyun had the very same dream. As a result, he restrained himself out of fear, and, for three years, nothing harmful occurred. Li thought that the dream must have been false, so he began to indulge in his old habits again. The following year on the third day of the third lunar month, he was on a pleasure boat on the Qujiang River with more than ten other men including Li Meng, Pei Shinan, and Liang Xiang. Famous courtesans from Chang'an had been selected and brought along. They were all drunk when the boat capsized and everybody drowned. (From *The Taiping Miscellany*.)

21. When Lou Shide was young he was felled by illness and dreamt that a man in purple robes came to summon him. He walked for more than a mile until he saw an official compound beside the road with a tall vermillion gate and a sign that read, "Bureau of the Underworld." Lou entered the compound. As the functionaries and guards made way, he saw a king and was told he was the "director of destinies" in charge of the registers of official positions and destinies among the living. There were also several thousand dossiers on a table. Beside these stood men dressed in green called "case administrators." Lou looked up his own name and the series of offices he was to hold: his position would reach that of chief bulwark of the state, and he would live to be eighty. Startled awake, he noticed that his illness had subsided. Later, after he took up his official career, he found that his offices all corresponded to what he had seen in the dream. When he had reached the position of preceptor of the western capital, he received an emissary dressed in yellow who came to summon him to the underworld. Lou said, "I have seen the register of the director of destinies, and I am supposed to enjoy even greater rank and longevity. Why am I being summoned prematurely?" The emissary in yellow said, "You wrongly killed an innocent man when you held a certain office. The chief commissioner has reduced both your official positions and longevity." Lou fell ill and died three days later. (From *Records from the Grand Hall*.)

22. Lü Yin dreamt during a nap that he was arrested and brought before a judge in the underworld. He said, "My mother is elderly and my children are young. There is no one else to take responsibility for my family." He pleaded his

case with great urgency. The judge ordered him sent to the king of the underworld. The king consulted his assistants, who told him, "This person has already utilized one substitute." When asked who the substitute had been, the reply was, "Kuai Shi." Lü Yin was living together with his brother-in-law Gu Hang at the time. As soon as he awoke, he told Gu about his dream. More than a month later, Lü died though he was not ill. (From *The Taiping Miscellany*).

23. Bo Shi's courtesy name was Mingqi. He lived in Yuzhang. At the time, Mei Xuanlong was serving as prefect and had already fallen ill. When Bo went to pay him a visit to inquire after his health, he told Mei, "Last night, I dreamt that you, sir, had sent someone to welcome me. He said that you would be paying me a call on the twenty-eighth." On the twenty-seventh, Bo suddenly died, and on the twenty-eighth, Mei died. (From *In Search of the Supernatural*.)

24. Wang Zhan, the magistrate of Qianhua District, retired from office and went to Jianye, where he moored his boat in the Qinhuai Quarter. He was gravely ill. He dreamt that someone in vermillion robes bearing an official document arrived and told him, "Your life is now over, and I have come to summon you." Wang replied, "I dare not avoid my destiny. However, this boat is too narrow, so I would prefer to use a wider one in order to cross over to the next world. Is this possible"? The functionary agreed and set five days hence for the appointed time. When Wang awoke, he went home and made funeral arrangements, taught his son the proper forms of mourning, and bid farewell to his relatives. At the appointed time, he lay down on his bed and died. (From *A Record of Inquests into Spirits*.)

25. Zhao Liangqi once dreamt that there were more than ten coffins *[guan]* arranged end to end. Zhao started at the easternmost one and stepped on each coffin until he reached the eleventh one, which broke when his foot went through it. Later, he held eleven offices *[guan]*, finally ending as secretariat drafter at which point he died. (From *A Record of Fates*.)

26. Gao Shi's courtesy name was Dafu. While serving as an administrator in Guangling, he dreamt that wood for coffins was piled high in a large hall reaching up to the roof. He also saw a coffin beside this that was extremely large and wide. He lay down in it, and there was plenty of room left over on all four sides. Indeed, he served in many offices and became supervisor of the Household of the Heir Apparent, which is a most lucrative and comfortable position. (From *A Record of Fates*.)

27. Li Fengji had a maid who dreamt that someone carried a coffin over behind the hall of the residence and said, "Put this on the ground." Soon it was moved into the hall. Not long afterward, Li became a secretariat drafter, and then a grand councilor. (From *A Record of Collected Strange Events*.)

28. Suo Chong dreamt that two coffins fell down from the sky in front of him. He asked Suo Dan about this and the latter replied, "The coffins symbolize official position. A high-ranking person in the capital will promote you. That there were two coffins means that you will be advanced twice." Not long afterward, Minister of Education Wang Rongshu ordered a governor to promote Suo Chong. The governor first appointed him to the Personnel Evaluation Section, and then he was awarded the "filial and incorrupt" degree. (From *History of the Jin Dynasty*.)

29. Yang Xiuzhi dreamt of traveling from east to west on a postal road north of the Yellow River. South of the road was a tomb that was extremely tall and large. Yang climbed atop the tomb and saw a bronze pillar whose base was in the form of a lotus. He stepped up onto the pillar's foundation from the northwest direction and pushed against the pillar, which turned to the right. Yang uttered a prayer, saying, "If this pillar makes three full turns, I will become one of the three dukes." The pillar then made three full turns and stopped. Later, this dream was indeed confirmed. (From *History of the Sui Dynasty*.)

30. When Zhu Zhaolin attended the official examinations during the Jingyou era [1034–1037], he dreamt that a coffin under construction was incomplete and left unfinished. That year he went to the capital and failed the examinations. Later, he ran afoul of someone powerful and was exiled. This confirmed his dream about the unfinished coffin. (From *History of the Song Dynasty*.)

31. Zhou Pan's courtesy name was Jianbo. In the first year of the Jianguang era [121 CE] when he was seventy-three years old, he assembled the students in the morning and lectured to them for the entire day. He told his two sons, "The other day, I dreamt that my former teacher Mr. Cili and I were lecturing in the southeast corner of a dark chamber. Doesn't his must mean that my life is over?" On the fifteenth day of that very month, he died without any sign of illness. (From *History of the Eastern Han Dynasty*.)

32. When Li Yuanzhong was about to serve in office, he dreamt that he entered his father's tomb holding a torch. He was startled awake in the night and was appalled by this dream. The next day, he told it to his teacher, who interpreted it, saying, "This is very auspicious, for it means that your glory will shine on your ancestors." In the end, it was just as he said. (From *An Encyclopedia of Paired Historical and Literary Citations*.)

33. Wen Xu's courtesy name was Cifang, and he served as commandant of Hujiang. He died valiantly while on duty and Emperor Guangwu of the Eastern Han ordered that he be buried beside the city wall in Luoyang. His eldest son, Shou, who served as administrator for the Marquis of Zouping, dreamt that Wen Xu told him, "I have been away for a long time and yearn to return to my hometown." Wen Shou then resigned his official position and requested permission to rebury his father in his hometown. (From Yuan Hong, *Annals of the Han Dynasty*.)

After Li Deyu died, he appeared to Linghu Tao in a dream and said, "Take pity on me, sir, and bury me in my hometown." Linghu discussed this with his son, Hao, and Hao replied, "Those in power resent him. Can it be done?" That night, Linghu Tao had the same dream again. He was frightened and said, "The Duke of Wei's [Li Deyu] *hun-* and *po*-souls are indeed fearsome. Disaster may befall us if we don't speak out." Consequently, he reported this matter to the emperor, who granted permission for the reburial. (From *New History of the Tang Dynasty*.)

CHAPTER 14

The *Feng* and Other Birds
鳳鳥

The *feng* is the bird of humaneness. Its virtue suffuses the tropics; its Way glorifies the heavens. No doubt this is because it possesses a divine spirit like the *lin*-beast and the dragon. Though the *feng* as well as lesser birds are all considered birds of the mortal world, one can distinguish specific meanings when they appear in dreams. Zhou Xuan's *Dream Manual* states, "A chicken symbolizes a soldier because it has a cockscomb and spurs. If one dreams of a rooster, then one will have anxieties about soldiers arriving."[1] Similarly, the crane and *fu*-duck are considered transcendent birds, the eagle and hawk as the birds of justice, the crow as the bird of filial piety, the pheasant as the bird of uprightness, the peacock as the bird of literary culture. The swan and swallow are regarded as signifying guests, the magpie as the bird of happiness, the osprey as indicating the distinction between male and female, and the wagtail as denoting the proper order among brothers. *Chi* and *fu*-owls are seen as birds of evil. Nevertheless, the significance of birds cannot really be categorized like this. Thus, Emperor Shizu of the Southern Qi dreamt that a *feng*-bird flew down to his residence at Qingxi, and the Liu Song dynasty yielded the throne to him.[2] There was a dream about a *feng*-bird resting in the courtyard of Duan Shaolian's home, and later he occupied the position of academician.[3] After his mother dreamt that *feng*-birds gathered on her body, Wang Yuanzhi was conceived, and Baozhi recognized that Wang would become a leader among transcendents.[4] After the mother of Xu Ling dreamt that *feng*-birds gathered on her left shoulder, she gave birth to him, and Baozhi exclaimed that he was actually a celestial *qilin*-beast.[5] Yang Xiong dreamt that he spit out a white *feng*-bird when he completed his "Rhapsody on the Sweet Spring."[6] After a dream about a red crow, the auspicious destiny of the Han dynasty was revealed in the birth of the Exalted Ancestor Zhijia.[7] After he dreamt that a purple bird flew down, Zhang's personal name was changed to Zhuo.[8] After a dream about a large bird that flew up high, Beizhulu's personal name was changed to Chong.[9] Luo Han dreamt of a colorful bird that entered his mouth; consequently, he became skilled in composing fine literary works.[10] After Mr. Sun dreamt that a pair of *feng*-birds gathered in his hands, he received the unfortunate news of the death of a parent.[11] After an empress dreamt of swallowing a golden chicken, she gave birth to the future Emperor Xingzong. This dream was a favorable omen indicating a sovereign of the Liao dynasty.[12] After a dream of a jade swallow entering her body, the mother of Zhang Yue became pregnant with him. This dream indicated a future grand councilor.[13] After Mistress Zhang dreamt of a flock of cranes, she gave birth to Zhang Jiuling.[14] After Mistress Shi dreamt about an emerald-green chicken, she gave birth to Xizi.[15] After Shao Yong dreamt that geese and cranes came to meet him, his years were numbered.[16] After Ouyang Xiu dreamt that a female crane flew away, his daughter died.[17] After a dream of a parrot with broken wings, the Prince of Luling was recalled to the court.[18] Though Li Baozhen dreamt that he traveled on a transcendent crane, he was never able to attain spiritual enlightenment.[19] When Shen Hui dreamt that he sat astride a *peng*-bird, he obtained a sign that he would place first in the official examinations.[20] When Zhuang Zhou dreamt that he was a butterfly, he understood the origin of the transformation of things.[21] The future King Wen began his rise as Earl of the West after he dreamt of a magpie biting hold of a vermillion document.[22] After Xu Zimu dreamt of a crow biting hold of a parasol with a long pole, he indeed came to a bad end.[23] The Southern Qi dynasty was established after a dream of an imperial robe made with peacock feathers.[24] But, a dream that a bird with golden wings devoured small dragons indicated why the Southern Qi would become weak.[25]

NOTES

1. From *Encyclopedia for Literary Composition*, chapter 91.
2. Emperor Shizu of the Southern Qi dreamt that a *fenghuang*-bird flew down from heaven in front of the study at his residence at Qingxi. Its wings measured more than one hundred feet across, and there were purple clouds under them. (From *History of the Southern Qi Dynasty*.)
3. Duan Shaolian was from Kaifeng. His mother dreamt that a *feng*-bird

stopped to rest in the courtyard of their house after which she gave birth to Duan. (From *History of the Song Dynasty*.)

4. When Wang Tanxuan, father of Wang Yuanzhi, was serving as prefect of Yangzhou, Yuanzhi's mother dreamt during a nap that *feng*-birds gathered on her body. Consequently she became pregnant. The Buddhist priest Baozhi told Wang Tanxuan, "A son will be born who will become a *fangshi*-wizard." Later, the court summoned Wang Yuanzhi to an audience, and he was posthumously given the name "Gentleman Who Has Ascended to Perfection." He lived to the age of one hundred and twenty-six. (From *Old History of the Tang Dynasty*.)

The mother of Wang Yuanzhi dreamt that divine *feng*-birds gathered on her body. Consequently she became pregnant. She also heard the sounds of birds from her abdomen. The Buddhist priest Baozhi said, "A son will be born who will become a leader among transcendents." (From *A Collection of Delectable Chicken Feet*.)

5. Xu Ling's courtesy name was Xiaomu. His mother Mistress Zang dreamt that multicolored clouds transformed into *feng*-birds and gathered on her left shoulder. Soon afterward, she gave birth to Xu Ling. When he was several years old, Baozhi rubbed his head and said, "He is an incarnate of a celestial stone *qilin*-beast." (From *History of the Chen Dynasty*.)

6. When Yang Xiong completed his "Rhapsody on the Sweet Spring," he dreamt that he spit out a white *feng*-bird [from *Master of the Golden Tower*]. When Yang Xiong wrote *The Book of the Great Mystery*, he dreamt that he spit out a white *feng*-bird. (From *Random Notes from the Western Capital*.)

7. The Duke of Feng's home was in Zhongyang Village, in Feng District in Pei. His wife dreamt that a red crow resembling a dragon played with her, and subsequently she gave birth to Zhijia. He became known as the Exalted Ancestor and the Supreme Exalted Emperor. (From *Annals of the Thearchs and Kings*.)

8. Zhang Zhuo's courtesy name was Wencheng. When he was a boy, he dreamt that a large, purple bird with multicolored markings flew down into the courtyard of his house. His grandfather told him, "A multicolored bird with red markings is a *feng*-bird. A bird with purple markings is a *yuezhuo*-bird. The *yuezhuo* assists the *feng*. My boy, your writings will achieve distinction in the imperial court." Consequently, this became his personal and courtesy names [Zhuo, from *yuezhuo*; and Wencheng, meaning "accomplished in literature"—*wen* also means "markings" or "patterns"]. (From *Old History of the Tang Dynasty*.)

9. Beizhulu Chong, whose courtesy name was Zihui, was from Shunyang in Deng. His father, Juqian, received an appointment in Jiangxi and took his family along with him. When Chong was born on a boat on the Gan River, a kettle emitted three sounds, which people considered an unusual sign. After his father's death, his family's fortunes declined. Beizhulu Chong returned to Jiangxi from Shunyang and studied with Xiao Keweng of Xinyu. Xiao dreamt one night that a large bird came to rest on his residence. Its wings covered the front of the building. The entire family was frightened, but he saw that it soared straight upward into the sky. The following day, Beizhulu Chong arrived. Originally, his personal name was Siwen, and his courtesy name was Bohe. Xiao changed Beizhulu's personal name to Chong [soaring straight upward] and also his courtesy name to Zihui [a multicolored pheasant] because of the dream. (From *History of the Yuan Dynasty*.)

10. Luo Han dreamt during a nap that a bird with unusual, colorful mark-

ings flew into his mouth. When he awoke, he told his aunt, Mistress Zhu, who said, "Since the bird has colorful markings, you will certainly produce literary works." From then on, his creative imagination grew day by day. (From *History of the Jin Dynasty.*)

11. There was a Mr. Sun who sought an official position and dreamt that a pair of *feng*-birds gathered in his hands. He consulted a fortune-teller, who said, "*Feng*-birds only alight on a sterculia tree and only dine on bamboo and fruits. Your Excellency will suffer a great misfortune, for if this doesn't signify the bamboo staff used in mourning a father, then it means the wooden staff used in mourning a mother." Later, Sun indeed suffered the misfortune of having to carry out the funeral of his mother. (From *Collected Records of Anomalies* [ca. 824].)

12. Lady Xiao, the future empress of Emperor Shengzong of the Liao, dreamt about a golden pillar that supported heaven. All the children tried to climb up it but couldn't. However, when she arrived there later, she and her servants all ascended. After a while, Lady Xiao entered the palace where she also dreamt that she shook the bed of Empress Dowager Chengtian and obtained a golden chicken, which she swallowed. Her skin took on a lustrous and felicitous appearance, prompting the empress dowager to comment in surprise at this unusual event, "It must mean the birth of an extraordinary son." Soon afterward, Lady Xiao gave birth to the future Emperor Xingzong. (From *History of the Liao Dynasty.*)

13. Zhang Yue's courtesy name was Daoji. His mother dreamt that a jade swallow *[yan]* flew from the southwest and entered her body. She became pregnant and gave birth to Zhang Yue. During the Kaiyuan era [713–741], he became secretariat director and was enfeoffed as Duke of Yanguo [the state of Yan]. (From *Old History of the Tang Dynasty.*)

14. Zhang Jiuling's courtesy name was Zishou [longevity]. His mother Mistress Zhang [fl. late 7th cent.] had dreamt that nine cranes flew down from the sky and gathered in the courtyard of her house. Therefore, she named him Jiuling [nine extra years]. (From *Old History of the Tang Dynasty*).

15. Xizi's surname was Shi. Her mother dreamt of an emerald-green chicken with multicolored markings that came down from the sky. After a while, it transformed into an owl and flew off. (From *Famous Chats from the Bureau of Writers.*)

16. Shao Yong took a nap and upon awakening said, "I dreamt that cranes and geese along with flags and banners came down from the sky to lead my spirit away. No medicine could chase them away." (From *The Valley Embroidered with Myriad Flowers.*)

17. When Ouyang Xiu was in Yiling, he visited the Jiang Shi Temple where he secretly prayed for an heir. A servant dreamt that a crane flew to where they were and said, "I am a female crane." Indeed, a daughter was born who was pretty and proper. When the girl was eight years old, Ouyang suddenly dreamt that a crane flew off. Several days later, she suddenly died. (From *Random Notes on Things Seen and Heard.*)

18. Empress Wu of the Tang [r. 690–705] dreamt about a parrot *[yingwu]* with august plumage, both of whose wings were broken. Secretary Di Renjie said, "The graph '*wu*' in parrot signifies Your Majesty's surname while the parrot with both wings broken is Your Majesty's second son, Prince Xiang of Luling. If Your

Majesty were to elevate the prince to become heir-apparent, his wings would be healed." (From *The Taiping Miscellany*.)

19. Li Baozhen enjoyed patronizing *fangshi*-wizards who claimed to be able to provide him with the drug of immortality. He supported someone named Ji Chang, who manufactured elixirs and told him, "If you ingest these, you will become a transcendent." Li appointed him to the staff of his private secretariat, where Ji Chang further enjoyed his friendship and confidence. One night, Li dreamt that he rode on a crane. He then had a statue of a crane carved, wore an outfit made of feathers, and practiced riding on the statue. Later, he became even more deluded and foolishly ingested more than twenty thousand pills. He could no longer eat and was on the point of death when a physician fed him a remedy of hog fat, grains, and parts of the lacquer tree, which relieved him somewhat. Ji Chang said, "You are going to become a transcendent, so why give up now?" So Li ingested three thousand more pills and died. (From *Bo and Kong's Encyclopedia*.)

20. For an explanation, see the commentary to Shen Hui's passing first in the examinations in the chapter, "The Official Examinations" [II:11n26].

21. For an explanation, see the commentary to Zhuang Zhou's dream that he was a butterfly in the chapter, "On General Analogies" [II:20n2].

22. When King Wen moved the capital from Cheng to Feng, he dreamt of a red bird biting hold of a vermillion document that entered Feng and stopped at his residence. (From *Annals of the Thearchs and Kings*.)

23. When Xu Zimu was young, he dreamt that a crow came down from the sky biting hold of a parasol with a long pole, which it erected in the front courtyard of his house. The crow then flew back up to the sky and returned with another parasol. When it was finished erecting three parasols in all, it finally uttered a loud, ugly squawk before departing. Xu indeed came to a bad end. (From Liu Yiqing, *A New Account of Tales of the World*.)

24. When the future Emperor Shizu dreamt that he was wearing a robe of peacock feathers, Yu Wen told him, "A peacock symbolizes noble rank and the colorfully patterned peacock feathers indicates an imperial robe." (From *History of the Southern Qi Dynasty*.)

25. Prince Zixia of Nanjun was the twenty-third son of Emperor Shizu. He was the youngest of the sons. The emperor dreamt that a bird with golden wings descended to the palace. It seized and devoured innumerable small dragons before flying upward to heaven. In the seventh year of the Yongming era [489], Zixia was executed, and he was but seven years of age. (From *History of the Southern Qi Dynasty*.)

CHAPTER 15

Animals
獸群

Among animals, the *qilin*-beast is the most auspicious. In the past, Confucius dreamt that a farm boy beat a *qilin,* and that he obtained a book in three chapters from it.[1] It was said that later, someone caught a *qilin* while hunting in the west; consequently Confucius wrote *The Qilin Classic.*[2] A bear was the divine form of Gun and also the ancestor of a nobleman of Jin. Thus, Duke Ping of Jin dreamt that a yellow bear entered his bedchamber.[3] Zhao Jianzi dreamt that he shot a bear at the residence of the supreme god Di.[4] These were recorded by Zuo Qiuming and Sima Qian, so they are reliable. Furthermore, the mother of Fu Jian dreamt that a giant bear took over her house.[5] The father of Lei Ji dreamt that a black bear was walking in the sky.[6] Is this not what the "Lesser Odes" meant when it stated that dreaming of bears was an auspicious sign for producing sons? The tiger is endowed with the seasonal *qi*-energy of autumnal death. It is chief among mountainous beasts.[7] It is also an ill omen of despotism and cruelty. Thus, Ying Huhai, the Second Emperor of Qin, dreamt that a tiger bit his left-side chariot horse.[8] Cao Shuang dreamt that tigers bit hold of Leigong, the God of Thunder.[9] Bandit Ni was born because of a dream about a white tiger.[10] Magistrate Zhou fell ill because he dreamt about a mother tiger.[11] The lion is outstanding among furry animals.[12] The elephant is basically the essence of the star Twinkling Brilliance.[13] Thus, Wang Jingze dreamt that he rode on a lion and attained the rank of a defender-in-chief.[14] Zhang Mao dreamt that he obtained an elephant and served as a commandery governor.[15] In the case of the birth of a Buddhist patriarch, it was a fulfillment of a dream of a white elephant.[16] The two domestic animals horse and ox are symbols of the creative cosmic principle *qian* and the receptive principle *kun,* respectively. Dream interpreters may correlate the horse with the agent "fire" and classify it under the trigram *Li:* "The Clinging." The ox is yin in nature and belongs to the category of demons in the ancestral temple. Therefore, when Huang Ping dreamt that a horse was dancing in his house, a fire broke out.[17] Emperor Gaozu of the Tang dreamt of horses flying in the sky and successfully established a dynasty.[18] Dong Feng dreamt that he rode a horse that halted in the middle of a stream and later had to bury his wife.[19] Liu Shu dreamt of a divine horse carrying a boy and later had a son.[20] Li Bolin dreamt of washing a horse.[21] Zhang Zhuo dreamt of riding on a donkey.[22] Jiang Wan dreamt of an ox-headed demon dripping blood and later advanced to become one of the three dukes.[23] Zhou Shan dreamt of an ox with a pair of tails and later lost his goods and money.[24] Magistrate Chen dreamt that he heard oxen speak while on the road.[25] Minister Zhang dreamt that he had mistakenly judged a case involving an ox.[26]

As for correlating the trigrams *Kan:* "The Abysmal" with the pig, *Gen:* "Keeping Still" with the dog, and *Dui:* "The Joyous" with the goat, all of these symbolic images are also domestic animals, yet they possess various meanings in dreams. Emperor Jing of the Western Han dreamt about a red hog that had descended.[27] An Lushan dreamt that he had been transformed into a black pig.[28] A prime minister of Yan dreamt that a pig changed into a tortoise.[29] Guan Yu dreamt that a pig bit his foot.[30] Mr. Pei dreamt that he shot a dog and later passed the official examinations.[31] Wang Dun dreamt that a dog bit him and then lost his life.[32] Magistrate Li dreamt of a gigantic sow and later became head of a military colony.[33] Xu Chao dreamt that he had been imprisoned after stealing a goat and later was enfeoffed in Chengyang.[34] Fuchai of Wu dreamt that black dogs ran howling about and was later destroyed by Gou Jian.[35] Zhang Tianxi dreamt that a green dog approached and bit him and was later defeated by Fu Jian.[36] Wu Jin dreamt of a white lamb and sired a virtuous empress in his later years.[37] Emperor Gaozong of the Southern Song dreamt of a white lamb and a filial son was born in the last month of his life.[38] The Yellow Emperor dreamt that he was herding ten thousand sheep and later obtained the services of Li Mu.[39] Mr. Li dreamt that he ate ten thousand sheep, and an extraordinary monk's interpretation was confirmed.[40] And, furthermore, the wolf possesses the essence of the agent "metal,"[41] and it considers the dog to be its uncle.[42] The deer contains the brilliance of the Big Dipper,[43] and the sheep is a friend. Thus, Zhang Ting dreamt that he feasted with someone dressed in gray, while a woman of Jin dreamt that she had an illicit encounter with someone wearing coarse yellow cloth—these are cases of wolves who are demons.[44] Shi Siming dreamt that when a deer died a stream dried up, and his life was over in an instant; Ji Shizhan dreamt about a pile of deer hides, and he received salaries from eleven different positions—these are cases of deer as omens.[45] In each case, dreams of animals should not be interpreted similarly based only on their species!

NOTES

1. Confucius dreamt that a farm boy beat a *qilin* and injured its front left leg. The boy said, "I am Red Pine." Confucius saw an animal like a roe deer with a goat's head and a single horn. Its tip was fleshy. He bound its injury with firewood. The *qilin* turned toward Confucius, covered his ears, and spit out a book in three chapters. Confucius studied the work closely. (From *The Right-Hand Concordance to the Book of Filial Piety*.)

2. Ju Shang captured a *qilin*. When Confucius observed it, he wept and said, "I am among men what the *qilin* is among animals. It appears but then dies, and its Way is extinguished." So he sang a song:

During the time of Yao and Shun
Qilin and *feng*-birds roamed about.
But now is not their time to appear.
Searching for them is futile, no doubt.
Oh *qilin*! Oh *qilin*!
My heart is worn out.

Because of this event, he compiled *The Spring and Autumn Annals* [a.k.a. *The Qilin Classic*]. (From *Anthology of the Kong Family Masters*.)

3. For an explanation, see the commentary to Duke Ping of Jin's dream about a bear in the chapter, "The Disciple of Emptiness" [I:5n18].

4. For an explanation, see the commentary to Zhao Jianzi's dream in the chapter, "Heaven" [II:1n12].

5. Fu Jian [r. 351–355], whose courtesy name was Jianye, was the third son of Fu Hong. His mother, Mistress Qiang, dreamt that a giant bear occupied her house, and she became pregnant. Her son became Emperor Gaozu of the Former Qin dynasty. (From *History of the Jin Dynasty*.)

6. Lei Ji's courtesy name was Zishu. His father's name was Derun, and his mother was Mistress You. Originally, Lei Derun lacked a son, so he silently prayed to a god and dreamt that a black bear was walking in the sky. Consequently, his wife became pregnant and gave birth to Lei Ji. (From *History of the Yuan Dynasty*.)

7. The tiger is a yang creature and chief of all the animals. (From *Penetrating Discussions about Environments and Local Cultures*.) The tiger is the lord of all mountainous animals. (From *Explanations and Analyses of Single and Composite Graphs*.)

8. The Second Emperor of Qin dreamt that a white tiger bit his left-side chariot horse and that he killed the tiger. He was very unhappy about the dream, and

a dream interpreter said, "There are evil influences by the Jing River." (From *Historical Records*.)

9. Cao Shuang dreamt that two tigers were biting hold of Leigong, the God of Thunder. The god was shaped like a bowl that could hold two liters, and the tigers set him down in the middle of the courtyard. Cao Shuang was appalled by this dream and consulted a diviner, the Director of the Imperial Observatory Ma Xun. Ma said, "You will face danger from soldiers within ten days." Indeed, Cao Shuang was killed by soldiers. (From *A New Account of Tales of the World*.)

10. Ni Wenjun, a bandit in Mianyang, was born in Huangpo. His mother dreamt that a white tiger entered her bedchamber and, subsequently, he was born. When he usurped a noble title and began to behave arrogantly without regard for authority, his mother dreamt that a white tiger died. He was then killed by a subordinate (from the *Master of Plants and Trees*).

11. Zhou Xiang loved to hunt. Later, when he had become magistrate of Fenyang, he dreamt that a mother tiger was chasing him. He awoke with fright and as a result fell ill. Later, an extraordinary monk passed by his door and said to an elderly neighbor, "This house contains demonic *qi*-energy." The elderly neighbor told this to Zhou Xiang, who summoned the monk to exorcise it. The monk set up an altar and, holding up a sword, uttered incantations. Suddenly, the sound of a tiger was heard beneath the bed where Zhou was lying. The monk spat water on it, and Zhou's illness gradually abated. (From *Events of the Tianbao Era*.)

12. It possesses the hardness of the essence of the agent "metal" and is outstanding among furry animals. (From Zhang Jiuling, "Encomium on a Lion.")

13. The rays of the star Twinkling Brightness disperse and become elephants. (From *The Movements of the Stars in the Dipper*.)

14. Wang Jingze dreamt that he rode on a multicolored lion. After Emperor Ming of the Liu Song assumed the throne, he appointed Wang general of the Bodyguards on Duty in the Hall. (From *History of the Southern Qi Dynasty*.)

15. Zhang Mao, whose courtesy name was Chengxun, dreamt when young that he obtained an elephant and asked the dream interpreter Wan Tui about it. Wan explained, "You, sir, will become a commandery governor but will end up badly." When asked the reason for this, Wan replied, "An elephant is a great beast *[shou]*, which sounds like 'governor' *[shou]*, so it is clear that you will become a commandery governor. However, an elephant is killed by men because of its tusks." The result was just as he predicted. (From *History of the Jin Dynasty*.)

16. At the time of the birth of the tenth Buddhist patriarch, Venerable Pārśva, his father dreamt that a white elephant entered through the door. (From *A Record of the Transmission of the Lamp*.)

17. Huang Ping dreamt that a horse was dancing in his house while ten men were clapping their hands at it. He asked Suo Dan about this, and Suo replied, "The horse denotes the agent 'fire,' and the dancing means an outbreak of fire. The men clapping at the horse are firemen." Before Huang reached home, a great fire had broken out. (From *History of the Jin Dynasty*.)

18. Emperor Gaozu of the Tang had dreamt that the sky was filled with innumerable flying thoroughbreds and that a man in the sky said, "These are the spirits of Your Excellency's body." When he finished, the horses flew into the fu-

ture emperor's body. After awakening, he summoned his son, the future Emperor Taizong, and told him, "My enterprise will succeed." (From *A Record of Collected Strange Events*.)

19. For an explanation, see the commentary to the entry about Feng Chang murdering Dong Feng's wife in the chapter, "Written Graphs" [II:10n17].

20. For an explanation, see the commentary to Liu Shu's dream about naming his son Yin in the chapter, "Gods and Strange Things" [II:12n70].

21. Mei Bocheng, the general of the Awe-Inspiring Army for Distant Regions, was skilled at interpreting dreams. An entertainer, Li Bolin, was traveling through Jingzhou seeking money and obtained one hundred *hu* in rice. When he was going to return home, he ordered his younger brother to collect the rice, but time passed, and the brother had still not arrived back home with it. One night, Li dreamt about washing a white horse. He paid a call to Mei Bocheng and asked him to interpret this. Mei said, "'White horse' [*baima* 白馬] is a phonetic recombination that indicates 'white rice' [*baimi* 白米]. You will have cause to worry due to wind and water." Several days later, news arrived that the boat carrying the rice had capsized in the Wei River. (From *Miscellaneous Morsels from Youyang*.)

22. Zhang Zhuo, whose courtesy name was Wencheng, dreamt that he was wearing crimson [i.e., red *(hong)*] clothes while riding on a donkey *[lü]*. In the dream, he thought to himself that this was strange: "I should be riding on a horse. Why am I wearing crimson and also riding on a donkey?" That same year, he passed the official examinations and was appointed minister of the Court of State Ceremonials *[honglüsi]*. He was also raised to the fifth-rank without having to undergo further examinations. This confirmed the dream. (From *Collected Records from Court and Countryside*.)

23. Jiang Wan dreamt one night that an ox-headed guardian was at his door dripping with blood. He was appalled by this and asked Zhao Zhi about its meaning. Zhao replied, "The horns and nose of an ox form an image of the graph *gong* 公 [duke]. The blood means that this matter will become clearly manifest. You, sir, will advance to become one of the three dukes." (From *History of the Shu Dynasty*.)

24. Zhou Shan was a merchant who traveled throughout the country. He dreamt of an ox with two tails that ran off and jumped into the water. Not long afterward, his boat encountered heavy winds and sank. He escaped with his life and nothing else, whereupon he realized that the graph for "ox" 牛 *[niu]* with two tails comprised the graph for "loss" 失 *[shi]*. (From *A Garden of Strange Events*.)

25. Magistrate Chen of Taining in Shandong dreamt that three oxen were blocking the road. They stood up on their hind legs and said, "Don't kill us!" The next day, a case about a sick ox reached Chen, who angrily said, "You have three oxen. Why is only one mentioned?" The man involved was dumbstruck. When an officer was sent to investigate, the dream was confirmed when it was found that the man had indeed tethered three oxen. (From *Yijian's Accounts*.)

26. For an explanation, see the commentary to the dream about Zhang Wenyi becoming a minister in the chapter, "The Official Examinations" [II:11n29].

27. Emperor Jing of the Western Han dreamt that a red hog descended right

through the clouds into the Pavilion for Adorable Blossoms. He awoke and observed that a red vapor like a cloudy mist had come and covered the doors and windows. Consequently, he changed the name from Adorable Blossoms to the Flourishing *Lan*-Flower Palace. Later, Madam Wang gave birth to the future Emperor Wu here. (From *A Record of Penetration into Mysterious Realms*.)

28. The *Events Concerning An Lushan* states that An Lushan dreamt one night that he had been transformed into a black pig with a dragon's head. Someone told this to Emperor Xuanzong [r. 712–756] who said, "This dragon-headed pig is incapable of becoming an emperor." (From *The Collected Works of Yao Runeng*.)

29. A compatriot presented the prime minister of Yan with a huge pig, which he ordered his cook to slaughter. The pig then appeared in the prime minister's dream and said, "Nature gave me the form of a pig to be fed with human garbage. But, thanks to your spiritual influence, I will now be reincarnated as the Earl of Lu Ferry." (From the *Master Fu*.)

30. The *History of the Wei Dynasty* states that Guan Yu dreamt that a pig bit his foot. (From *Bo and Kong's Encyclopedia*.)

31. For an explanation, see the commentary to the dream about shooting a dog with a bow and arrow in the chapter, "Utensils and Things" [II:7n23].

32. Wang Dun dreamt that dog descended from the sky and bit him. Right after that, he died. (From *History of the Jin Dynasty*.)

33. Li Qutan of Raozhou was in line for an official appointment and dreamt one night about a gigantic sow. Li Xianyao interpreted it, saying, "A sow is the head *[zhu]* of a group of piglets *[tun]*. You, sir, will become the head of a military colony *[tunzhu]*." A few days later, events turned out as predicted. (From *Records from Inside and Outside the Court*.)

34. Xu Chao dreamt that he was imprisoned after having stolen a goat *[yang]*. He consulted Yang Yuanzhen, who replied, "You will obtain the post of magistrate of Chengyang [a homophone for 'succeeding in obtaining a goat']." Later, he was enfeoffed as the Marquis of Chengyang. (From *Miscellaneous Morsels from Youyang*.)

35. Fuchai, King of Wu, dreamt one night about three black dogs. They were howling in the south and howling in the north, and the fire had gone out under the cooking vessels. When he awoke, the king gathered his officials and told them his dream, but none of them could interpret it. So, he summoned Gongsun Sheng. When Gongsun was summoned, he bid his wife farewell, saying, "I have been summoned because of an evil dream, yet how can I deceive him? I will surely be killed by the king." When Gongsun arrived, he was told about the dream and replied, "My lord will be defeated. The howling dogs mean that no one will preside in the royal ancestral temple, and the absence of fire beneath the cooking vessels means that there will be no food for the sacrifices." The king indeed became angry and killed him, but when the army of Yue arrived, the king said to those attending him, "I was wrong to kill Gongsun Sheng. Can you summon him from the beyond?" They called to him thrice, and thrice he responded. But the state of Wu was destroyed by Yue. (From *Yue's Destruction of Wu*.)

36. When Zhang Tianxi was in Liangzhou, he dreamt that a green dog with a long body came toward him from the south and tried to bite him, but he jumped

up on the bed to avoid it. Later, Fu Jian [r. 357–385] dispatched Gou Chang, who wore a green robe and attacked from the south. Gou broke through Zhang's gate and defeated him. (From Guo Jichan, *Collected Stories of Anomalies*.)

37. For an explanation, see the commentary to Wu Jin's dream about a peony in the chapter, "Plants and Trees" [II:18n16].

38. Emperor Gaozong of the Southern Song dreamt that the god Lord of Cuifu bestowed a white lamb on him, saying, "You will obtain a filial son." This was a genuine omen of the future Emperor Xiaozong. He was born on the sixth day of the sixth lunar month. (From *A Touring Guide to West Lake*.)

Emperor Xiaozong was the son of Prince Xiu [later Emperor Gaozong]. The prince's lady was Mistress Zhang [fl. 12th cent.]. She dreamt that someone hugging a lamb presented it to her saying, "This is a sign." Before long, she became pregnant by herself in the official Green Pine-Needle Residence in Xiuzhou. A red light filled her bedroom as if the sun was in the middle of it. (From *History of the Song Dynasty*.)

39. For an explanation, see the commentary to the dream about Li Mu in the chapter, "The Disciple of Emptiness" [I:5n2].

40. Li Deyu summoned a monk to tell his fortune. The monk replied, "Your Excellency will suffer misfortune and be forced to journey myriad miles south. You are fated to consume ten thousand sheep in your life and have thus far eaten nine thousand five hundred." Li replied, "I once dreamt that I had traveled to Mount Jin where more than ten shepherds greeted me saying that these were sheep for me to eat. I kept silent and never told anyone about this." Ten days later, someone gave Li four hundred head of sheep. Li was shocked and replied, "I won't eat them." The monk said, "Since the sheep have arrived, they count as your possessions." Soon afterward, Li was demoted to serve as vice prefect of Chaozhou, then demoted again to revenue manager of Yazhou, after which he died. (From *A Record of Inquests into Strange Events*.)

41. A white wolf is the essence of the agent "metal." (From *Illustrations of Auspicious Anomalies*.)

42. The dog is the uncle of the wolf, and whenever a wolf meets a dog, it quickly bows down as if respectfully greeting it. (From *Miscellaneous Morsels from Youyang*.)

43. When the star Flickering Brilliance disperses its rays, they become deer. (From *The Movements of the Stars in the Dipper*.)

44. Zhang Ting [n.d.] dreamt that the Marquis of Ba arranged a feast and invited the Lord of Canglang, who arrived dressed in gray *[cang]* with a powerful appearance. Zhang was startled awake and realized that he had seen a wolf *[lang]* lying down in front of him. This was probably the "Lord of Canglang" [also a nickname for a wolf]. (From *Records from the Grand Hall*.)

The wife of Huang Zhang, a commoner from Mount Shen in Jinzhou, suddenly dreamt that a man dressed in coarse yellow cloth with a very narrow waist detained and seduced her. After they coupled twice, he departed, and she subsequently became pregnant. She loved to eat raw meat and would lick her chops and gnash her teeth while her personality became cruel and heartless like that of a wolf. She gave birth to two wolves who left as soon as they were born. Her husband beat her to death. (From *A Record of Inquests into Spirits*.)

45. Shi Siming loved the comic routines of actors. They were always by his side whether he was eating or sleeping, but the actors hated him because he was cruel. One night, Shi was startled awake and, sitting up in bed, began railing and shouting. An actor asked him the reason for this, and he answered, "I dreamt that a herd of deer was crossing a stream. The deer all died and the stream dried up. What does this mean?" Suddenly, he fell over. The actors said to each other, "Isn't he about to meet his end?" In a little while, the soldiers of Luo Yue entered. (From *Bo and Kong's Encyclopedia*.)

Ji Shizhan dreamt that he had obtained a pile of deer hides. He counted them and found that they amounted to eleven pieces. Then, he awoke and was overjoyed, saying "'Deer' *[lu]* has the same sound as 'official salary' *[lu]*. I will be serving in eleven different positions!" In the course of his official career, he had already served in nine positions when he was concurrently appointed to two commanderies. He was appalled by this development and died soon afterward. (From *History of the Southern Dynasties*.)

CHAPTER 16

Dragons and Snakes
龍蛇

Dreams of dragons and snakes are recorded in biographies and records, so there is evidence for discussing them. There are those who dreamt about a dragon and were then blessed with a son bestowed from on high. For example, Lady Bao of the Western Han dynasty dreamt that a green dragon leaned on her abdomen, and later she gave birth to the Prince of Dai.[1] Empress Dowager Li of the Jin dynasty dreamt that two dragons used her knees as a pillow, and she gave birth to Emperor Xiaowu.[2] The Prince of Pu dreamt that a dragon fell onto his robes and begat Emperor Yingzong of the Northern Song.[3] Consort Huang dreamt that a dragon was inserted into her body and then gave birth to Emperor Duzong of the Southern Song.[4] Duke Feng's wife dreamt about a crow that resembled a dragon and later gave birth to the Exalted Ancestor Zhijia.[5] Empress Gao of the Northern Wei dreamt that the sun transformed into a dragon, and she later gave birth to Emperor Shizong.[6] Empress Lou of the Northern Qi dreamt of four dragons.[7] And Empress Chen of the Southern Qi dreamt of "Little Dragon."[8] There are those who dreamt of dragons and fulfilled these signs of nobility such as Emperor Guangwu of the Eastern Han, who dreamt of riding a red dragon up to heaven.[9] Emperor Taizu of the Southern Qi dreamt that he was riding on a green dragon while chasing after the sun.[10] Liu Muzhi dreamt that his boat was supported by white dragons, and later he was summoned to serve Emperor Wu of the Liu Song.[11] Zhao Ruyu dreamt that he was carrying a white dragon on his back and later became an official of Emperor Lizong of the Southern Song.[12] Xun Boyu dreamt that six dragons came out of the armpits of an emperor of the Southern Qi.[13] Teng Juan dreamt that Wu Cheng transformed himself into a red dragon.[14] Emperor Yizu of the Southern Tang dreamt that he disrobed and caught a dragon, later obtaining the future Emperor Liezu. Liezu dreamt of a dragon coiled around the railing of the palace, and obtained the future Emperor Yuanzong.[15] As for the Yellow Emperor's dream of a dragon who gave him a white diagram[16] and Wang Jixin's dream that a dragon spit out *The Book of Chess*,[17] these revealed a divine and marvelous pattern and were disclosed through nature's transformations. *Random Notes from the Western Capital* states that Dong Zhongshu dreamt that a *jiao*-dragon entered his body, and then he composed the *Luxuriant Dew of the Spring and Autumn Annals*—doesn't this indicate a similar origin?

And yet, there are also cases of dreams of dragons that are inauspicious, such as when Guo Yu dreamt that a dragon terminated its flight at a building when he was about to die.[18] When Zhang Wenbiao was about to suffer defeat, he dreamt that a dragon emerged from his collar.[19] Liu Xun of the princely house of Jin'an dreamt that he rode on a headless dragon and, indeed, he ominously met with a sudden death.[20] Sun Xiu and the mother of Tao Hongjing both dreamt of riding on a dragon without a tail, and indeed this was a sign of having no descendants.[21] However, at the time of Wu Cheng's birth, an old woman next door dreamt of a writhing creature descending into a pond. Whether it was a dragon or a snake is difficult to determine.[22]

The snake is also a type of dragon, and its significance in dreams varies. Thus, Duke Wen of Qin dreamt that a yellow snake extended down from heaven.[23] Duke Wen of Jin dreamt that a giant snake was blocking the road.[24] Liu Zhen dreamt that a snake grew legs.[25] The Marquis of Sui dreamt that a snake repaid him with pearls.[26] Tang Cong dreamt that a snake wound itself around his body and then created a style of cursive script.[27] Fan Yanguang dreamt that a snake entered his abdomen, and consequently he harbored an extraordinary ambition for power.[28] Before Li Xiong of Western Shu was born, a giant snake appeared in his mother's dream.[29] When Yao Guang of the Southern Qi was defeated, a group of snakes appeared in the dreams of the city's residents.[30] And yet, *The Book of Songs* states that the poisonous *hui*-snake is an auspicious sign of the birth of a daughter, so how could these examples exhaust all possible meanings?

NOTES

1. Lady Bao dreamt one night that a green dragon leaned on her abdomen. Emperor Gaozu of the Western Han said, "This is a sign of nobility. I will fol-

low his example with you." After he favored her for a single night, she gave birth to a son who became the Prince of Dai. (From *Historical Records*.)

2. Empress Dowager Li dreamt several times that two dragons used her knees as a pillow and that the sun and moon entered her body. Subsequently, she gave birth to Emperor Xiaowu of the Eastern Jin as well as to Prince Wenxiao of Guiji and Princess Chang of Poyang. (From *History of the Jin Dynasty*.)

3. Emperor Yingzong of the Northern Song was the thirteenth son of Prince Anyi of Pu. Originally, Prince Anyi dreamt that two dragons together with the sun fell down and that he caught them in his robe. (From *History of the Song Dynasty*.)

4. Emperor Duzong of the Southern Song was the son of a younger brother of Emperor Lizong. His father Yurui succeeded to the title of Prince Rong, and Emperor Duzong was born in Prince Rong's residence. His mother, Mistress Huang, who was Consort of Qiguo, dreamt of a god in a colorful gown holding a dragon, which he inserted into her body. Soon afterward, she became pregnant. (From *History of the Song Dynasty*.)

5. For an explanation, see the dream about encountering a red crow in the chapter, "The *Feng* and Other Birds" [II:14n7].

6. Empress Gao of the Northern Wei dreamt that the sun transformed into a dragon that wound itself around her body several times. Before long, she gave birth to Emperor Xiaowen. (From *History of the Northern Wei Dynasty*.)

7. When Empress Lou of the Northern Qi was carrying the future Emperor Wenxiang, she dreamt of a severed dragon. When she was carrying the future Emperor Wenxuan, she dreamt of a giant dragon whose head and tail extended between heaven and earth and whose appearance startled everyone when it opened his mouth and moved its eyes. When she was carrying the future Emperor Xiaozhao, she dreamt of a dragon writhing on the ground. When she was carrying the future Emperor Wucheng, she dreamt of a dragon entering the sea. (From *History of the Northern Qi Dynasty*.)

8. Emperor Wu of the Southern Qi, whose posthumous name was Ze, courtesy name was Xuanyuan, and childhood name was Longer [little dragon], was born in a residence in Qingxi in Jiankang. That night, both Empress Chen and Empress Liu dreamt of a dragon perching on the roof. (From *History of the Southern Qi Dynasty*.)

9. For an explanation, see the commentary to the dream where Guangwu's generals all urged him to proclaim himself emperor in the chapter, "Heaven" [II:1n5].

10. When the future Emperor Taizu of the Southern Qi was seventeen years old, he dreamt that he was riding on a green dragon westward while chasing after the sun and only stopped when the sun was about to set behind a mountain. When he awoke, he was frightened by this. A family member consulted a dream interpreter, who said that it was a sign of the highest nobility. Su Kan said that green was the color of the agent "wood" and that the setting sun signified the declining destiny of the Liu Song dynasty. (From *History of the Southern Qi Dynasty*.)

11. For an explanation, see the commentary to the dream about sailing on

the ocean, viewing a beautiful peak, and responding to a summons to the imperial court in the chapter, "Mountains and Rivers" [II:4n1].

12. For an explanation, see the commentary to the dream of ascending the throne in white clothes in the chapter, "Heaven" [II:1n6].

13. In the seventh year of the Taishi era [471] of the Liu Song dynasty, Xun Boyu dreamt that the future Emperor Taizu of the Southern Qi boarded a boat at Beizhu in Guangling, and that he saw folded wings below both the emperor's armpits. When Xun asked when he would spread the wings, His Majesty replied that he would do so in three years. While still dreaming, Xun stated that he was an exorcist and uttered spells for the emperor's sake. After he uttered six spells, six dragons emerged from the emperor's armpits with their wings spread out. Then they returned to him and folded up their wings. In the fifth year of the Yuanwei era [477], Emperor Taizu said to Xun, "Your dream turned out to be accurate." (From *History of the Southern Qi Dynasty.*)

14. Wu Cheng [fl. early 10th cent.] in his early days devoted himself to study. During the time of King Wenmu of Wu-Yue, Teng Juan, an official in the west administration, dreamt that Wu Cheng transformed himself into a red dragon and went off toward the south. Teng then told this dream to someone else who said, "I cannot fathom this fellow Wu." But later, when Wu succeeded in Fuzhou, the dream was confirmed. (From *The Complete History of the Wu-Yue Dynasty.*)

15. Emperor Yizu of the Southern Tang dreamt that he encountered innumerable yellow dragons when he approached a great body of water. Yizu disrobed and entered the water, emerging with a dragon that he had captured. He was startled by this. Not long afterward, the future Emperor Liezu was captured, whom he subsequently adopted as a son. (From *Conversations by a Fishing Jetty.*)

Emperor Liezu of the Southern Tang dreamt during a nap that a yellow dragon was coiled around the railing of the palace. Its scales glistened brilliantly. Upon awakening, he sent someone to inspect the front hall of the palace where Prince Qi was leaning against the railing. The scene in back of him accorded with the dream, so Liezu said, "Heaven's intentions are not casually disclosed." Within ten days, he established Prince Qi as the heir-apparent, who was posthumously known as Emperor Yuanzong. However, the prince continued to use the title of his fiefdom. (From *Recent Events of the Southern Tang Dynasty.*)

16. For an explanation, see the commentary to the dream of the Register-Diagram in the chapter, "The Disciple of Emptiness" [I:5n2].

17. Wang Jixin dreamt that a green dragon spit out *The Book of Chess* in nine volumes and gave it to him. He immediately became expert at the game. (From *The Secrets of Chess.*)

18. Guo Yu dreamt that he was riding a green dragon up to heaven when it reached a building *[wu]* and terminated its flight. He said, "A flying dragon terminating its flight at a building means that I *[wu]* will die." (From *History of the Jin Dynasty.*)

19. Zhang Wenbiao was from Wuling. He revolted, seized Tanzhou, and killed Hengzhou Army Adjutant Liao Jian. He was hesitating as he was about to attack Changsha when a military officer dreamt that a dragon emerged from Zhang's collar. Zhang was delighted and said, "This is a mandate from heaven."

After he was defeated, his decapitated head was exposed in Langling. (From *Annals of Chu*.)

20. Liu Xun, the son of the Prince of Jin'an, erected an altar at Xunyang. As soon as he had ascended to the throne as emperor, he told his closest officials, "Last night, I dreamt that I was riding on a dragon upward to heaven, but when I looked closely at it, I couldn't see that it possessed any head at all." Everyone's expression changed, and none could reply. Editorial Director Sun Yi said, "*The Book of Changes* states that the appearance of a flight of dragons without heads is auspicious." Everyone was greatly pleased at this. But, before long, the army of Shen You arrived, burned down the palace, captured Liu Xun, and executed him. (From *History of the Song Dynasty*.)

21. Sun Xiu dreamt of riding a dragon upward to heaven, but when he looked closely, he was unable to see any tail on it. Indeed, he became emperor but had no descendants. (From *History of the Wu Dynasty*.) The mother of Tao Hongjing dreamt that she rode on a green dragon without a tail. Tao never married nor had any children. (From *History of the Chen Dynasty*.)

22. Wu Cheng [1249–1333], whose courtesy name was Youqing, was from Chongren. On the night before he was born, an old woman next door dreamt that a writhing creature descended into a pond next to her house. (From *History of the Yuan Dynasty*.)

23. Duke Wen of Qin dreamt that a yellow snake extended down from heaven to earth and its mouth reached Fuyan. Duke Wen asked Historian-Astrologer Shi Dun, who replied, "This is a sign from a supreme god. Your Excellency should sacrifice to him." Therefore, an altar was established at Fuyan, and three kinds of animals were offered up to the White Emperor. (From *Historical Records*.)

24. When Duke Wen of Jin was out hunting, an advance guard came back and told him, "There is a giant snake ahead as high as a levee stretched across the way." Duke Wen withdrew and improved his government. Three days later, he dreamt that heaven had killed the snake while uttering, "How dare you block the way of a sagely ruler?" Duke Wen awoke and ordered someone to inspect the place. The snake was already decaying. (From Jia Yi, *New Writings*.)

When Duke Wen of Jin went forth, a giant snake blocked the way, extending across it. Duke Wen returned and cultivated his virtue. He sent an official to guard the snake, and the official dreamt that heaven had killed the snake while uttering, "How dare you block the way of the ruler of Jin?" When he awoke, he inspected the snake, but the snake had already died. (From *A Record of Manifold Things*.)

25. Liu Zhen of Wei, whose courtesy name was Gonggan, once dreamt that a snake grew four legs. He killed it because it failed to show him respect. (From *Bo and Kong's Encyclopedia*.)

26. When the Marquis of Sui went to Qi, he encountered a snake on the way that had blood on its head. He applied some medicine to it and left. That night, he dreamt that he stepped on a snake. He was startled awake whereupon he found a pair of pearls. (From *Exquisite Words on the Origins of Surnames*.)

27. Tang Cong dreamt that a snake wound itself around his body. Subsequently, he imitated its form to create a style of "snake-cursive" script. (From *History of the Jin Dynasty*.)

Dragons and Snakes

28. Fan Yanguang was serving as military commissioner of Tianxiong when he dreamt that a giant snake entered his abdomen through his navel. It had entered halfway when he pulled it out and rid himself of it. He asked Scholar Zhang, a wizard in his establishment, about this. Zhang replied, "The snake is a species of dragon. A snake entering the abdomen is an auspicious sign of a king." From this time on, Fan harbored extraordinary ambitions for power. (From *History of the Five Dynasties.*)

29. Li Xiong's mother Mistress Luo dreamt that a giant snake wrapped itself around her body. Subsequently, she became pregnant and fourteen months later gave birth to Li. Later, he usurped the throne in Shu. (From *History of the Jin Dynasty.*)

30. Yao Guang, Prince of Shi'an during the Southern Qi dynasty, rose in revolt and was defeated after four days. The inhabitants of the city all dreamt that a group of snakes appeared climbing up the city walls on all four sides. (From *History of the Southern Dynasties.*)

CHAPTER 17

Turtles and Fish
龜魚

Turtles, fish, flies, and ants all derive their *qi*-energy from yin and yang, and survive by dwelling in water or on land. The *Master Who Embraces Simplicity* states that roosters possess the courage to strike at obstacles, pheasants have the pride to dominate a marsh, ants know how to capture the weak, and bees can strategize to attack the isolated. It is also said that when King Mu of the Zhou campaigned in the south, his entire army underwent a transformation. All the noble men turned into gibbons and cranes, while petty men became insects and grains of sand. Aren't these cases of each conforming to his type? In antiquity, Lord Yuan of Song dreamt that a divine tortoise appeared who was an emissary to Hebo, God of the Yellow River.[1] Gao Lu dreamt that a tortoise lost its life at the court of the Former Qin dynasty.[2] Liu Zan dreamt of a golden turtle, and then his literary talent progressed.[3] Mei Yaochen dreamt of a yellow turtle and begat a son.[4] A prime minister of Yan was rewarded with a pearl that glowed in the dark.[5] Han Yu wrote a poem about a Daoist.[6] Wan Bi caught a famous turtle and dreamt that it asked to be returned to the river.[7] Chunyu Fen saw a desiccated turtle but was dreaming about a mountain where he had gone hunting.[8]

Yet, in investigating the symbolic images found in *The Book of Changes,* one finds that turtles are associated with the trigram *Li:* "The Clinging" and fish are associated with *Sun:* "The Gentle." How could the appearance of fish in dreams be limited to the poetic device of a dream of many fish to indicate a year of abundant harvest? Emperor Wu of the Western Han dreamt that a fish requested that he remove the hook from its mouth, and he received pearls.[9] The wife of Hu Anguo dreamt that a fish jumped into a basin of water, and then her nephew was born.[10] Prefect Liu Zhiheng dreamt that fish begged him for their lives.[11] This was the same as the dream of District Magistrate Ashili, when a fish asked him to forbid any further catches.[12] In one case, the fish resulted in an increase in wealth, in another, in the drowning of people. Such is the difference between understanding a dream or not.

As for insects, there are indeed a multitude of types. The image of flies resting on a fence was used by a poet as a criticism. Thus, Prince He of Changyi dreamt that piles of fly dung had accumulated on the steps.[13] He Yan of the Ministry of Personnel dreamt that flies gathered on his nose.[14] These were both omens of slander. Maggots gather in groups that do not disperse. They symbolize the mass of common people. Thus, the future Empress Ma dreamt that flying insects entered her skin.[15] Emperor Gaozu of the Tang dreamt that a group of maggots was devouring his body.[16] All these were confirmed by the attainment of noble rank. As for ants, which are a class of stinging insects, they, too, designate kings. He who received the command to serve as prefect of Nanke maintained a well-ordered administration.[17] Someone who floated on a reed in the river was able to repay a favor by boring a hole into a prison cell.[18] Though these may only be allegories composed by literary men, it is significant that they occurred within the world of dreams.

NOTES

1. Lord Yuan of Song dreamt in the middle of the night that someone with unbound hair peered through the side-door of his chamber and said, "I come from the Cailu Depths. I was on my way to God of the Yellow River, Hebo, as an emissary from the Yangzi River when I was caught by the fisherman Yu Ju." Lord Yuan awoke and had someone interpret the dream who stated, "This was a divine tortoise." Lord Yuan asked, "Is there a fisherman named Yu Ju?" His attending officials answered, "Yes, there is." Lord Yuan ordered him to appear at court and obtained from him a white tortoise five feet in circumference. He could not decide whether to kill it or not when a diviner said, "Kill the tortoise and use it to divine an auspicious omen." So, the tortoise's entrails were cut out, and each of the seventy-two holes drilled in its plastron produced an accurate divination. Confucius said, "This divine tortoise could appear in Lord Yuan's dream, but it couldn't escape Yu Ju's net. It knew how to produce seventy-two correct divinations, but couldn't avoid the catastrophe of having its entrails cut out." (From the *Master Zhuang*.)

2. A man from Gaoling dug a well and found a large tortoise three feet around with patterns of the eight trigrams on its back. Fu Jian [r. 357–385] ordered his grand diviner to have a pond dug to care for it and had it fed grains. Later, it died, and its bones were buried in the Imperial Ancestral Temple. That night, An-

cestral Temple Aide Gao Lu dreamt that the tortoise said to him, "I was returning to the Jiangnan region when unfortunately I lost my life at the court of the Former Qin." Another person in the dream told Gao, "Such tortoises live for three thousand six hundred years and then die. After their death, evil portents appear that are omens of the destruction of the state." Before long, Fu Jian was defeated. (From *History of the Jin Dynasty*.)

3. For an explanation, see the commentary to the dream about swallowing a golden turtle in the chapter, "Food and Clothing" [II:6n9].

4. Mei Yaochen, whose courtesy name was Shengyu, dreamt one day before his son was born that a Daoist presented him with a turtle. He wrote "A Poem Harmonizing with Ouyang Xiu's 'Poem on a Son's First Bath'" that went, "Last night, I dreamt of someone in a sleeveless robe, who gave me a little yellow turtle alongside a river. Suddenly, the next day, my wife went into labor, and delivered a boy with beautiful eyebrows." (From *The Valley Embroidered with Myriad Flowers*.)

5. A man of Yan presented King Zhao of Yan with a huge pig that was one hundred and twenty years old. He said that it was an immortal pig, but all the officials told the king, "This pig is useless." So, the king ordered his chef to cook it. After the pig died, it appeared to the Prime Minister of Yan in a dream, saying, "Thanks to Your Excellency's spiritual influence, I have been able to undergo reincarnation and am now the Earl of Lu Ferry." When the prime minister traveled to Lu Ferry, he encountered a red turtle biting hold of a pearl that glowed in the dark, which the turtle presented to him. (From *Master Fu*.)

6. Meng Jiao, whose courtesy name was Dongye, became a presented scholar at the age of fifty and begat three sons, all of whom he lost within several days of one another. He had no other descendants and was overcome with grief. Han Yu wrote a poem alluding to this which included the lines, "Then, they summoned a giant, divine tortoise, rode upward on the clouds, and knocked at the gate of heaven." One night, Meng had a dream about a Daoist in a black robe and cap who strode right into his house and thrice repeated to him words from heaven. Bowing in thanks to the Daoist, he ceased grieving and was overjoyed. (From *The Collected Works of Han Changli*.)

7. Wan Bi caught a famous turtle when he was in Jiangnan. He kept it at home and prospered. Later he dreamt that the turtle said, "Send me back to the river." But he didn't listen and killed it. Soon thereafter, he himself died, and his family's fortune declined. (From *The Book of Wan Bi*.)

8. Chunyu Fen dreamt that he was hunting on Divine Tortoise Mountain in the west of the country. The mountain's peaks were lofty and its rivers and marshes were extensive. He led his subordinates in a hunt that lasted through the night before returning. After awakening, he was exploring a deep hole in the ground while following a stream to its origins when he came across a desiccated turtle. Its shell was moistened by dripping rainwater and had grass growing on top of it—it was the Divine Tortoise Mountain where he had gone hunting. (From Li Gongzuo, "Biography of the Prefect of Nanke.")

9. *Mr. Xin's Record of the Three-Qin Region* states that Lake Kunming leads into White Deer Plain. A man from the plain was fishing, but his line snapped and so he left. The fish appeared to Emperor Wu of the Western Han in a dream,

asking that the hook be removed from its mouth. Three days later, the emperor was on an outing on the lake and saw a large fish with a hook. The emperor said, "Doesn't this confirm my dream from the other day?" He removed the fishhook and released the fish. Later, when he made another excursion along the lakeshore, he found a pair of brilliant pearls. The emperor said, "Isn't this a reward from the fish from a while ago?" (From *Events from the Imperial Capital*.)

10. Hu Yin, whose courtesy name was Mingzhong, was the son of the younger brother of Hu Anguo. At the time of Hu Yin's birth, his mother already had many sons and did not want to raise him. The wife of Hu Anguo dreamt that a large fish jumped into a basin of water. She rushed over to get the child and adopted him as a son. (From *History of the Song Dynasty*.)

11. For an explanation, see the commentary to the dream about two carp in the chapter, "Longevity and Destiny" [II:13n10].

12. In the north of Dingtao District in Caozhou is a small lake where local residents earn a living by gathering oysters and turtles. In the second year of the Zhenglong era [1157] under the enemy ruler Wanyan Liang, an ethnic Jurchen named Ashili was serving as the district magistrate. He dreamt that someone in a green robe, black hat, black shoes, and a leather belt holding an audience tablet paid him a formal visit. The man accused the local people of catching and killing members of his clan, and he requested that the magistrate forbid this. Ashili agreed to this in the dream. The next night he dreamt this again, but no one knew what it meant. When it turned to spring and the fishermen along the lakeshore were increasing day by day, there appeared a gigantic creature six or seven feet long resembling a *jiao*- or *chi*-dragon. It surged over the waves and spewed forth clouds, smashing everything along the shore of the lake. The people all fled in fear, and more than half of them drowned. Then the meaning of the magistrate's dream was understood. (From *Gazetteer of Shandong*.)

13. Prince He of Changyi dreamt that fly dung was piled on the east and west palace steps, weighing more than five or six hundred pounds. Prince He asked Gentleman of the Interior Gong Sui about this, and Gong replied, "There are many close to the throne [*jiexia*, literally, 'on the palace steps'] who are slandering you. I recommend that you drive them away." Prince He did not heed his words and finally was removed from his position. (From *History of the Western Han Dynasty*.) Fly dung piled on the steps of the palace means that the ruler is following the slanderous remarks of his officials. (From Wang Chong, *Judicious Discussions*.)

14. Minister of Personnel He Yan dreamt that scores of flies came and settled on his nose. He tried to chase them away, but they wouldn't leave. Later, he was assassinated. (From *History of the Three Kingdoms*.)

15. During the Yongping era [58–75 CE] of Emperor Ming of the Eastern Han, an official memorialized that an empress should be established. His Majesty had not yet issued a reply when the Empress Dowager said, "Lady Ma's virtue is chief among those in the rear palace." Subsequently, she was raised to her exalted rank. Several days earlier, the future Empress Ma had dreamt that myriad small flies descended on her body, entered her skin, and then flew away. (From *History of the Eastern Han Dynasty from the Dongguan Pavilion*.)

16. When the future Emperor Gaozu of the Tang was going to lead his army

forth, he dreamt one night that he had died and that his body fell off the bed where it was devoured by a mass of maggots. Buddhist Master Zhiman said, "Your Excellency will conquer the world. 'Death' means 'corpse' *[bi]* and 'falling off the bed' means 'below' *[xia]*—that is the same sound as *bixia* [Your Majesty]. These are symbols of attaining supremacy. That a mass of maggots was devouring you means that the millions of common people will flock to you. (From *A Record of Collected Strange Events*.)

17. Chunyu Fen was drinking beneath a sophora tree. When he became drunk, he lied down and dreamt of two emissaries who said, "The Land of the Peaceful Sophora has issued an invitation to you." They pointed to the old sophora, saying, "This is the Great Land of the Peaceful Sophora." Its kings told him, "The Commandery of Nanke is not well governed, and We ask that you, Our minister, serve as prefect there." After many days, he reached the commandery. After he awoke, he investigated the opening beneath the sophora and realized that the clumps of earth were shaped like city walls and palaces. There were two large ants—these were the kings. Another hole led directly upward into the southern branch of the tree—this was the Commandery of Nanke [literally, "southern tree branch"]. (From *A Record of Strange Things Heard*.)

18. Dong Zhaozhi of Dangyang once took a boat to cross the Qiantang River. In the middle of his crossing he saw an ant atop a short reed. It walked to the tip of the reed, then turned back and walked toward the other end, appearing quite terrified. Dong said, "It is afraid of dying." He wanted to pick up the reed and bring it onto the boat, but those on board said, "This thing is poisonous and stings. It should be stepped on and killed." Dong took pity on it, though, and prevented them from harming it. That night, he dreamt that a gentleman in a black gown followed by several hundred people came to thank him, saying, "I was careless and fell into the river and am embarrassed that you should have had to trouble yourself to save me. I am the king of these insects, and if you are ever in need, be sure to let me know." Dong became involved in an affair that led to his imprisonment. The ant led a multitude of other ants to bore a hole into the prison cell, enabling Dong to escape. (From *Qi Xie's Records*.)

CHAPTER 18

Plants and Trees
草木

Every plant and tree that appears in dreams has a correlation. Liu Xiang said that the mind is correlated with the jujube and the liver is correlated with the elm. Zhou Xuan's *Dream Manual* states that the pine corresponds to the ruler among men, so that dreaming about a pine means that one is going to meet a ruler. It also states that the elm symbolizes a ruler's virtue, which is the highest order of humaneness, so that a dream of gathering elm leaves means one will receive favor from a ruler, and a dream of dwelling in an elm tree means one will be promoted to a high-ranking office.[1] Moreover, it states that the willow symbolizes an emissary, so that a dream of holding a willow branch means one will be appointed as an emissary.[2] And, furthermore, it states that grain is a form of wealth produced in fields, so that a dream of grain means the *qi*-energy of wealth is growing.[3] Now, Zhou Xuan was an expert at interpreting dreams. Although his manual has not survived in its entirety, one may gather its general approach from these examples.

In antiquity, Taisi dreamt of brambles in the Shang palace courtyard and catalpas planted by the Crown Prince of the Zhou.[4] Thus was the fall and rise of these dynasties decisively indicated. Ding Gu dreamt of a pine, and this was an auspicious omen of nobility.[5] Zhang Zhai dreamt of a juniper, and it was a sign of misfortune.[6] After Zhang Zhihe's mother dreamt that a maple tree grew from her abdomen, his fame reached the "Palace of Maples" [the emperor].[7] After dreaming that a willow tree fell down, Liu Zongyuan became prefect of Liuzhou.[8] After Fu Sheng dreamt of a giant fish eating rushes, it was understood that he would be deposed.[9] A dream that moxa grew all over the river confirmed that a member of the Xiao family would triumph as emperor.[10] Madam Li dreamt of two papaya trees.[11] Liu Chaolin dreamt of two pomegranate trees.[12] Murong Shaozong dreamt of garlic.[13] The mother of Shen Caizhi dreamt of a fungus.[14] Emperor Xuanzong of the Tang dreamt of wisteria blossoms.[15] Wu Jin dreamt of peonies.[16] Liu Hao dreamt of grain beneath a fence.[17] Cai Mao dreamt of grain growing on top of a great hall.[18] Liu Lingzhe dreamt of bamboo shoots and was able to cure his mother of her ailment.[19] Zhang Zhichun dreamt of fine fruit, and indeed a worthy descendant was then born.[20] When Erzhu Zhao led forth his army, he dreamt that he had pulled out every stalk of *malin*-rush.[21] After Liu Changyan failed the official examinations, he dreamt that he had flown into a blossom on a *citong*-tree.[22] Worthy Lady Yin dreamt of eating a delicious melon whose seeds came from Penglai.[23] "Filial Son" Song dreamt that he had obtained a melon, which he then offered it to his mother. The incident was publicized during the Later Wei dynasty.[24] Fu Jian dreamt of a city filled with vegetables and concluded that it would be difficult to for a general to conquer.[25] Wang Rong dreamt about chopping blocks made of mulberry wood and lost his children one after another.[26] Scholar He dreamt that wood from a paulownia tree could be used to make a Buddhist image, and found the best material on a neighbor's property.[27] Zhang Xun dreamt that a section of bamboo sprouted in his courtyard, and he rapidly rose in position, though not for long.[28] Although it is said that plants do not have emotions, they appear in dreams and can be interpreted as symbolic images.

NOTES

1. Both examples are recorded in *Encyclopedia for Literary Composition*, chapter 88.
2. *Encyclopedia for Literary Composition*, chapter 89.
3. *Encyclopedia for Literary Composition*, chapter 85.
4. For an explanation, see the commentary to dreams of pines, junipers, and oaks in the chapter, "The Disciple of Emptiness" [I:5n12].
5. For an explanation, see the commentary to the dream of the graph for "pine" as composed of the graphs "eighteen" and "duke" in the chapter, "Forms and Appearances" [II:5n10].
6. For an explanation, see the commentary to the dream in which the graphs for a "man" climbing up a "mountain" indicate "misfortune" in the chapter, "Written Graphs" [II:10n10].
7. Zhang Zhihe, whose courtesy name was Zitong, was from Jinhua. His mother dreamt that a maple tree grew from her abdomen and then gave birth to him. At first, his name was Guiling. When Emperor Suzong of the Tang appointed

him an academician awaiting orders, he bestowed upon Zhang the name "Zhihe." (From *New History of the Tang Dynasty*.)

8. Liu Zongyuan was recalled to the capital after serving as vice prefect of Yongzhou. He consulted a fortuneteller about his destiny, saying, "My surname is Liu [willow]. Last night, I dreamt that a willow tree fell over. Isn't this unlucky?" The fortuneteller said, "When alive, it is a willow tree. After falling down, it becomes willow wood. 'Wood' *[mu]* has the same sound as 'prefect' *[mu]*. You will become prefect of Liuzhou [willow prefecture]." (From *A Record of Collected Strange Events*.)

9. The Fus in earlier generations were chiefs among the Western Rong people. At first, they settled in Puchi and took Pu [rushes] as their surname. Fu Hong was the first to change it to Fu in response to a prophecy. Fu Hong's son was Fu Jian [r. 351–355], and Fu Jian's son was Fu Sheng. After Fu Sheng ascended the throne, the officials and the common people both suffered from his murderous cruelty. Fu Sheng dreamt that a giant fish ate the rushes. Later, he was indeed killed by his cousin Fu Jian [r. 357–385]. (From *History of the Jin Dynasty*.)

10. Ji Sengzhen dreamt that wormwood and moxa grew all over the river. Startled by this, he spoke openly about the dream. Xiao Daocheng, the future Emperor Taizu of the Southern Qi, said, "Poets gather artemisia *[xiao]* and moxa is a kind of artemisia. When artemisia grows, it blocks the flow of the current *[duanliu]*. You, sir, must not publicize this, for *duanliu* sounds like 'supplanting the Liu Song dynasty' *[dai Liu (Song)]*." (From *History of the Southern Qi Dynasty*.)

11. Madam Li, the mother of Shao Yong, became ill and lost weight, so a doctor prescribed medicine for her. Madam Li dreamt about two papaya trees flanking the gate to a courtroom. The one on the right had already withered. Shao's father fetched the medicine and ordered that she take it. When her time arrived, she gave birth to a boy and a girl. The boy was Shao Yong, but the girl was stillborn. (From *Mr. Shao's Records*.)

12. Liu Chaolin of Nancheng was a gentleman of upright character. One night, he dreamt that he arrived at a place where there were two pomegranate trees. He found money in a pit beneath them amounting to a thousand strings of cash. He thought to himself that he had never harbored any wayward ideas, so he wondered how he could have arrived at such a place. Not long afterward, Dai Xunsi invited him to become the family tutor and educate his sons and nephews with an annual salary of one thousand strings of cash. When Liu entered the study of the house, he saw two pomegranate trees growing in the courtyard exactly like the ones in his dream. Ten years later, he passed the official examinations in the year *wuxu*. (From *Yijian's Accounts*.)

13. Murong Shaozong had a number of nightmares and was appalled by each of them. He privately told his close officials, "For several years now I have continually had dreams of 'garlic-hair' [prematurely grey hair]. Last night, I dreamt that it was all gone. 'Garlic' *[suan]* sounds the same as 'lifespan' *[suan]*. Does the disappearance of the garlic mean that my life will soon be over?" Not long afterward, he went with Liu Feng to an embankment and boarded a warship. A

violent wind broke a hawser and the ship was blown over to the enemy-held city. Murong realized that he could not escape capture, jumped into the water, and drowned. (From *An Encyclopedia of Paired Historical and Literary Citations*.)

14. Shen Caizhi was from Luoyang. His mother, Mistress Yang, dreamt that she had swallowed a fungus and became pregnant, hence his name Caizhi [gathering fungus]. Emperor Xuanzong of the Tang [r. 712–756] dreamt one night that in Hunan there was a Retired Gentleman of the White Clouds [Shen Caizhi], and he subsequently summoned him to the capital. In their discussion, they found that they were in complete agreement. Shen returned to his home in the mountains and before long became a transcendent. (From *Old History of the Tang Dynasty*.)

15. For an explanation, see the commentary to the dream about eating the stamens of wisteria blossoms in the chapter, "Food and Clothing" [II:6n14].

16. Empress Wu [1115–1197], consort of Emperor Gaozong of the Southern Song, was the daughter of Gentleman of Militant Assistance Wu Jin. Wu Jin once dreamt that he arrived at a pavilion whose placard bore the inscription "Assisting Good Health" *[shikang]*. Next to the pavilion peonies had been planted, only one of which had blossomed, and beneath this blossom was a white sheep. After he awoke, Wu Jin regarded this as quite strange. The empress was born in the year *yiwei* [1115, the year of the sheep]. She was accepted into the palace when she was fourteen. The future Emperor Gaozong was then Prince Kang [good health], so this confirmed "Assisting Good Health." (From *History of the Song Dynasty*.)

17. Liu Hao was extremely filial in taking care of his grandmother, but his family was poor. He dreamt that someone told him, "There is grain beneath the western fence." He dug and found fifteen *zhong* of grain and an inscription that read, "Seven years of grain weighing more than one hundred *dan* for a filial grandson." Liu Hao was able to live off it for seven years before it was exhausted (from *History of the Jin Dynasty*).

18. For an explanation, see the commentary to the dream where the graphs "losing" and "grain" combine to make "official salary" in the chapter, "Written Graphs" [II:10n14].

19. For an explanation, see the commentary to the dream about an old man dressed in yellow in the chapter, "Gods and Strange Things" [II:12n25].

20. For an explanation, see the commentary to the dreams about Confucius's spirit in heaven in the chapter, "Gods and Strange Things" [II:12n66].

21. When Erzhu Zhao led forth his army to quell a rebellion, he dreamt that his late father had climbed up on a hill and observed that all the fields around had been harvested—only the stalks of *malin*-rushes still remained. When his father asked why these hadn't all been pulled out, his close officials said that they were too firmly rooted and couldn't be dislodged. He looked at Erzhu Zhao and ordered him to pull them out from the roots. Erzhu Zhao immediately eliminated all of them wherever he went. (From *History of the Wei Dynasty*.)

22. Liu Changyan from Quanzhou wrote a poem on failing the official examinations that went, "It was only a 'Butterfly Dream' in the night; happily fluttering about, I flew into a blossom on a *citong*-tree." (From *Random Notes from a Green Box of Knowledge*.)

23. Worthy Lady Yin of Emperor Ming of the Eastern Han dreamt of eating a delicious melon. At that time, a foreign melon called "piercing yin" arrived at the court from Dunhuang. An elder remarked that a Daoist had obtained the seeds of this melon from Penglai and that eating the melon could banish hunger. (From *Wang Zinian's Recovered Records*.)

24. During the Later Wei dynasty, the mother of Song Qiong fell ill and longed for melon during the eleventh lunar month. Song Qiong dreamt that someone gave him a melon, and when he awoke, he found a melon in his hands. At the time, this was proclaimed to be a divine response to his filial piety. (From *Exceptional Dreams*.)

25. When Fu Jian [r. 357–385] was about to launch a southern military campaign, he dreamt of a city overgrown with vegetables *[cai]*. His empress said that when there is a lot of food *[cai]* served, it difficult to judge which dish is best [*jiang,* a homonym for "general," i.e., a general will face difficulties]. (From *The Taiping Miscellany.*)

26. Wang Rong dreamt that someone gave him seven chopping blocks, which he stored inside his clothes. Upon awakening, he found them. A dream interpreter said, "A chopping block is made from the mulberry tree [*sangzi,* a homonym for 'the death of a child']." Afterward, he buried seven sons and daughters, both younger and older ones. (From *A Garden of Strange Events*.)

27. When He Jingshu was young, he made a vow to make a Buddhist image out of sandalwood, but could not find the material for it. He dreamt that a Buddhist monk told him, "The paulownia trees of the He family behind the district office would be excellent." When he awoke, he searched there in accordance with the dream and indeed obtained wood. (From *A Record of Auspicious Signs*.)

28. Zhang Xun dreamt that a single section of bamboo sprouted forth in his courtyard and asked Zhu Fadu about it. Zhu said, "You will rapidly rise to an exalted position, though not for long." Indeed, it turned out just as he said. (From *A Garden of Strange Events*.)

CHAPTER 19

Reward and Retribution
施報

Reward and retribution is an eternal principle at work throughout the realms of the living and the dead. Whenever someone has accumulated good or bad actions, plenty of blessings or misfortunes will ensue. Wherever forms or sounds exist, they are inseparable from shadows and echoes. Therefore, kindnesses dispersed far and wide will certainly result in receiving demonstrable assistance, while cruelty and harm toward innocent people will lead to death from hidden forces. In the past, Wei Ke married off his father's concubine, and an old man weaving grass by the roadside appeared to him.[1] Li Jue assisted the poor, and his name was inscribed on a stone wall in a cave residence of transcendents.[2] The wife of Chen Wu offered libations of tea at an ancient tomb and obtained a hundred thousand strings of cash.[3] A maid in the Zhou family picked thorns out of a skull and obtained a pair of gold bracelets.[4] How could these result from deliberately searching for profit throughout this immense world, or just be absurd tales designed to delude ordinary people? Then there are such cases as the grievance of the Zhao clan, when an ancestor beat his breast after being granted revenge by the supreme god Di.[5] The cruelty meted out to Hun Liangfu caused him to unbind his hair and cry out to heaven.[6] After Yao Chang killed Fu Jian, the latter led demons to attack him.[7] Tao Ji executed a musical performer, but she obtained justice by accusing Tao before heaven.[8] After Emperor Ling of the Eastern Han killed Empress Song, heaven expressed its fury.[9] The Dethroned Emperor of the Liu Song dynasty killed a palace woman, and an eloquent woman unleashed disaster upon him.[10] Gao Ang killed Metropolitan Governor Nu and found himself dripping with blood.[11] Houmochen Yue killed Heba Yue and then suffered from a nervous disorder.[12] Xu Wen exhumed the corpse of Zhu Jin. He fell ill because of this, so he reburied Zhu.[13] Zhang Cou collected the hair of Yan Gaoqing, had a vision in a dream, and built a memorial temple.[14] Mrs. Peng had a penchant for killing people and died at the hands of a dishonorable slave.[15] Hu Du slandered her husband and died during pregnancy.[16] Shang Zhongkan reburied a coffin that had been carried off by water.[17] Zou Zhan reburied a corpse located underground to the west.[18] Assistant Magistrate Zhou was buried under a sack of earth, but the two thieves were unable to hide from their crime.[19] After Liu Chang buried some dry bones, a group of ghosts thanked him for his kindness.[20] The Prince of Chengyang took revenge for Kou Zuren's enmity.[21] King Wen of the Zhou agreed to bury someone with the rites of a sovereign.[22] Time does not permit me to record many other examples like these.

Even miniscule things such as insects may owe their lives to grand gestures of empathy, as when Dong Zhaozhi ferried over an ant.[23] The father of Fang Xiaoru burned snakes.[24] Liu Zhiheng set fish free.[25] Pei Anzu granted life to a pheasant.[26] An old monk fed a mynah bird.[27] Magistrate Li interred a sheep.[28] The Diamond Immortal recited an incantation for a spider.[29] Huan Miao saved a duck.[30] In each case, they were moved to repay the dreamer, and there were verifications of these auspicious or disastrous consequences. How much truer this is in the area where humans and ghosts arise and submit, or at the border where vigorous essences and *hun*-souls undergo transformations! Therefore, it is said that heaven's net is wide and the human mind is not easily deceived. Gods report the goodness of the radiantly virtuous; demons spy on the households of the shady and immoral. Whenever such things take form in dreams, aren't there always efficacious confirmations?

NOTES

1. For an explanation, see the commentary to Wei Ke's dream about an old man in the chapter, "The Disciple of Emptiness" [I:5n25].
2. During the Tang dynasty, Li Jue [n.d.] from Guangling sold grain for a living. He was filial in serving his parents and liked to aid the poor. At that time, Grand Councilor Li Jue [785–853] was in charge in Huainan and dreamt that that he entered a cave residence of transcendents. There, he saw his name written in gold graphs on a stone wall, whereupon he felt quite pleased with himself. But then three transcendent youths told him, "This is the commoner Li Jue [n.d.] from Guangling, not you, sir." (From *The Comprehensive Gazetteer*.)
3. The wife of Chen Wu of Yanxian was widowed while young and lived with her two sons. She enjoyed drinking tea. There was an ancient tomb on the grounds

of her house, and every time she drank tea, she would first offer some there. One night, she dreamt that someone came to thank her, saying, "Though I lie buried here in this moldering earth, how could I forget my debt of gratitude to you for sustaining me?" The next morning, she found a hundred thousand strings of cash in her courtyard. They seemed to have been buried for a long time, and yet the strings themselves were new. (From *A Garden of Strange Events*.)

4. A maid in the Zhou family of Chenliu would go into the hills to gather firewood. She dreamt that a woman said to her, "Thorns have been growing in my eyes. I beg you to remove them, and I will generously reward you." The maid then discovered a skull in a decaying coffin which had grass growing through the eye sockets. She plucked it out and then found a pair of gold bracelets at her home. (From *A Record of an Expedition*.) *Bo and Kong's Encyclopedia* states that thorns were growing in the eye sockets and that upon her return home, she received a reward of gold bracelets.

5. Duke Jing of Jin killed Zhao Tong and Zhao Kuo. Later, he fell ill and dreamt that a giant demon with unbound hair was beating his breast and leaping about, saying, "Killing my descendants was an unjust deed. The supreme god Di has granted me revenge." (From *Zuo's Narratives*.)

6. For an explanation, see the commentary to Duke Zhuang of Wei's dream of Hun Liangfu in the chapter, "The Disciple of Emptiness" [I:5n21].

7. When Yao Chang fell seriously ill, he dreamt that Fu Jian [r. 357–385] dispatched a celestial emissary and several hundred demon soldiers to break into Yao's encampment. Yao was frightened and fled into his palace where an attendant harbored Yao and tried to stab the demons. But the attendant struck Yao in his genitals by mistake. The demons said to each other, "He has been struck in the most life-threatening place." When the spear was pulled out, more than twenty gallons of blood issued forth. Yao awoke in a panic and subsequently developed a tumor on his genitals. A physician lanced it and drained his blood, just as in the dream. (From *History of the Jin Dynasty*.)

8. When Tao Ji served as prefect of Moling, he wrongly killed a musical performer. Later, he dreamt that she came and said, "I accused you before heaven and obtained justice. Now, I have come to take you." She jumped into his mouth and in an instant, Tao was dead. (From *A Record of an Expedition*.)

9. Emperor Ling of the Eastern Han dreamt that Emperor Huan angrily said to him, "What crime did Empress Song commit for you to listen to the evil son of a concubine and deprive her of her life? Prince Kui of Bohai was so grieved that he voluntarily went into exile, and still he was executed. Now, both Empress Song and Prince Kui have accused you before heaven and the supreme god Di has expressed his fury. Your crimes will be difficult to pardon, so investigate the truth of this extraordinary dream." After the emperor awoke, he asked Xu Yong, the supervisor on the left of the Palace Guard, about the dream. Xu replied, "In the past, Duke Jing of Jin punished someone unjustly and dreamt of a giant demon with unbound hair stretching down to the ground. Heaven always discerns the truth because it is hard for ghosts and spirits to bring false charges. It would be proper to move the graves of the deceased to pacify their aggrieved *hun*-souls." The emperor refused to listen to this advice, and not long afterward, he, too, died. (From *History of the Eastern Han Dynasty*.)

10. The Former Dethroned Emperor of the Liu Song enjoyed going to the Bamboo Forest Pavilion in the Flower Grove Garden where he had naked women chase after one another. There was a woman who refused to obey, so he had her executed. One night, he dreamt that he was visiting the women's quarters where another woman berated him, saying, "You are perversely cruel and immoral. You won't live to see the grain ripen next year." When the emperor awoke, he was angry. He found someone in the palace resembling the one in the dream and had her killed. That night, he again dreamt that the woman he had just killed berated him, saying, "You wrongly murdered me, and I have already accused you before the supreme god Di." Before long, he was indeed killed by Shou Jizhi and others. (From *History of the Liu Song Dynasty*.)

11. Gao Ang was commander-in-chief and fought against Emperor Wen of the Zhou, who defeated him at Mangyin. Gao was then killed. Before this, Gao ordered Metropolitan Governor Nu to command the Western Army. However, Nu, with the aid of a maidservant, stole Gao's sword and fled. Gao captured Nu and eventually killed him. Nu had said to him, "I rescued you three times when you were in dire straits. How can you execute me over such a trivial matter?" Then, Gao dreamt one night that Nu appeared and smeared blood all over him so that Gao was dripping with blood. When Gao awoke, he was so angry that he ordered someone to break both of Nu's shinbones. At that time, Liu Taobang was in Bohai and also dreamt about Nu, who told him that he had brought a grievance against Gao and had obtained justice: Gao Ang would be dealt with by the rebels. When Gao went into battle, indeed, he met with catastrophe. (From *History of the Northern Dynasties*.)

12. After Houmochen Yue killed Heba Yue, he suffered from a nervous disorder and was never the same again. Every time he fell asleep he dreamt that Heba said to him, "Where are you off to, brother? I will always follow you, so you need never leave me." As a result, he was never at peace and finally was defeated. (From *History of the Northern Dynasties*.)

13. When Zhu Jin died, his body was left by the north gate of Guangling, so he was buried by a passer-by. At that time, many of the common people were suffering from malaria. They all took earth from his grave and ate it, which was said to provide an instant cure. New earth was piled on the grave until it became a tall mound, but Xu Wen and others disliked this. They exhumed his corpse and cast it into the Lake of the Lord of Thunder. After this, Xu fell ill and dreamt that Zhu had shot him with a bow and arrow. Xu was terrified and fished out Zhu's bones, burying them beside the lake and establishing a memorial temple there. (From *History of the Five Dynasties*.)

14. Yan Gaoqing was killed and his head was exposed at a crossroads where no one dared to collect it. There was someone named Zhang Cou, who collected Yan's hair and reported this to the supreme god in heaven. That evening, he had a dream from the supreme god Di. After awakening, Zhang built a memorial temple where he made offerings to Yan. (From *New History of the Tang Dynasty*.)

15. At the beginning of the Jianwu era [25–55 CE] of Emperor Guangwu of the Eastern Han, Governor of Yuyang Peng Chong revolted and proclaimed himself King of Yan. Peng's wife had a penchant for killing people so that his close officials feared for their lives. She had many nightmares, which made her even more

suspicious and fearful. Before long Peng Chong's slave Zimi and two others bound and decapitated him while he was in bed. They took his head together with that of Mrs. Peng, left the city, and surrendered to the emperor, who enfeoffed Zimi as "Marquis of Dishonor." (From *History of the Eastern Han Dynasty*.)

16. Yelü Shucheng was slandered by his wife Hu Du so that he was accused of a crime and lost his official position. He often dreamt about occupying the position of secretary. A skillful dream interpreter Hu Lügu interpreted it, saying, "You would have attained the position of secretary, but you became a criminal because of your wife." When Yelü pursued the matter legally, he found he was entitled to divorce her. It just so happened at this point that Hu Du was pregnant, but she died without giving birth. When an autopsy was performed, it was observed that her child's hands were holding onto her heart. Knowledgeable people said that this was retribution for slandering her husband. (From *History of the Jin [Jurchen] Dynasty*.)

17. When Shang Zhongkan was in Dantu, he dreamt of a person who said, "You, sir, have an altruistic heart. Can you extend your benevolence to my withered bones and move me to a high and dry place?" The next day, a coffin was indeed carried by water to where Shang was. He retrieved it and reburied it atop a tall hill. That night, he dreamt that the man came to thank him. (From *Exceptional Dreams*.)

18. For an explanation, see the commentary to the dream about the characters "earth," "west," and "tiles" in the chapter, "Written Graphs" [II:10n31].

19. Assistant Magistrate Zhou of Taoxian in Jizhou was sent on official business to Linyu during the Xianqing era [656–660] of the Tang dynasty. He took along two assistants. Zhou was traveling with a substantial amount of money, and the two men killed him by crushing him under a sack of earth, stealing the money. Toward the end of the year, Zhou's wife dreamt about the incident as well as the location where the thieves were hiding. She then accused them before the court, and the truth was revealed. The money was still there and the two thieves were executed. (From *A Book of Good Deeds*.)

20. When Liu Chang first fortified the city of Pingliang, he found that the remains of officers and soldiers had not been buried after the alliance was broken off. Liu then ordered them interred. At night, he dreamt that a crowd of spirits visited him to offer thanks. Liu made this known to Emperor Dezong of the Tang, who issued a proclamation mourning them. The emperor also donated several hundred sets of clothes, and officials contributed coffins. (From *Old History of the Tang Dynasty*.)

21. Prince Hui of Chengyang had sought refuge with Kou Zuren, magistrate of Luoyang. Kou learned that Erzhu Zhao wanted to arrest Prince Hui, so Kou had him decapitated and sent his head to Erzhu. Erzhu dreamt that Prince Hui said to him, "I have more than a hundred pounds of gold and a horse at Kou Zuren's house—you may take possession of these." Erzhu then had Kou's head tied to a tree and weighed down his feet with rocks, whipping him while demanding the gold and horse. Kou died, and people said at the time that it was Prince Hui's retribution. (From *History of the Northern Wei Dynasty*.)

22. King Wen of the Zhou dreamt that someone climbed up on the city wall and shouted out, "I am the withered bones lying in the northeast corner. Hurry

and bury me with the rites of a sovereign." King Wen replied, "Agreed." When he awoke, he summoned a functionary and commanded him to bury the bones with the rites of a sovereign. The functionary suggested, "Let him be buried with the rites of a grandee instead." But King Wen replied, "I have already promised him this in my dream." When the common people heard about it, they said, "Since our sovereign shows such concern for the withered bones of the dead because of a dream, imagine how much more concern he has for the living." (From Jia Yi, *New Writings*.)

23. For an explanation, see the commentary to the dream of an ant floating on a reed in a river in the chapter, "Turtles and Fish" [II:17n18].

24. Before Fang Xiaoru was born, his father had divined an auspicious day to bury his grandfather. That night, he dreamt that someone in a vermillion robe knelt before him, saying, "I have learned that you intend to bury your grandfather on such-and-such a mountain. Nine branches of my family have been dwelling there for several hundred years. I hope you might delay the interment for three days so that we can move away." The next day, the father dug a pit and found more than a thousand red [*chi*] snakes, one of which was several dozen feet long. Fang Xiaoru's father allowed them all to be burned. Several days later, Fang Xiaoru was born, and he resembled a snake in that he possessed a forked tongue that could lick his nostrils. Later, he was exterminated [*chi*], along with nine branches of his family. (From *Conversations Gathered by a Solitary Tree*.)

25. For an explanation, see the commentary to the dream about two carp in the chapter, "Longevity and Destiny" [II:13n10].

26. For an explanation, see the commentary to the dream about a man in an embroidered robe bowing in thanks in the chapter, "Mountains and Rivers" [II:4n7].

27. At the Stonewall Temple in Bingzhou during the Tang dynasty, a mynah bird built a nest in an eave, and two chicks were born. An old monk fed it leftovers whenever he had some, but when their wings had almost fully grown, they fell to earth and died. The monk buried their bodies and that night dreamt that two small boys told him, "Formerly, we were minor sinners who were punished by being given the form of mynah birds. Now, as a result of listening to your recitation of the sutras, we are to receive human form. In ten months, we are destined to be reborn near the temple in such-and-such a household, with such-and-such a surname, in such-and-such a village." The monk awaited the time and went to the house to make inquiries. Indeed, twin boys had been born. A month later, he called to them as if they were the two mynah chicks, and both boys answered him. (From *Collected Biographies of Transcendents*.)

28. During the Tang dynasty, a certain magistrate of Huojing named Li was visiting the home of an office manager in the locality and spent the night. The host intended to kill a sheep for a banquet. The sheep was pregnant. Li dreamt that a woman in a white dress leading two children knelt before him and begged him for their lives. Li awoke but couldn't understand the reason behind the dream. After going back to sleep, he again dreamt that the woman said to him, "I am already dead. Formerly, I was the wife of the office manager. There was a servant girl pregnant with two children who died after she was beaten. I deceived my husband by telling him that the maid stole my gold hairpin and gold box.

Now, my death has expunged her grievance. The gold hairpin and box are hidden among the roof brackets on the western side of the chamber." Li was startled awake and asked his host if he had killed a white sheep with two fetuses. He then told him about his recent dreams, and they searched among the roof brackets. Indeed, they found the lost objects and immediately buried the sheep. (From *A Record of Retributions*.)

29. The Diamond Immortal was a Buddhist monk from the Western Region. He lived in Qingyuan Gorge and could utter incantations in Sanskrit. There was an old spider who had become a demon. The Diamond Immortal uttered an incantation to cause him to cast off his form. One night, he dreamt that an old man offered him cloth in thanks, saying, "I am the spider. I would like to present this to you, Master, to be made into a robe as a reward for your good deed." When he awoke, he found the cloth beside him. It was exquisite and unlike anything in this world. After it was made into a robe, he found that dust never clung to it. (From *The Taiping Miscellany*.)

30. Huan Miao was from Ru'nan Commandery. He intended to send four black ducks to someone as a gift when he dreamt that four men in black robes begged him for their lives. He awoke and suddenly saw that the ducks were about to be killed, so he spared them. He bought some meat instead. After that, he dreamt that the four men came to thank him. (From *A Record of Ghosts and the Living*.)

CHAPTER 20

On General Analogies
泛喻

Employing general analogies is not as good as incisive thinking and broad critiques are not as good as concise explanations. The omens that appear in dreams involve events that range from the infinitesimal to the boundless. Unless one utilizes concise explanations based on incisive thinking, such dreams will destabilize one's spirit and dissipate one's will. Thus, Wei Jie became befuddled when he tried to comprehend dreams as thoughts because his efforts at incisive thinking were insufficient. But Yue Guang was skilled at examining people and obtained the principle for a concise explanation of Wei's illness.[1] Master Zhuang said, "When I was dreaming, I didn't know it was a dream. But, after I awoke, I realized it was a dream." This is a statement of being conscious of having dreamed. It is not a statement about dreaming of dreaming or being conscious of waking consciousness. He who understands what it is to dream of dreaming or is conscious of waking consciousness has attained knowledge of the causes behind life and death and comprehends where things begin and end. For a dream is also a kind of consciousness, while waking consciousness is also a kind of dreaming. Examples of dreams that are like waking consciousness are Master Zhuang's dream of himself as a butterfly and Prince Zhongzhuang of the Liang dynasty's dream of himself as a fish and a bird.[2] An example of waking consciousness that is like a dream is the grand historian's dream of straw dogs that Zhou Xuan interpreted.[3] As for the youth Lu, who received a pillow in Handan and experienced success and an entire lifetime before the millet was fully cooked,[4] and Yang Guozhong, who obtained the pillow from Kucha that enabled one to encounter transcendents, cross the seas, and travel to di-

251

vine realms[5]—these show that the universe of space-time is just a pillow and that success, failure, glory, and disgrace occur between entering and leaving the holes in the pillow's sides. When Wang Qi said that it was all just like the success or failure experienced in a dream, was he not absolutely correct?[6] Alas! Dreams cannot be sought by simply going through the hole in a pillow! *The Book of the Spiritual Pivot* states that when excessive *qi*-energy attacks internally, it must manifest itself in the form of dreams. Such dreams can be stopped by purging any overabundance and tonifying any deficiency.[7] *The Inner Canon of Medicine* says that lesser yin syncope causes bizarre dreams while acupuncture performed in the wrong season causes people to develop a penchant for dreaming. Thus, it is necessary to combine the five diagnostic methods to understand the condition of the pulse.[8] Furthermore, there is confirmation of the efficacy of praying for dreams at the Temple of the Transcendents at Nine Carp Lake. No doubt, the divinities of the rivers and sacred mountains understand human fortunes. Therefore, they send dreams disclosing omens.[9] Also, a plant found in Ronggao can be used to interpret dreams. Why should yarrow and other kinds of divining stalks be the only kinds used to communicate with the human mind?[10]

When the first emperor of the Northern Wei dynasty issued a proclamation to execute the Buddhists, it maintained that the dream of Emperor Ming of the Eastern Han about a gold figurine was the result of a delusion.[11] It was certainly a valid argument for exposing this heresy. The complete circumstances surrounding a dream must be interpreted. Why else would King Wen have bowed with respect when he received an auspicious dream even though the Zhou dynasty had triumphed and his government was flourishing?[12] Why else did Emperor Shizu of the Jin, confused by all the specious advice surrounding him, have his dreams divined before deciding to go into battle?[13] Ever since a favorite of the ruler of the state of Wei slandered Taishu Wei and forced him into exile, the practice of interpreting dreams became unreliable.[14] Ever since the rebel An Lushan used a dream to deceive the emperor about An's establishment of temples,[15] and the wife of Yang Guozhong cited a dream to deceive her husband when she gave birth to a son,[16] some dreams have been impossible to interpret correctly. How lamentable! Is this because dreams are no longer efficacious? I have transcribed these "lofty principles," but am I dreaming, or am I awake? As I do not possess complete consciousness of myself, this may all very well be a dream. Gentlemen in later generations might try perusing these lofty principles and lend an ear to these earlier dreams of mine.[17]

On General Analogies 253

NOTES

1. Wei Jie asked Yue Guang, "What makes dreams?" Yue answered, "Dreams are thoughts." Wei said, "How can dreams be thoughts when the body or spirit has never experienced such things?" He spent the entire day trying to think about this but could not understand it. As a result, he became ill. Yue then called for his carriage and went to examine him closely. After Wei recovered, Yue sighed, "This worthy gentleman's ailment must have been in the region below the heart." (From *History of the Jin Dynasty*.)

2. Once, I, Zhuang Zhou, dreamt I was a butterfly, a butterfly fluttering about. I felt completely happy and did not know that Zhuang Zhou existed. Suddenly, I awoke and was surprised to realize I was Zhuang Zhou. But, I did not know if I was Zhuang Zhou who had dreamt he was a butterfly or a butterfly dreaming he is Zhuang Zhou. There must be some difference between these two. This is what is called "the transformation of things." (From "Discussion on Equalizing Everything" in the *Master Zhuang*.)

Prince Zhongzhuang of the Liang said, "I once dreamt that I was a fish who then transformed into a bird. How happy I felt while dreaming! But after I awoke, how anxious I felt as a human!" (From *History of the Liang Dynasty*.)

3. Zhou Xuan's courtesy name was Konghe. The grand historian asked him the meaning of a dream about straw dogs, and Zhou replied, "It means you will obtain food and drink." Another day, he again asked the meaning of another dream about straw dogs, and Zhou replied, "You will fall from your carriage and break a foot." Another day, he again asked the meaning of yet another dream about straw dogs, and Zhou replied, "There will be a destructive fire." The grand historian said, "On these past three occasions when I consulted you, there never were such dreams. I was just testing you. How were you able to provide interpretations that were confirmed in each case?" Zhou replied, "Divine spirit was aiding you, and this was indistinguishable from a dream." (From *History of the Wei Dynasty*.)

4. During the Kaiyuan era [713–741] of the Tang dynasty, Old Man Lü, a Daoist, was resting at an inn in Handan where he met a young man, Scholar Lu, who lamented that he was poor and in dire straits. The innkeeper was just then steaming some millet as the old man gave Scholar Lu a pillow, saying, "Use my pillow and you will experience all the glory you desire." The young scholar lay down on the pillow and dreamt that he entered it through one of the holes in its side. He arrived back home where he married a woman from the Cui family who was quite beautiful. The next year, he earned the presented scholar degree and eventually rose to the position of secretariat director, dying at the age of eighty. When he awoke, he observed that the old man was still beside him and that the millet was not yet fully cooked. He thanked Lü by saying, "Through this experience, sir, you have restrained my desires." (From *The Comprehensive Gazetteer*.)

5. The land of Kucha presented a pillow to the court that appeared to be made of agate, yet was warm and lustrous like jade. When Emperor Xuanzong of the Tang [r. 712–756] used it, he was able to travel to the ten continents and the three divine islands, so it was called the "Pillow for Traveling to Encounter Transcendents." Later, he bestowed the pillow on Yang Guozhong. (From *Events*

of the Tianbao Era.) A poem by Li Bo included the lines, "Let's leave the amber pillow where it lies, there is still time for more dreams to arrive."

6. During the Taihe era [827–835], Wang Qi failed the official examinations and wound up as a staff retainer in Heshuo, where he often would complain about those in power at the imperial court. He wrote a poem that went, "I urge you not to brag about being outstanding, success or failure in a dream is never real." (From *New Writings from Nanbu.*)

7. The Yellow Emperor asked, "What can be done about the spreading of excessive *qi*-energy"? Qibo replied, "When excessive energy enters the body from outside, it does not take up a fixed abode. When it overflows into the *zang*-organs, it does not settle in any definite place. It circulates together with the nutrient and defense systems and flutters about with the *hun*- and *po*-souls. This causes restless sleep and a penchant for dreaming. When excess *qi*-energy spreads into the *fu*-organs, there is an external overabundance and an internal deficiency. When *qi*-energy spreads into the *zang*-organs, there is an internal overabundance and an external deficiency. If one purges the overabundance and tonifies the deficiency, then one can stop such dreams. (From *The Book of the Spiritual Pivot.*) See the chapter "Influences and Abnormal Conditions" for dreams due to overabundant or deficient *qi*-energy [I:10].

8. Insufficient yin syncope causes bizarre dreams and, at its extreme, leads to mental confusion. The pulse in the three yang channels is interrupted and becomes weak in the three yin channels. Therefore, the sage utilizes diagnostic methods to restore the balance between yin and yang. If one does not lose sight of the individual nature of the patient, this way will result in a clear and detailed examination. (From "Discussion on Diagnostic Methods for Abundance or Decline of *Qi*-Energy" in *The Inner Canon of Medicine.*)

During the autumn season, if one applies acupuncture to the points appropriate for the summer season, then the illness will not be cured. It will induce in the patient a greater desire to sleep and, moreover, a penchant for dreaming. (From "Discussion of the Essentials of Diagnosis and of the Meridian System" in *The Inner Canon of Medicine.*)

9. The Temple of Lady Transcendent He is located at Nine Carp Lake in the northeast of Xianyou District where Lady He and nine transcendents are sacrificed to. Whenever the triennial examinations are held, local scholars pray for dreams here, and there are always efficacious responses. (From *The Comprehensive Gazetteer.*)

10. The dream-plant *[mengcao]* is found in the west of Ronggao. Its stalks resemble yarrow. By wearing it close to one's chest while interpreting a dream, one will know if the dream signifies catastrophe or good fortune. (From *Wang Zinian's Recovered Records.*)

11. The "Proclamation on the Execution of the Buddhists" by Emperor Shizu of the Northern Wei stated, "In the past, a deluded sovereign of the Eastern Han dynasty insanely believed in heterodox and false doctrines and recklessly exploited a dream in order to serve foreign demons, thereby upsetting the constancy of heaven. From remote antiquity on, there has never been such a thing within the nine provinces of Our land. The Buddhists expound wild and exaggerated doctrines not founded on human nature so that everyone in these decadent times is

mesmerized by them. Thus, the true teachings are not practiced. The rites and morality have suffered great damage as this demonic way spreads like wildfire, and the rule of the king is considered worthless. Ever since, every era has experienced disaster and chaos, punishments must be carried out, and the common people are dying. It is all because of this. I have received direct authority from heaven to eliminate the false and establish the true, to expunge the foreign gods and destroy their traces. Government officials should issue orders to the armies and regional inspectors to destroy and burn all false objects, Buddhist images, and foreign sutras produced over the years, and to bury alive all Buddhist priests, regardless of age. Issued in the third lunar month of the seventh year of the Taiping zhenjun era [April-May 446]." (From *History of the Northern Wei Dynasty.*)

12. For an explanation, see the commentary to the dreams announcing heaven's will in the chapter, "Auspicious Events" [I:9n2].

13. When the Jin dynasty first arose, Emperor Shizu had his dreams interpreted to predict victory or defeat before going into battle with the enemy. (From "Treatise on the Five Agents" in *History of the Jin [Jurchen] Dynasty.*)

14. Duke Zhuang of Wei had a dream of his interpreted. One of his favored courtiers had sought some wine from Taishu Wei but could not obtain it. So, together with the dream interpreter, the courtier slandered him to the duke. Taishu was driven out and fled to the state of Jin. (From *Zuo's Narratives.*)

15. An Lushan led an army to attack the Qidan people. Upon his return, he memorialized the throne, "I dreamt that Li Jing and Li Ji requested that your humble official institute sacrifices to them, so I established temples in the northern commanderies. Subsequently, divine fungus was seen growing in Liang." In this way, his exaggerated, deceptive, and presumptuous words were not suspected. (From *Old History of the Tang Dynasty.*)

16. When Yang Guozhong was sent on a mission to the Jiangzhe region, his wife longed for him intensely. Time passed, and she fell ill. Suddenly, during a nap one day, she dreamt that she had relations with him. She consequently became pregnant, giving birth to a son whom she named Fei [impending dawn]. When Yang returned home, his wife told him all about the dream, and he said, "This undoubtedly resulted from an emotional stimulation due to the mutual longing between husband and wife." However, everyone at the time ridiculed him. (From *Events of the Tianbao Era.*)

17. "The emperor had heard about the empress's earlier dream." Yan Shigu commented that this meant that he wrote down what his ears had heard. (From "Biography of Empress Wang, wife of Emperor Jing" in *History of the Western Han Dynasty.*)

List of Sources

Following standard practice in encyclopedias, Chen Shiyuan usually identified his sources by title only, often using abbreviations. In a few cases, he also indicated the author as well. The entries below generally follow the titles as cited by Chen unless corrected by me for obvious errors. A question mark appears after a source that remains problematical. Chen undoubtedly had access to books and editions that are no longer extant today, but many had already disappeared by the sixteenth century. Some of these survived only as citations in later compendia. Usually, he indicated the original source regardless of how he obtained the material though, occasionally, he only indicated the later compendia in which these texts appear. Additional bibliographical information has been provided where possible. In the case of a source that can only be identified as a citation in another work, I have provided a reference to its appearance in compendia Chen made use of or might have consulted.

Accounts of Anomalies 志怪 (*Zhiguai*, mid-4th–early 5th cent.), traditionally attributed to Kong Yue 孔約 (n.d.).
Accounts of Strange Things 述異記 (*Shuyiji*), by Zu Chongzhi 祖沖之 (429–500).
Accounts of Unique and Strange Things 獨異志 (*Duyizhi*, ca. 865–ca. 873), by Li Rong 李冗 (fl. 865).
Additional Records 補錄記 (*Buluji*, Five Dynasties), also titled *Additional Records and Biographies* 補錄記傳 (*Bulu jizhuan*), anon., cited in *Taiping Miscellany*, q.v., chapter 278.
Annals of Chu 楚紀 (*Chuji*), by Liao Daonan 廖道南 (d. 1547).
Annals of the Han Dynasty 漢紀 (*Hanji*), also titled *Annals of the Eastern Han Dynasty* 後漢紀 (*Houhanji*), by Yuan Hong 袁宏 (327–376).
Annals of the Song Dynasty 宋紀 (*Songji*) [?].
Annals of the Thearchs and Kings 帝王世紀 (*Diwang shiji*), by Huangfu Mi 黃甫謐 (215–282).
Anthology of the Kong Family Masters 孔叢子 (*Kongcongzi*, 3rd cent.), anon.
Apocrypha to The Book of Ritual 禮緯 (*Liwei*, Han dynasty), anon.

Apocrypha to The Spring and Autumn Annals 春秋緯 (*Chunqiuwei*, Han dynasty), anon.

"Author's Introduction" 自敘 ("Zixu"), in *Collected Poems of Su Dongpo* 東坡詩集 (*Dongpo shiji*), by Su Shi 蘇軾 (1037–1101).

"The Awakening in Cheng" 程寤 ("Chengwu"), in *Zhou Dynasty Documents Recovered from a Tomb*, q.v.

"The Beck" 斯干 ("Sigan"), "Lesser Odes" 小雅 ("Xiaoya"), in *Book of Songs*, q.v.

A Biographical Encyclopedia According to Surnames 氏族大全 (*Shizu daquan*, Yuan dynasty), anon.

Biographies of Divine Transcendents 神仙傳 (*Shenxianzhuan*, 317), by Ge Hong 葛洪 (ca. 283–343 or 363).

Biographies of Eminent Elders of the Past from Changsha 長沙耆舊傳 (*Changsha qijiuzhuan*, Jin dynasty [265–420]), by Liu Huo 劉彧 (n.d.).

Biographies of Eminent Elders of the Past from Yidu 益都耆舊傳 (*Yidu qijiuzhuan*), by Chen Shou 陳壽 (233–297).

Biographies of Eminent Worthies of the Past from Guiji 會稽先賢傳 (*Guiji xianxianzhuan*, 3rd cent.), by Xie Cheng 謝承 (n.d.).

"Biographies of Empresses and Consorts" 后妃傳 ("Houfeizhuan"), in *New History of the Tang Dynasty*, q.v.

Biographies of Exalted Recluses 高士傳 ("Gaoshizhuan"), by Huangfu Mi 黃甫謐 (215–282).

Biographies of Extraordinary People 異人傳 (*Yirenzhuan*, n.d.), cited in *Valley Embroidered with Myriad Flowers*, q.v., part I, chapter 20.

Biographies of Foreigners 外夷傳 ("Waiyizhuan"), in *History of the Southern Qi Dynasty*, q.v., chapter 58.

Biographies of Officials According to Historical Period 職官分紀 (*Zhiguan fenji*), by Sun Fengji 孫逢吉 (fl. 1086–1093).

Biographies of the Fan Family 范氏家傳 (*Fanshi jiazhuan*, Song dynasty), cited in *Valley Embroidered with Myriad Flowers*, q.v., part I, chapter 18.

"Biography of Empress Wang, wife of Emperor Jing 孝景王后傳 ("Xiaojing wanghouzhuan"), in *History of the Western Han Dynasty*, q.v.

"Biography of Gao Pian" 高駢傳 ("Gao Pianzhuan"), in *New History of the Tang Dynasty*, q.v.

"Biography of the Prefect of Nanke" 南柯太守傳 ("Nanke taishouzhuan"), by Li Gongzuo 李公佐 (ca. 770–ca. 848).

"Biography of Zheng Xie of the Palace Gate" 青瑣鄭獬傳 ("Qingsuo Zheng Xiezhuan"), cited in *Valley Embroidered with Myriad Flowers*, q.v., part I, chapter 23.

Bo and Kong's Encyclopedia 白孔六帖 (*Bo Kong liutie*), by Bo Juyi 白居易 (772–846), supplemented by Kong Chuan 孔傳 (fl. 1127–1162).

The Book of Changes 易經 (*Yijing*, ca. late 9th cent. BCE–Han dynasty), anon.

A Book of Good Deeds 為善書 (*Weishanshu*) [?], also recorded in *Collected Stories of Retribution from the Netherworld* 冥報拾遺 (*Mingbao shiyi*, ca. 663), by Lang Yuling 郎餘令 (ca. 614–681), cited in *A Grove of Pearls in the Dharma Garden*, q.v., chap. 92.

The Book of Ritual 禮記 (*Liji*, Eastern Han dynasty), anon.

List of Sources

The Book of Songs 詩經 (*Shijing*, ca. 11th–7th cent. BCE), anon.
The Book of the Great Mystery 太玄經 (*Taixuanjing*, ca. 7–1 BCE), by Yang Xiong 揚雄 (53 BCE–18 CE).
The Book of the Long-Willow Method 長柳經. See *Gan De's Long-Willow Method of Dream Interpretation,* also *Yellow Emperor's Long-Willow Method of Dream Interpretation.*
The Book of the Spiritual Pivot 靈樞經 (*Lingshujing*, 2nd–1st cent. BCE), also titled *The Yellow Emperor's Book of the Spiritual Pivot* 黃帝靈樞經 (*Huangdi lingshujing*), anon.
The Book of Wan Bi 萬畢傳 (*Wan Bizhuan*, Western Han dynasty), by Liu An 劉安 (ca. 179–122 BCE), cited in *Historical Records,* q.v., chapter 128.
The Bookcase of the Clouds 雲笈經 (*Yunjijing*, 1019), also titled *The Bookcase of the Clouds with the Seven Labels* 雲笈七籤 (*Yunji qiqian*), by Zhang Junfang 張君房 (fl. 1008–1025).
Casual Chats from Army Headquarters 戎幕閑談 (*Rongmu xiantan,* 831), by Wei Xuan 韋絢 (796–ca. 866).
Casual Chats of a Herd-boy 牧豎閑談 (*Mushu xiantan,* ca. 976–997), by Geng Huan 耿煥, a.k.a. Jing Huan 景煥 (fl. 965–984).
Casual Conversations from the Jade Hall 玉堂閑語 (*Yutang xianyu*), by Wang Renyu 王仁裕 (880–956).
"The Cautions of King Wen" 文儆 ("Wenjing"), in *Zhou Dynasty Documents Recovered from a Tomb,* q.v.
"The Cautions of King Wu" 武儆 ("Wujing"), in *Zhou Dynasty Documents Recovered from a Tomb,* q.v.
The Central Concordance to The Book of Filial Piety 孝經中契 (*Xiaojing zhongqi,* Han dynasty), anon.
The Central Omens in The Documents of Antiquity 尚書中候 (*Shangshu zhonghou,* Han dynasty), anon.
"The Charge to Yue" 說命 ("Yueming"), *Documents of the Shang Dynasty* 商書 (*Shangshu*), in *Documents of Antiquity,* q.v.
A Chart of the Life of Confucius 孔演圖 (*Kongyantu,* Han dynasty), also titled *A Chart of the Life of Confucius in the Spring and Autumn Annals* 春秋演孔圖 (*Chunqiu yankongtu*), anon.
Chats on Past and Contemporary Poetry 古今詩話 (*Gujin shihua,* Song dynasty), anon., cited in *Valley Embroidered with Myriad Flowers,* q.v., part I, chapter 1.
Chats on Poetry from Rongtang 蓉塘詩話 (*Rongtang shihua*), by Jiang Nan 姜南 (fl. 1506–1519).
Chats on Poetry from the Western Capital 西京詩話 (*Xijing shihua,* Song dynasty), anon., cited in *Valley Embroidered with Myriad Flowers,* q.v., part I, chapter 26.
"A Classfication of Dreams" 夢列 ("Menglie"), in *Discussions from a Gentleman in Hiding,* q.v.
Collected Biographies of Transcendents 仙傳拾遺 (*Xianzhuan shiyi*), by Du Guangting 杜光庭 (850–933).
Collected Conversations 談叢 (*Tancong*), cited as *A Concourse of Conversations*

談藪 (*Tansou*, Sui dynasty), by Yang Jiesong 陽玠松 (n.d.), in *The Imperial Digest of the Taiping Era* 太平御覽 (*Taiping yulan*, 984), by Li Fang 李昉 (925–996), chapter 4.

Collected Essentials about the Six Categories of Graphs 六書精蘊 (*Liushu jingyun*, 1540), by Wei Xiao 魏校 (1483–1543).

Collected Policies and Achievements 謨烈輯遺 (*Molie jiyi*, Ming dynasty) [?].

Collected Records from Court and Countryside 朝野僉載 (*Chaoye qianzai*), by Zhang Zhuo 張鷟 (657–730).

Collected Records of Anomalies 集異記 (*Jiyiji*, ca. 824), by Xue Yongruo 薛用弱 (fl. 824).

Collected Records of Anomalies 集異記 (*Jiyiji*, ca. 871), by Lu Xun 陸勳 (fl. 871).

Collected Records of Transcendents 集仙錄 (*Jixianlu*), by Du Guangting 杜光庭 (850–933).

Collected Stories from Jade Stream 玉溪編事 (*Yuxi bianshi*), by Jin Liyong 金利用 (fl. 934–965).

Collected Stories of Anomalies 集異傳 (*Jiyizhuan*), by Guo Jichan 郭季產 (Liu Song dynasty).

Collected Trifles from the Studio of Honesty 謇齋瑣綴錄 (*Jianzhai suochuolu*), by Yin Zhi 尹直 (1427–1511).

Collected Works from West River 西江集 (*Xijiangji*), by Wang Renyu 王仁裕 (880–956).

Collected Works of Han Changli 韓昌黎集 (*Han Changliji*), by Han Yu 韓愈 (768–824).

Collected Works of Siru 四如集 (*Siruji*), by Huang Zhongyuan 黃仲元 (1231–1312).

Collected Works of Song Jinglian 宋景濂文集 (*Song Jinglian wenji*), by Song Lian 宋濂 (1310–1381).

Collected Works of Su Dongpo 蘇東坡文集 (*Su Dongpo wenji*), by Su Shi 蘇軾 (1037–1101).

Collected Works of Yao Runeng 姚汝能集 (*Yao Runengji*), by Yao Runeng (fl. 762–779).

A Collection of Delectable Chicken Feet 雞跖集 (*Jizhiji*), cited in *Valley Embroidered with Myriad Flowers*, q.v., part I, chapter 18.

A Collection of Ivory Bodkins 佩觽集 (*Peixiji*), by Guo Zhongshu 郭忠恕 (d. 977).

A Collection of Strange Tales 異聞集 (*Yiwenji*, 874–875), by Chen Han 陳翰 (n.d.).

A Commentary on Su Dongpo's Poems 坡詩注 (*Po shizhu*), cited in *Valley Embroidered with Myriad Flowers*, q.v., part I, chapter 26.

Commentary on The Book of Songs 詩箋 (*Shijian*), by Zheng Xuan 鄭玄 (127–200).

Commentary on The Government Organization of the Zhou Dynasty 周禮注 (*Zhoulizhu*), by Zheng Xuan 鄭玄 (127–200).

The Compendium of Master Yan 宴子春秋 (*Yanzi chunqiu*, Warring States period), traditionally attributed to Yan Ying 宴嬰 (d. 500 BCE), but anon.

The Compendium of Mr. Lü 呂氏春秋 (*Lüshi chunqiu*, ca. 239 BCE), attributed to Lü Buwei 呂不韋 (d. 235 BCE) et al.

A Compendium on Tea 茶譜 (*Chapu*), cited in *An Encyclopedia from Mount Tianzhong* 天中記 (*Tianzhongji*), by Chen Yaowen 陳耀文 (fl. 1550), chapter 44.

List of Sources

The Complete Book on Writing 翰墨全書 (*Hanmo quanshu*, ca. 1307), also titled *A Newly Compiled Complete Book on Writing Arranged by Categories* 新編事文類聚翰墨全書 (*Xinbian shiwen leiju hanmo quanshu*), by Liu Yingli 劉應李 (fl. 1274).

Complete History of the Wu-Yue Dynasty 吳越備史 (*Wu-Yue beishi*, Song dynasty), by Fan Jiong 范坰 (n.d.) and Lin Yu 林禹 (n.d.).

Comprehensive Annals of the Ming Dynasty 皇明通紀 (*Huangming tongji*), also titled *Comprehensive Annals of the Ming Dynasty for Use in Government* 皇明資治通紀 (*Huangming zizhi tongji*), by Chen Jian 陳建 (1497–1567).

The Comprehensive Gazetteer 一統志 (*Yitongzhi*, 1461), also titled *The Comprehensive Gazetteer of the Great Ming*, 大明一統志 (*Da Ming yitongzhi*), by Li Xian 李賢 (1408–1467) et al.

The Comprehensive Mirror 通鑒 (*Tongjian*), also titled *The Comprehensive Mirror for Aid in Government* 資治通鑒 (*Zizhi tongjian*), by Sima Guang 司馬光 (1019–1086).

A Comprehensive Record of Strange Things 括異志 (*Kuoyizhi*), by Zhang Shizheng 張師正 (1016–ca. 1099).

A Concordance to the Divine Significance of The Book of Filial Piety 孝經援神契 (*Xiaojing yuanshenqi*, Han dynasty), anon.

A Continuation of A Garden of Strange Events 續異苑 (*Xuyiyuan*, ca. late 5th–early 7th cent.), anon.

A Continuation of A Record of Fates 續定命錄 (*Xudingminglu*, ca. 837–ca. 841), by Wen Yu 溫畬 (fl. 820–ca. 841).

A Continuation of A Record of Manifold Things 續博物志 (*Xubowuzhi*), by Li Shi 李石 (1108–after 1177).

A Continuation of A Record of Strange Events 續異記 (*Xuyiji*, late Liang or Sui dynasty), anon.

A Continuation of A Record of Strange Things 續怪錄 (*Xuguailu*), anon.

A Continuation of Accounts of Strange Events 續異錄 (*Xuyilu*), anon.

A Continuation of the History of the Han Dynasty 續漢書 (*Xuhanshu*), by Sima Biao 司馬彪 (d. 306).

A Continuation of the History of the Jin Dynasty [265–420] 續晉書 (*Xujinshu*), cited as *A Continuation of the Spring and Autumn Annals of the Jin Dynasty* 續晉陽秋 (*Xujin yangqiu*), by Tan Daoluan 檀道鸞 (Liu Song dynasty), in *The Imperial Digest of the Taiping Era* (*Taiping yulan* 太平御覽, 984), by Li Fang 李昉 (925–996), chapter 400.

A Continuation of The Treasury of Rhymes 續編韻府 (*Xubian yunfu*), by Bao Yu 包瑜 (fl. 1450–1456).

Conversations by a Fishing Jetty 釣磯立談 (*Diaoji litan*), by Shi Xubai 史虛白 (890–961).

Conversations from the Feudal States 國語 (*Guoyu*, Warring States period), anon.

Conversations Gathered by a Solitary Tree 孤樹裒談 (*Gushu poutan*), by Li Mo 李默 (fl. 1521–ca. 1566).

Conversations of a Guest in a Thatched Pavilion 茅亭客話 (*Maoting kehua*), by Huang Xiufu 黃休復 (fl. 1001–ca. 1021).

Conversations of Zhou 周語 (*Zhouyu*), in *Conversations from the Feudal States*, q.v.

Critical Rankings of Poets 詩品 (*Shipin*), by Zhong Rong 鍾嶸 (fl. 502–519).

Destinies Revealed by the Yellow River Diagram 河圖著命 (*Hetu zhuming*, Han dynasty), anon.

"Discussion of the Essentials of Diagnosis and of the Meridian System" 診要經絡論 ("Zhenyaojingluo lun"), in *Inner Canon of Medicine*, q.v.

"Discussion on Equalizing Everything" 齊物論 ("Qiwulun"), in *Master Zhuang*, q.v.

"Discussion on Diagnosing Overabundance and Deficiency of *Qi*-Energy" 方盛衰論 ("Fangshengshuai lun"), in *Inner Canon of Medicine*, q.v.

"Discussion on the Importance of Detecting the Subtle Vigor of the Pulse" 脈要精微論 ("Moyaojingwei lun"), in *Yellow Emperor's Inner Canon of Medicine*, i.e. *Inner Canon of Medicine*, q.v.

Discussions from a Gentleman in Hiding 潛夫論 (*Qianfulun*, ca. 111–152 CE), by Wang Fu 王符 (ca. 90–165 CE).

Discussions in the White Tiger Hall 白虎通 (*Bohutong*, ca. 79 CE), traditionally attributed to Ban Gu 班固 (32–92 CE).

The Divine Matchmaker's New Book 月老新書 (*Yuelao xinshu*, Southern Song dynasty), anon.

"The Diviner of Dreams" 占夢 ("Zhanmeng"), in *Government Organization of the Zhou*, q.v.

The Documents of Antiquity 尚書 (*Shangshu*, Zhou dynasty), anon.

Documents of the Zhou Dynasty 周書 (*Zhoushu*, late 4th–1st cent. BCE), also titled *Zhou Dynasty Documents Recovered from a Tomb* 汲冢周書 (*Jizhong zhoushu*), q.v.

Dream Manual 夢書 (*Mengshu*), traditionally attributed to Zhou Xuan 周宣 (d. ca. 239), but probably anon.

"A Dream of Brushes" 夢筆記 ("Mengbiji," 1226), by Huang Yuan 黃淵 (n.d.).

"Dreams Caused by Excessive and Perverse Energies" 淫邪發夢 ("Yinxie fameng"), in *The Yellow Emperor's Book of the Spiritual Pivot*, i.e. *Book of the Spiritual Pivot*, q.v.

"The Eldest Prince of King Wen" 文王世子 ("Wenwang shizi"), in *Book of Ritual*, q.v.

Elegant Chats from a Commandery Studio 郡閣雅談 (*Junge yatan*), by Wu Shu 吳淑 (fl. mid-10th cent.).

"Encomium on a Lion" 獅子贊 ("Shizizan"), by Zhang Jiuling 張九齡 (673 or 678–740).

Encyclopedia for Literary Composition 藝文類聚 (*Yiwen leiju*, 604), by Ouyang Xun 歐陽詢 (557–641) et al.

An Encyclopedia of Paired Historical and Literary Citations 事類合璧 (*Shilei hebi*, 1257), also titled *An Encylopedia of Important Paired Historical and Literary Citations Past and Present* 古今合璧事類備要 (*Gujin hebi shilei beiyao*), by Xie Weixin 謝維新 (n.d.).

The Encyclopedic History of Institutions 通典 (*Tongdian*, ca. 801), by Du You 杜佑 (735–812).

"Epitaph for Li Xuzhong" 李虛中墓銘 ("Li Xuzhong muming"), in *Collected Works of Han Changli*, q.v.

"Essay on the Double Seventh Festival" 乞巧文 ("Qiqiaowen"), also titled "Re-

ply on the Double Seventh Festival 乞巧對 ("Qiqiaodui"), in *The Collected Works of Sun Kezhi* 孫可之集 (*Sun Kezhiji*), by Sun Qiao 孫樵 (fl. 855).
Events Concerning An Lushan 安祿山事跡 (*An Lushan shiji*), by Yao Runeng 姚汝能 (fl. 762–779).
Events from the Epoch of the Three Sovereigns and Five Thearchs 三五歷記 (*Sanwu liji*, Wu dynasty) by Xu Zheng 徐整 (n.d.).
Events from the Imperial Capital 三輔皇圖 (*Sanfu huangtu*, Tang dynasty), anon.
Events of the Kaiyuan Era 開元遺事 (*Kaiyuan yishi*), also titled *Events of the Kaiyuan and Tianbao Eras*, q.v.
Events of the Kaiyuan and Tianbao Eras 開元天寶遺事 (*Kaiyuan tianbao yishi*), by Wang Renyu 王仁裕 (880–956).
Events of the Tianbao Era 天寶遺事 (*Tianbao yishi*), also titled *Events of the Kaiyuan and Tianbao Eras*, q.v.
Excellent Stories of the Sui and Tang Dynasties 隋唐嘉話 (*Sui Tang jiahua*), by Liu Su 劉餗 (fl. 742–755).
Exceptional Dreams 夢雋 (*Mengjuan*), by Liu Can 劉燦 (fl. 888–904).
Explanations and Analyses of Single and Composite Graphs 說文解字 (*Shuowen jiezi*, 100 CE), by Xu Shen 許慎 (n.d.).
Exquisite Words on the Origins of Surnames 姓源珠璣 (*Xingyuan zhuji*, ca. 1432), by Yang Xinmin 楊信民 (d. 1450).
An Extensive Record of Anomalies 廣異記 (*Guangyiji*, 806), by Dai Fu 戴孚 (ca. 724–ca. 794).
Extensive Records 廣記 [?].
Famous Chats from the Bureau of Writers 翰府名談 (*Hanfu mingtan*), by Liu Fu 劉斧 (fl. 11th cent.).
"The First Month" 正月 ("Zhengyue"), "Lesser Odes" 小雅 ("Xiaoya"), in *Book of Songs*, q.v.
Five Classics 五經 (*Wujing*), i.e. *Book of Songs, Documents of Antiquity, Book of Changes, Book of Ritual, Spring and Autumn Annals*, all q.v.
Forest of Jottings 志林 (*Zhilin*), also titled *Dongpo's Forest of Jottings* 東坡志林 (*Dongpo zhilin*), by Su Shi 蘇軾 (1037–1101).
Friendly Discussions at Cloud Stream 雲溪友議 (*Yunxi youyi*), by Fan Shu 范攄 (fl. 877).
Gan De's Long-Willow Method of Dream Interpretation 甘德長柳占夢 (*Gan De changliu zhanmeng*, Zhou dynasty), traditionally attributed to Gan De 甘德 (n.d.).
A Garden of Stories 說苑 (*Shuoyuan*), by Liu Xiang 劉向 (ca. 79–ca. 6 BCE).
A Garden of Strange Events 異苑 (*Yiyuan*), by Liu Jingshu 劉敬叔 (ca. 390–ca. 470).
Gathered Talks 摭言 (*Zhiyan*), by Wang Dingbao 王定保 (870–ca. 954).
Gazetteer of Changsha 長沙府志 (*Changsha fuzhi*).
Gazetteer of Hangzhou 杭志 (*Hangzhi*), cited in *Touring Guide to West Lake*, q.v.
Gazetteer of Shandong 山東通志 (*Shandong tongzhi*).
Gazetteer of the World during the Taiping Era 太平寰宇記 (*Taiping huanyuji*, 976–983), by Yue Shi 樂史 (930–1007).
A Giant Divination Tortoise for the Imperial Library 冊府元龜 (*Cefu yuangui*, 1013), by Wang Qinruo 王欽若 (962–1025) et al.

The Government Organization of the Zhou 周禮 (*Zhouli*, ca. 3rd cent. BCE), anon.

"The Grand Diviner" 大卜 ("Taibu"), in *Government Organization of the Zhou*, q.v.

Grand History 路史 (*Lushi*, 1170), by Luo Mi 羅泌 (n.d.).

"The Great Commentary" 大傳 ("Dazhuan," Han dynasty), in *Book of Changes*, q.v.

"The Great Plan" 洪範 ("Hongfan," Warring States period), in *Documents of Antiquity*, q.v.

"Green Diagram" 綠圖 ("Lütu").

A Grove of Pearls in the Dharma Garden 法苑珠林 (*Fayuan zhulin*, 668), by Daoshi 道世 (ca. 600–683).

The Guideways Through Mountains and Seas 山海經 (*Shanhaijing*, Warring States-Han), anon.

Historical Records 史記 (*Shiji*, ca. 91 BCE), by Sima Tan 司馬談 (d. ca. 110 BCE) and Sima Qian 司馬遷 (ca. 145–ca. 86 BCE).

"Historical Records" 史記 ("Shiji"), in *Zhou Dynasty Documents Recovered from a Tomb*, q.v.

History of the Chen Dynasty 陳書 (*Chenshu*, 622–629), by Yao Cha 姚察 (533–606) and Yao Silian 姚思廉 (d. 637).

History of the Eastern Han Dynasty 後漢書 (*Houhanshu*, 3rd cent.), by Xie Cheng 謝承 (n.d.).

History of the Eastern Han Dynasty 後漢書 (*Houhanshu*, 445), by Fan Ye 范曄 (398–445).

History of the Eastern Han Dynasty from the Dongguan Pavilion 東觀漢記 (*Dongguan hanji*, ca. 72–ca. 220), by Liu Zhen 劉珍 (d. after 126) et al.

History of the Five Dynasties 五代史 (*Wudaishi*, 974), by Xue Juzheng 薛居正 (912–981).

History of the Jin Dynasty 晉書 (*Jinshu*, 646), by Fang Xuanling 房玄齡 (578–648).

History of the Jin [Jurchen] Dynasty 金史 (*Jinshi*, 1344), by Toghto [Tuotuo] 脫脫 (1313–1355).

History of the Later Zhao Dynasty 趙書 (*Zhaoshu*), by Tian Rong 田融 (fl. 4th cent.).

History of the Liang Dynasty 梁書 (*Liangshu*, 636), by Yao Cha 姚察 (533–606) and Yao Silian 姚思廉 (d. 637).

History of the Liao Dynasty 遼史 (*Liaoshi*, 1344), by Toghto [Tuotuo] 脫脫 (1313–1355).

History of the Liu Song Dynasty 宋書 (*Songshu*, 492–493), by Shen Yue 沈約 (441–513).

History of the Northern Dynasties 北史 (*Beishi*, 659), by Li Yanshou 李延壽 (fl. 618–76).

History of the Northern Qi Dynasty 齊書 (*Qishu*, 636), compiled by Li Delin 李德林 (530–590) and Li Boyao 李百藥 (565–648).

History of the Northern Wei Dynasty 魏書 (*Weishu*, 554), by Wei Shou 魏收 (506–572).

History of the Northern Zhou Dynasty 後周書 (*Houzhoushu*, 636), by Linghu Defen 令狐德棻 (583–661).

List of Sources

History of the Shu Dynasty 蜀志 (*Shuzhi*, 297), by Chen Shou 陳壽 (233–297).
History of the Song Dynasty 宋史 (*Songshi*, 1345), by Toghto [Tuotuo] 脫脫 (1313–1355).
History of the Southern Dynasties 南史 (*Nanshi*, 659), by Li Yanshou 李延壽 (fl. 618–676).
History of the Southern Qi Dynasty 南齊書 (*Nanqishu*, 537), by Xiao Zixian 蕭子顯 (489–537).
History of the Sui Dynasty 隋書 (*Suishu*, 636), by Wei Zheng 魏徵 (580–643).
History of the Three Kingdoms 三國志 (*Sanguozhi*, 297), by Chen Shou 陳壽 (233–297).
History of the Wei Dynasty 魏志 (*Weizhi*, 297), by Chen Shou 陳壽 (233–297).
History of the Western Han Dynasty 漢書 (*Hanshu*, 92 CE), by Ban Gu 班固 (32–92 CE).
History of the Wu Dynasty 吳志 (*Wuzhi*, 297), by Chen Shou 陳壽 (233–297).
History of the Yuan Dynasty 元史 (*Yuanshi*, 1370), by Song Lian 宋濂 (1310–1381).
Illustrations of Auspicious Anomalies 瑞應圖 (*Ruiyingtu*), cited in "Memorial of Congratulations on the Appearance of a White Wolf Written on Behalf of Prefect Cheng of Weizhou" 為魏成使君賀白狼表 ("Wei Weizhou Cheng shijun he bailangbiao"), by Cui Rong 崔融 (653–706).
In Search of the Supernatural 搜神記 (*Soushenji*, ca. 335–ca. 349), by Gan Bao 干寶 (ca. 286–ca. 349).
"Influences and Abnormal Conditions" 感變篇 ("Ganbianpian"), in *Book of the Spiritual Pivot*, q.v.
The Inner Canon of Medicine 內經 (*Neijing*, ca. 2nd-1st cent. BCE), also titled *The Yellow Emperor's Inner Canon of Medicine* 黃帝內經 (*Huangdi neijing*), anon.
Intrigues of the Warring States 戰國策 (*Zhanguoce*, Warring States-late 1st cent. BCE), compiled by Liu Xiang 劉向 (79–8 BCE).
Investigations of Strange Events 甄異記 (*Zhenyiji*) [?].
Jottings from the East Belvedere 東軒筆錄 (*Dongxuan bilu*), by Wei Tai 魏泰 (fl. 11th–12th cent.).
Judicious Discussions 論衡 (*Lunheng*, ca. 70–80 CE), by Wang Chong 王充 (27–ca. 100 CE).
Laozi 老子 (3rd cent. BCE), also titled *The Way and Its Power* 道德經 (*Daodejing*), traditionally attributed to Lao Dan 老聃, a.k.a. Li Dan 李聃, Li Er 李耳 (trad. fl. late 6th–early 5th century BCE), but anon.
Leisure Notes from a Country Man 野人閑記 (*Yeren xianji*, 965), by Geng Huan 耿煥, a.k.a. Jing Huan 景煥 (fl. 965–984).
Leisurely Reading 閑覽 (*Xianlan*, Song dynasty), by Chen Zhengmin 陳正敏 (n.d.).
"Lesser Odes" 小雅 ("Xiaoya"), in *Book of Songs*, q.v.
The Literary Mind and the Carving of Dragons 文心雕龍 (*Wenxin diaolong*), by Liu Xie 劉勰 (ca. 466–ca. 538).
Liuchi duizhu 柳尺對主 [?].
Long Conversations by Thunder Lake 震澤長語 (*Zhenze changyu*), by Wang Ao 王鏊 (1450–1524).

The Lotus Sutra 法華經 (*Fahuajing*, 406), also titled *Scripture of the Lotus Blossom of the Fine Dharma* 妙法蓮華經 (*Miaofa lianhuajing*), translated by Kumārajīva, a.k.a. Jiuluoshi 鳩羅什 (ca. 350–410).

"Luo River Text" 洛書 ("Luoshu").

Luxuriant Dew of the Spring and Autumn Annals 春秋繁露 (*Chunqiu fanlu*, late 2nd cent. BCE), by Dong Zhongshu 董仲舒 (179–104 BCE).

Master Fu 符子 (*Fuzi*, Jin dynasty [265–420]), by Fu Lang 符朗 (n.d.).

Master Hanfei 韓非子 (*Hanfeizi*), by Han Fei 韓非 (ca. 280–ca. 233 BCE).

Master Lie 列子 (*Liezi*, ca. 4th cent.), traditionally attributed to Lie Yukou 列禦寇 (trad. fl. 400 BCE), but anon.

Master Mo 墨子 (*Mozi*, ca. late 4th cent. BCE), traditionally attributed to Mo Di 墨翟 (fl. late 4th cent. BCE).

Master of Huainan 淮南子 (*Huainanzi*, ca. 139 BCE), compiled under Liu An 劉安 (ca. 179–122 BCE).

Master of Plants and Trees 草木子 (*Caomuzi*), by Ye Ziqi 葉子奇 (fl. late 14th cent.).

Master of the Golden Tower 金樓子 (*Jinlouzi*, ca. 523), by Xiao Yi 蕭繹 (508–554), a.k.a. Prince Yi of Xiangdong 湘東王繹.

Master Shi 尸子 (*Shizi*), by Shi Jiao 尸佼 (ca. 390–ca. 330 BCE).

The Master Who Embraces Simplicity 抱朴子 (*Baopuzi*), by Ge Hong 葛洪 (ca. 283–343 or 363).

Master Xun 荀子 (*Xunzi*), by Xun Qing 荀卿 (ca. 335–ca. 238 BCE).

Master Yang 揚子 (*Yangzi*, ca. 9 CE), also titled *Master Yang's Exemplary Sayings* 揚子法言 (*Yangzi fayan*), by Yang Xiong 揚雄 (53 BCE–18 CE).

Master Zhuang 莊子 (*Zhuangzi*, ca. 3rd cent. BCE), traditionally attributed to Zhuang Zhou 莊周 (trad. fl. 4th cent. BCE), but anon.

"Memorial Requesting a Court Audience" 清朝覲表 ("Qingchaojinbiao"), by Liu Yuxi 劉禹錫 (772–842).

"Memorial Requesting a Court Audience Composed for Vice Censor-in-chief Cui" 為崔中承請朝表 ("Wei Cuizhongcheng qingchaobiao," 816), by Liu Zongyuan 柳宗元 (773–819).

Mencius 孟子 (*Mengzi*, late 4th cent. BCE), traditionally attributed to Meng Ke 孟軻 (fl. ca. 320 BCE), but anon.

Miscellaneous Morsels from Youyang 酉陽雜俎 (*Youyang zazu*, ca. 850), by Duan Chengshi 段成式 (803–863).

A Miscellany from Duyang 杜陽編 (*Duyangbian*), also titled *Duyang zabian* 杜楊雜編), by Su E 蘇鶚 (fl. 886).

The Movements of the Stars in the Dipper 運斗樞 (*Yundoushu*, Han dynasty), also titled *The Movements of the Stars in the Dipper in the Spring and Autumn Annals* 春秋運斗樞 (*Chunqiu yundoushu*), anon.

Mr. Liu's Accounts of Past Events 柳氏舊聞 (*Liushi jiuwen*), by Li Deyu 李德裕 (787–849).

Mr. Lü's Readings of The Book of Songs 呂氏讀詩記 (*Lüshi dushiji*), by Lü Zuqian 呂祖謙 (1137–1181).

Mr. Shao's Records 邵氏錄 (*Shaoshilu*, 1132), also titled *Mr. Shao's Records of Things Heard and Seen* (*Shaoshi wenjianlu* 邵氏聞見錄), by Shao Bowen 邵伯溫 (1056–1134).

List of Sources

Mr. Sun's Illustrations of Auspicious Things 孫氏瑞應圖 (*Sunshi ruiyingtu*, Liang–Chen dynasties), by Sun Rouzhi 孫柔之 (n.d.).

Mr. Wang's Record of Things Heard and Seen 王氏聞見錄 (*Wangshi wenjianlu*, 941), by Wang Renyu 王仁裕 (880–956).

Mr. Xin's Record of the Three-Qin Region 辛氏三秦記 (*Xinshi sanqinji*), by Mr. Xin 辛 (possibly Jin dynasty [265–420]).

Narrations of Strange Events 述異記 (*Shuyiji*), anon. [?].

A New Account of Tales of the World 世說新語 (*Shishuo xinyu*, ca. 430), by Liu Yiqing 劉義慶 (403–444).

New Discussions 新論 (*Xinlun*, 26 CE), by Huan Tan 桓譚 (ca. 23 BCE–56 CE, or ca. 43 BCE–28 CE).

New History of the Tang Dynasty 新唐書 (*Xintangshu*, 1060), by Ouyang Xiu 歐陽修 (1007–1072).

A New Version of Mr. Zhou's Manual for Interpreting Dreams 新集周公解夢書 (*Xinji Zhougong jiemengshu*, 966), traditionally attributed to Zhou Xuan 周宣 (d. ca. 239), but anon.

New Writings 新書 (*Xinshu*), by Jia Yi 賈誼 (201–169 BCE).

New Writings from Nanbu 南部新書 (*Nanbu xinshu*, ca. 1008–ca. 1016), by Qian Yi 錢易 (983–after 1017).

The Newly Expanded Treasury of Rhymes 新增韻府 (*Xinzeng yunfu*), possibly an expanded edition of *Assembled Jade Words in the Treasury of Rhymes* 韻府群玉 (*Yunfu qunyu*), by Yin Shifu 陰時夫 (fl. 13th cent.) [?].

"No Sheep?" 無羊 ("Wuyang?"), "Lesser Odes" 小雅 ("Xiaoya"), in *Book of Songs*, q.v.

Notes Compiled While Weary from Traveling 倦遊錄 (*Juanyoulu*), by Zhang Shizheng 張師正 (fl. 1059–1099).

"The Oaths of Tai" 泰誓 ("Taishi"), in *The Documents of Zhou* 周書 (*Zhoushu*), in *Documents of Antiquity*, q.v.

Ocean of Chapters According to the Five Sounds 五音篇海 (*Wuyin pianhai*), by Han Xiaoyan 韓孝彥 (fl. 12th cent.).

Ocean of Jade 玉海 (*Yuhai*), by Wang Yinglin 王應麟 (1223–1296).

An Ocean of Rhymes 韻海 (*Yunhai*) [?].

Old History of the Tang Dynasty 舊唐書 (*Jiutangshu*, 945), by Liu Xu 劉昫 (887–946).

Omitted History of the Tang Dynasty 唐闕史 (*Tangqueshi*, 884), by Zhang Yanxiu 張彥休 (854–?).

An Outline of History 史略 (*Shilue*), by Gao Sisun 高似孫 (fl. 1184).

Ouyang Xiu's Remarks on Poetry 歐陽詩話 (*Ouyang shihua*), by Ouyang Xiu 歐陽修 (1007–1072).

Past and Present Records about the Five Agents from the Tang Dynasty 唐古今五行記 (*Tanggujin wuxingji*), by Dou Weiwu 竇維鋈 (n.d.), cited in *Taiping Miscellany*, q.v., chapter 142.

Past Events from the Eastern Studio 東齋遺事 (*Dongzhai yishi*) [?].

Penetrating Discussions about Environments and Local Cultures 風俗通義 (*Fengsu tongyi*, ca. 194–ca. 204), by Ying Shao 應劭 (ca. 140–ca. 204).

"A Poem Harmonizing with Ouyang Xiu's 'Poem on a Son's First Bath,'" 和永叔洗兒詩 ("He Yongshu xiershi"), by Mei Yaochen 梅堯臣 (1002–1060).

"Poem on Ascending to Heaven" 昇天詩 ("Shengtianshi"), by Li He 李賀 (790–816).

Poems and Their Events 本事詩 (*Benshishi*), by Meng Qi 孟棨 (fl. 875–ca. 904).

The Poems of Wang Jiefu 王介甫詩 (*Wang Jiefu shi*), by Wang Anshi 王安石 (1021–1086).

Precedents of Emperor Wu of the Western Han 漢武故事 (*Hanwu gushi*, ca. 3rd cent.), anon.

"A Preface to a Poem" 詩序 ("Shixu"), cited in *Valley Embroidered with Myriad Flowers*, q.v., part I, chapter 18.

"Preface to Rhapsody on Mount Luofu" 羅浮山賦序 ("Luofushanfu xu"), by Xie Lingyun 謝靈運 (385–433).

"Preface to Rhapsody on the Gaotang Shrine" 高唐賦序 ("Gaotangfu xu"), traditionally attributed to Song Yu 宋玉 (ca. 290–ca. 223 BCE).

The Private History of the Guardian of the City Gate 關令內傳 (*Guanling neizhuan*, Northern and Southern dynasties), by Mr. Guigu 鬼谷先生 (n.d.), cited in *Encyclopedia for Literary Composition*, q.v., chapter 78.

"Proclamation on the Execution of the Buddhists" 誅戮沙門詔 ("Zhulu shamenzhao"), by Emperor Shizu of the Northern Wei 魏世祖 (r. 423–451), in *History of the Northern Wei Dynasty*, q.v.

A Profusion of Primal Qi and Ruling Mandates in The Spring and Autumn Annals 春秋元命苞 (*Chunqiu yuanmingbao*, Han dynasty), anon.

Pure Conversations from Yuhu 玉壺清話 (*Yuhu qinghua*, 1078), also titled *Unofficial History from Yuhu* 玉壺野史 (*Yuhu yeshi*), by Wenying 文瑩 (n.d.).

Qi Xie's Records 齊諧記 (*Qi Xieji*), by Dongyang Wuyi 東陽無疑 (fl. 1st half of 5th cent.).

The Qilin Classic 麟經 (*Linjing*), i.e. *Spring and Autumn Annals*, q.v.

Random Notes 雜記 (*Zaji*, Jin dynasty [265–420]), anon.

Random Notes from a Green Box of Knowledge 青箱雜記 (*Qingxiang zaji*), by Wu Chuhou 吳處厚 (fl. 1053–ca. 1093).

Random Notes from the Western Capital 西京雜記 (*Xijing zaji*), traditionally attributed to Liu Xin 劉歆 (53 BCE–23 CE) or Ge Hong 葛洪 (ca. 283–343 or 363).

Random Notes on Things Seen and Heard 見聞雜錄 (*Jianwen zalu*), cited in *Valley Embroidered with Myriad Flowers*, q.v., part II, chapter 29.

Recent Events of the Southern Tang Dynasty 南唐近事 (*Nantang jinshi*, 977), by Zheng Wenbao 鄭文寶 (953–1013).

"A Record of a Dream of Brushes" 夢筆記 ("Mengbiji," 1226), by Huang Yuan 黃淵 (n.d.).

A Record of a Purposeful Mind 存心錄 (*Cunxinlu*), by Wu Chen 吳沉 (d. 1386) et al.

"A Record of a Strange Dream" 異夢記 ("Yimengji," ca. 827), also titled "A Record of a Dream in Qin" 秦夢記 ("Qingmengji"), by Shen Yazhi 沈亞之 (781–832).

A Record of an Expedition 述征記 (*Shuzhengji*, Jin dynasty [265–420]), by Guo Yuansheng 郭緣生 (n.d.).

A Record of Auspicious Signs 貞祥記 (*Zhenxiangji*) [?], also cited as *A Record of Signs from the Unseen Realm* 冥祥記 (*Mingxiangji*), by Wang Yan 王琰 (ca. 454–early 6th cent.), cited in *Taiping Miscellany*, q.v., chapter 276.

List of Sources

A Record of Cautionary Examples 鑒戒錄 (*Jianjielu*), by He Guangyuan 何光遠 (fl. ca. 938).
A Record of Collected Strange Events 紀異錄 (*Jiyilu*, ca. 968–976), by Qin Zaisi 秦再思 (fl. 981).
A Record of Communications with the Other World 通幽記 (*Tongyouji*), by Chen Shao 陳劭 (fl. ca. 780–805).
A Record of Dunhuang 敦煌錄 (*Dunhuanglu*), by Liu Bing 劉昞 (fl. early 5th cent.).
A Record of Events from the Eastern Studio 東齋記事 (*Dongzhai jishi*, ca. 1078–1085), by Fan Zhen 范鎮 (1008–1089).
A Record of Fates 定命錄 (*Dingminglu*), by Lü Daosheng 呂道生 (fl. ca. 827–840).
A Record of Festivals 歲時記 (*Suishiji*), cited in *Valley Embroidered with Myriad Flowers*, q.v., part II, chapter 4.
A Record of Ghosts and Other Strange Things 幽怪錄 (*Youguailu*), by Niu Sengru 牛僧孺 (779–847).
A Record of Ghosts and the Living 幽明錄 (*Youminglu*), by Liu Yiqing 劉義慶 (403–444).
A Record of Guiji 會稽記 (*Guijiji*, Liu Song dynasty), by Kong Lingfu 孔靈符 (n.d.).
A Record of Inner Light 葆光錄 (*Baoguanglu*, ca. 997–1022), by Chen Zuan 陳纂 (n.d.).
A Record of Inquests into Spirits 稽神錄 (*Jishenlu*, 935–955), by Xu Xuan 徐鉉 (917–992).
A Record of Inquests into Strange Events 稽異錄 (*Jiyilu*) [?].
A Record of Linyi 林邑記 (*Linyiji*, ca. Northern and Southern Dynasties), anon., cited in *Taiping Miscellany*, q.v., chapter 276.
A Record of Longcheng 龍城錄 (*Longchenglu*), traditionally attributed to Liu Zongyuan 劉宗元 (773–819).
A Record of Manifold Things 博物志 (*Bowuzhi*), by Zhang Hua 張華 (232–300).
A Record of Mist and Flowers 煙花錄 (*Yanhualu*), cited in *Valley Embroidered with Myriad Flowers*, q.v., part I, chapter 23.
A Record of Mr. Wang's Conversations, 王氏談錄 (*Wangshi tanlu*), by Wang Zhu 王洙 (997–1057), compiled by Wang Qinchen 王欽臣 (fl. ca. 11th cent.).
A Record of Penetration into Mysterious Realms 洞冥記 (*Dongmingji*, ca. 6th–7th cent.), also titled *A Record of Emperor Wu of the Han's Penetration into the Mysteries of Outlying Realms* 漢武別國洞明記 (*Hanwu bieguo dongmingji*), traditionally attributed to Guo Xian 郭憲 (ca. 26 BCE–ca. 55 CE), but anon.
A Record of Retributions 報應錄 (*Baoyinglu*), by Wang Gu 王轂 (fl. 898).
A Record of Romances 抒情記 (*Shuqingji*), cited as *Romantic Poems* 抒情詩 (*Shuqingshi*), in *Taiping Miscellany*, q.v., chapter 279.
A Record of Selected Strange Events 甄異記 (*Zhenyiji*), by Dai Zuo 戴祚 (late Eastern Jin dynasty [317–420]).
A Record of Stories 說錄 (*Shuolu*) [?].
A Record of Strange Events 異錄 (*Yilu*) [?].
A Record of Strange Things Heard 異聞錄 (*Yiwenlu*), cited in *Valley Embroidered with Myriad Flowers*, q.v., part I, chapter 3.

A Record of Textual Studies 丹鉛錄 (*Danqianlu*), by Yang Shen 楊慎 (1488–1559).

A Record of the Excellent Conversations of Liu Binke 劉賓客嘉話錄 (*Liu Binke jiahualu*, 856), by Liu Yuxi 劉禹錫 (772–842), compiled by Wei Xuan 韋絢 (fl. ca. 821–ca. 859).

A Record of the Founding Destiny of the Ming Dynasty 皇明啟運錄 (*Huangming qiyunlu*, Ming dynasty), by Shao Xiang 邵相 (n.d.).

A Record of the Lands South of Mount Hua 華陽國志 (*Huayangguozhi*), by Chang Qu 常璩 (fl. 265–316).

A Record of the Transmission of the Lamp 傳燈錄 (*Chuandenglu*, ca. 1004–1007), by Daoyuan 道原 (n.d.).

"A Record of Three Dreams" 三夢記 ("Sanmengji," ca. 809–826), by Bo Xingjian 白行簡 (775–826).

A Record of Unusual Things Heard 聞奇錄 (*Wenqilu*, late Tang dynasty), anon.

A Record of Wu 吳錄 (*Wulu*, before 14th cent.), by Zhang Bo 張勃 (n.d.).

Recorded Stories 傳載 (*Chuanzai*, Tang dynasty), also titled *Recorded Stories of the Great Tang Dynasty* 大唐傳載 (*Datang chuanzai*), anon.

Records from the Grand Hall 宣室志 (*Xuanshizhi*, ca. 852), by Zhang Du 張讀 (834–after 881).

Records from the Treasure Cabinet 寶櫃記 (*Baoduji*, Ming dynasty), anon.

Recovered Biographies of Transcendents 仙傳拾遺 (*Xianzhuan shiyi*), by Du Guangting 杜光庭 (850–933).

Recovered Records from the Daye Era 大業拾遺 (*Daye shiyi*), also titled *A Record of Southern Mists and Flowers* 南部煙花錄 (*Nanbu yanhualu*), traditionally attributed to Yan Shigu 顏師古 (581–645), but anon.

Reliable Accounts of the Kaiyuan and Tianbao Eras 開天傳信記 (*Kaitian chuanxinji*), by Meng Qi 孟棨 (fl. 875–ca. 904).

Remarks While at Leisure from Watering the Fields 灌畦暇語 (*Guanqi xiayu*, Tang dynasty), anon.

"Rhapsody on a Dream" 夢賦 ("Mengfu"), by Wang Yanshou 王延壽 (fl. mid-2nd cent. BCE).

"Rhapsody on the Gaotang Shrine" 高唐賦 ("Gaotangfu"), traditionally attributed to Song Yu 宋玉 (ca. 290–ca. 223 BCE).

"Rhapsody on the Goddess" 神女賦 ("Shennüfu"), traditionally attributed to Song Yu 宋玉 (ca. 290–ca. 223 BCE).

"Rhapsody on the Great Man" 大人賦 ("Darenfu"), by Sima Xiangru 司馬相如 (179–117 BCE).

"Rhapsody on the *Peng*-bird" 大鵬賦 ("Dapengfu"), by Shen Hui 沈晦 (1084–1149).

"Rhapsody on the Sweet Spring" 甘泉賦 ("Ganquanfu"), by Yang Xiong 揚雄 (53 BCE–18 CE).

"Rhapsody on the Two Capitals" 兩都賦 ("Liangdufu"), by Sang Yue 桑悅 (1447–1513).

The Right-Hand Concordance to the Book of Filial Piety 孝經右契 (*Xiaojing youqi*, Han dynasty), anon.

Secrets of Chess 棋訣 (*Qijue*), cited in *A Deep Ocean of Records* 記纂淵海 (*Jizuan yuanhai*), by Pan Zimu 潘自牧 (fl. 1196), chapter 88.

List of Sources

Six Classics 六經 (the *Five Classics*, q.v., plus *The Book of Music* 樂經 (*Yuejing*, Zhou dynasty).

The Spring and Autumn Annals of Han and Jin 漢晉春秋 (*Han Jin chunqiu*), by Xi Zuochi 習鑿齒 (d. ca. 384).

The Spring and Autumn Annals of Wu and Yue 吳越春秋 (*Wu Yue chunqiu*), traditionally attributed to Zhao Ye 趙曄 (fl. 40–80 CE).

The Spring and Autumn Annals 春秋 (*Chunqiu*, Warring States period), anon.

Stories of Encounters with Divine Transcendents 神仙感遇傳 (*Shenxian ganyuzhuan*), by Du Guangting 杜光庭 (850–933).

A Summary of Ritual 禮統 (*Litong*), by He Shu 賀述 (Liang dynasty).

A Summary of the Canons of the Three Kingdom, 三國典略 (*Sanguo dianlue*), by Qiu Yue 丘悅 (fl. early 8th cent.).

"Summer Officials" 夏官 ("*Xiaguan*"), in *Government Organization of the Zhou*, q.v.

A Supplemental History 逸史 (*Yishi*), by Lu Zhao 盧肇 (fl. 843–ca. 873) .

The Sutra of the Buddha of Measureless Life 無量壽經 (*Wuliangshoujing*, ca. 252), traditionally translated by Sengkai of Sogdiana, a.k.a. Kang Sengkai 康僧鎧.

The Taiping Miscellany 太平廣記 (*Taiping guangji*, 978), by Li Fang 李昉 (925–996).

"Tan Gong" 檀弓 ("*Tan Gong*"), in *Book of Ritual*, q.v.

A Touring Guide to West Lake 西湖遊覽志 (*Xihu youlanzhi*, 1547), by Tian Rucheng 田汝成 (1526–1547).

Transcriptions of Historical Events 史節鈔 (*Shijiechao*) [?].

Transmissions of Unique Events 傳奇 (*Chuanqi*), by Pei Xing 裴鉶 (825–880).

"Treatise on Arts and Literature" 藝文志 ("*Yiwenzhi*"), in *History of the Western Han Dynasty*, q.v.

"Treatise on Astronomy" 天文志 ("*Tianwenzhi*"), in *History of the Western Han Dynasty*, q.v.

Treatise on Astronomy in an Era of National Revival 中興天文志 (*Zhongxing tianwenzhi*, Northern Song dynasty), anon.

"Treatise on the Five Agents" 五行志 ("*Wuxingzhi*"), in *History of the Jin [Jurchen] Dynasty*, q.v.

Trifling Conversations 瑣語 (*Suoyu*, Warring States period), anon.

Trifling Discussions of Su Dongpo's Poetry 胅說坡詩 (*Cuoshuo Poshi*), by Zhang Junfang 張君房 [?].

Trifling Words from Beimeng 北夢瑣言 (*Beimeng suoyan*), by Sun Guangxian 孫光憲 (d. 968).

True Stories from a Government Minister 尚書故實 (*Shangshu gushi*), by Li Chuo 李綽 (ca. 805–ca. 862).

An Unofficial Biography of Emperor Wu of the Western Han 漢武帝內傳 (*Hanwudi neizhuan*, late Eastern Han dynasty), anon.

An Unofficial History of Jiangnan 江南野史 (*Jiangnan yeshi*, Song dynasty), by Long Gun 龍袞 (n.d.).

An Unofficial Record from Mount Xiang 湘山野錄 (*Xiangshan yelu*, ca. 1068–1077), by Wenying 文瑩 (n.d.).

Unworldly Chats 麈談 (*Zhutan*) [?].

The Valley Embroidered with Myriad Flowers 錦繡萬花谷 (*Jinxiu wanhuagu*, 1188), anon.

Wang Zinian's Recovered Records 王子年拾遺記 (*Wang Zinian shiyiji*), by Wang Jia 王嘉 (d. before 393).

"The World Inside a Pillow" 枕中記 ("*Zhenzhongji*"), by Shen Jiji 沈既濟 (ca. 740–ca. 800).

The Yellow Emperor's Book of the Spiritual Pivot. See *Book of the Spiritual Pivot.*

The Yellow Emperor's Inner Canon of Medicine. See *Inner Canon of Medicine.*

The Yellow Emperor's Long-Willow Method of Dream Interpretation 黃帝長柳占夢 (*Huangdi changliu zhanmeng*, Zhou dynasty), anon.

"Yellow River Diagram" 河圖 ("*Hetu*").

The Yellow River Diagram Offered as an Aid to the Emperor 河圖挺佐輔 (*Hetu tingzuofu*, Han dynasty), anon.

Yijian's Accounts 夷堅志 (*Yijianzhi*, ca. 1142–1202), by Hong Mai 洪邁 (1123–1202).

The Younger Dai's Book of Ritual 小戴禮記 (*Xiaodai liji*, Eastern Han dynasty), traditionally attributed to Dai Sheng 戴聖 (1st cent. BCE), but anon.

Yue's Destruction of Wu 越絕書 (*Yuejueshu*), by Yuan Kang 袁康 (fl. 40 CE).

Zhou Dynasty Documents Recovered from a Tomb 汲冢周書 (*Jizhong zhoushu*, late 4th–1st cent. BCE), also titled *Recovered Documents of the Zhou Dynasty* 逸周書 (*Yizhoushu*), anon.

Zuo's Narratives to the Spring and Autumn Annals 春秋左傳 (*Chunqiu zuozhuan*, Warring States period), traditionally attributed to Zuo Qiuming 左丘明 (trad. fl. 5th cent. BCE), but anon.

Index

altars, 6n5, 71n18, 73n23, 89n2, 145n40, 164n27, 196n10, 223n11, 232nn20,23. *See also* sacrifices; temples
ancestors, 56n3, 71n20, 72n22, 74n26, 87n15, 103, 106n12, 121, 143n23, 144n30, 174n24, 193, 196n10, 205n68, 206n78, 209, 214n32, 216, 217n7, 220, 225n35, 228, 235n2, 244
animals, 220–227. *See also individual species*
armies, 67, 73n25, 92, 109, 112n10, 124n19, 125n24, 127n34, 132n7, 133n11, 145n38, 151n19, 153n34, 170, 175n26, 177, 195n9, 225n35, 232n20, 234, 237n16, 240, 242n21, 247n11, 255n15. *See also* soldiers
armor, 73n23, 147, 148n3, 153n34, 188n44, 206n77
asterisms. *See* stars
aunts, 114n28, 218n10

bandits, 136n35, 189n46, 196n16, 202n53, 220, 223n10
beards (including moustaches and whiskers), 69n8, 112n10, 130, 133n11, 134n17, 135n27, 176n33, 177, 179n3, 194n4, 200n42
bears, 66, 67, 71n18, 76n32, 97n18, 106n12, 220, 222nn5,6
beasts, 90n5, 145n36
bedrooms, 70n14, 92, 104n2, 110n3, 111n6, 134n18, 147, 150n17, 156n26, 200n44, 202n58, 206nn76,77, 220, 223n10, 226n38, 235n1

beds, 74n26, 111n6, 136n33, 157n18, 168n36, 192, 193, 196n18, 197nn22,26, 205n68, 218n12, 223n11, 226n36, 238n16, 248n15
birds, 66, 67, 71n18, 73n23, 86n14, 95n5, 166n31, 168n37, 215–219, 234, 251, 253n2; *chi-* and *fu-*owl 鴟, 鵩, 215, 218n15; chicken, 111n5, 215, 216, 218nn12,15; crane, 165n29, 194, 207n80, 215, 216, 218nn14,16, 17; crow, 90n6, 162n15, 215, 216, 217n7, 219n23, 228; duck, 250n30; eagle, 215; *feng-* and *fenghuang*-bird 鳳, 鳳凰, 116, 117n12, 215, 216, 216n1–217n6, 217n8, 218n11, 222n2; *fu*-duck 鳧, 215; goose, 73n23, 216, 218n16; hawk, 215; *luan*-bird 鸞, 167n35; magpie, 215, 216; mynah 249n27; osprey, 215; parrot, 216, 218n18, 219n19; peacock, 215, 216, 219n24; *peng*-bird 鵬, 178, 184n26; pheasant, 74n26, 140, 145n34, 146n45, 215, 216, 217n9, 245; swallow, 154, 155n9, 215, 216, 218n13; swan, 215; vermillion bird 朱雀 *(zhuque)*, 187n39; wagtail, 215; *yuezhuo*-bird 鷾鷿, 217n8; *yiyu*-bird 鶂鶂, 88, 90n6
birth (including pregnancy), 56n5, 70nn11,12–14, 72n22, 74n26, 75n28, 78, 79n2, 80, 97n18, 103, 108, 109, 110, 110nn2–5, 111nn6,7, 112n15, 113n16,17, 114nn28–30, 115, 116, 116nn1,2, 117n6,8,9,12, 118n19, 120, 124n17, 127nn34,39, 129n48, 130, 132n3, 133nn10,15,

273

birth (including pregnancy) *(continued)*
134n16, 136n33, 139, 140nn2,6,
141n10, 143nn22–25, 144nn27,28,
145n35, 146nn42,43, 147, 148,
149n8, 150n17, 151nn18,20,21,
152n26, 154, 155nn1–5,8,9,
156n13, 157n20, 158, 160n4,
173n19, 180n10, 193, 194, 194n1,
203n62, 204n67, 205nn68–71,
206nn75–78, 207nn79–81, 208,
209n1, 215, 216, 217nn3–5,7,9,
218nn12,13, 220, 222nn5,6,
223n10, 225n27, 226nn38,44, 228,
229, 230nn1,2,4,6–8, 232n22,
233n29, 234, 236n4, 237n10, 240,
240n7, 241n11, 242nn14,16, 245,
248n16, 249nn27,28, 252, 255n16.
See also reincarnation
blood, 92, 131, 136n35, 173n17,
189n46, 202n53, 224n23, 232n26,
244, 246n7, 247n11
boats, 66, 68n2, 69n5, 92, 103, 104n3,
105n9, 122n1, 126n30, 130,
133nn13,15, 134n16, 136n32,
147, 148, 151n24, 152n27,
153nn31,32, 34, 157n22, 166n30,
177, 180n11, 185n31, 186n34,
190n50, 192, 212n20, 213n24,
217n9, 224nn21,24, 228, 231n13,
238n18, 241n13
body, 25, 55–56, 56n5, 57n9, 60,
62n6, 68n3, 69n8, 71n19, 73n24,
74nn26,27, 78, 79nn2,3, 5, 80,
91–94, 94n1, 95nn3,4, 96n11,
97n18, 108, 109, 110nn1–4,
111nn5–7, 112nn13, 113nn16,17,22,
114nn28,29, 115, 116, 116n2,
117nn8,9,12, 118n18, 122n2, 130,
131, 132nn5,10, 133nn11,13,15,
134nn16,19, 135nn23,24,
136nn29,31, 139, 140n6,
143nn22,23, 145n41, 146nn43,45,
147, 150n17, 151n18, 152n26,
153n32, 154, 155nn3,9, 156n11,
157n22, 158, 160n5, 175n31,
186n33, 187n38, 194, 195n8,
198n33, 199n38, 207nn80,81,
211n17, 215, 216, 217nn4,5,
218n13, 223n18, 225n36, 226n44,
228, 229, 229n1, 230nn2,4,6,
232n27, 233nn28,29, 235, 235n1,
237n15, 238n16, 239, 240n7,
247n13, 252, 253n1, 254nn7,8,10.
See also specific body parts
bones and skeletons, 26, 92, 179n5, 244,
245, 246n4, 247n13, 248nn17,22
Book of Changes, The 易經 *(Yijing)*,
59n5, 99n18, 138, 140n4, 141n8,
159, 164n24, 172n17, 191, 203n61,
208, 210nn7,8, 204n66, 232n20,
234. *See also* trigrams
Book of Documents, The 書經 *(Shujing,*
a.k.a. *Documents of Antiquity* 尚書
[*Shangshu*]), 67, 191, 204n66
Book of Songs, The 詩經 *(Shijing)*, 67,
76n32, 97n18, 191, 204n66, 220,
229
books, 51, 58n1, 66, 67, 68n2, 69nn5,7,
70n15, 87n16, 89n2, 116, 118n19,
123n13, 124n18, 130, 131, 136n34,
138, 140n3, 142n17, 143n20,
146n42, 149n9, 159, 160n3, 165n30,
168n39, 185n30, 191, 192, 202n57,
204n66, 207n79, 209, 217n6, 220,
222n1, 229, 231n17, 234, 252. *See
also specific titles;* dream manuals;
texts
boys (including youths), 66, 67, 69n5,
70n10, 75n27, 90n5, 106n12,
112n10, 114n30, 127n38, 130,
131nn2,9, 134n25, 139, 140nn2,7,
141nn8,11, 142nn18,19, 143n25,
144n27, 146n43, 151n18, 156n11,
158, 159n3, 160nn4,5, 165n29,
176n33, 179n4, 192, 193, 197n26,
200n41, 203n63, 205n70, 206n75,
207n79, 209n2, 217n8, 219n25,
220, 221, 222n1, 236n4, 241n11,
245, 245n2, 249n27
brains, 72n21, 97n18, 130
brothers, 3, 75n27, 153n32, 159,
167n34, 170, 172n17, 175n28,
179n4, 204n65, 211nn17,18,
213n22, 215, 224n21, 230n4
brushes, ii, 113n17, 134n17, 139,
144n34, 158–168, 161n9, 174n24,
210n5
Buddha, 40n39, 131, 136n34, 140n1,
195n8
Buddhism (including Buddhist monks
and priests), 21, 40n39, 41nn41,42,
66, 68n1, 78, 114n29, 117n10, 121,
125n21, 138, 140n1, 141nn7,11,
142n17, 147, 148, 150n15,
152nn25,28, 154, 155n2, 157n22,
162n17, 169, 174nn21,22, 178,
184n29, 186n35, 194, 194n3,
195n8, 206nn78,79, 215, 217nn4,5,
220, 223n16, 238n16, 240, 243n27,
245, 249n27, 250n29, 252, 254n11.
See also Buddha; reincarnation;
temples
burials and funerals, 19, 73n25, 86n14,
94, 107n15, 129n46, 141n13,

Index

146n41, 153n32, 156n12, 164n27, 165n28, 175n31, 176n33, 177, 179n5, 180n12, 199n39, 200n45, 204n65, 205n74, 209, 211n17, 213n24, 214n33, 218n11, 221, 245, 246nn3,9, 247n13, 248nn17, 20, 249nn22,24,27, 250n28. *See also* coffins; tombs
buttocks, 91, 92, 131, 137n37

carriages and chariots, 15, 25, 60, 61n4, 68n2, 70n10, 96n10, 109, 113nn20,23, 145n37, 148, 152nn25,27, 153n33, 164nn25,27, 168n36, 169, 172n15, 173n18, 198n33, 199n40, 220, 222n8, 253nn1,3
cat, 188n43
caves, 68n3, 120, 192, 199n37, 203n62, 244, 245n2
chess 圍棋 *(weiqi)*. *See* games
children, 78, 79nn3,4, 110, 127n39, 151n20, 155n2, 181n13, 194n1, 207n80, 218n12, 249n28. *See also* boys; daughters; girls; sons
Chinese characters. *See* graphs
cities and towns, 69n8, 92, 107n17, 121, 122nn1,8, 123nn10,13, 124n19, 125nn22,27, 126n31, 127nn38,39, 128nn41,44, 139, 144n32, 147, 151n19, 152n27, 156n12, 158, 160n4, 163nn19,20, 165nn28,30, 166n31, 167n34, 168n36, 170n2, 179n6, 180n9, 181n15, 183n24, 184nn28,29, 187n39, 188nn41,45, 191, 194n4, 200n41, 202n53, 203nn60,62, 209, 212n18, 214n33, 219n22, 229, 233n30, 238n17, 240, 241n8, 242n13, 243n25, 248nn15,20,22. *See also* villages
clothes, 4, 93, 94, 96n14, 112n11, 119n20, 124n14, 127n38, 129n46, 138, 139, 142n17, 161n15, 169, 173n18, 175n25, 187n36, 192, 197nn20,25, 198n34, 199n38, 203n63, 210n6, 221, 224n22, 226n44, 229, 243n26, 248n20: belts and sashes, 95n5, 105n3, 147, 156n14, 237n12; blouse, 163n18; collars, 146n45, 162n15, 229, 231n19; Daoist, 141n7, 146n43, 165n29, 194n3; embroidered, 69n5, 93, 122n7, 139, 140, 144nn31,32, 146n42,45, 152n25; feathered, 136n31, 139, 144n34, 216, 219nn19,24; foreign-style, 107n17; gowns and robes, 86n12, 90n5, 103, 105n6, 124n17, 125n27, 128n45, 139, 145nn39–41,43, 151n19, 170n2, 191, 192, 194n3, 195n10, 197n21, 198n32, 200n42, 204n67, 205n69, 206nn75,76,78, 207n81, 209n4, 210n6, 212n21, 213n24, 226n38, 228, 230nn3,4, 236nn4,6, 237n12, 238n18, 249nn24,28, 250nn29,30; hats, 75n27, 90n5, 103, 104n3, 115, 116n3, 124n17, 125n27, 128n45, 129n46, 139, 143n23, 145n37, 146n43, 151n19, 162n15, 165n29, 170n2, 193, 195n10, 197n21, 199n39, 200n42, 203n63, 204n67, 205n69, 206nn75,78, 211n14, 236n6, 237n12; imperial, 146n42, 216, 219n24; shirts, 105n3, 155n10, 203n63; shoes, 127n36, 139, 145n38, 198n33, 237n12; silk, 118n19, 144n31, 165n28; skirts, 116n1, 139, 145n35; sleeves, 51, 69n8, 86n12, 90n5, 114n30, 139, 144n31, 161n10, 236n4; trousers, 112n12; upper garments, 143n24, 144n34. *See also* armor
clouds, 60, 61n4, 112n15, 115, 116, 117n12, 118nn16,18,19, 122n7, 124n17, 125n26, 133n13, 138, 152n27, 162nn15,17, 164nn25,27, 170n2, 174n22, 192, 194n1, 197n22, 199n36, 216n2, 217n5, 225n27, 236n6, 237n12, 242n14
coffins, 93, 96n11, 122n4, 142n18, 153n32, 156nn11,12, 177, 180n12, 203n62, 209, 213nn25–28, 214n30, 246n4
concubines, 72n22, 73n25, 74n26, 114n29, 151n20, 159, 166nn31,32, 194, 205n74, 244, 246n9
Confucianism, 66, 76n29, 131n2, 132n9, 149n9, 160n5, 176n33, 204n66. *See also* Confucius; filial piety
Confucius 孔子 (551–479 BCE), 66, 69n10, 70nn14,17, 76n29, 78, 86n14, 87n16, 97n18, 116, 146n42, 149n8, 158, 160n5, 176n33, 193, 198n28, 204n66, 220, 222nn1,2, 235n1
courtesans, 174n24, 212n20
courtyards, 70nn12,14, 89n2, 110n3, 113n19, 116n1, 117n7, 157n20, 168n36, 199n36, 215, 217nn3,8, 218n14, 219n23, 223n9, 239, 240, 241n12, 243n26, 245n3
cousins, 159, 168n37, 173n18, 196n10, 202n52, 241n9

crime, 75n27, 93, 95n7, 106n12, 126n29, 127n34, 134n20, 137n36, 169, 172n17, 173n18, 176n33, 185n29, 199n38, 201n49, 202nn52,53, 212nn20,21, 221, 224n25, 225n34, 238n18, 244, 245, 246nn5,8,9, 247nn10,11, 248nn16,19. *See also* execution; murder; revenge; robbery
crying, 73n24, 78, 85n5, 91, 93, 96nn13,14, 130, 134n18, 164n27, 165n28, 167nn32,35, 174n19, 200n46, 201n51, 209, 212nn19,20, 222n2

dancing, 74n27, 93, 130, 162n16, 221, 223n17
Daoism (including Daoists and Daoist priests), 10, 51, 55–56, 79nn1,2, 84–85, 86nn13,14, 87nn15,16, 104, 107n17, 126n29, 128n42, 134n20, 138, 140nn4,7, 142n43, 146n43, 148, 149n8, 152n27, 159, 165n29, 176n33, 185n30, 188n44, 193, 194, 194n3, 197n20, 200n41, 202n57, 205n73, 206n75, 207nn79,80, 219n19, 229, 234, 236nn4,6, 242nn14,22, 243n23, 251, 253n4. *See also* "Dream of a Butterfly"; Master Zhuang; temples; transcendents
daughters, 67, 69n8, 74n26, 76n32, 109, 111n6, 114n28, 116, 118nn13,19, 127n39, 136nn33,35, 155n2, 161n11, 165n28, 166n32, 172n17, 203n62, 206n75, 210n6, 216, 218n17, 229, 241n11, 243n26
death, 62nn6,9, 71nn18,19, 72n20, 72n21, 73nn23,24, 74n26, 75n27, 78, 79n2, 80, 82n7, 85n5, 86n14, 96n15, 104, 106n12, 107nn14,15, 118n14, 120, 122nn2,4,7, 126n30, 127nn32,34,37,39, 128nn41–44, 129nn46,48, 131, 132n5, 133n13, 134nn18,20,21, 135n24, 136nn29,33,35, 141n9, 142nn16,18, 143n21, 144n27, 145n38, 146n45, 148, 149nn5,10, 150n11, 151n19, 152nn27,28, 153nn32,34, 154, 155n10, 156n11, 157n18, 159, 161nn9,13, 163nn19–22, 164nn23,24, 165n28, 166nn31,32, 167nn33,34, 171nn2,10, 172nn15,17, 174nn20,21,23, 175n24, 176n33, 177, 180n7, 183n23, 186n34, 187n40, 188nn41,42, 189n6, 192, 193, 195n9, 196n16, 197n20, 198nn27,30,33, 199nn38,39, 200nn40,41,43–46, 201nn47,48,50–52, 202nn53–55, 203n62, 204n66, 205n74, 208, 209, 210nn4,5,7, 211nn13,17, 212nn18,19,21, 213nn22–25, 214nn31,33, 216, 218n17, 219nn19,23,25, 220, 221, 222, 222n2, 223nn9,10,15, 225nn32,35, 226nn40,44, 227n45, 229, 231n18, 232nn19,20, 234, 235nn1,2, 236nn5–7, 237nn12,14, 238n16, 240, 241nn9,11, 244, 245, 246nn8,9, 247nn10,11,13, 248nn16,21, 249nn24,27,28, 251, 253n4, 255n11. *See also* burials; coffins; crime; destiny; drowning; longevity; murder; tombs; underworld
deer, 93, 95n7, 174n20, 196n19, 221, 222, 222n1, 226n43, 227n45, 236n9
demons, 3, 26, 60, 71n18, 73n23, 75n27, 88, 89n3, 90nn4,5,8, 94, 96nn15,16, 97n17, 98n18, 126n31, 129n46, 131, 135n25, 178, 191, 192, 195n7, 197n21, 198nn28,29, 203n62, 221, 222, 223n11, 244, 245, 246nn5,7,9, 250n29, 254n11. *See also* ghosts; spirits
destiny, 62n6, 63, 64n3, 83n12, 111n6, 115, 116, 133n13, 139, 142n43, 146n43, 154, 156n17, 161n11, 163n22, 165n29, 170, 191, 209–214, 241n8. *See also* longevity
Di 帝 (supreme god), 70n16, 75nn27,28, 76n30, 89n2, 97n18, 103, 104, 106n12, 107n16, 126n29, 128n42, 133n13, 142n15, 144n27, 156n17, 163n20, 194n3, 199n35, 210n6, 220, 244, 246nn5,9, 247nn10,14
divinations, 58, 58n1, 59nn2,4–6, 63–65, 67, 72nn21,22, 73n24, 74n26, 76n33, 172n17, 223n9, 235n1. *See also* spirit-mediums; trigrams
doctors, 75n27, 94, 96n14, 106n12, 142n15, 211n17, 219n19, 241n11, 246n7
dogs, 93, 106n12, 148, 151n23, 169, 171n13, 182n19, 189n49, 221, 225nn32,35,36, 226n42, 251, 253n3
doors, 61n2, 71n18, 75n27, 129n46, 170, 171n10, 175n28, 186n34, 189n47, 192, 223n11, 16, 224n23, 225n27, 226n36, 235n1, 236n6, 241n11, 247n13

Index

dragons, 66, 68nn2,3, 70n14, 74n27, 103, 104n2, 105nn5,6,8, 107n16, 110n5, 111n6, 118n19, 121, 122nn1,7,9, 123n11, 135n26, 141n11, 145n34, 162n15, 163n20, 166n32, 168n40, 177, 180n7, 182n18, 185n31, 192, 195n7, 196n10, 198n31, 215, 216, 217n7, 219n25, 225n28, 228–233, 237n12
dream manuals, 4–5, 58, 58n1, 68n2, 69n7, 87n16, 99n18, 130, 215, 239
"Dream of a Butterfly" 蝴蝶夢 (Hudiemeng), cover, 9–10, 216, 242n22, 251, 253n2
dream-plant 夢草 (mengcao), 252, 254n10
drinking. *See* eating and drinking
drought, 60, 97n18, 119n20, 120, 122n9, 222, 227n45
drowning, 92, 120, 122n4, 143n25, 202n52, 212n20, 235, 237n12, 242n13
drums, 66, 68n3, 90n5, 126n31, 164n27
Duke of Zhou 周公 (fl. 1046–1032 BCE), 71n20, 78, 89n2, 97n18, 193, 198n28, 203n61
dukes, 85n5, 89n2,133n10, 169
—pre-Qin: Guo, 191, 195n5; Jin, 66, 67, 71n18, 72n21, 73n24, 75nn27,28, 76n33, 94, 97n17, 107n15, 137n37, 220, 229, 232n24, 246nn5,9; Lu, 67, 71n20, 74n27, 130; Qi, 108, 112n9, 121, 133n11, 193; Qin, 106n12, 165n28, 229, 232n23; Shan, 137n37; Song, 66, 71nn18,20; Wei, 67, 72nn21,22, 108, 111n8, 121, 255n14; Zheng, 75n28; Zhu, 74n26
—post-Qin: Han, 171n5, 217n7; Shu, 221, 224n23; Chen, 189n49; Northern Wei, 171n2; Sui, 209, 214n29; Tang, 107n141, 148, 152n27, 214n33, 218n13; Song, 133n13, 139, 145n39, 160n4, 206n75; Yuan, 204n66. *See also* Duke of Zhou
dynastic change and succession, 64n8, 68n3, 69nn4,9, 70n10, 71n18,20, 72n22, 73n23, 75n28, 88, 89n2, 97n18, 103, 104n2, 105n5, 107n12, 108, 110, 121, 122n8, 127n36, 131, 134nn18,22, 136n32, 137n37, 139, 142n14, 143n20, 145n37, 148, 149nn4–6,10,11, 152n25, 159n1, 169, 170n2, 173n19, 188n40, 191, 194nn3,4, 198n32, 202n55, 209, 215, 216, 219nn18,24, 221, 224n18, 230n10, 231nn13,15, 232n20, 233n29, 236n2, 238n16, 239, 241nn9,10, 255n13

earls, 67, 71n19, 85n5, 94, 97n17, 116, 117n11, 216, 225n29, 236n5
ears, 56n5, 62n6, 128n40, 130, 132n5, 170, 175n32, 177, 179n4, 222n1
earth, 19, 55, 56nn1,3–5, 57n8, 60, 61nn2,5, 62n6, 64nn2,3, 68n2, 71n19, 73n23, 80, 81nn3,5,6, 82n7, 83n8, 85, 85n3, 86n8, 87n15, 94n1, 104n1, 105n11, 109, 112n13, 120, 121, 123n11, 124n20, 125n22, 128n45, 129nn47,48, 138, 139, 143n20, 151nn19,23, 157n18, 164n27, 165n28, 169, 170, 170n2, 175n31, 188n44, 201n47, 213n27, 230n7, 232n23, 234, 236n8, 238n17, 245, 246n3, 247n13, 248n19, 249n24, 249n27, 253n5. *See also* caves; five agents; islands; lakes; mountains; oceans; rivers
eating and drinking, 51, 71n19, 75n27, 92, 93, 94, 96nn13,14, 108, 109, 111n5, 112n11, 113n24, 115, 117n8, 118n16, 124n18, 125n24, 129n2, 134n20, 138, 139, 140nn3,4,6, 141n7–11,13, 142nn16–19, 143nn20–23, 147, 149n4, 152n26, 154, 155nn2,4, 161n11, 162n17, 166nn31,32, 169, 171n9, 175n25, 183n24, 185n31, 189n49, 197n21, 200n41, 203nn61,62, 211n17, 212n20, 218n12, 219nn19,25, 221, 226nn40,44, 227n45, 230n7, 238n17, 240, 241n9, 242n14, 243n23, 245n3, 247n13
elders, 66, 67, 70n14, 76n34, 150n14, 152n26, 161n13, 242n23. *See also* old men
elephants, 220, 223nn13,15,16
elixirs. *See* medicine
emperors, 61n4, 78, 79n6, 84, 89n3, 103, 104, 104n1, 113n22, 150n16, 232n20; (arranged by dynasty) Qin, 191, 192, 195n7, 198n33, 220, 225n8; Han, 14, 40n39, 103, 105nn3,5, 107n16, 110n2, 121, 132n5, 139, 171n5, 191, 193, 195n8, 196n19, 202n57, 204n65, 214n33, 217n7, 221, 224n27, 228, 229n1, 243n23, 244, 246n9, 247n15, 252, 254n11, 255n17; Xin, 114n28; Wei, 109, 112n,13, 15, 146n42, 147, 149n4, 154, 157n19; Wu, 110n4, 159n1, 176n33, 193,

emperors *(continued)*
  202n58, 232n21; Jin, 108, 134n18, 161n9, 173n19, 198n30, 228, 230n2; Han-Former Zhao, 108, 111n5, 192, 195n9; Former Qin, 176n33, 192, 195n10, 220, 221, 222n5, 226n36, 235n2, 240, 243n25, 244, 246n7; Later Yan, 176n33; Southern Yan, 208, 211n18; Western Liang, 161n13; Liu Song, 104n2, 121n1, 187n40, 223n14, 228, 231n13, 244, 247n10; Southern Qi, 104n2, 120, 121n6, 127nn36,38, 131, 134n21, 135nn23,24, 139, 140n2, 144n34, 158, 215, 216n2, 219n24, 228, 230n8, 239, 241; Liang, 103, 104n2, 110, 114n29, 120, 123n10, 127n32, 138, 143n21, 145n37, 149nn5,10, 154; Chen, 108, 109, 112n11, 153n34, 178, 189n49; Northern Wei, 111n6, 112n10, 170n2, 192, 200n42, 228, 230n6, 252, 254n11; Northern Qi, 117n10, 139, 145n35, 230n7; Northern Zhou, 247n11; Sui, 120, 122n8, 131, 135n32, 159, 166n30; Tang, 107n14, 113n18, 133n15, 138, 143n20, 144n31, 145n40, 152n25, 187n37, 189n46, 190n51, 193, 202nn54,55, 221, 223n18, 235, 237n16, 240n7, 242n16, 248n20; Liao, 111n7, 216, 218n12; Later Liang, 96n9; Later Jin, 154, 156n14, 202n58; Southern Tang, 131, 134n22, 228, 229, 231n15; Later Zhou, 105n8; Song, 17, 103, 105nn4,6, 106n10, 108, 110n3, 120, 122n9, 141n7, 144n28, 145n39, 178, 184n25, 189nn48,49, 193, 202nn58,59, 204n67, 209n4, 221, 226n38, 228, 230nn3,4, 252, 255n15; [Jurchen] Jin, 252, 255n13; Yuan, 205n68, Ming, 17, 26, 178, 190n50, 191, 194n4. *See also* Emperor Taizu; Emperor Wu; Emperor Xuanzong; Shun; Yao; Yellow Emperor
Emperor Taizu of the Ming 明太祖 (r. 1368-1398), 17, 26, 121, 125n24, 139, 143n23, 191, 194n3
Emperor Wu of the Western Han 漢武帝 (r. 141-87 BCE), 108, 110n3, 120, 122n7, 139, 193, 204n64, 234, 236n9
Emperor Xuanzong of the Tang 唐玄宗 (r. 712-756), 17, 24, 86n12, 108, 112n12, 120, 121, 122n5, 125n26, 128n45, 138, 141n14, 148, 178, 186n36, 189n46, 191, 192, 193, 197n21, 199nn36,37, 203n63, 225n28, 240, 242n14, 253n5
empresses (including other palace women of rank): 114n25, 170n2; (arranged by dynasty) Zhou: 66, 70n12, 89, 239; Han, 68n3, 103, 105n7, 108, 109, 110n2, 163n18, 228, 229n1, 235, 237n15, 240; 243n23, 244, 246n9, 255n17; Xin, 114n28; Wei, 157n19; Jin, 173n19, 228, 230n2; Former Qin, 240n25; Northern Wei, 111n6, 114n28, 228, 230n6; Eastern Wei, 114n28; Southern Qi, 138, 140n2, 154, 155n5, 228, 230n8; Liang, 109, 114n29; Northern Qi, 109, 154, 228, 230n7; Tang, 107n14, 133n15, 147, 149n6, 151n20, 218n18; Song, 108, 110n3, 139, 144n28, 228, 230n4, 242n16; Liao, 111n7, 216, 218n12; Ming, 139, 143n23
entertainers, 96n13, 98n18, 224n21, 227n45, 244, 246n8
eunuchs, 135n24, 186n36, 189n46
executions, 135n24, 137n36, 150n11, 171n10, 176n33, 192, 195n5, 198n33, 199nn38,40, 200n44, 202n52, 219n25, 232n20, 244, 246n9, 247n10, 248n19. *See also* murder
exile, 74n26, 75n27, 94, 97n17, 126n29, 134n20, 135n27, 152n28, 176n33, 214n30, 246n9, 252, 255n14
exorcisms, 88, 89n3, 90nn4,5,7,8, 195n7, 223n11, 231n13, 245, 250n29
eyes, 51, 55, 56n5, 62nn6,7, 66, 68nn4,7, 71n19, 74n26, 96n9, 114n29, 115, 116n1, 131, 134n17, 135n25, 138, 142n17, 201n47, 207n79, 230n7, 236n4, 246n4

faces, 131, 133nn11,12, 134nn17,18, 135n25, 136n33, 141n11, 156n17, 161n11, 187n38, 195nn5,9, 210n6
fangshi-wizards. *See* spirit-mediums
farmers and farming, 75n27, 156n17, 220, 222n1
fate. *See* destiny
fathers, 67, 74n25, 111n6, 113nn17,19, 114n28, 117n7, 135n27, 139, 141n13, 142nn15,17, 143n25, 144nn27,30, 156n12, 157n20, 163n21, 173n18, 174n22, 178, 180n13, 184n27, 186n34, 187n39, 193, 194, 196n12, 201n49, 202n52,

Index

204n66, 205nn70,71, 74, 75, 206nn76,78, 207nn79,81, 209, 210n6, 211n13, 212n18, 214nn32,33, 217nn4,8,9, 220, 222n6, 223n16, 230n4, 241n11, 242nn16,21, 244, 249n24

feet and legs, 62n6, 68n2, 70n10, 72n22, 92, 93, 104n2, 121, 125n24, 131, 134n17, 135n23, 137n38, 139, 169, 171n9, 186n34, 202n53, 221, 222n1, 224n25, 225n30, 228, 229, 230n2, 232n25, 247n11, 253n3

fields and countryside, 92, 95n7, 115, 120, 122n6, 123n10, 169, 173n18, 174n20, 239, 242n21

filial piety, 61n4, 139, 141n11, 142n15, 16, 145n41, 178, 186n36, 205n74, 215, 221, 226n38, 240, 242n17, 243n24, 245n2

fire, 62n6, 91, 92, 94n2, 96nn12,14, 111n8, 115, 116, 117n11, 125n21, 127n34, 135nn24,27, 142n18, 170, 171n10, 175n26, 177, 209, 214n32, 221, 223n17, 225n35, 232n20, 249n24, 253n3, 255n11. *See also* five agents

fish, 26, 67, 68n2, 76n32, 86n14, 93, 111n5, 130, 154, 155n10, 162n15, 164n25, 195n7, 208, 210n10, 234–238, 239, 241n9, 245, 251, 252, 253n2, 254n9

fishing, 66, 69nn8,9, 234, 235, 235n1, 236nn7,9, 237n12

five agents (i.e. metal, wood, water, fire, earth), 56n5, 62n6, 74n27, 80, 81nn4,5, 82n7, 98n18, 127n36, 221, 223nn12,17, 226n41, 230n10

floods, 69n5, 70n13, 120, 122n8, 202n58

flowers, ii, 70n11, 121, 126n29, 156n11, 158, 160n8, 165n28, 166n31, 179n5, 203n62, 225n27, 240, 247n10: cassia, 159, 167n35; camellia, 163n18; *citong*-tree blossom 刺桐, 242n22; *lan*-flower 蘭, 68n2, 72n22, 225n27; lotus, 138, 140n7, 141n8, 169n15, 214n29; orchid 蘭, 143n23; peony, 240, 242n16; sophora tree blossom, 159, 168n36; trumpet vine, 161n11; wisteria, 138, 142n14, 240

flying, 70n14, 81, 83n9, 86n14, 91, 92, 95n5, 106n11, 128n41, 144n34, 152nn26,27, 163n20, 165n29, 166n31, 168n38, 184n26, 195n8, 215, 217nn8,9, 218nn10,17, 221, 223n18, 229, 231n18

food and drink, 69n10, 75n27, 91, 93, 95n2, 96n13, 129n 47, 134n20, 138–139, 140nn2,4, 141nn7,14, 144n27, 147, 150n12, 169, 172nn13–15, 173n18, 175n25, 197n25, 203n62, 211n17, 219n19, 225n35, 226n44, 242n17, 243n25, 249nn27,28, 250n30, 253n3. *See also* grains; tea; wine

foreign lands, 66, 68n2, 86n14, 87n14, 151n24, 156n13, 162n15, 195n8, 250n29, 251, 253n5

foreigners (including other non-Han ethnicities), 69n5, 71n19, 72n21, 86nn12,14, 106n12, 108, 112n10, 144n30, 151n24, 171nn7,12, 193, 198n33, 199n37, 205n68, 235, 237n12, 241n9, 250n29, 254n11, 255n15

fortune-tellers, 218n11, 226n40, 241n8

friends, 87n14, 120, 122n4, 123n12, 126n28, 127n32, 128n46, 153n31, 159, 167n33, 180n7, 188n41, 193, 199n39, 200nn43–45, 201n51, 219n19, 221

funerals. *See* burials

Fuxi 伏羲 (mythical sage-king), 193, 203n61

gall-bladder, 62n6, 92
games, 138, 143n20, 147, 149nn5,6,8, 229, 231n17
gardens, 112n12, 145n39, 163n20, 168n37, 247n10
gates, 70n10, 71n18, 75n27, 90n8, 104, 106n11, 124n19, 125n27, 128nn40,46, 134n16, 161n15, 164n27, 170n2, 171n10, 173n18, 197n19, 202n53, 212n21, 226n36, 236n6, 241n11. *See also* doors
genitals, 92, 131, 137n36, 246n7
ghosts, 19, 26, 86n10, 94, 96n16, 169, 171n2, 176n33, 245, 246n9, 247n12, 249n28. *See also* demons; spirits
girls, 156n12, 198n34, 241n11. *See also* daughters; children
glyphomantic dreams 拆字夢 (*chaizi-meng*), 19, 42nn55,56, 68n2, 70n10, 121, 122n3, 123n9, 124n20, 127n36, 132nn4,7, 133n10, 143n24, 145n36, 150n13, 151n23, 169–176, 177, 179n4, 211nn12,14, 224nn23,24. *See also* graphs
goats, 169, 171n5, 221, 222n1, 225n34, 226nn38,40, 242n16, 245, 249n28

gods and goddesses (including lesser divinities), 8, 60, 61n5, 67, 69n9, 70nn14,16, 73n23, 75nn27,28, 76n30, 88, 89n2, 90nn5,8, 97n18, 103, 104, 106n12, 107nn16,17, 108, 110nn2,3, 111n8, 112n11, 113nn15,17, 118n20, 121, 122n7, 126nn27,29, 128nn42,44,45, 129n48, 130, 131, 133nn13,15, 134n20, 135nn27,28, 137n37, 139, 141n10, 142n15, 143n23, 144n27, 145n38, 146n43, 147, 150nn11,17, 151nn19,23, 24, 153n34, 154, 155nn4,8, 156n17, 158, 160, 160nn4,5, 161n15, 163n20, 173n19, 176n33, 178, 179, 183n24, 184nn27–29, 189n48, 190n51, 191–207, 209n4, 210nn5,6, 211n15, 212n21, 220, 222n6, 223n9, 226n38, 230n4, 232n23, 234, 235n1, 245, 247n13, 252, 255n11. *See also* Di

gold, 69n5, 70n10, 92, 121, 122n2, 126n27, 128n45, 138, 141n9, 150n17, 152n27, 154, 155n11, 156n13, 165nn28,29, 181n17, 189n50, 192, 193, 195nn8–10, 196n13, 198n32, 202n58, 204n67, 205n68, 206n77, 216, 218n12, 219n25, 234, 244, 245n2, 246n4, 248n21, 249n28, 252

grains, 70n15, 75n27, 93, 96n14, 139, 141n7, 143n22, 144n27, 169, 172n14, 173n18, 219n19, 224n21, 235n2, 239, 240, 242n17, 245n2, 247n10, 251, 253n4

grandfathers, 113n19, 180n13, 207nn80,81, 211n13, 249n24

grandmothers, 208, 209n4, 242n17

grandsons (including great-grandsons), 72n22, 75n27, 168n37, 193, 201n47, 208, 242n17

graphs, 3, 39n28, 51, 68n2, 69n5, 70nn10,14,15, 75n28, 77n35, 79n3, 83n10, 85n6, 86n12, 88n1, 89n3, 93, 97n18, 112n15, 114n30, 121, 122n8, 124n18, 125n22, 126n28, 127n32, 136n32, 137n38, 138, 140n3, 141n7, 143nn20,21, 145nn38,40, 149nn4,6, 150nn12,16, 153nn31,32, 156n14, 159, 161n11, 163nn21–23, 164n27, 169–176, 179nn1,3,6, 180n12, 181nn16,17, 182nn18–20, 183n21, 184n25, 186n35, 187nn36,37, 188nn43,45, 189n50, 196nn12,15, 198n32, 203n63, 204n66, 205n72, 208, 210nn5,10, 218n18, 223n15, 224nn21,22, 225nn33,34, 226n44, 227n45, 229, 231n18, 232n27, 238n16, 241nn8,10,13, 242nn16,17, 243nn25,26, 244, 245n2, 249n24. *See also* glyphomantic dreams; names

hair, 57n6, 68n4, 72n21, 75n27, 95n5, 118n20, 131, 136nn30,35, 137n38, 139, 144n34, 162n16, 186n35, 195n5, 198n33, 200n42, 201n47, 202n53, 235n1, 241n13, 244, 245, 246nn5,9, 247n14. *See also* beards

halls, 70n17, 73n23, 89n2, 99n18, 111n6, 121, 126nn27,28,30, 127nn36,37, 128n45, 160n3, 162n15, 163n20, 165nn29,30, 167n33, 170n2, 171n14, 178, 181n14, 184n25, 189n48, 195n8, 204n64, 213nn26,27, 231n15, 240

hands and arms, 73n24, 75n28, 103, 104, 105nn7,10, 106n11, 108, 110nn2,3, 111n5, 112nn11,15, 113n20, 117n8, 119n20, 123n11, 130, 131, 132nn3,5, 134n17, 135n24, 136n31,32, 140n3, 147, 150n15, 156n11, 174nn22,24, 176n33, 179nn4,5, 211n17, 216, 218n11, 223n17, 228, 231n13, 243n24

hare, 167

heads, 62n6, 69n7, 73n24, 90n6, 109, 113n18, 123n11, 127n38, 130, 131, 132n7, 134nn17,22, 135nn23,26, 158, 159n1, 169, 172n15, 173n18, 174n20, 175n28, 177, 179n5, 180n7, 189n46, 225n28, 230n7, 232nn19,20, 26, 247n14, 248nn15,21

heart, 62n6, 75n27, 91, 92, 94n2, 105n5, 130, 132n9, 136n31, 161n11, 164n27, 166n32, 222n2, 248nn16,17, 253n1

heaven, 55, 56nn1,3–5, 57n8, 60, 61nn2,3, 62n6, 64nn2,3,6, 65n9, 66, 68n3, 72nn21,22, 74n26, 75n27, 80, 81nn3,5,6, 82n7, 85, 85n3, 86n8, 87n15, 88, 89nn2,3, 94n1, 103–107, 109, 111n8, 112nn11,12, 114n26, 115, 116n2, 118n14, 121, 126n28, 128n45, 137n37, 140nn4,6, 143n23, 144nn27,34, 145n40, 152nn26,27, 159, 162n15, 167n35, 169, 170n2, 171n7, 184n24, 192, 193, 195n5, 198nn32,33, 199n35, 203n62, 205nn68,69,74, 209, 215, 216n2, 217n5, 218n12, 219n25,

Index

228, 229, 230n7, 231n15, 18, 19, 232nn20,21,23,24, 236n6, 244, 245, 246nn8,9, 247n14, 254n11. *See also* sky
historian-astrologers, 64n8, 72n22, 73nn24,27, 89n2, 99n18, 195nn5,9, 232n23
horns, 123n11, 130, 132n7, 169, 170, 171n5, 174n20, 222n1, 224n23
horses (including donkeys and mules), 25, 69n8, 125n24, 128nn40,41,46, 147, 149n4, 152n27, 168n36, 171n10, 172n17, 186n34, 187n39, 189n49, 192, 193, 194n4, 198nn30,33, 203n59, 205n70, 220, 221, 222n8, 223nn17, 18, 224nn21,22, 248n21
houses, 19, 109, 116, 121, 122n4, 127n32, 131n3, 133n13, 135n27, 136n32, 142nn15,17, 147, 149n8, 165n29, 167n32, 171n10, 174n22, 201n48, 203n60, 205nn70,75, 211n17, 217n3, 218n14, 219n23, 220, 221, 222n5, 223nn11,17,18, 232n22, 236nn6,7, 241n12, 245n3, 246n4, 248n21, 249n27. *See also* residences
hunger, 93, 95n2, 96n14, 123n10, 142n14, 243n23
hunting, 73n23, 95n7, 96n13, 130, 220, 223n11, 232n24, 234, 236n8
husbands, 159, 164n28, 169, 173nn17,18, 174n20, 209, 245, 248n16, 249n28, 252, 255n16

ice, 115, 116, 117n13
illness (including deformity and injury), 59n4, 70n10, 71n18, 72n22, 73nn24,25, 74n26, 75nn27,28, 88, 90nn4,5, 91–94, 94nn1,2, 95nn3,4, 96n14, 97n18, 105n10, 106nn11,12, 107n17, 108, 112n9, 114n29, 121, 122nn2,9, 123n11, 126nn29,31, 129n47, 132nn3,5, 134nn18,20, 136nn31,34, 138, 140nn1,7, 142nn15–18, 148n2, 149n10, 153n33, 157n18, 165n29, 166n31, 174n23, 186n34, 189n49, 192, 193, 197n25, 201n48,52, 202nn54,58, 204n66, 205n69, 209n4, 210n8, 211n17, 212n21, 213nn23,24, 223n11, 224n25, 240, 241n11, 243n24, 244, 245, 246nn5,7, 247nn12,13, 251, 252, 253n1, 254nn7,8, 255n16
ink, 64n4, 138, 140n3, 158–168, 178, 187n38

insects, 10, 67, 76n32, 91, 94n2, 159, 168n36, 216, 234, 235, 237nn13–15, 238n16–18, 242n22, 245, 250n29, 253n2. *See also* "Dream of a Butterfly"
intestines, 92, 124n18, 130, 134n16
islands, 70n11, 153n32, 157n22, 168n39, 243n23, 253n5

jade, 68n4, 69n5, 70n14, 71n19, 73n24, 75n27, 81, 83nn10,11, 85n5, 121, 123n11, 124n17, 125n26, 126nn28,29, 128, 138, 141n10, 144n27, 145n35, 154, 155nn5,8–10, 156n14, 158, 159, 160n5, 162n15, 163n20, 164n27, 165n28, 167n35, 192, 198nn32,33, 199n35, 207n80, 210n5, 216, 218n13, 253n5
jewelry and ornaments, 75n27, 81, 154, 155n5, 156n11, 162n15, 164n27, 165n28, 167n35, 244, 246n4, 249n28. *See also* gold; jade; pearls

kidneys, 62n6, 91, 92, 94n2
kings, 25, 40n36, 61n4, 64n6, 65n9, 79n6, 81, 82n7, 84, 85n3, 88, 89n1, 154n24, 169, 171n5, 212n21, 213n22, 233n28, 235, 238nn17,18, 255n11: (arranged by dynasty or state) early dynasties: Xia, 66, 69nn5,7, 116, 118n20, 139, 143n22, 191; Shang, 3, 63, 66, 67, 68n3, 69n7, 76n30, 105nn6,7, 133n11, 147, 148n1, 178; Zhou, 15–16, 63, 64n7, 65n8, 66, 67, 69nn8,9, 70n16, 75n28, 76n32, 88, 89n2, 97n18, 109, 110n1, 120, 122n6, 131, 136n31, 173n17, 193, 203n61, 208, 216, 219n22, 234, 245, 248n22, 252; pre-Qin states: Chu, 8, 71nn19,20, 192, 197n22; Dai, 107n12; Wu, 164n27, 203n61, 221, 225n35; Yan, 236n5; Zhao, 107n12, 158, 161n11; post-Qin states and dynasties: Linyi, 156n13; Han-Former Zhao, 108, 111n5; Former Liang, 201n47; Shu, 118n14, 186n34; Wu, 110, 159n1, 202n58; Wu-Yue, 231n14; Yan, 247n15. *See also* emperors; Shun; Yao

lakes and ponds, 107n16, 123n13, 160n3, 162n15, 164n26, 168n37, 181n16, 202n58, 229, 232n22, 235n2, 236n9, 237n12, 247n13, 252, 254n9

laughter, 51, 73n24, 78, 86n12, 90n6, 91, 98n18, 134n17, 140n3, 148n1, 198nn27,34
leopard, 93
lightning (including thunder), 66, 68n1, 69n7, 92, 115, 116nn1–3, 123n11, 220, 223n9, 247n13
lions, 161n15, 220, 223n12, 237n12
literary accomplishment, 109, 113n17, 116, 118n16, 120, 124n18, 126n29, 132n5, 133n13, 134n17, 138, 140n3, 141nn7,9, 146n42, 147, 151nn18,19, 155, 155n1, 157n22, 158–159, 159n3, 160nn4–6,8, 161nn9,10,12,15, 163nn18–20, 164nn24,27, 168n37, 39, 184n26, 192, 196n12, 215, 216, 217n8, 218n10, 220, 222n2, 229, 232n27, 236n4. *See also* official examinations
liver, 55, 62n2, 91, 92, 130, 239
Long-Willow Method, 58, 58n1, 130
longevity, 55, 66, 70n16, 117n7, 154, 157n21, 159, 163n22, 175n24, 185n29, 204n66, 209–214, 216, 217n4, 218n14, 241n13, 253n4. *See also* death; destiny; numbers
lords, 66, 121, 121nn42,47, 139, 146n43, 151n19, 153n34, 192, 193, 194, 197n20, 204n65, 207nn79,80, 234, 235n1, 247n13
lunar lodgings. *See* stars
lungs, 62n6, 91, 92, 130

maidservants (including wet nurses), 84, 140n2, 183n24, 201n50, 210n6, 213n27, 244, 246n4, 247n11, 249n28
magic diagrams and talismans, 63, 64n2, 66, 68n2, 131, 134n20, 135n25, 138, 140n6, 141n7, 229
marquises, 74n25, 192, 196n19, 201n47, 214n33, 225n34, 226n44, 229, 232n26, 248n15
marriage, 69n8, 73n25, 74n26, 93, 105n8, 106n12, 107n14, 115, 116, 118n13, 127n39, 164n28, 168n38, 169, 174n20, 199n35, 203n62, 210n6, 212n19, 232n21, 244, 248n16, 253n4
Master Zhuang 莊子 (Zhuang Zhou 莊周, trad. fl. 4th cent. BCE), cover, 10, 251, 253n2
Master Zhuang 莊子 *(Zhuangzi)*, 130
medicine (including elixirs of immortality), 129n47, 131n2, 132n9, 135n25, 136n31, 138, 139, 140n1, 142nn15,17,18, 143nn20,23, 176n33,

187n37, 203n63, 218n16, 219n19, 232n26, 241n11, 247n13
menservants, 84, 173n18, 186n34, 201n51, 218n17. *See also* maidservants; slaves
merchants, 173n18, 186n34, 224n24, 245n2
metals, 92, 147, 150n11, 174n21, 214n29. *See also* five agents; gold
military officials, 68n2, 74n25, 103, 105n5, 107n14, 109, 113n21, 124n14, 125n22, 139, 141n11, 144n30, 145n38, 147, 148, 149n3, 152n27, 153n34, 174n22, 178, 179n5, 181n14, 185n31, 187n40, 188nn43,44, 189nn47,49, 191, 193, 196nn10,15, 198n27, 201n49, 203n60, 206n77, 210n6, 220, 223n14, 224n21, 233n28, 240, 243n25, 247n11. *See also* armies; soldiers
mind, 25, 26, 62n8, 76n29, 79nn2–5, 97n18, 131, 132n9, 133n13, 136n29, 168n39, 239, 245, 251, 253n1
mirrors, 55, 57n8, 131, 134n19, 135n26, 147, 148, 151n21, 154, 156n11, 169, 173n17, 174n21
money and wealth, 61n4, 62n9, 93, 96n11, 112n12, 120, 122n4, 123n10, 135n25, 137n35, 150n16, 154–155, 156n12, 157nn17–19, 169, 171n14, 178, 180n7, 181n16, 189n46, 192, 196n18, 201n52, 205n74, 208, 209, 209n1, 210n6, 211n13, 213n26, 217n9, 221, 224n21, 235, 236n7, 239, 241n12, 244, 246n3, 248nn19,21
monkeys, 173n18, 234
monks (other than identifiably Buddhist or Daoist, q.v.), 114n29, 136n32, 141n11, 178, 184n29, 185n30, 201n52, 221, 223n11, 226n40, 249n27
moon, 51, 61n4, 66, 69nn5,8, 71n19, 74n27, 80, 81, 81n3, 82nn6,8, 83n10, 89n1, 108–110, 110n1, 112, 113n21, 114nn25,26,28–30, 121, 125n26, 148, 152n25, 162n17, 165n28, 167n35, 170n2, 184n28, 230n2
mothers, 66, 70nn11,13,14, 77nn13,14, 78, 103, 105n8, 108, 109, 111nn5,7, 112nn10,15,16, 114nn28,30, 115, 116nn1,2, 117nn6,8,9,12, 118n14, 121, 124n17, 130, 131, 133n10, 134nn16,20, 136n33, 137n36, 138,

Index

139, 140n6, 141nn8,10,11, 142nn15,18, 144n28, 145n35, 146nn42,43, 147, 149n8, 150n17, 151nn18,20,21, 152n26, 154, 155nn1–5, 156n13, 158, 160n4, 163n20, 189n47, 192, 193, 194, 194n1, 197n25, 202n52, 204n67, 205n68, 69, 206nn75–77, 207nn79–81, 208, 209nn1,2,4, 210n6, 211n17, 212n22, 215, 216, 216n3, 217nn4,5, 218nn10,11,13–15, 220, 222n5, 223nn10,11, 229, 230n4, 232n21, 233n29, 237n10, 239, 240, 240n7, 241n11, 242n14, 243n24

mountains and hills, 61nn4,5, 66, 68n3, 69n5, 71n18, 90nn6,8, 92, 109, 112n15, 113n20, 119n20, 120, 121, 122nn1–5,7, 123nn11,13, 124nn16,19, 125n24, 128nn42,43,45, 136n35, 141n7, 155n8, 157n20, 162n17, 164n26, 169, 170, 171nn10,12, 175n26, 177, 178, 180n7, 181n19, 182n19, 184nn28, 29, 192, 193, 194, 194n1, 196nn18,19, 197nn21,22,25, 198n31, 200n41, 202n58, 203n63, 205n75, 206nn75,76,78, 207nn79,80, 210n5, 220, 222n7, 225n27, 226nn40,44, 230n10, 234, 236n8, 242nn14,21, 246n4, 248n17, 249n24, 252

mouths, 62n6, 93, 112n11, 116, 130, 131, 131n2, 134nn17,21, 141n11, 143n21, 154, 156n26, 194n1, 216, 218n10, 226n44, 230n7, 232n23, 234, 237n9, 246n8, 249n24

murder and killing, 72n21, 73n23, 74n26, 75n27, 91, 95n2, 96n9, 107n12, 127n34, 131, 135n24, 143n21, 145n38, 150n11, 153n34, 169, 170n2, 172nn15,17, 173n18, 189n46, 192, 199n38, 200n43, 202nn52,53, 205n73, 212n21, 223nn9,10,15, 225n35, 226n44, 235nn1,2, 236nn5,7, 237nn12,14, 241n9, 244, 245, 246n5, 246nn8,9, 247nn10–12,14,15, 248nn19,21, 249nn24,28, 250n30, 252, 254n11. See also crime; executions

music, 25, 91, 106n12, 120, 124n17, 125n26, 126n30, 147, 149n10, 151n18, 159, 161n11, 162n16, 163nn20,23, 164n27, 165n28, 168n40, 177, 180n9, 192, 199n36. See also entertainers; singing; songs

names, 71n19, 72n22, 74n26, 75n28, 97n18, 109, 112n15, 113n17, 114n30, 115, 117nn6,7, 122nn5,8, 124n17, 126n28, 133n13, 141n7, 144n27, 145n41, 149n3, 151n21, 156n13, 162n17, 169, 173n19, 175n26, 176n33, 177–178, 179nn5,6, 180nn12,13, 181nn14,15,17, 182nn18–21, 183nn22,24, 184n25, 186n34, 187n36, 189n50, 192, 193, 194, 196nn12,13,15–17, 204n66, 205nn69,70,74, 206nn76,77, 209n2, 212n21, 216, 217nn4,8,9, 218n14, 225n27, 230n8, 240n7, 241nn8,9, 242n14, 247n27, 255n16

nephews, 75n27, 187n37, 234, 237n10, 241n12

nightmares, 39n30, 60, 65n9, 80, 81n1, 88, 89n3, 90nn4–7, 241n13, 247n15

nobles, 25, 71n20, 73nn23,24, 89n3, 114n25, 131, 136n26, 198n32, 219n24, 220, 223n10, 228, 229n1, 239. See also specific ranks

noses, 62n6, 74n26, 131, 134n17, 135n28, 224n23, 235, 237n14, 249n24

numbers (including calendrical and other calculations), 55, 56nn2,5, 62n6, 63, 70n16, 80, 81nn5,6, 82n7, 83n8, 87n15, 89n1, 105n11, 111n6, 117n5, 127n36, 133n10, 143n19, 150n14, 152n28, 165n29, 169, 170, 170n2, 174nn23,24, 176nn32,33, 179n2, 182n17, 183nn22,23, 192, 195n9, 198n28, 204n66, 208, 209n4, 210nn5,7,8, 211n12, 213n25, 218n14, 226n38, 227n45, 242nn16,17, 243n26, 249n24

oceans and seas, 69n8, 90n8, 120, 121, 121n1, 125n21, 135n35, 145n35, 148, 151n24, 191, 195n7, 204n65, 230n7, 251

official examinations and degrees, xvi, 113nn15,19,24, 115, 116, 117nn5,10, 118n18, 123n11, 144n32, 148, 150n14, 151n23, 155nn1,4, 160nn3,4, 162n15, 163n23, 166n31, 167n34, 169, 171n13, 174n23, 175nn26,32, 177–190, 192, 202n53, 203n62, 205n74, 209, 213n28, 214n30, 216, 221, 224n22, 236n6, 240, 241n12, 242n22, 253n4, 254n6,9

official position, 68n2, 69n8, 73n23, 74n26, 76n30, 93, 96n11, 104, 104n3, 105n9, 109,

official position (continued)
113nn15,18–20,23,24, 114n25,
115, 116n3, 117n10, 120, 121,
122nn1,3, 123nn10,11, 126nn28,29,
127n34, 128n43, 129n46, 130,
131, 132n3, 134n18, 135nn24–28,
137nn36,38, 139, 141nn8,11,
143n25, 144nn27,30–32,
145nn36,39, 146nn41,42, 149n3,
150nn11,13–16, 151n18, 152n25,
153nn31,33, 154, 155nn1,9,
157n20, 160nn3,4, 169, 171n2,
172n14, 174nn22,23, 175nn25,28,32,
178, 181n16, 182n20, 184nn27,28,
185nn29–33, 186nn34,35,
187nn36–40, 188nn41–45,
189nn46–49, 190n50, 192, 193,
196nn10,15, 197n20, 201nn46,47,51,
205n72, 206n76, 207n81, 209,
211n15, 212n21, 213nn25–28,
214nn29,33, 215, 216, 218nn11,13,
220, 222, 223n15, 224n22,
225nn33,34, 226n40, 227n45,
228, 231n14, 235, 237n13, 238n17,
239, 240, 240n7, 241n8, 243n28,
248n16, 251, 253n4. *See also*
military officials; prime ministers
old men, 51, 67, 69n8, 74n25, 87n16,
115, 117n7, 118n20, 132n9, 140n7,
161n12, 174n24, 178, 184n28, 192,
193, 197n24, 200n42, 203n63,
205nn69,74, 209n2, 244, 250n29,
253n4. *See also* elders
old women, 105n9, 229, 232n22
omens, 26, 51, 60, 64n6, 65n9, 68n3,
69n8, 70n10, 73n24, 76n32, 80,
85n3, 88, 88n1, 89n3, 108, 111nn5,6,
115, 116, 124n20, 132n7, 134n16,
136n32, 142n14, 144n27, 147,
151n23, 156n14, 158, 172n17, 177,
179, 191, 195n9, 214n26, 216, 220,
222, 226n38, 230n10, 233n28, 235,
235n1, 236n2, 239, 251, 252
oxen, 74n26, 109, 121, 128n40, 144n27,
185n29, 202n53, 220, 221,
224nn23–25

pagoda, 121, 125n21
palaces, 26, 67, 69n7, 71n18, 72n21,
75n27, 76n32, 86n12, 89n2, 90n5,
105nn4,5,7, 106n10, 110n3, 111n6,
112n12, 113n15, 114n29, 120,
121, 122n5, 123n11, 125nn24,26,
126nn28,30, 128n45, 133n15,
134n18, 135n27, 139, 145n39,
148, 152n27, 159, 160n3, 161n15,
162n17, 163n20, 164nn26,27,

165n28, 167n35, 170n2, 172n14,
175n25, 178, 180n9, 184n25,
185nn32, 35, 190n51, 195n8,
198n33, 199n37, 200n41,
204nn64,67, 218n12, 219n25,
225n27, 226n38, 229, 230n4,
231n15, 232n20, 237n13, 238n17,
239, 242n16, 246n7, 247n10
pavilions, 26, 120, 128n45, 150n14,
166n31, 182n20, 186n36, 225n27,
242n16, 247n10
pearls, 71n19, 85n5, 129n47, 138,
142n19, 143n22, 154, 155nn1–4,
164n27, 165n28, 229, 232n26,
234, 236n5, 237n9
pigs, 221, 224n27, 225nn28–30,33,
236n5
pillars, 66, 70n17, 78, 209, 214n29,
218n12
pillows, 51, 93, 134n18, 156n14,
172n17, 197n22, 228, 230n2,
251, 252, 253nn4,5
plants, 92, 164n27, 165n28, 239–243:
artemesia, 241n10; bamboo, 98n18,
197n25, 218n11, 240, 243n28,
247n10; birthwort root, 129n47;
brambles, 170, 176n33, 208, 239;
brush, 95n7; cardamom, 129n47;
dates, 129n47; duckweed, 162n15;
eggplant, 26; divine fungus, 121,
126n30, 240, 242n14, 255n15;
divine herb, 138, 142n19, 255n15;
dream-plant 夢草 (*mengcao*), 252, 254n10;
fruits, 204n66, 218n11; garlic, 240,
241n13; grass, 74n25, 127n38,
148n2, 158, 159, 168n37, 169,
173n18, 174n22, 236n8, 244;
licorice root, 187n37; *malin*-rushes
馬藺, 240, 242n21; melons, 72n21,
240, 243nn23,24; moxa, 239,
241n10; mushroom, 92; reeds,
88, 90n8, 136n32, 235, 238n18;
rhubarb, 138, 142n16; rushes,
239, 241n9; sedge, 165n27; sesame,
138, 140n2; thorns, 246n4; thorny
bushes, 93; vegetables, 125n22, 138,
142n18, 178, 184n25, 240, 243n25;
vines, 72n21, 119n20, 142n14;
wormwood, 241n10; yarrow stalks,
208, 252, 254n10. *See also* flowers;
grains; trees
poetry, 76nn32–34, 118n16,
123nn11,13, 124n18, 125n21,
126nn27,30, 132n5, 138,
140n3, 143n19, 149n8, 151n19,
152n27, 155n9, 158–159,
160nn4,5,8, 161nn12,15, 162n17,

Index

163nn18–20,22,23, 165nn28,29, 166nn31,32, 167nn33–35, 168nn37–39, 179n5, 180n11, 184n26, 192, 193, 197n22, 198n29, 200n43, 206n77, 215, 217n6, 220, 234, 236nn4,6, 241n10, 242n22, 254nn5,6. *See also Book of Songs*; songs
poison, 138, 142n18
poverty and financial decline, 62n9, 117n10, 143n25, 154n17, 184n28, 185n31, 186n34, 189n47, 236n7, 242n17, 244, 245n2, 253n4. *See also* money
pregnancy. *See* birth
prime ministers, 68n2, 74n26, 75n27, 81, 82n7, 90n8, 95n7, 97n18, 115, 123n11, 130, 144n27, 175n28, 221, 225n29, 234, 236n5
princes
—pre-Qin: Song, 71n20; Zhou, 89n2, 239
—post-Qin: Han, 110n2, 136n30, 192, 197n24, 228, 230n1, 235, 237n13, 246n9; Wei, 112n13; Jin, 134n18, 203n60, 230n2; Northern Wei, 111n6, 170n2, 245, 248n21; Later Yan, 212n18; Southern Qi, 200n41, 219n25, 233n30; Liang, 127n32, 139, 145n37, 147, 149n5, 251, 253n2; Tang, 97n18, 107n14, 133n15, 149n6, 152n25, 202nn54,55, 216, 218n18; Later Liang, 96n9; Later Shu, 174n24; Later Tang, 141n11; Southern Tang, 131, 135n22, 231n15; Song, 105n6, 106n10, 110n3, 189n48, 193, 204n67, 226n38, 230nn3,4, 232n20, 242n16
princesses (including other wives of princes), 134n35, 159, 166n32, 204n67, 226n38, 230n2
prisoners, 73nn23,25, 86n12, 93, 94, 97n17, 113n15, 125n24, 127n37, 137n36, 139, 143nn21,23, 169, 172n17, 176n33, 196n16, 201n51, 221, 225n34, 231n15, 235, 238n18, 247n11

qi-energy 氣, 55, 56nn2–5, 61n5, 78, 79n3, 85n3, 90n4, 91, 92, 94, 95n3, 115, 116, 117n4, 130, 141n7, 170n2, 220, 223n11, 23, 239, 252, 254n7
qilin-beast 麒麟 (a.k.a. *lin*-beast 麟), 70nn10,14, 132n7, 215, 217n5, 220, 222nn1,2
queens, 151n24, 161n11

rain and storms, 59n4, 60, 61n5, 62n6, 69n8, 92, 93, 97n18, 115, 116, 116nn1,3, 118, 119n20, 141n11, 156n11, 162n16, 165n29, 167n32, 188n44, 197n22
rainbows, 70n11, 81, 83n10, 116, 118n14, 141n11
rebels, 41n47, 86n12, 112n10, 113n15, 127n36, 132n7, 171nn5,10, 200n43, 225n28, 233n30, 247nn11,15, 252, 255n15
reincarnation, 114n29, 194, 197n20, 200n41, 206n77, 207n80, 208, 217n5, 225n29, 231n19, 236n5, 249n27
residences, 71n18, 75n27, 90n8, 98n18, 104, 106n12, 107nn14,17, 110n3, 116n1, 121, 123nn9,10, 124n15, 126n28, 136n35, 146n43, 155n10, 165n28, 169, 172n17, 189n48, 198n31, 202n54, 204n67, 209, 213n27, 215, 216n2, 217n9, 219n19, 220, 226n38, 230nn4,8, 244, 245n2. *See also* houses; palaces
resurrection and revival, 146n45, 203n62, 208, 211n17
revenge and retribution (including punishment), 75n27, 94, 96n16, 212n21, 244–250
reward and repayment (including gratitude), 19, 74n25, 123n10, 140, 140n1, 141n13, 145n45, 165n29, 170n2, 189n49, 194, 210n6, 211nn10,13,15, 229, 232n26, 236n5, 237n9, 243n24, 244–250
rice. *See* grains
rivers and streams, 61n5, 63, 64n2, 66, 67, 68n2, 69nn5, 9, 70n19, 71n19, 73n24, 75n27, 85n5, 91, 94n2, 115, 116nn1,3, 118n20, 120, 122n9, 124nn14–18, 125n24, 128nn40,45, 133n13, 136n32, 138, 141n11, 142n19, 148, 153nn31,34, 159, 164n27, 166n30, 168n38, 169, 172n17, 178, 184n27, 185n31, 189n50, 191, 192, 194, 207n80, 212n20, 217n9, 221, 222, 223n8, 224n21, 227n45, 234, 235, 236nn4,7,8, 238n18, 239, 252. *See also* Yangzi; Yellow River
robbery, 156n11, 172n17, 173n18, 225n34, 245, 247n11, 248n19
rocks. *See* stones
roofs, 8n3, 92, 127n32, 128n45, 158, 141n11, 158, 161n9, 162n15, 172n14, 176n33, 203n59, 213n26, 230n8, 249n27, 250n28

sacrifices (including offerings and prayers), 3, 71n18, 73n24, 75n27, 89n2, 90n5, 99n18, 103, 107nn14,15, 110n5, 111n5, 116, 117n7, 118n20, 121, 129n47, 141n9, 145n40, 148n1, 150n11, 153n32, 157n18, 163n23, 165n39, 168n39, 184nn24,28, 191, 194n1, 195n7, 197n25, 198nn30,34, 199nn37,40, 200nn42,44, 202nn58,59, 203n64, 206nn75,76, 207n79, 210n4, 214n29, 218n17, 222n6, 225n35, 232n23, 244, 246n3, 247n14, 252, 254n9, 255n15. See also altars; temples
seas. See oceans
sexual relations, 72n22, 74n26, 75n27, 114n29, 156n12, 197nn22,23, 205n68, 221, 226n44, 230n1, 255n16
scholars, 89n3, 115, 118n13, 131, 132nn6,9, 135n25, 154, 158, 159, 163n23, 164n27, 168n39, 201n49, 203n62, 233n28, 253n4, 254n9. See also students
shamans. See spirit-mediums
sheep, 25, 68n2, 76nn32,33, 221, 226nn38,40, 242n16, 245, 249n28
Shun 舜 (trad. r. late 3rd–early 2nd millennium BCE), 66, 68nn3,4, 222n2
silk (including cloth), 81, 83n11, 89n1, 118n19, 120, 122n3, 126n28, 154, 155, 157nn21,22, 161n12, 165n28, 170, 188n45, 208, 250n29
singing, 73n24, 74n27, 85n5, 91, 93, 127n34, 128n43, 130, 158, 161n11, 162n16, 163n18, 168nn36,37, 189n46, 222n2. See also songs
sisters, 127n39, 143n25, 201n49
sky, 61n4, 70n14, 81n3, 89n1, 96nn12,14, 106n11, 111n6, 115, 117n7, 118nn16,20, 126n27, 127n32, 139, 146n43, 147, 151n19, 162n15, 167nn32,35, 170n2, 194n3, 209, 213n28, 218nn14–16, 219n23, 220, 221, 222n6, 223n18, 225n32. See also heaven
slaves, 87n14, 245, 248n15. See also maidservants; menservants
snakes, 67, 70n10, 76n32, 93, 95n5, 126n31, 140, 142n14, 228, 229, 232n22–233n30, 245, 249n24
snow, 116, 118n20, 135n27, 162n18, 165n28
soldiers, 73n25, 112n12, 125n24, 127n34, 139, 147, 148, 150n16, 152n25, 170, 174n22, 175n26, 176n33, 178, 179n5, 185n31, 187n40, 188nn43,44, 189n46, 192, 195n9, 196nn10,15,16, 197nn21,26, 198nn27,30, 199n40, 200n43, 201n49, 202nn53,58, 205n75, 206nn75,77, 210n6, 214n33, 215, 220, 221, 223n9, 224n21, 225n35, 227n45, 231n19, 232nn20,24, 233n28, 234, 237n16, 240, 242n21, 243n25, 246nn7,11, 248n20, 255n11. See also armies; military officials
songs, 130, 158, 159, 161n11, 162n16, 164n27, 165n28, 189n46, 222n2, 223n17. See also poetry; singing
sons, 71n18, 72n22, 73nn23–25, 75n28, 76n32, 97n18, 103, 104n2, 105n8, 106n12, 110nn3,5, 114n29, 116n1, 118nn13,14, 120, 121, 123n10, 124n17, 127n34, 128nn42–44, 129n48, 139, 140n7, 141nn10,11, 142n17, 143nn24,25, 144nn27,30, 145nn37,41, 146n2, 147, 149n6, 151n21, 152nn25,27, 153n32, 154, 155n2, 156n13, 157n18, 162n16, 167n33, 168n37, 169, 170n2, 172n17, 173n19, 174n24, 176n33, 178, 183n23, 186nn34,36, 191, 193, 194, 194n1, 200n46, 201nn47,50,52, 204n66, 205nn68–70,73,74, 206n75, 207n79, 208, 209nn1,2, 211nn13,18, 212n20, 213n24, 214nn31,33, 217n4, 218nn12,18, 219n25, 220, 221, 222nn5,6, 224n18, 226n38, 228, 230nn1,3,4, 231n15, 232n20, 234, 236nn4,6, 237n10, 240, 241nn9,11,12, 243n26, 245n2, 246n9, 252, 255n16
souls 魂魄 (hun and po), 55, 56n5, 57nn6,7,9, 58, 60, 62nn6,7, 79n1, 84, 96n15, 126n27, 159, 168n38, 176n33, 191, 193, 209, 214n33, 245, 246n9, 254n7
spirit 神 (shen), 25, 26, 55, 56, 56n5, 57nn8,9, 58, 59nn5,6, 60, 61n2, 62nn6,8, 64n3, 68n2, 71n18, 78, 79nn1,3,5, 80, 84, 94, 98n18, 105n5, 125n24, 132n5, 168n37, 178, 186n33, 193, 200n44, 212n18, 215, 216, 218n16, 223n18, 251, 253n1
spirit-energy 神氣 (shenqi), 60
spirit-mediums, 73n24, 75n27, 88, 90nn4,5, 116n1, 129n48, 131,

Index

134n21, 178, 184n27, 197n22, 217n4, 219n19, 233n28, 241n8
spirits 神 *(shen)*, 86n10, 107n14, 132n5, 133n11, 195n7, 246n9, 248n20. *See also* demons; ghosts; gods
spirit-wandering 神遊 *(shenyou)*, 55, 60, 68n2
spleen, 91, 92, 94n2
Spring and Autumn Annals, The 春秋 (*Chunqiu*, including *Zuo's Narratives* 春秋左傳 [*Chunqiu Zuozhuan*]), 66, 67, 76n33, 180n13, 204n66, 222n2
stars and other astronomical phenomena, 59n4, 60, 61nn4,5, 63, 64n6, 66, 69n9, 70n11, 74n27, 75n28, 80–81, 81n3, 82nn6,8, 83nn9, 12, 89n1, 90n4, 115, 117nn4–10, 134n19, 138, 141n13, 143n22, 170n2, 177, 179n2, 188n44, 190n51, 192, 195n9, 197n20, 199nn36,37, 220, 221, 223n13, 226n43. *See also* moon; sun
stomach, 92, 109, 113n24, 124n18, 130, 131, 132nn5,10, 134nn19,20, 140n3, 148
stones and rocks, 68n3, 69n5, 105n7, 120, 124nn17,18, 128n45, 147, 150n12, 154, 162n17, 163n20, 178, 183n24, 188n44, 196n18, 199n37, 203n63, 217n5, 244, 245n2, 248n21, 253n5. *See also* jade
students, 132n9, 168n38, 181n15, 182n19, 202n62, 214n31, 217n9
Su Shi 蘇軾 (1037–1101), 24–25, 128n42, 159, 163n23, 194, 206n79
sun (including eclipses and halos), 63, 64n6, 66, 69n8, 71n19, 74n27, 80, 81, 81nn3,6, 82n8, 83nn10,12, 89n1, 90n4, 104n2, 108–114, 121, 139, 145n35, 148, 150n17, 152nn25,26, 156n11, 159, 162n15, 163n22, 166n32, 169, 170n2, 172n17, 174n20, 181n17, 226n38, 228, 230nn2,3,6,10

tables, 129n46, 174n24, 187n38, 212n21
tails, 71n18, 74n27, 90n6, 105n8, 171n5, 174n20, 221, 224n24, 229, 230n7, 232n21
talismans. *See* magic diagrams
tea, 162n18, 168n39, 187n38, 244, 245n3
teachers, 96n10, 132n9, 180n13, 202n62, 209, 214nn31,32, 217n9, 241n12
temples and shrines, 69n4, 71n20, 74n26, 107n14, 119n20, 121, 128nn40,45,46, 129n47, 133n13, 136n32, 140nn1,7, 142n17, 148, 150n11, 151n24, 152n27, 157n22, 160nn3,5, 163n23, 174nn22,24, 178, 183n23, 184nn27–29, 196n19, 199n40, 202nn57–59, 203n60, 204n66, 211n14, 218n17, 221, 225n35, 235n2, 245, 247nn13,14, 249n27, 252, 254n9, 255n15. *See also* altars; sacrifices
terraces, 26, 120, 121, 162n17, 194n3, 197n22, 206n78
texts: 70n14; 194: biography, 206n77; commentary, 204n66; dynastic statutes, 89n2; epitaph, 165n28; essays, 168n36, 176n33; examination list, 181n16; funerary proclamation, 161n9; inscriptions, 156nn11,14, 163n21; letters, 163n21, 168n38, 176n33, 200n41, 242nn16,17, 244, 245n2; memorials to the throne, 113n18, 140n4, 190n51, 198n28, 203n63; official documents, 122n7, 129n46, 161n9, 178, 186n34, 188nn41,42, 197n20, 210n5, 213n24, 216, 219n22; proclamations, 248n20, 252, 254n11; records, 69n4, 159, 160n5, 163n20, 164nn25,26, 200n4; registers and ledgers, 126n28, 187n38, 192, 196n13, 209, 212n21; report, 174n23. *See also* books; "Dream of a Butterfly"; magic diagrams; poetry; trigrams
thirst, 62n9, 140n1, 125n24, 187n38
thunder. *See* lightning
tigers, 88, 90n8, 93, 131, 135n26, 194n1, 195n5, 220, 222nn7,8, 223nn9–11
toads, 26, 142n18, 159, 167n35
tombs, 90n4, 156n11, 159, 168n39, 170n2, 171n10, 176n33, 179n5, 200n42, 209, 214nn29,32, 244, 245n3
towers, 26, 120, 121, 126nn29,31, 127nn34,38, 147, 152n27, 158, 161n18, 163n20, 165n28, 166n31, 167n35, 189n46
transcendents *(xian* 仙*)*, 90nn4,5, 109, 116n1, 121, 124n17, 125n26, 126n28, 128n41, 129n48, 131, 134n20, 136n31, 138, 140n6, 143n43, 146n43, 147, 161n15, 163n23, 167n35, 176n33, 192, 193, 194n3, 199nn36,37, 203n62, 215, 216, 217n4, 219n19, 242n14, 244, 245n2, 251, 252, 253n5, 254n9. *See also* Daoism

travel, 15–16, 68n2, 69nn5,8, 71n20, 74n26, 75n27, 92, 104, 106n12, 107n17, 116n3, 121, 122n5, 123n13, 124n14, 125n16, 126n29, 128n40, 129n48, 134n20, 135n27, 136n32, 144n32, 148, 150n12, 152n27, 163n23, 164nn25,27, 166n31, 171n9, 172n17, 173n18, 174n21, 176nn32,33, 179, 182n20, 184nn24,26, 187n39, 190n51, 193, 196n18, 197n22, 199nn36,37, 200n43, 201n48, 202nn52,59, 203n63, 214n29, 216, 224nn21,24, 226n40, 236n5, 246n9, 251, 252, 253n5, 255n14

trees, 79n2, 90n8, 92, 93, 128n45, 132n9, 146n45, 151n24, 154, 169, 171n7, 179n5, 184n27, 211n17, 239–243, 248n21; catalpa, 70n12, 89n2, 239; citong-tree 刺桐, 240, 242n22; crabapple, 166n31; cypress, 138, 141n7; elm, 62n6, 239; jujube, 62n6, 239; juniper, 66, 70n12, 89n2, 171n10, 239; lacquer, 219n19; maple, 130, 239, 240n7; mulberry, 142n15, 208, 211n12, 240, 243n26; oak, 66, 70n12, 89n2; papaya, 240, 241n11; paulownia, 161n13, 240, 243n27; peach, 90n8; pine, 66, 70n12, 89n2, 132n10, 169, 171n10, 226n38, 239; pomegranate, 240, 241n12; sandalwood, 145n41, 243n27; sophora, 66, 159, 169, 170n2, 238n17; sterculia, 218n11, willow, 120, 124n14, 130, 165n28, 167n32, 239, 241n8

trigrams and hexagrams, 58, 59nn2,4–6, 63, 64nn5,8, 72nn21,22, 122n2, 138, 140n4, 164n24, 171n10, 172n17, 191, 195n9, 203n61, 208, 210nn7,8, 220, 221, 234, 235n2. See also Book of Changes

turtles and tortoises, 58, 59nn2,4,6, 63, 64nn3,4, 67, 68n2, 76n32, 138, 141n9, 181n16, 221, 225n29, 234, 235n1–236n8

types of dreams, 80–84, 91–99. See also nightmares

uncles, 142n17, 186n34, 207n80, 221, 226n42

underworld, 128n43, 166n32, 167n34, 199n39, 200n41, 201nn47,50, 209, 211n13, 212nn21,22, 225n35. See also tombs

usurpers, 108, 116, 149nn4,11, 223n10, 233n29, 247n15

utensils and vessels, 98n18, 147–153: basins, 143n25, 154, 156n14, 234, 237n10; bronze and lacquer vessels, 60, 105n6, 147, 148n1, 149n9; bowls, cups, and pots, 96n14, 98n18, 141n10, 147, 150n11, 217n9, 225n35; chopping blocks, 240, 243n26; chopsticks, 138, 141n10, 154; containers, 106n12, 135n28, 142nn18,19, 145n36, 146n42, 187n38, 223n9, 249n28; dippers and ladles, 51, 112n13; hammer, 161n13; incense burners, 114n29, 147, 150n17; mortars, 66, 70n13, 147, 150n12; staves, 175n25, 203n60. See also brushes; mirrors; pillows; weapons

vapors 氣 (qi), 60, 66, 70n10, 80, 81n3, 83n10, 203n63, 225n27

vigorous essence 精 (jing), 55, 56nn4–5, 57n8, 59n6, 60, 61nn3,6, 62n7, 64n3, 96n15, 109, 111n5, 112n14, 113n16, 120, 124n17, 150n17, 245

villages, 70n13, 184n29, 203n62, 249n27

walls, 73n23, 92, 121, 123n11, 126n27, 127n38, 167n35, 197n26, 214n33, 233n30, 238n17, 244, 245n2, 248n22

war, 59n4, 69n7, 71n19, 72nn21,23, 73n25, 74n27, 75n28, 85n5, 86n12, 92, 96n9, 97n18, 106nn11,12, 108, 109, 112n10, 117n11, 121, 122n1, 124nn16,19,20, 125nn22,24, 131, 132n7, 133n11, 136n35, 141n11, 145n38, 148n2, 151n19, 152n27, 153n34, 171nn9,10, 174n22, 188n44, 194n4, 195nn9,10, 198n33, 200n43, 205n73, 206n78, 221, 225n35, 226n36, 231n19, 233n30, 234, 236n2, 240, 242n21, 243n25, 247nn11,12,15, 252, 255nn13,15

water, 60, 61n4, 62n6, 66, 70n13, 86n14, 92, 96n12, 107n16, 113n23, 120, 121, 123nn10,11, 124nn15,17,18, 125n24, 126n30, 134n20, 138, 141nn9,11, 142n17, 143n25, 145n36, 153n31, 156n11, 162n15, 166nn31,32, 169, 170, 172n17, 174n22, 184n27, 186n34, 202n52, 223n11, 224nn21,24, 231n15, 234, 236n8, 237n10, 242n13, 245, 248n17. See also drowning; five agents; floods; lakes; oceans; rain; rivers

Index

weapons: ax, 195n5; bow and arrow, 148, 151nn23,24, 169, 181n16, 195n7, 247n13; dagger, 3, 73n24, 130; crossbow, 68n2; halberd, 189n46; knife, 132n9, 147, 150n13, 169, 170, 174n22; spear, 246n7; sword, 96n6, 113n15, 134nn21,22, 149n5, 162n15, 162n32, 173n18, 188n44, 194n4, 205n73, 223n11, 247n11

wells, 109, 112n12, 122n5, 165n28, 199n38, 211n12, 235n2

wind, 51, 60, 61n5, 62n6, 66, 68n2, 69n7, 70n10, 92, 97n18, 115, 116, 116n1, 121n1, 133n13, 151n24, 161n13, 162nn16,17, 164n27, 165nn28,29, 166nn30–32, 184n26, 186n34, 224nn21,24, 241n13

windows, 86n12, 111n6, 136n34, 139, 144n27, 166n32, 198n34, 205n68, 225n27

wine, 51, 96n13, 161nn11,15, 162n17, 166nn31,32, 183n24, 189n49, 200n43, 203n61, 212n20, 255n14

wings, 106n11, 165n29, 231n13

wives, 3, 74n26, 75nn27,28, 95n7, 110nn4,5, 114n28, 118n13, 127nn34,39, 128n43, 129n48, 131, 135nn24,26, 136nn33–35, 143nn22,24, 144n27, 150n12, 159, 161n11, 165n28, 166n31, 168n38, 169, 172n17, 173n18, 174n20, 176n33, 183n24, 192, 199n35, 207n79, 209, 211n17, 212nn18–20, 217n7, 221, 222n6, 225n35, 226n44, 234, 236n4, 237n10, 244, 245, 245n3, 247n15, 248nn16,19, 249n28, 252, 255n16. *See also* concubines; empresses; princesses

wolves, 169, 171n9, 221, 222, 226nn41,42,44

women, 26, 67, 69n8, 70nn11,12, 74n26, 89n2, 105n9, 109, 120, 129n47, 130, 145n36, 147, 151n19, 154, 156nn11,12, 158, 159, 161nn11,15, 162n16, 163n18, 164n27, 165n28, 170, 193, 197n22, 198n24, 201n50, 209n1, 216, 221, 229, 232n22, 244, 246n4, 247n10, 249n28, 253n4. *See also* concubines; courtesans; daughters; empresses; girls; maidservants; mothers; old women; princesses; sisters; wives

wood, 88, 90n8, 95n7, 128n45, 148n1, 158, 161n13, 170, 174n23, 177, 179n1, 188n44, 213n26, 222n1, 240, 241n8, 243n27, 245n4. *See also* five agents

Yangzi River 長江 (Changjiang), 128n40, 133n13, 136n32, 178, 184n27, 235n1

Yao 堯 (trad. r. late 3rd millennium BCE), 66, 68nn3,4, 105n7, 120, 121, 166n32, 191, 194n1, 222n2

Yellow Emperor 黃帝 (Huangdi, mythical sage-king), 15, 66, 68n2, 69n5, 70n11, 87nn14,15, 90n8, 221, 229, 254n7, 229, 254n7

Yellow River 黃河 (Huanghe), 63, 64n2, 67, 68n2, 73n24, 75n27, 120, 122n9, 138, 141n11, 191, 192, 198n30, 214n29, 234, 235n1

yin and yang 陰陽, 55, 56nn2,5, 57n8, 61nn2,3, 62n8, 63, 64n3, 78, 79n5, 80, 81n3, 82nn6,7, 90n4, 91, 94n2, 95nn3,4, 97n18, 109, 112nn9,14, 114n25, 116, 118n13, 139, 143n24, 163n23, 173n17, 198n28, 221, 222n7, 234, 243n23, 252, 254n8

Zhou Xuan 周宣 (d. ca. 239), 4, 215, 239, 251, 253n3

Text: 10/13 Sabon
Display: Sabon
Compositor: Integrated Composition Systems

www.ingramcontent.com/pod-product-compliance
Lightning Source LLC
Chambersburg PA
CBHW030525230426
43665CB00010B/764